FOUNDERS OF FAITH

The Parallel Lives of God's Messengers

Harold Rosen

Bahá'í
PUBLISHING

Wilmette, Illinois

Bahá'í Publishing
415 Linden Avenue, Wilmette, Illinois 60091-2844

13   12   11   4   3

Library of Congress Cataloging-in-Publication Data

Rosen, Harold, 1947–
   Founders of faith : the parallel lives of god's messengers / Harold Rosen.
      p. cm.
   Includes bibliographical references.
   ISBN 978-1-931847-78-0 (pbk. : alk. paper) 1. Religious leaders. I. Title.
   BL72.R67 2010
   200.92'2—dc22

                              2010027599

Cover design by Robert A. Reddy
Book design by Patrick Falso

Contents

Acknowledgments

Any gift this book may offer is primarily due to the divine wisdom of the Founders of Faith—Moses, Zoroaster, Krishna, Buddha, Christ, Muḥammad and Bahá'u'lláh. They have been my primary inspirers as I tried to open myself to the Word and Spirit that has transformed our world. Indeed, I now believe that most of humanity's advancement through the ages has been inspired by these revelatory Teachers, who progressively conveyed the highest truths and loftiest ideals. Any weakness of this book, on the other hand, is my own responsibility, and I look forward to the continuing process of learning from mistakes and correcting them.

Without the loving and skilled support of my wife, Wendy Rosen, and that of my parents, Mary and Larry Williams, I could not have completed this work. My dear wife often believed in me more than I believed in myself, replacing my intermittent doubts and sense of "maybe" with a more confident "yes of course." In recent years, my dear parents provided a warm and stimulating home away from home where extended periods of study and writing were possible, offering countless forms of assistance and encouragement. My dear sisters, Debi Madden and Cory Going, also cheered me on and deepened the family support which led to this book's completion.

Because this book grew out of courses that I designed and taught, I wish to thank all my students collectively—they appreciated, challenged, and modified my material in various ways over the years. I am grateful to the institutions and administrators who sponsored some of my teaching in the Vancouver, Canada area, including, Alan Aberbach of the Simon Fraser University Seniors Program, Don Black of the University of British Columbia Continuing Studies Program, Elizabeth Dennis and Dave Wyatt of the University of the Fraser Valley, and Bill McKitrick of the West Vancouver Community Learning Program. My gratitude also extends to the various churches, community centers, libraries, and Bahá'í Local Spiritual Assemblies that sponsored and hosted my courses.

Acknowledgments

Because the topic of this work is quite broad—world religions and world history—it is impossible to identify all the people who supported and influenced its development. Nonetheless I wish to acknowledge a special few who deserve a degree of credit for whatever merits this book may contain.

I appreciate the past support of my Unitarian friends and colleagues: Lynn Sabourin, Brian Kiely, and Phillip Hewett; the support of my multifaith friends: John Wong, David Spence, and Barry Cooke; and the support and inspiration of far-flung academic colleagues: Nick Gier, William Hatcher, John Hatcher, Robert Stockman, and Moojan Momen.

I appreciate the continuing support of my Bahá'í friends: the Majzub family, the Azizi family, the Greenall family, the Kiai family, the Sarvian family, the Fatheazam family, Barbara Matthews, Sylvester Scott, Gerri Graber, Gina Devlin, Brian Murdoch, David Bowie, and Norma Hoyle.

I appreciate the moral support of several members of the Furutan Academy: Shahrokh Monjazeb, Mark Keedwell, Jack McLean, and Peter Terry.

I have learned a great deal from several religion scholars and researchers: Huston Smith, Mircea Eliade, John Bowker, Ninian Smart, Keith Crim, Hasan Balyuzi, Udo Schaefer, Julio Savi, Peter Smith, and Dan Popov.

I have benefited from the perspectives of several philosophers, theologians, and ethical thinkers: Plato, Plotinus, Immanuel Kant, Georg Hegel, John Stuart Mill, Alfred North Whitehead, Paul Tillich, Teilhard de Chardin, Martin Buber, Albert Schweitzer, Henry Nelson Wieman, John Rawls, and John Hick.

I have benefited from the perspectives of several sociohistorical interpreters: Arnold Toynbee, Pitirim Sorokin, Peter Stearns, Karen Armstrong, and Douglas Martin.

I admire the work of several international interfaith advocates: Marcus Braybrooke, Hans Kung, Diana Eck, Robert Traer, and William Swing.

I admire several figures who have crossed over from their home faith traditions, and then returned, enriched by their interfaith encounters: Mohandas Gandhi, Thomas Merton, and Thich Nhat Hanh.

I have been inspired by several thoughtful visionaries, past and present: Hildegard of Bingen, Teresa of Avila, Ṭáhirih of Persia, Sophia Lyon Fahs, Barbara Marx Hubbard, and Linda Kavelin Popov.

Finally, I would like to thank my editors, Terry Cassiday and Ariana Brown, and their coworkers at the Bahá'í Publishing Trust for their sublime patience and consummate skill in bringing this work to useful completion.

Note on Approach and Style

Within this book we will capitalize terms such as Founders and Revealers, along with all related pronouns, because these Figures are the very center of this study, and They are held to be the most transformative forces in world history. This practice encourages mutual reverence and assigns equal dignity to each of the Founders. It also helps to clarify the intended and often complex communication between God and humanity that we find in the collective body of the world's religious literature. We will use italics for all scriptural quotations and visionary passages, as well as for essential descriptions of the twenty-five parallels or patterns linking the Founders.

- 1 -

Finding Hope in an Anxious World

Conscious human life is like eating the fruit of the tree of the knowledge of good and evil. The fruit of this tree may prove delicious, or it may prove bitter. Tasting this fruit teaches us that there is both good and bad in the world, as well as countless other moral and spiritual consequences in between. The consequences are both personal and social, for we are both private and public beings. Greater awareness of these consequences can lead to either heightened joy or pain. Wherever we turn, we are faced with degrees of choice and responsibility—for better or worse.

An endless array of questions confronts us throughout our lives. What is expected of me, and is this what I expect of myself? Should I opt for safety, or take the risks of new experience? How might I respond to people, and what relationships will I encourage? Which of my interests will I pursue next? What capacities call for development? Should I follow the faith of my parents, seek alternatives, or neglect religion and spirituality altogether? What skills and knowledge might I acquire? Which paths of service and livelihood will I walk? Should expedience or principle guide my steps? How can I best educate my children? Which is the priority for my nation—economic development, environmental protection, ethnic harmony, cultural advancement, or international peace?

Such questions are inescapable. Consciousness includes the awareness of choice, and choice imposes responsibility upon us, and responsibility often brings anxiety in its wake. These realities—consciousness, choice, responsibility, and anxiety—seem to be among the key descriptors of human nature.

Many of our choices have distinctly moral and spiritual dimensions. At one extreme, we may sink into depths of anxious sinfulness, if not sheer terror, over something we have said or done that later fills us with guilt, anger, or fear. It is not only others who become defensive about beliefs and

5

ways of life, sometimes resorting to violence above rational persuasion. We, too, might succumb to fear and desperation in our decision-making and, in highly pressured circumstances, be tempted to commit shameful acts. But as human beings, we can also make dramatic turns toward the high road of principles, ideals, and aspirations—attaining heights of loving joy, productive engagement, and creative fulfillment. Ideals and virtues have spread to our whole world, so models of excellence can be found in each society and culture. Nobility and inspiration can lead us to praiseworthy endeavors and the building of a more beautiful world.

Between these depths of sinfulness and heights of virtuousness are a wide set of intermediate options and conditions. Individually and collectively, we attempt to escape from consciousness, to avoid bewilderment and challenges, to choose comfort over growth. We often settle for material survival routines, suspending the questions of ultimate meaning and purpose, indulging in whatever means of entertainment may be economically available. And so we can drift in a state of partial consciousness, uncertain morality, and clouded spiritual vision—without direction or sense of calling.

Religion as an Attempt to Address Anxiety

Traditionally, it has been religion that awakened humanity to invisible possibilities, providing us with conscious direction and hope vis-à-vis the challenges and perplexities of our existence. But religion, being an interaction between divine and human realms, shows the influence of both infinite grandeur and finite frailty. Religion can bring out humanity's best, including moral uprightness, spiritual transcendence, and cultural refinement. But religion can also lose its effectiveness over time to guide us along the right path. When this happens, we can easily succumb to our worst failures, and religion can become tainted with human limitations and evil decision-making. Religion, in its "earthly" dimensions, declines inevitably to the point of needing divine renewal. This strange rhythm of heavenly and earthly counterpoint, this dialectic of rising and falling religions and civilizations, has given human history its decisive shape—for better or worse.

The anxieties of human consciousness are responses to both outer and inner conditions. Outwardly, events in today's world are rightly described as disturbing and often frightening. In the opening decades of the third millennium, religiously motivated violence often dominates the news. Commentators on current events allude to the clash of civilizations, especially that between the Christian West and the Islamic Middle East. Images abound of explosions causing innocent civilian death.

Beyond this religious "war," many other problems are also apparent. The gap between the extremes of wealth and poverty is widening. The faces of starving children remain in our mind's eye long after the television is turned off. Many thoughtful, informed people conclude that the long-feared economic or environmental collapse has indeed begun. When we see these disturbing images on TV and in magazines, many questions come to mind. Was it inevitable that capitalism, like communism, would prove to be a shallow ideology? How close to the end of the fossil fuel supply have we come? Have we set irreversible and inevitably destructive processes in motion? Could governmental anxieties reach the point where weapons of mass destruction are used indiscriminately?

Believers in the Jewish, Hindu, Buddhist, Christian, and Islamic faith traditions may be wondering if their own religious civilization is in a stage of decline. Secular values alone seem paramount on the world stage. To an alarming degree, moral idealism has become very weak, and in many regions, creative spiritual vision has become a faint memory. Believers among established religions see no obvious signs of the Day of God or the Golden Age promised in their scriptures. Many traditional religious beliefs seem to contradict the scientific description of the universe. Old cosmologies, as traditionally interpreted, have been completely outgrown. Those who do not identify with any particular faith and expect technology and the economy to provide a good life for everyone are also deeply disenchanted. Prejudices of many varieties divide humanity and obstruct our search for cooperative solutions to global problems. And there are a growing number of New Age seekers who desperately await the unified consciousness that will usher in a truly global community.

These outwardly oriented anxieties have counterparts in our inner world. Feeling a sense of being unsafe, if not in immediate danger, many of us go through periods of feeling left out, unloved, and simply not counted as significant players in the drama of life. At times, we feel utterly incompetent and incapable of learning, incapacitated, and left behind in the ever-quickening pace of social and economic development. Often we feel that we have failed as students, spouses, parents, and coworkers, not knowing where to turn for guidance we can trust. Many religious institutions and spiritual movements seem hypocritical and shallow. As years go by, we may feel further and further away from earlier dreams of developing and expressing our creative potential. Given the frustrations and injustices that abound, failing health and waning energies that come with aging, we may begin to conclude that God does not exist, that life is meaningless, and that there is no realistic hope of abundant eternal life beyond this fleeting world. When these anxieties begin to take hold, hope dwindles and despair mounts.

The Priority of Religious Hope

Hope is a universal need. We cannot become fully human without it. Precisely because we human beings are acutely aware of time and unfolding processes, hope is essential to all higher human functioning. It is a positive orientation to the future, providing constructive motivation in the present, as well as a useful interpretation of the past. Hope reframes personal mistakes as learning experiences, collective problems as evolutionary drivers, crises as opportunities, breakdowns as preludes to breakthroughs, and darkness as motivation to discern more light. We do well to remember the famous observation of Alexander Pope in the early eighteenth century: "Hope springs eternal in the human breast."

Traditionally, religion has addressed our need for hope in the face of all the inner and outer anxieties of the human condition. Religious belief may be understood as a very important "if"—the provisional hypothesis that human life is meaningful because it is part of a larger and more significant whole. Religion, generally speaking, declares that if God, or an Ultimate Realm, really exists; if this divine power is creative and benevolent and almighty; if He speaks to us and provides for us; if we can understand what is said; if we can accept the grace of divine sustenance and mould ourselves virtuously; if we can learn and grow and come to reflect heavenly qualities in this lifetime; if we can cooperate with divine guidance, envisioning and working toward a better world, then there is hope because the world is ordered and purposeful. Life has purpose and beauty, prayer and meditation are effective, all human beings are children of God, and we are brothers and sisters who are interdependent with one another, comprising together a united world family. Each of us is dignified and vital, and the future is promising. History and religion are ultimately progressive, prophetic visions are essentially true, and our existence and the universe as a whole are evolutionary and developmental.

Even if one is not ready to embrace these traditional religious beliefs personally, it might be possible to entertain them as provisional hypotheses so as to gain insight into religious experience and the role of religion in world history. Stepping into the religious frame of reference may illumine the sacrifices and idealism that have generated some of the most significant turning-points of humanity's journey across the ages.

A Hopeful Book, Reviewing Humanity's Spiritual Progress

This book was written with great hope for humanity's progress and with a strong desire to contribute to interfaith understanding and global cooperation. It grew out of a lifelong fascination with the idea of unity in diversity—the discovery of common ground and interdependence across religious, cultural, and national boundaries, and building on this discovery to help make a more just, peaceful, and creative world. This book's global emphasis was influenced by work and travel in the United States, Canada, Mexico, England, Greece, Israel, India, China, Japan, Korea, and Turkey.

This book also grew out of my study of the human sciences and my twenty-five-year Unitarian Universalist ministry, during which I engaged in extensive interfaith activities, along with eager study of the world religions and their respective founders and scriptures. This book reflects my experience as a community interfaith educator, grateful to many and varied students. Finally, the pages before you reflect my becoming a member of the Bahá'í Faith, hearing its call to investigate truth independently and glimpsing its all-embracing vision of humanity's past, present, and future. Though others more competent will soon surpass this effort, I feel called to share what I see now—trying not to get lost in the trees but rather to survey the forests with an eye for useful and general truths about humanity's endowment and prospects.

This book is for those who want to renew their hope for humanity on an informed and reasonable basis; those who want to rise above cynical, pessimistic, and partisan attitudes in their assessment of religion; those who intuit that, despite great dangers faced today, a positive and transformative breakthrough is emerging; those who want to see religion and science as complementary partners, rather than antagonists, in establishing an ever-advancing global civilization; and those aspiring to be better world citizens or international bridge-builders.

In this book the term "we" usually refers to readers, as well as to all the people who would be willing to entertain the hypothesis of progressive revelation—the idea that God or the realm of ultimate truth periodically reveals or discloses new guidance to humanity by means of revelatory teachers Who founded new scriptural traditions and generated new civilizations. The term "we" will sometimes also refer to humanity as a whole, because the focus of this work is world religion and world history viewed as a common heritage.

This book is for those who feel lured to the process of dialogue and the creative ideals embedded in unity in diversity; those who suspect that humanity's commonalities are more abiding and significant than our differences; those who prefer to build upon common ground rather than accentuate differences; those interracial and multicultural activists who are discovering the motivational importance of spiritual vision; and those who sense that if certain foundational virtues were practiced widely, our world would be transformed for the better.

My Spiritual Journey

A few of the developments in my process of becoming a Bahá'í may cast light on the methodology and rationale of this study. In the summer of 1996, I made an interfaith pilgrimage to Oxford and Seoul, where I met many enthusiasts for global cooperation and participated in their devotions. It was soon after this that I began to take a different approach to the major faith traditions. Before this time, I had adopted a kind of anthropological perspective on the teachings of other faiths, and had tried to understand them from a safe distance. I did not anticipate being changed in any significant way by exposure to these teachings. But then the world's scriptures, including the Bahá'í writings, began to speak to me personally and spiritually. I became a more open-minded and open-hearted seeker of higher truth. I began to hear the same voice behind all of the scriptures, as if the same story were being revealed, and as if a common body of sequential guidance were being offered to humanity as a whole.

Another key turning point for me was gaining some insight into the giant puzzle of history's civilizations. I had long been fascinated by the whole concept of civilizations, broadly conceived as mountain ranges of human achievement. How had these mighty structures arisen? Were there significant patterns in their development? Why did they fall? How do they arise anew? What roles does religion play in this earth-changing sequence? Is a new civilization arising today out of the ashes of two devastating wars involving both the Western and Eastern hemispheres?

I was thinking of civilization in general as the highest collective achievement of a sizeable portion of humanity, bringing certain images to mind: religiously inspired architecture, beautiful gardens and parks, kind and trustworthy people in all walks of life, schools and universities, flourishing arts and sciences, widely shared prosperity marked by fair commerce and trade, respect and care for the earth, creative development and opportunity for all levels of society, effective social services, a just legal system underlying a wise and humane government, dignity and moderation in all quarters, and spiritual reverence and philosophical reflection.

I adopted the Bahá'í view of history, which is reflected in this study. The Founders of the world's religions seem to be the very hinges of history—the establishers of the highest civilizations, effectively generating new worlds of meaning and purpose for humanity. The deep, transformative impact of religious Founders is briefly described in this quotation.

> "He was in the world, and the world was made by Him." The promised Manifestation of God appears; a community of believers forms around this focal centre of spiritual life and authority; a new system of values begins to reorder both consciousness and behaviour; the arts and sciences respond; a restructuring of laws and of the administration of social affairs takes place. Slowly, but irresistibly, a new civilization emerges, one that so fulfils the ideals and so engages the capacities of millions of human beings that it does indeed constitute a new world, a world far more real to those who "live, move, and have their being" in it than the earthly foundation on which it rests. Throughout the centuries that follow, society continues to depend for its cohesion and self-confidence primarily on the spiritual impulse that gave it birth.[1]

This is a concise summary of formative patterns enabling us to learn effectively from humanity's past. Progressive revelation unlocks the mystery of the rise and fall of civilizations. The Founders' teachings help us discern where tragic mistakes were made, to celebrate virtuous achievement, to embrace the latest divine guidance, and then hopefully to co-establish a glorious future. We explore this hope-giving pattern in detail in the exciting journey ahead. The intimate connection between civilization and religion will be identified, and key dynamics specified.

This book is for students of religion and history seeking a more integrative or unified perspective; those seeking a more global view of today's moral and spiritual challenges; those who suspect that religion loses its purity when it departs too far from the spirit of its Founder; those who have wondered how such Figures as Buddha, Jesus, and Muḥammad would regard each other were They to meet face-to-face; and those who suspect that all the great Prophets were like teachers in a vast school—educators of humanity.

Twenty-Five Patterns in the Lives of the Founders

The first four chapters of this book introduce the motivations, working assumptions, and hypotheses of this study as a whole. They offer a glimpse of the lofty station of the Divine Messengers. They describe progressive revelation as a new paradigm for understanding religion and history. They present twenty-five patterns or parallels discovered in the lives and teachings of the Founders of great religions. These patterns are briefly illustrated by applying them to the lives of Moses, Zoroaster, Krishna, Buddha, Jesus, Muḥammad, and Bahá'u'lláh. A rationale for selecting these Figures and not others is offered.

The patterns explored include, among others: continuity with previous dispensations, prophetic fulfillment, transformative teaching, establishing new sociolegal guidelines, renewing universal virtues, overcoming powerful opposition, claiming and exemplifying a dual station, promising a future Redeemer, and generating civilization anew. The introductory chapters also reflect on the significance of the twenty-five parallels, the extent to which they link and unite humanity's most essential religious heritage, along with some of their implications for global understanding.

The same twenty-five parallels are then developed in more detail in succeeding chapters to tell Their world-changing stories and to clarify the abiding principles of each of the Messengers of God. Surprising links, interconnections, and commonalities among religious heritages appear in clear relief. Chapters 5 and 6 focus on Moses and His teaching, including key developments in the Jewish Faith. Chapters 7 to 18 address—with comparable outlines and corresponding scriptural quotations—Zoroaster, Krishna, Buddha, Christ, Muḥammad, and Bahá'u'lláh. The interdependence, complementary nature, and ultimate unity of major world religions come into view. Humanity's religious history is presented as successive chapters in a book of divine providence, as a way of both testing and presenting the hypothesis of progressive revelation. All of this illustrates the coming paradigm-shift in humanity's self-understanding and aspiration.

This book is for faithful religious adherents or spiritual practitioners who are now seeking wider horizons; those who are disenchanted with traditional religions but wish to identify and preserve the universal content of humanity's spiritual heritage; those wishing to reduce religious prejudice, especially at a time when this barrier poses such danger to global security; those who wonder how there can be so many religions, if God and truth are ultimately one; and those who suspect that a single Source may have inspired the various religious systems in humanity's journey through time.

Hope is indeed a universal need and an essential theme of religion. "Most religions contain teachings that anticipate a time, beyond the present era of suffering and injustice, when human history will be consummated by a decisive act of God."[2] Hope is also an assumption of evolutionary understanding, a "given" of developmental theory, and a discernible reality despite the atrocities of humanity's past—the troubled and even tragic character of human existence up until this day of maturation. Hope is a lesson of history when interpreted with divine guidance, showing that vast and glorious realities lie ahead for humanity.

This book is for those who are blessed with hope, and for those who desperately thirst for hope; those who reflect thoughtfully on the big picture for humanity across the ages; those who take seriously the patterns and directions of our cultural and spiritual evolution; those starting to embrace history's great civilizations as a common heritage and a continuing story; those who believe that humanity's technological progress must now be brought under moral and spiritual discipline and be redirected for the benefit of all people; those engaged in business and commerce, and desiring to operate by the highest standards ever known; and those in all walks of life who sense that a truly global civilization is emerging today, and are eager to contribute to a more unified world.

Visions of Hope

I cherish the hope that some day, primary selections from all the world's scriptures will be bound in one volume and will be taught to all children everywhere. The present work is a humble and preliminary contribution to the arduous process of bringing forward that day of global religious education. The Bahá'í writings speak of a time when spiritual understanding will far surpass where we are today. *"The newly born babe of that Day excels the wisest and most venerable men of this time, and the lowliest and most unlearned of that period shall surpass in understanding the most erudite and accomplished divines of this age."*[3] In the meantime, we can reappraise world religion and world history, identify universal teachings and patterns, make peace between religions, and then align ourselves with the new divine guidance that will lead us to one world.

In the face of many historic trials, frustrations, and failures, visions of hope that seem divinely inspired have sustained humanity through the ages. Such visions have given the world's peoples renewed purpose and courage, guiding them to arise with virtue and prepare for a better day. There are passages from many of the world's faith traditions that speak of this hope.

And I saw that the sacred hoop of my people was one of many hoops that made one circle, wide as daylight and as starlight, and in the center grew one mighty flowering tree to shelter all the children of one mother and one father.[4]

The greatness of the kingdoms under the whole of heaven shall be given to the people of the saints of the Most High; their kingdom shall be an everlasting kingdom, and all dominions shall serve and obey them.[5]

Then will all men come together in the greatest joy. . . . All men will become of one voice and give praise with a loud voice. . . . Their weapons smashed, will all be made powerless. . . . Then will the final Resurrection take place.[6]

The minds of the people shall become pure as flawless crystal, and they will be as if awakened at the conclusion of a night. And these men . . . will thus be transformed.[7]

In those days, brethren, there will arise an Exalted One. . . . He will be . . . Fully Awakened, abounding in wisdom and goodness, happy, with knowledge of the worlds, unsurpassed as a guide to mortals. . . . The Law, lovely in its origin, lovely in its progress, lovely in its consummation, will he proclaim, both in the spirit and in the letter; the higher life will he make known, in all its fulness and in all its purity.[8]

When the Great Tao [Unity] is realized, the spirit of openness and fairness will prevail all under the sky. The men of talents, virtue, and ability shall be chosen equally, and sincerity and harmony shall be cultivated.[9]

Then I saw a new heaven and a new earth. . . . And I saw the holy city, new Jerusalem, coming down out of heaven from God. . . . And the city has no need of sun or moon to shine upon it, for the glory of God is its light.[10]

Even as We produced the first Creation, so shall We produce a new one: a promise We have undertaken: truly shall We fulfill it.[11]

The Promised One of all the world's peoples hath now been made manifest. . . . The tabernacle of unity will be upraised on the heights of the world, and the banners of the universality of all humankind will be unfurled on the peaks of the earth.[12]

- 2 -
Founders of Faith:
Mediators between Divine and Human Realms

If we think of religion as a relationship, a connection, an interaction between divine and human realms, this raises immediate questions to thoughtful minds. How do we conceive of a divine realm? Is it merely a product of wishful thinking? Since there are so many ideas about this realm, how do we discern its true nature? Who or what would bridge the gap between an Infinite Eternal Being and finite creatures like us—if anyone or anything? Independent of the claims of religion itself, is there any reason to believe in divine reality? Can religion be understood without a concept of the divine? What are the consequences of disbelief in God? If there are Mediators between God and humanity, how might we recognize Them as authentic? What would be Their essential qualities and achievements? What grounds might there be for following one Mediator rather than another? What role might such a Figure play in history?

The God Hypothesis

We offer no systematic argument for the existence of God but rather offer some major reasons given for religious belief, both within and outside of religious traditions. Common observation of nature and the details of science point to a universe that is highly ordered. This makes it seem unlikely that the universe has come about as a result of purely accidental processes. And since the universe also displays areas of considerable contingency or randomness, it cannot be completely explained as necessarily determined. This leaves the possibility that the universe is continually created and sustained by an Infinite Source, with degrees of freedom built into the process.

Other forms of reasoning have made belief in God seem plausible to the large majority in history. Since all phenomena are caused, the universe as a whole probably has a first cause—something was needed to spark the creation of the universe. Since all natural phenomena show various degrees of design, the universe as a whole probably has a designer. Since all systems seem to require an external source of energy, the universe as a whole probably requires an infinite energy source, or it would have wound down by now. Since morality exists and seems indispensable in human life, there is probably a just standard and a judge with the power to enforce rules. Since beauty predominates over ugliness in the creation, there is probably a fashioner of beauty who has shared aesthetic capacity with us.

Before addressing those who resist using the God hypothesis, we will consider a few more evidences or arguments for the existence of God that are persuasive for many people worldwide. Since human evolution has resulted in an extremely complex and improbable being, it was probably fashioned by a deliberate intelligence. Since we perceive many kinds of imperfections, there is probably a higher order of being to which we compare these imperfections. If we recognize weakness, we probably sense a greater power. If we discover ignorance, we probably assume a higher truth. If we behold ugliness, we probably presuppose a vision of beauty. If we are repelled by acts of evil, we probably embrace a standard of good. And if we understand that we are finite creatures, we probably envision an infinite creator.

But some thoughtful persons object to these forms of reasoning, saying there are some very well-known phenomena that make the existence of God unlikely. They point to the toll of undeserved suffering in the world, to historic atrocities committed in the name of God, to the confusion surrounding even the meaning of the term *God,* as well as to the progress of science over the last 400 years in explaining things without recourse to God. To these objections we reply that the freedom allowed by God to human beings gives them capacity for evil. Suffering is a consequence of both natural law and human choice. Atrocities done in the name of God are the responsibility of the perpetrators, not of God; just as atrocities committed with the power of science do not make science itself culpable. An explanatory pluralism would allow us to investigate the teachings and claims of religion by identifying factors that could be categorized as biochemical, psychological, and socioeconomic, as well as philosophical and religious. Each of these disciplines and investigative tools has its merits.

To disbelievers in God who wish to understand religion better, we ask for a suspension of disbelief long enough to investigate the God hypothesis fairly. What developments in history and social evolution are illumined with the

God hypothesis? If God has revealed guidance to humanity at intervals of 500 to 1000 years, and if humanity's response has been both positive and negative, does this cast explanatory light on the history of civilizations? Does it provide a way of evaluating the lessons of the past and discerning proper directions for the future? If we can suspend disbelief when we see a movie or read a novel, then we can similarly open our minds to phenomena of religion as understood by communities of believers and as explained in original scriptures. The belief in God enables us to identify protagonists and antagonists in the building of religious civilizations and also suggests a general direction for history, toward ever larger circles of unity, cooperation, and progressive advancement.

Belief in God is also important on a deeply personal level. It can bring us a sense of self-transcendence, opening us to revelatory wisdom designed to activate humanity's higher capacities. If God exists and has a plan for humanity, it behooves us to align ourselves as completely as possible with this plan—both for ourselves as individuals and as members of the world family. And there is a potential danger in disbelieving in God. There is the chance of losing all sense of moral or spiritual authority, leaving us vulnerable to destructive ideologies that promise material and political power. Such ideologies argue that the end justifies the means—an attractive, erroneous view, luring us onto the wrong side of history and crippling humanity's spiritual evolution.

Personal and Impersonal Concepts of the Divine

It must be quickly pointed out that for many, the distinction between personal and impersonal concepts of the divine is crucial. For those who prefer a more abstract kind of thinking and lean toward scientific explanations, and for those who find Eastern thought more palatable, including Hindu and Buddhist teachings and a "new age" worldview, impersonal concepts of the divine are often more attractive. To such persons, the term *God* may seem inescapably anthropomorphic and patriarchal, or it may appear the product of childish, wishful thinking. They prefer meditation and contemplation to prayer and worship. Other terms for a greater being or force, such as *Ultimate Reality* or *Higher Power*, may seem preferable to them, and they may be willing to use other abstract terms as well. From this perspective, though there may be a moral / spiritual order of some kind, it is best not to call it *God*.

Other kinds of persons consider this kind of language and approach too cool and distant, unable to inspire loyalty and devotion. For them, metaphorical language feels more welcoming and interactive. They are more comfortable with terms such as *Creator, Provider, Lord,* and others. Prayer and worship seem more appropriate approaches to the Divine Being than rational reflection or meditative practice. It has been frequently pointed out that the scriptures of Judaism, Christianity, and Islam—though impersonal concepts are not completely absent from them—are more personal and concrete in their imagery of the divine.

But if we accept the notion that human minds and hearts are limited in what they can understand and embrace, that we all fall far short of any final comprehension or absolute control, that mysteries and wonders will always be part of human experience, then the issues surrounding personal and impersonal terms for the divine diminish in importance. From this perspective, faith is necessary because we will always be surrounded by significant unknowns, despite the continuing advance of human learning. As Bahá'u'lláh taught on this point, *"To every discerning and illuminated heart it is evident that God, the unknowable Essence, the Divine Being, is immensely exalted beyond every human attribute, such as corporeal existence, ascent and descent, egress and regress."*[1] This is grounds for humility and a deeper solidarity among those who differ in their beliefs. But it also suggests that many notions of God are projections of our limited conceptual powers—idols of thoughts and emotional needs, conjectures that say much more about us than about the divine nature. Disbelief in idolatrous notions of God is a step toward a more advanced ethical and spiritual orientation.

The Mediator Hypothesis

If it is understood that creatures cannot fully understand their Creator, any more than a house can grasp the intellect of its architect or the skills of its builder, then it becomes clear that help is needed in bridging the gap between human experience and the divine. Finite minds can never completely grasp an infinite mind, comprehend the dynamics of creation and emanation, describe with any accuracy the levels of reality, nor design a system that fully develops individual souls and transforms societies into lofty civilizations. Without assistance from higher and greater vantage-points, progress and fulfillment will forever elude us. This kind of awareness brings us to the threshold of the Mediator hypothesis: humanity's cultural and spiritual evolution seems to require guidance and illumination.

We can approach this conclusion with a brief survey of nature's levels: mineral, vegetable, animal, and human. Early in life we begin to distinguish rocks and other physical objects from simple forms of life, such as house-plants, flowers, and pets. We learn that living things are more complex and higher than nonliving things. Plants and animals are seen to have powers of growth and sensation, making them superior in capacity to earth and stone. We are also taught to ponder and appreciate differences between humans and animals. Humans can think, reason, speak, and make choices; we can discover and fashion things of use and beauty; and we can envision higher realms calling for our higher capacities of learning, aspiration, and service.

Poetic and mythic wisdom depict humanity as a world between the beasts and the gods, with built-in characteristics of both the lower and higher orders of being. Realms of ascending complexity surround us. Under ordinary circumstances, we can choose between developing our animal-like nature on one hand, or our ethical and spiritual capacities on the other. We can move backward or forward in the cosmic hierarchy.

Just as human parents and teachers are required to nurture our individual human powers and faculties, so are Divine Teachers required to elevate large portions of humanity as a whole. How can we explain humanity's episodic progress in understanding the invisible realms of science, mathematics, ethics, metaphysics, and divine attributes without Guides to show us what was hidden from our minds and hearts?

If there are levels of reality higher than human, we are dependent on those levels for advancement in understanding and capacity. When we view ourselves as the center and apex of creation, without higher authority and aspiration, we fail to develop and advance, and tend to sink into material selfishness and abasement. But with lessons from levels or beings above us, we enjoy break-throughs in personal aspiration and the social order. Higher values, broader understandings, renewed institutions, elevated art forms, and higher systems of justice and service bring a dramatic quickening for many peoples and nations. Such is the Mediator hypothesis, an outlook attempting to show why renewed religion is essential to the civilizing process and to spiritual progress.

Qualities and Descriptors of Divine-Human Mediators

Presumably, an infinite and all-powerful Being could have chosen to enlighten humanity all at once, but the history of religions shows that this option was not selected. Humanity's overall spiritual progress has been incremental and developmental, with many regressions and declines in this heartrending story. The divine method of educating humanity seems to reflect an amazing degree of patience, with intermittent lessons offered through certain Figures, several of Whom are identifiable historical Personages. What are the essential qualities and descriptors of these Mediators, Whose teachings and missions have marked history as clearly as the highest mountain ranges mark the surface of the earth?

They are greater than human, clearly manifesting divine qualities, while also being human and subject to the conditions of earthly existence. This difficult-to-fathom set of traits has made Them easily misunderstood and controversial Figures. But if They were not divine to some degree, we would not have been transformed by Their influence, and if They were not human, we would have been less likely to have understood Their messages and exemplary actions. Whereas human mortals—even great ones like Plato, Shakespeare, and Beethoven—have limited influence touching on a certain set of cultural domains, the Founders' influence cuts across all aspects of human functioning: individual and social, moral and intellectual, artistic and legal, and technical and spiritual. The educative, hope-giving, and exalted roles of the Founders are briefly described in this quotation.

> The Prophets and Founders of the world's great religions have assured Their followers of the existence of God and have led them to love and worship Him. Thus, for thousands of years, throughout the various ages until the present day man's efforts to understand his Creator have been illumined by the lives and teachings of these great Beings. . . .
>
> The Manifestations of God, by virtue of the Holy Spirit which animates Them, dwell in a kingdom of Their own far above the world of humanity and dominate the destiny of mankind. Though basically human, They abide in the realms of the Spirit beyond the reach of man.[2]

It is instructive to ponder some of the titles and descriptors that have been generated in Their wake. In various religious scripture, for example, one finds names such as the Friend of God, Exemplar of Righteousness, Revealer of Eternal Truth, Supreme Teacher, Enlightened One, Spiritual Physician, Word Made Flesh, Light of the World, Prince of Peace, Best-Beloved of

God, and Mirror of Divine Perfection. Who could evoke such reverence and adulation?

Unlike human beings, the knowledge of these Personages is innate rather than the result of learning, experimentation, and reasoning. They see and shape the heart of human reality. Their advent is a renewal of previous divine visitation. Their speech becomes the archetype of beautiful and uplifting literature deemed revelatory or the Word of God. Their impact on society is similar to the influence of the sun upon the earth—seasons and dispensations depend on nearness to and remoteness from Them. Their teachings are universal and eternally true, as well as adapted to cultural needs and historical contingencies of Their day. They awaken souls, quicken multitudes, and transform vast regions. Their missions overcome unprecedented degrees of oppression, persecution, and injustice. They have authority to abrogate the old and outdated, and to inaugurate the new and creative. Their civilizations, at their height, offer the clearest glimpses of the highest human potential and an earth made heavenly. Their legacies endure beyond any reasonable historical expectation. They prophesy dispensational Successors Who carry humanity forward and upward.

Those Who Taught Humanity and Illumined Our World

In this book we focus on those religious Figures who we know enough about to designate as originators or generators of the highest levels of civilization over the last 3500 years. Theirs are the "higher religions," according to the notable historian Arnold Toynbee. The primary Figures of this study include Moses, Krishna, Zoroaster, Buddha, Christ, Muḥammad, and Bahá'u'lláh. They are the Founders of Faith. *Faith* is understood here as a generic term for the sequential building of a common or a complementary body of moral and spiritual guidance offered by the Founders. The particular religious civilizations associated with these Figures show some significant advances over their predecessors in the areas of spiritual, social, and material development.

Thoughtful questions might be raised about four of the seven Figures we will explore. Some might reasonably point out that Buddha did not affirm a personal God, Zoroaster's current following is small, Krishna is identified with only one expression of the multifaceted Hindu Faith, and the Faith generated by Bahá'u'lláh is not well known yet. Therefore, one might question whether these four Figures should be placed on the same level as Moses,

Christ, and Muḥammad. But in the chapters dealing with these four Figures, all of these points will be directly addressed, and it will be made clear how Their lives exemplify twenty-five patterns providing telling evidence that They established major religious civilizations.

For present purposes, our seven central Figures are treated as functionally equivalent in spiritual station. They may have been called a Founder, a Divine Educator, a Revealer, an Intermediary, a Prophet, a Messenger, a Savior, the Word of God, an Avatar, an Incarnation, an Enlightened Being, a Manifestation of God, or by a number of other names or titles. Their particular titles and attributes are related to the unique cultural and scriptural traditions in which They play so momentous a part. In the unity paradigm we develop in the next chapter, Their powers and functions appear equal and interdependent. The Founders' universality and transformative power have been described as follows,

> The Manifestation of God is the Archetype, and His life is the supreme pattern. His vision, not arrested by time and space, encompasses the future as well as the past. He is the only and the necessary link between one period of social evolution and another. Without Him history is meaningless and coordination is impossible. Furthermore, the Manifestation of God releases deep reservoirs of spiritual power and quickens the forces latent in humanity.[3]

The general outlook of the twentieth century historian Arnold Toynbee seems consistent with the perspective of this study on the causes of the rising and falling of major civilizations. According to Toynbee, the Figures we are calling Founders of Faith and Divine Messengers were the originators and generators of the highest civilizations. The nearly thirty civilizations that Toynbee identified showed a pattern of development powered by spiritual vision and purpose and a pattern of decline brought on by the breakdown of such vision and purpose. Declines were rarely complete. Instead, a creative minority built a new order from the best elements of the old, combined with fresh inspiration.

In this view, religion is the directing force in history. History is not shaped primarily by economic or political forces, but by spiritual forces. Civilizations rise by responding successfully to challenges under the guidance of creative, visionary Founders. Civilizations decline when leaders lose the original vision and sink into the sins of nationalism, militarism, and materialism. Toynbee said that the emergence of "higher religion" can be seen as a new departure in human history. He said, "they are not parasites on dying civilizations," but rather "are themselves societies of a new and distinctive species; their purpose is to enable men to find a direct personal relation with the transcendent reality in and behind and beyond the Universe, though so far they have fallen short of their spiritual aspirations." This has happened because "some have been betrayed by their institutionalization into becoming rigid in structure and intolerant in outlook." Toynbee then goes on to describe what he classifies as a "higher religion." He says, "The principal higher religions that still survive are Hinduism, Judaism, Zoroastrianism, Buddhism, Christianity, and Islam."[4] Elsewhere in his writing, Toynbee described the Bahá'í Faith as tolerant and global minded, like the more humane expressions of the major world religions.[5] When Toynbee stepped back to evaluate whether religion had been a source of progress, he came to a very positive conclusion.

> The recurrent vicissitudes of civilization have carried the higher religions forward in a movement that has been, not cyclical, but progressive. If we ask ourselves why the descending movement in the revolution of the wheel of civilization has carried the chariot of religion forward and upward, we shall find our answer in the truth that religion is a spiritual activity.[6]

Distinguishing Sunlight from Moonlight

It is reasonable to ask why certain other figures have not been included in this study. Confucius and Lao Tzu are central to Chinese culture. Mahavira is the revered founder of the Jain faith. Guru Nanak, founder of the Sikh faith, is viewed as an exalted being by many of his devotees. Joseph Smith is declared a prophet by the Latter Day Saints. Black Elk has been considered a visionary holy man by many Native North Americans since the late nineteenth century. And neo-oriental gurus and new age teachers like Yogananda, Krishnamurti, Gurdjieff, Steiner, Sai Baba, and Eckhart Tolle have been revered by millions. Can they justifiably be interpreted as equal in importance to the Founders?

From our perspective, these spiritual leaders were influential sages, synthetic reformers, seers, mystics, and teachers of moral and spiritual wisdom. They have not claimed to fulfill scriptural prophecy, offering the world new revelations, nor did they convincingly define themselves as Mediators

25

between divine and human realms. They did not claim to offer new laws of divine guidance as a basis for a new religious civilization. On the contrary, each of them can be properly seen as contributing within the boundaries of previous faith traditions. Though some of their followers experienced harassment, they have not been systematically and continuously persecuted, as was the case with major world religions. For such reasons we do not view them as Founders.

As sages, they developed the wisdom tradition inherited from their forbearers. As seers and visionaries, they offered illuminating imagery and may have even been clairvoyant, able to perceive beyond the natural range. As mystics, they were deepened spiritual practitioners who elevated consciousness of the unity of all things. As reformers, they distinguished the pure essence of their inherited faith tradition, and removed some malpractices that appeared. As prophets, they warned of new divine initiatives soon to come. As new age gurus, they integrated spiritual wisdom of the ages with modern scientific ideas. Though these are clearly contributions to our planetary culture, and though they reflect spiritual light from many sources, they are not implementers of new divine laws, nor do they generate a new departure in history.

The Founders can be compared to the light of the sun. They are not the sun itself, but are Mirrors reflecting the light and energy of the sun. Like the sun, They are Each an independent source of light that illumines the earth and the world of humanity. The moon, another heavenly body that emits light, is dependent upon and reflects the light of another heavenly body, namely the sun. The Founders are often identified as God Himself because They bring divine light to humanity and generate new religious civilizations. They are much greater than mystical and visionary "moons," for example minor prophets and philosophical teachers, who reflect the light of previous illuminations. They are much greater than reformers in that They initiate the pure teaching that reformers return to and develop. By comparing these religious figures to the sun and moon, we can better understand the role they play in world history, and we can deepen our sense of God's educational plan for humanity.

Progressive Revelation:
New Paradigm for Understanding
Religion and History

Progressive Revelation—the prospect that humanity is guided regularly with messages from the divine realm—may be among the most significant ideas of the new millennium. This idea is far greater in its implications than we can adequately introduce in this chapter. However, we make an initial attempt to describe its key elements and appreciate its main applications, for it offers a new paradigm for understanding both world religion and world history. Progressive revelation casts light on the relationships between the Founders and their religious traditions on one hand, and the evolution of civilizations and the development of humanity on the other. It is a revolutionary idea with the potential to unify many peoples, fields of learning, and perspectives.

We employ several hypotheses or paradigms about religion and history that help to explain their enigmas, resolve some perplexities, and provide hope for humanity. We attempt to account for the basic contours of humanity's past, present, and future using several working assumptions for which there is good evidence. We explore the "greatest stories ever told" in ways that show their intimate connections and compatibility with widely recognized standards of reason. We strive to show that various religious systems are complementary and ultimately unified, in the same way that various sciences are interdependent and viewed as integral.

Paradigms as Explanatory Hypotheses

Until the 1960s the term *paradigm* was unfamiliar to most people and not commonly used in the English-speaking world. It had a narrow technical usage in the fields of grammar and rhetoric, pointing to linguistic forms illustrating a set of elements in an exemplary way. But due mostly to the philosopher and historian of science, Thomas Kuhn, paradigms became associated with conceptual models that form the basis of a scientific theory.[1]

The notion of paradigms suddenly became popular in the 1970s and was used broadly to describe conceptual frameworks that guide common understanding. A shift in such a framework was seen as marking a revolution in thought, soon to be followed by significant changes in practice as well. The oil crisis of the early 1970s, for example, was said to bring a paradigm-shift toward the development of renewable fuels and sustainable economic practices. The tearing down of the Berlin Wall in 1989 was said to mark a paradigm-shift in geopolitical thought from a superpower standoff to a more multilateral world. In the last several decades, the build-up of international law, the acceleration of the interfaith movement, and books that describe the dovetailing of frontier science and new age spirituality have all become linked to paradigm-shifts in common discourse, and they are highlighted in the media.

For this study we consider a paradigm-shift to be a new explanatory hypothesis connecting the dots more thoroughly than before, illuminating the phenomena being studied in a fresh way, while catalyzing creative action toward a more universal ideal. Major paradigm-shifts in understanding world religion and world history emerged in the early nineteenth centuries. Such shifts of perception have accelerated up until our present day. Religions and civilizations can be interpreted in relation to one another by using the paradigms of *Isolationism, Exclusivism, Inclusivism, Pluralism, Universalism,* and *Progressivism.* Progressivism might also be called the "unity paradigm," and it is central in the teachings of the Bahá'í Faith.

What is Revelation? How Can it be Progressive?

Revelation is the unveiling, disclosure, or renewal of divine wisdom. It is regarded as moral and spiritual guidance offered to humanity through Mediators between the ultimate and human realm. It is recorded in the scriptures or holy writings of major world religions. Throughout history, revelation has been understood as a gift to those who would "hear and see" (Matthew 11:4) what the Mediators came to teach us. Revelation is conceived of as the invisible made visible, the potential made actual, the latent made manifest. It has been praised as the music of the spheres, the heavenly chorus, the path of Cosmic Law, the Eternal Truth, breezes of the Holy Spirit, the foundation of the Celestial Kingdom, the City of God, and the Divine Word. Some believe that revelation has come to an end with the advent of their own body of scriptures. We maintain that revelation comes intermittently to humanity and will never stop coming.

With respect to the paradigm of progressive revelation, it is reasonable to ask: How could a new revelation catalyze social and material developments on the part of people unaware of this new revelation? By what mechanisms can an invisible realm impact the visible world? Admittedly, the impact of revelation is difficult to grasp or even to visualize with the mind's eye, so we need an explanatory hypothesis. Does it make any sense to say a supposedly heavenly power influences the earthly lives and activities of those who deny the very existence of such a power? Even assuming that a majority of humanity believes in God, how can we understand the process by which Spirit—the renewing of the Word of God—guides humanity's contributions to the historical process? What is the ultimate source of creative innovations—are they human, divine, or a product of divine / human interaction?

One of the patterns we will explore in the teachings of the Founders is concerned with four levels of reality. The revelatory realm can be understood as above the human realm, and events taking place there have powerful, transformative effects here on individuals who receive the new revelation. Early followers build a community of faith that, over several centuries of development, comes into social and political power. As a new faith arises, positive human capacities are quickened, and a new civilization takes shape—with intellectual, scientific, artistic, and cultural innovations appearing in its wake.

We might approach this idea about the impact of revelation by observing that the human mind is receptive to ideas spoken and written, as well as to ideas unattached to voices and written language. The mind can reflect abstractions, intuitions, and images whose origins may be completely unknown. We can reflect and express moral and spiritual qualities that are far from tangible. We can discern patterns and significances transcending the immediate content of our experiences. We can also discover realities previously unknown to us. These are fairly recognizable aspects of the human experience, which suggests the distinctively spiritual nature of human beings.

Such familiar processes suggest that the human mind is influenced by purely conceptual and non-physical currents of information and power. Though details of this human receptivity remain obscure, few would deny that we are gifted with intellectual, moral, and spiritual capacities. Lofty ideals can guide our behavior and move us to make great sacrifices. Potent ideas integrate wide areas of our experience. Virtues inspire our decision-making. Spiritual teachings shape our thought and action. Revelation catalyzes creative social developments—as in the wide range of arts, sciences, technical innovations, and cultural expressions—that we associate with the civilization-building process. Humanity will come to understand these complex causal relations more deeply in the future.

In the meantime, it is tempting to consider certain metaphors to aid us in interpreting the influence of the latest world religion. Humanity's global capacities may be seen as a set of gems that have only begun to be polished; we must rediscover the discipline of polishing our rough gems. We are like a package of seeds that has, for several centuries now, been relatively deprived of the nutrients provided by a spiritual sun and moral soil but whose source of light and warmth has now returned. We are like mirrors that have been angled so as to reflect narrower dimensions of the material world but that can now turn toward more expansive spiritual realms. We are like radios suddenly empowered to receive a greater range of wave-patterns but that are in need of an Interpreter or Guide for all this new information.

We can also observe that humanity today is disenchanted with the old order of national sovereignty, but we have yet to embrace the new order of world citizenship. Most essentially, we are creatures fashioned for self-transcendence and ever-wider circles of relationship, poised to rediscover ways to move closer to our Creator and to fulfill our potential. Whatever image or paradigm we choose to explain a new revelation, we can expect that, as in the past, social disequilibrium and transformative cultural breakthroughs will come. A day of judgment is also a day of renewal. A time of crisis is a time of opportunity. Where there is new light, areas of darkness appear in clearer relief. Processes of disruption and destruction are accompanied by processes of integration and advance.

A Working Description of Progressive Revelation

For today's world, the phenomena of progressive revelation—the historic lives, messages, and legacies of Founders—seem especially telling and transformative. We will examine the periodic sets of moral and spiritual guidance erupting onto the stage of history. The notion of the oneness of God has implications more vast and profound than humanity can fathom. It means truth is one, though it will never be fully and finally grasped by finite creatures, who may therefore continue to improve in every way and make prog-

Bottom paragraph: later scriptures can be used to interpret earlier scriptures.

ress indefinitely. It suggests that the complementary nature of religion and science will become increasingly clear through the ages to come. Appreciating the singleness of God can lead to a recognition of unity as the new paradigm for all fields.

The hypothesis of progressive revelation suggests that when a major portion of humanity needs a new religion, when the previous one in the chain has lost its potency, and when adherents are disillusioned and adrift, God sends a new Messenger. Each revelation is progressive in that it elevates humanity, propelling us forward after inevitable periods of decline. Each religious civilization at its zenith makes moral, spiritual, and intellectual advances over its predecessors. However, the prejudices of the adherents of one faith usually prevent them from perceiving these patterns. Religious leaders usually resist the new revelation because it threatens their social status, while exposing their ignorance and corruption. Eventually, a creative minority catalyzes a social transformation that historians call a new civilization.

Progressive revelation is the claim that all religions are essentially one, and differences among them are attributable to varying requirements of the cultural and historical contexts in which they were born. It means that all Founders—Moses, Zoroaster, Krishna, Buddha, Christ, Muḥammad, and Baháʼuʼlláh—were united in their divine aspects and spiritual teachings. They were prophetically linked agents of a single providential plan. Their authority was given to Them by God, and Each had equal access to infinite wisdom and power. But They were also distinct in Their human temples. They were historically separate, addressing different cultural contexts.

The relationship between great historic religions, then, under the progressive unity paradigm, may be likened to links in a chain, classes in a graded school, dawning-points of the sun, or stages in a lifespan—infancy, childhood, youth, and adulthood. Religions may also be compared to widening social circles of historical development—self, family, tribe, village, city, nation, empire, and finally, the world. These analogies suggest an evolutionary process where advances in complexity and sophistication are achieved as higher capacities develop and creative potentialities unfold.

As noted previously, if God is the source of all genuine revelations, then later scriptures can be used to interpret earlier scriptures. The significance of this principle is often undervalued. It means our understanding of Abraham, for example, can deepen and expand with revelations that came after the scriptures of ancient Israel. Christian, Islamic, and Baháʼí scriptures enrich our grasp of the significance of Abraham as the father of many nations, peoples, and religions. Later scriptures unlock mysteries of prophetic passages in earlier scriptures, clearing away dogmas that build up when a single body of scripture is taken as the final word of God.

Even though the spiritual virtues emphasized in succeeding revelations are the same abiding universal principles (such as devotion, loving-kindness, justice, peace, wisdom, and trustworthiness), the social and material guidelines in each revelation are indeed distinct from their predecessors. Without these new guidelines, there could be no progress and renewal. This means that some differences between religions are divinely sanctioned—that is, later social and economic teachings abrogate earlier ones that correspond to them most closely. Legal and ritual guidelines change from dispensation to dispensation. Islam, for example, abrogated the earlier Christian and Jewish tolerance of drinking alcoholic beverages, and it changed the point of adoration from Jerusalem to Mecca. The Bahá'í Faith has abrogated the Islamic prohibition of usury and changed the direction of prayer from Mecca to 'Akká, Israel.

Many differences that appear between major religions are not divinely sanctioned. Rather, they result from human misinterpretation, institutional rigidity, and abuse of power. Ritual and theological doctrines within faith traditions often become increasingly prejudicial, superstitious, and exclusionary. Though they were never part of the Founders' intent, dogmas are later perceived as essential, becoming a basis for sectarian divisions and hostilities. We review the more troublesome distortions of original scriptural guidance in upcoming chapters. Here we simply observe that progressive revelation seems to be the divine method of renewing moral and spiritual guidance. It reforms and corrects social and material guidance in appropriate stages, preparing humanity as a whole to co-establish an ever-advancing civilization. Such principles help unify humanity's spiritual heritage and explain apparent contradictions.

Paradigms for Interpreting World Religion

It is probable that most people throughout history have thought of religion in the singular. That is, religion meant for them "my religion," and it was hardly distinguishable from the way of life and the guiding beliefs of "my people." This means that for most human beings during most of our time on earth, there has been little or no attention given to other peoples' religions.

We might call this perspective *Isolationism,* suggesting a kind of cultural and intellectual vacuum that did not stimulate spiritual reflection and religious philosophizing. Although the number of civic and religious leaders, as well as traders, may have begun to rise significantly in the Axial Age, centered about 2,500 years ago, the multitudes did not have to face the implications of other religions and civilizations until medieval times and the Age of Exploration.

Today it is commonly observed that there is great variety among members of any given faith tradition regarding how other faith traditions are evaluated. Christians, for example, range from a very conservative or fundamentalist perspective at one end of the spectrum to a more liberal or universal perspective at the other. Stricter Christians might believe that there is no truth or abiding value outside their own community—an *Exclusivist* position with regard to other religions. Moderate Christians might believe there are noteworthy ethical and spiritual principles outside their own faith tradition, but perhaps these moderates would quickly add that their own religion is *inclusive* of all the highest truths and values that might be found elsewhere. Liberal Christians usually differ from both the *Exclusivist* and *Inclusivist* perspectives, declaring that each religious perspective has its distinctive truths and worthwhile values—a *Pluralist* position with regard to other faith traditions. These examples of varying perspectives within Christian faith tradition would also apply to Jews, Hindus, Buddhists, Muslims, and Bahá'ís as well.

Diana Eck, a notable interfaith researcher at Harvard University, has been credited with the initial clarification of these three views of other faiths: *Exclusivism* essentially says "my religion is the only true one"; *Inclusivism* concludes that "my religion contains the truth of all others"; and *Pluralism* declares that "each religion has its own respectable truth and values."[2] Most interfaith advocates have adopted Eck's view of these vantage points on the presence of other communities of faith. Most investigators of interfaith relations assume these three views are comprehensive, and they adequately describe in logically exhaustive categories the basic perspectives people may have on other faiths.

It is said that if *Exclusivists* show interest in the interfaith arena, it is to prepare for a more informed and effective approach to their conversion-oriented teaching programs and missionary work. When *Inclusivists* participate in interfaith events, this is seen as their attempt to learn more about how their own faith tradition is the culmination of all other ethical and spiritual initiatives. And when *Pluralists*—probably representing the majority of interfaith participants—step into the interfaith arena, this is viewed as a genuine give-and-take process, a true dialogue leading to mutual discovery, cooperation, and transformation.

One distinctive type of *Pluralism* emphasizes that the many different spiritual perspectives are best interpreted as reflections of one Source from which they have all arisen. Many Theosophists, Sufis, Sikhs, religious liberals, and new age seekers embrace this perspective, which might be termed *Universalist.* It suggests that we step outside of our particular traditions as often as possible and adopt a more spiritually cosmopolitan outlook, seeing the same divine signature written in all spiritual literature and activity. *Universalists* claim that higher perception enables us to see commonalities as more deeply grounded in the human condition than the barriers and divisions that separate us.

For many years I shared the standard threefold assessment of interfaith dynamics—the view that there are three main paradigms—*Exclusivism, Inclusivism,* and *Pluralism*—so we must choose one. I embraced a *Pluralist / Universalist* worldview. But then in the mid-1990s, my experience in interfaith gatherings, as well as my study of world scriptures, helped me see that *Pluralism* and *Universalism,* though much better than conflict, cannot lead to the higher understanding and commitment needed to transform global society toward a united world. To me, it began to feel as if the same Voice were speaking through the world's scriptures down through the ages, in sequence, and now once again had spoken through the Bahá'í Faith. This Voice has shown sensitivity to humanity's varying historical settings, providing one light that reconciles seemingly irreconcilable differences that have given history its tragic but progressive character.

Progressivism as a religious worldview sees major religions as linked and sequential, as part of a divine plan to educate humanity. This perspective contains elements of *Inclusivism* and *Pluralism.* Like *Inclusivism,* it sees its own faith as a culmination of previous religious eras, but unlike *Inclusivism,* it says that higher revelations and wider loyalties will definitely unfold in the future. Like *Pluralism* and *Universalism,* it sees many virtues in the family of faiths, but unlike *Pluralism* and *Universalism, Progressivism* feels obligated to unite under the highest of all authorities—God's latest guidance. *Progressivism* says that all religions have one Source, and so will eventually merge, but they should be guided by the latest revelation. When humanity learns to see beyond cultural particulars, discerning that revelations are offered at intervals of about 500 to 1000 years, then both earlier and later religions appear more clearly as part of one providential process that is deeply developmental. ₁₂ -₂₇

Other Working Hypotheses Regarding Religious Interpretation

A major hypothesis we employ is that what operates behind these phenomena is a unique Source and Revealer of guiding truth. We both assume and explore evidence that God or some sort of Ultimate Reality exists as the Creator of the universe—an unlimited store of power, knowledge, and goodness—a view that for many minds is compatible with authentic scriptures and is also amenable to the hypothetical inquiries of science. Beliefs influence behavior and therefore have social impact that can be systematically investigated. Science looks for ever more inclusive explanations of phenomena in the natural and social worlds, and it is methodologically obliged to remain provisional in its conclusions.

Because there would be an unbridgeable distance between an infinite God and merely finite human creatures, and because there would be no way for human beings to know about such an Exalted Being, we explore the possibility that God sends Mediators from time to time. We identify Figures that appear partly human and partly divine, and Who seem to be direct vehicles of revelation. They claim to be humanity's access to moral and spiritual guidance. Though our understanding of God can never be complete, human understanding can make infinite progress, both through the discovery of patterns and processes in the natural world and human society, as well as through guidance from an Unknowable Source.

An important distinction in interpreting the teachings of Revelers, and one deemed necessary by the contemporary mind, is the distinction between *literal* and *figurative* meanings. The world's scriptures contain "true stories" that can be corroborated to some degree by scientific historical methods. Examples are Buddha's establishing a new religious movement in the Ganges Plain, Jesus' generating a movement that challenged and eventually overcame the Jewish and Roman establishments, and Muḥammad's uniting the tribes of Arabia under a renewed form of belief in one God. These depictions contain historical truth.

But the world's scriptures also contain "stories of truth," that are meant to be understood in symbolic and spiritual ways. These latter stories refer to largely spiritual significances. The Garden of Eden story, for example, may cast light on the transition from pre-history to history, the roles of choice and guiding values in human existence, as well as generational dynamics and foundational views of a single divine reality. Figurative stories are often not useful for a detailed historical or scientific understanding, but they do provide moral and spiritual guidance, while inspiring new forms of art and offering hope to the faithful. When the complementary purposes of these two kinds of stories—literal and figurative—are borne in mind and fully appreciated, then the complementary nature of the relationship between religion and science can be maintained with intellectual integrity.

It is often the case that a later set of scriptures comments on an earlier set. Thus we find commentary in the Qur'án about stories in the Christian and Jewish scriptures, as well commentary in the Buddhist scriptures about the Hindu scriptures. If the same one God is the source of all authentic scriptures, as this study assumes, then our understanding of humanity's spiritual heritage will undergo a liberating kind of paradigm shift when our investigation becomes illumined and deepened by interfaith encounter and multi-scriptural research. Such comparative appreciation can be a gateway to a more peaceful, just, and united world community.

Religion can be defined in two basic ways. It may be viewed as *divine guidance* through authoritative Revealers. But as a worldly phenomenon, religion is culturally defined and historically developed, so it may be understood as *human aspiration*—reaching toward, failing to attain, and sometimes tragically distorting the highest ideals ever conceived. Because religion is both a transcendent and a worldly phenomenon, it is ambiguous and a source of intense controversy and confusion. Quite reasonable people can argue across perplexing sociocultural divisions. One side earnestly believes that religion is the source of the highest good, while the other side sees it as the source of the gravest evil. But when religion is understood as a developmental phenomenon—pure in its spiritual origins and emergence, yet humanly corruptible in its maintenance and declining stages—confusion subsides, and interreligious unity becomes possible.

Human nature, in this perspective, spans a continuum from material to spiritual. We are essentially *spiritual beings*—with divinely-given capacities to discern ever deeper truths, to design ever more useful instruments, to fashion ever more beautiful forms, and to express ever higher virtues. But we are also volitional creatures that can allow ourselves to fall far short of our creative potential. Ours is the choice at every turn, for better or worse, and we can even sink to the darkest and most immoral depths imaginable.

Paradigms for Interpreting World History

History will be viewed in this study as a drama in which religion plays the most significant role, leading humanity to the greatest achievements as well as the vilest depravities. Civilization—a development (or misuse) of humanity's spiritual, social, and material capacities—is the major agent or player on the stage of world events. Civilization is a measure of collective human capacity, both for better and worse. At its best, civilization is an authentic and faithful response to revelatory guidance. At its worst, civilization becomes a tool of oppression, militarism, materialism, and moral degradation. Religion proves to be a positive and civilizing force in its stages of birth, growth, and renewal. But it also proves to be a retarding and corrupting influence in its stages of stagnation and decline.

The six paradigms we mentioned above with respect to religion also have corresponding or parallel application in the field of history. What have ordinary people, not leaders or scholars, understood about world history down through the ages? The *Isolationist* paradigm explained the development of the world from a single tribal, regional, or national perspective. Such accounts were dominant until the Axial Period (800 to 200 BCE) during which the four earliest civilizations—Mesopotamian, Egyptian, Indian, and Chinese—came into significant interaction. The next paradigm of world history might be termed *Exclusivist* because other peoples and cultures were recognized but were assumed to be misguided. Late classical and medieval times, as well as the Age of Exploration, brought the *Inclusivist* sense that other civilizations have offerings of genuine worth but that overall those other cultures are incomplete and not as good as one's own culture.

In the last 500 years, during which the West began to dominate the rest of the world economically and politically, the *Pluralist* and the *Universalist* paradigms have emerged. Many ordinary citizens of modernizing societies have the *Pluralist* view that many different peoples and cultures live side by side and that therefore societies must be broadly egalitarian in relation to each other. The world is seen as increasingly interdependent. A significant minority, however, has adopted a *Universalist* perspective, concluding that our commonalities are more deeply grounded than our differences, that traditional revelatory systems will become relics of a bygone age, and that a planetary culture will emerge almost unconsciously.

The advocates of *Progressive Unity* see the world as uniting in more intentional and authoritative ways than do the *Universalists*. The *Progressivist* paradigm claims that unity is the paramount task for humanity in this current millennium. Acts that oppose world unity will bring grievous consequences, while building unity will bring unprecedented prosperity and advancement to humanity and the whole global community. Science and religion will become thoroughly complementary in their functions, a world commonwealth will emerge, and its foundations will be both pragmatic and spiritual.

All the above paradigms about God, religion, scripture, human nature, history, and the future will be explored and applied in succeeding chapters. Can these frameworks help us make sense of the dramatic panorama of world history? Can they assist us in identifying hopeful commonalities and vexing differences found in the family of world religions? Might they help explain the seeming collapse of once great civilizations? Do they cast any light on the moral / spiritual vacuum that many people experience today? Can they help halt the current materialistic slide, providing insight on the needed reconciliation between science and spirituality? Can they steer us away from chaos and disaster and guide us toward greater global maturity? Such questions are inescapable for thoughtful and responsible people today, and we seek useful answers in the journey before us. Our effort, if successful, will amount to a philosophy of global religion and an educational program faithful to the original teachings of major religions, yet will also remain compatible with an open-minded scientific outlook.

Preview of Common Patterns in the Greatest Stories Ever Told

The Founders' stories are the greatest stories ever told—inspiring billions of people over the last 3,500 years, commanding devotion and dedication, moulding character and conduct, guiding morality and family life, founding legal systems and institutions, generating literature and other art forms, and shaping education and philosophical reflection. It appears that the highest ideals and most useful guidance humanity has known came through these Founders of the world's religions. We develop our personal and collective capacities most effectively and creatively when we align our wills with Their teachings. No other figures in history have had more influence and impact on the building of civilizations and the transformation of souls.

In the next chapter, brief summaries are offered of twenty-five common patterns or parallels found in the world's religions. Hopefully they serve as observable links between the world's major religious heritages. These same twenty-five patterns are elaborated in the fourteen succeeding chapters. A *pattern* in the sense we use this term refers to a significant regularity or exemplary model that stands out clearly in the lives and teachings of the Founders, if we study Them with open minds and hearts. A pattern is an order of events or arrangement of ideas associated with each Teacher that has a discernible shape. Patterns are motifs or models in Their lives and legacies that are clearly comparable. When we contemplate these regularities, we discover their power to guide our conduct and elevate our aspiration.

We will show that each facet of the Founders' backgrounds, each episode in Their missions, each category of Their teaching, and each primary achievement in Their legacies are intimately related and help illumine one another. These linked patterns, when deeply absorbed, can startle our souls and shatter our prejudices. They can illuminate the contours of history, deepen interfaith compassion, sharpen intellectual understanding, and inspire greater global cooperation. The patterns are like well-paved but seldom used roads between religious cultures. They are like strong cable-bridges over turbulent rivers that have intimidated those who have tried to cross them. They are common ground and shared entry-points for serious reflection, dialogue, and consultation.

These parallels point to a common Source beyond human consciousness. The truths revealed in these stories are viewed not merely in the factual or historical sense but as containing moral and spiritual lessons that, when combined with the universal principles taught by the Founders in complementary ways, have given purpose to human life and direction to the evolution of civilization. These life stories are referred to by some sociologists of religion as *symbolic biographies* and are viewed as "important not *merely* to the degree that they are factual. The mytho-historical form of the saving stories is designed to communicate and to evoke the significance of the founder's revelation in the persons who hear it." Such a story "teaches, commands, enlightens, and reveals the transformation of human existence. The story is true or is accepted as true of the human condition and of the way to salvation or liberation."[3]

My understanding of the Founders' patterns has been deeply influenced by one of Bahá'u'lláh's works titled The Kitáb-i-Íqán, or "The Book of Certitude."

I find especially useful and inspiring the suggestions that we approach all scriptures with a sense of spiritual detachment, receptivity, and purity of heart; ponder the reasons why the Founders were deemed threats to the religious leaders of their day, which resulted in severe persecution and social disequilibrium; view such terms as *life, death, resurrection, sun, moon, stars,* and *earth* symbolically—as figurative and spiritual references, rather than literal and physical references; acknowledge that Founders spoke of Themselves as divine and unified with each other, on one hand, and as human and distinguished from each other, on the other—their differences being effective responses to varying historical and cultural conditions; see four factors as likely evidence of their divine unity: 1) Their ability to reveal supplementary and new scriptural verses, 2) Their steadfastness in the face of enormous opposition, 3) the potency of Their lives and revelations to evoke great sacrifices toward the founding of new civilizations, 4) Their capacity to interpret, fulfill, and announce prophecies of one another; recognize that Founders function as Mediators between spiritual reality and material reality; and accept later scriptures as authoritative in interpreting earlier scriptures.

Interfaith Understanding and the Building of a More United World

Let us conclude this chapter with a quick look at some of the practical implications of the patterns among the Founders becoming widely known, whether or not the ultimate explanation is universally agreed upon. One positive outcome might be called spiritual—glimpsing the unique and ultimate realm from which the great religions have emerged, and allowing ourselves to be transformed thereby. Our reverence for God, or whatever other name by which we refer to a greater being or reality, is greatly enhanced when taking all of the Founders' lives and teachings into account, rather than just one of Them, or trying to ignore Them altogether in a secular fashion.

Another set of results might be called *intellectual.* Greater sensitivity to the patterns among the Founders would enable us to distinguish reform movements from advents of major new religious dispensations, to clarify the distinctiveness and complementary functions of the major religions, to integrate our understanding of religious history as a whole, and to appreciate more fully the role of religion in giving direction to history. A final set of useful implications might be called *moral.* Acknowledging all Founders as our Teachers would help us embrace basic ethical principles upon which cultural advancement depends, establish a culturally fair global curriculum, improve interfaith harmony, and in the language of the Founders, "build the kingdom of heaven on earth."

Our hope is that evidence for the patterns will be deemed substantial and become widely available to the world's reading public. This would improve the prospects for interfaith understanding, international cooperation, and intercultural befriending. If religious education becomes more global in its content, and if intercontinental communication and transportation continue to improve, then religious prejudices will definitely subside. This will enable a more cooperative humanity to remove barriers to the formation of a united and peaceful world.

- 4 -
Parallels and Patterns Linking the Founders

Twenty-five parallels or patterns link humanity's religious heritage, follow-ing a roughly chronological order. The first four concern the background of the Founder—the traditional antecedents, spiritual ancestry, and cultural context that are essential to understanding His arising onto the stage of world history. The next eight describe the Founder's mission—the basic narrative account of pursuing a divine calling, facing enormous challenges, and ulti-mately attaining a great triumph for a sizeable portion of humanity. The next eight relate to His teachings, or lessons of guidance, that are soon deemed the Word of Truth, with the ability to save individual souls and transform a wide social milieu. The last five show His legacy—the enduring institutional influence of the Founder and His endowment to posterity.

1 – Continuity with Previous Dispensations
Each Founder arose from a lineage of other revered Figures who purified, supplemented, and passed on an ancient body of revealed guidance.

> Religions do not spring up without a root in this world. Each great founder of religion has acknowledged his debt to his spiritual forebears, whose teachings and traditions he cherishes and passes on anew.[1]

> Each of the founders reveals something new and thus is a reformer, but he is at the same time reannouncing or reenacting an ancient, primor-dial truth.[2]

Those who study religions soon see they are related as parent to child. The Aryan-Vedic contributors to the Hindu Faith gave birth to the Zoroastrian and Buddhist Faiths; the Jewish Faith gave birth to the Christian Faith; these latter two gave birth to the Islamic Faith, which gave birth to the Bahá'í

Faith. Each Founder spoke in terms familiar to the followers of the preceding religion, using concepts, symbols, and traditions deeply significant to Their followers. Predecessors were duly praised. Bahá'u'lláh summed up this vital continuity: *"All the Prophets are Temples of the Cause of God, Who have appeared clothed in divers attire."*[3]

The background of Moses (ca. 1500 BCE) included Abraham (ca. 2000 BCE), known as the "father of many nations," through whom *"all the families of the earth shall bless themselves,"*[4] as well as Joseph (ca. 1850 BCE), who rose to great heights in Egypt, assuring the people that God would revisit them and lead them to the Promised Land.[5] Zoroaster's background (ca. 1000 BCE) included various civilizations—Sumerians, Elamites, and other Mesopotamians—generally polytheistic, though there were monotheistic influences through figures such as Yima, Spitama, and Manuschir. Krishna's background (ca. 1100–1400 BCE) included the Aryan-Dravidian encounter (ca. 1500 BCE) resulting in diverse yet surprisingly unified religious patterns, including Avatars or divine incarnations such as Rama, who strengthened monotheistic influences without eliminating the gods. Buddha's background (ca. 500 BCE) included the previous Buddha Kassapa, the breakdown of Krishna's devotional synthesis, regression to rigid ritualism, as well as the intellectual and spiritual revolt that produced the Upanishads, a collection of Hindu scriptures (ca. 750 BCE). Christ's background (6 BCE–30 CE) included Israel's trials from Moses' day and David's united kingdom, through the divided kingdom, the Babylonian exile, Hellenistic domination, as well as prophets such as Isaiah revealing messianic visions. Muḥammad's background (570–632 CE) included the instability of ancient Arabia; the heritage of Abraham, Hagar, and Ishmael who established Mecca and the Kaaba; regression into polytheism; domination by Persians and Byzantines, as well as Jewish and Christian influence. Bahá'u'lláh's background (1817–1892 CE) included the Zoroastrian heritage of Persian kings, Davidic heritage through Cyrus' wife Rahab, and rising and falling Islamic dynasties, especially the Persian Qajar dynasty and its S͟hí'ah clergy.

2 – Arising to Guide Humanity in the Worst of Times

The Founders emerged in a context of intolerable oppression and degradation.

> The scriptures of the different religions are unanimous in describing the degraded state of the world prior to the coming of the saviour . . . More

emphasis is placed, however, in these prophecies on the deterioration of the moral and spiritual state of humanity . . . In particular, the social structures that maintain stability of society . . . are predicted to become destabilized.[6]

Founders always arise in the darkest of days, when saving messages and transformative guidance seem absolutely essential for human survival. They come at the end of long declines, when a moral and spiritual change is widely demanded. Their settings effectively dramatize the power of God to overcome great obstacles. Moses came to the stage of religious history under the oppressive yoke of the Egyptian Pharaoh who no longer favored Joseph's people, and had begun to make their burdens unbearable. Zoroaster's context was dominated by the injustice of violent, raiding nomads and the corruption of superstitious, dogmatic Persian priests. In Krishna's day, the notorious tyrant King Kamsa oppressed all of northern India, keeping people in constant fear and dread. Buddha arose at a time of profound restlessness, exploitation, and violence that had developed in the Ganges plain. The context for Christ's emergence was Roman / Herodian oppression, intense messianic expectation, and sectarian tensions among Jews. Muḥammad arose during conditions later described as the Arabian "days of ignorance," which included inter-tribal raiding and violence, poorly distributed wealth, female infanticide, as well as deeply entrenched superstition. Though Persia had a glorious and relatively peaceful past, Bahá'u'lláh arose at a time of widespread political and religious corruption in the Iranian Qajar Dynasty.

3 – Advent Prophesied and Expected

Each Founder was specifically predicted and expected to arise as part of a grand redemptive scheme.

> The scriptures of most religions tell of holy figures who recognize the station and destiny of the divine educators years before the start of their ministries.[7]

> There is often a precursor, a holy figure who recognized the prophet-founder when the latter was only a child or who prophesied to the people that his advent was imminent.[8]

The veil between the earthly and heavenly realms seems to be more permeable just prior to the coming of the Founders. Spiritually perceptive souls announced the gift about to be offered to humanity. Moses was expected, not only through Joseph's assurance about the Promised Land, but because soothsayers had warned Pharaoh that a child had been born who would control the kingdom's fate and its slaves. Zoroaster was among the longed-for series of ancient Persian revealers from Gayomart's (which may be a reference to Adam's) and Yima's (which may be a reference to Noah's) lineage. Before Krishna's birth, people longed for an Avatar, a term that can be translated as a deity or incarnation. A heavenly voice warned King Kamsa, Krishna's uncle, that his nephew would kill him and vanquish evil. Before Buddha's birth, hope for another Enlightened One had intensified, and one great seer, Asita, prophesied that young Gautama would become either a world ruler or a world redeemer. Christ was heralded by John the Baptist, enjoining Israel's repentance and promising that *"He who is coming after me is mightier than I."*[9] The arising of Muḥammad as a Prophet was foretold by pagan soothsayers, some Jewish leaders, the Christian monk Bahira, and Salman the Persian. Bahá'u'lláh claimed to bring the fulfillment of age-old prophetic promises. The Báb (1819–50) heralded "Him Whom God shall make manifest," or the "Promised One of All Ages." Bahá'u'lláh claimed to fulfill Jewish expectation of the Messiah, Zoroastrian expectation of the Future Savior, Hindu expectation of Kalki or the Tenth Avatar, Buddhist expectation of Maitreya, Christian expectation of the Return of Christ, and Islamic expectation of the Mahdi.

4 – Auspicious Signs, Birth, and Intimations of Greatness

Heavenly signs heralded the coming of humanity's spiritual kings. Their births and upbringing revealed a process of divine intervention. In Their youth and young adulthood, the Founders showed spiritual signs of future greatness.

Twofold signs, in the visible and the invisible heaven, have announced the Revelation of each of the Prophets of God.[10]

Miraculous stories are related about the birth and childhood of each of these figures. . . . Common features include some form of divine

46

intervention in the process of conception, and the infant speaking from inside the womb or immediately after birth and possessing a miraculous degree of prescience and wisdom. . . .

Despite these stories of birth and infant miracles, it would appear that these figures grow to adulthood leading ordinary lives.[11]

Portents of beyond-human powers and destiny are among the relatively scant details of the Founders' early years provided in the various scriptural traditions. These stories provide an effective link between the accounts of Their births and Their moments of call or awakening.

As an infant Moses was set afloat on the Nile River to escape Pharaoh's wrath, but God led Him to Pharaoh's daughter and a royal Egyptian education. Zoroaster was born of a virgin who drank a sacred mixture containing His own preexistent, eternal seed, and then later in His life He became a seeker of wisdom and prepared for a career of moral discernment. As a child, Zoroaster received divine protection from evil forces, and in His youth He chose the "sacred girdle" rather than land, seeking righteousness in solitary communion with God. Krishna was conceived in a dungeon, even though His parents were bound to separate pillars; and then, according to His own command, He was reared by foster parents as a cowherd. As a divine incarnation, Krishna slew demons, bested the gods, and enchanted villagers with His flute playing. Before Buddha's birth, His mother dreamed a white elephant (a symbol of divine power and purity) entered her womb; and upon His birth, He said, *"For enlightenment I was born."*[12] As a youth, Buddha felt compassion for small creatures in a plowed field, and meditation on their suffering brought Him profound insights, which led Him to new Dharma (Truth). Christ was born of a virgin who was described as a *"handmaid of the Lord"*[13] and was parented by a carpenter from David's line. He fulfilled prophecy about a virgin's son and His birth was celebrated by a *"heavenly host."*[14] Other signs included the star seen by wise men from the East, and youthful dialogue between Jesus and teachers in the temple. Muḥammad descended from Abraham, and His mother heard a voice telling her she would give birth to the lord of the Arabs while seeing a light issuing from her womb. Other signs included Muḥammad's support of the league of the virtuous as a youth, and His equitable proposal for relocating the Black Stone in the Kaaba. Bahá'u'lláh was born of noble Persian lineage, which included the last Sasanian king as well as Zoroaster. Some of those who knew Him had dreams of His future sovereignty, and He knew many things not taught and solved problems as a youth that caused observers to marvel.

5 – Divine Commission

Dramatic events marked decisively the beginning of the Founders' earthly missions. Momentous initiatory events signalled an awakening to Their divine callings: "In many cases the beginning of their vocations is marked by a 'call' or 'illumination' experience of great intensity."[15] Divine commissioning events were impressive and luminous signs for both believers and unbelievers that new, world-transforming happenings were taking place.

Moses saw a burning bush, heard a divine command to deliver His people from bondage, and led them to the Promised Land. Zoroaster was led by an archangel to the heavenly court to receive His divine commission, and He found so much light there that shadows were absent. Krishna's divine calling required Him to leave His rural home, move to the city of Mathura, kill the tyrant King Kamsa, and restore righteousness. Buddha's call to truth led Him to go forth from pleasure palaces to forests and eventually to attain enlightenment under the Bodhi Tree. While Christ was being baptized by John, the Holy Spirit descended as a dove, and a heavenly voice declared *"with Thee I am well pleased."*[16] Muḥammad received His divine commission through the archangel Gabriel on Mount Hira when He was commanded to *"Proclaim! (or Read!) in the name of thy Lord."*[17] Bahá'u'lláh saw a vision of the Maid of Heaven in a dungeon proclaiming that He would emerge *"victorious by Thyself and by Thy pen."*[18]

6 – Struggling in Solitude

Soon after Their divine callings, the Founders experienced doubt, temptation, or a significant period of spiritual testing that was undertaken alone. Each conquered His human self, and became a perfect servant of the divine cause.

> Most of these figures appear, following this initiatory experience, to have had doubts or to have felt the need for a period of solitude during which they prepared themselves for their mission.[19]

48

The founders of all the great religions go through a period of solitude in the course of which they often have to endure hardships or internal struggles with doubts, evil suggestions, or even demonic forces.[20]

There was always a transition period between the Founders' commission experiences and the declaration of Their new religious era—an interval allowing for a shift from primarily human activities and roles to divinely powered ministries.

Moses voiced deep concerns about His ability to fulfill His commission, saying *"I am not eloquent"* [21] and asking by what authority He would speak. He made the solitary journey back to Egypt, contemplating His new responsibilities and bestowals. Zoroaster was tempted by the Evil Spirit to renounce the new faith. He wandered in the wilderness and sometimes feared that He was failing to fulfill God's assignment. Krishna's greatest weakness was love for those who loved Him. He said, *"the only thing that can bind Me is the power of love,"* [22] and He struggled with the temptation to return to His childhood village. Buddha's doubts and trials haunted Him during an intense six-year search; and even upon finally attaining enlightenment, the Evil One tempted Him with desires, fears, and questions about the futility of teaching. After baptism, Christ was *"led up by the Spirit into the wilderness to be tempted by the devil"* offering Him *"all the kingdoms of the world."* [23] After His calling, Muḥammad thought He had been possessed by evil spirits and sought the assurance of His first wife, Khadijah. Later, He overcame the temptation to compromise with Meccan polytheists. After the troubled start of His ministry in Baghdad, Baháʼuʼlláh abandoned the city to pursue mystical solitude in the mountains of Kurdistan, where He *"contemplated no return."* [24]

7 – Declaration and First Followers

A private declaration by the Founders, followed by a public declaration, yielded initial devotees, followers, and supporters.

Following the initiatory event, these figures did not go out immediately and proclaim their mission to the world. Rather, they gathered around themselves a small group of disciples . . . . It was only at a later stage that these prophet-founders of new religions made a more public declaration of their missions.[25]

49

The developmental nature of the Founders' ministries was accented by having an interval between Their embracing of a divine station and its socially visible expression, as if to grow into Their divine calling.

Moses won the support of Aaron (his brother) and all the elders of the people of Israel, telling them what God had commanded, and later He told Pharaoh to *"Let my people go."*[26] Zoroaster's first group of followers were King Vishtaspa and his royal court in Balkh (northeastern Iran), followed later by proclamations to other leaders. Krishna chose Arjuna, Yudhishthira, three other Pandava brothers, and Drapaudi to be the primary instruments of restoring righteousness to India. Later, He declared His spiritual station to kings. Buddha's first followers were five monks befriended during His period of austerities; later, Sariputta and Mogallana became leading disciples, and two kings, Bimbisara and Pasenadi, became loyal supporters. Christ chose Peter, Andrew, and ten other disciples as *"fishers of men,"*[27] and later made His mission known to Jewish and Roman leaders. Muḥammad's initial declaration and followers included only family and close friends; but three years later, He made a public declaration to Meccan leaders, and later in Medina, addressed the emperors of His day. Bahá'u'lláh declared to a small group of followers in the Garden of Riḍván outside Baghdad that He was "Him Whom God shall make manifest," and He later declared His station to the most influential of the world's political and religious leaders.

8 – Overcoming Powerful Opposition

The Founders courageously faced strong external and internal opposition, and They overcame seemingly insurmountable obstacles. Leaders of the older religion were especially obstructive.

Leaders of religion, in every age, have hindered their people from attaining the shores of eternal salvation, inasmuch as they held the reins of authority in their mighty grasp. Some for the lust of leadership, others through want of knowledge and understanding, have been the cause of the deprivation of the people.[28]

The activities of each of the prophet-founders set off a reaction in the form of internal and external opposition to them and their teaching. The internal opposition arose from within the ranks of the disciples and followers and was an act of betrayal caused usually by motives of fear, jealousy or envy. . . .

The external opposition to these prophet-founder figures occurred because, through their teaching, they had each challenged the social order. Those with the greatest vested interest in the maintenance of that order, the rulers and the religious leaders, opposed them.[29]

If objective observers in the time of a new Founder were asked to wager for or against the infant faith, their rational calculations would make them bet against it. When religious and civil leaders conspire against a new cause, especially when they gain help from the Founder's followers, what earthly power could explain their failure to eliminate the new faith? Such considerations lead us to conclude that divine assistance is a factor in the rise of new world religions. Moses' chief opposition came from Pharaoh, murmurers among His followers, and worshippers of the golden calf; but these moments of opposition were made into opportunities to clarify and strengthen the Faith. Zoroaster struggled triumphantly with wizards and sorcerers, His own misguided magi, as well as invading Turanians. Strong initial and continuing resistance helped to illuminate the contrast between Zoroaster's "good religion" and the surrounding superstition and malevolence. Krishna's primary enemies were the kings Kamsa and Jarasandha, and the prince Duryodhana who led the opposition in the Mahabharata War; but they were made vehicles for positive social and spiritual change. Buddha's primary internal opposition came from His cousin Devadatta, while Prince Ajatasattu was His greatest external threat; but resistance ultimately strengthened the Sangha's ability to live and teach the Dharma. Christ's external opposition was chief priests (Sadducees), learned Pharisees, and Roman officials; and His strongest internal opposition was Judas; but their evil accented the goodness and power of the Gospel. Muḥammad's external opposition was posed by Meccan leaders; His internal opposition was led by Ibn Ubayy and the hypocrites, and also came from treacherous Jews in Medina who colluded with the Meccans and the hypocrites. But such testing merely strengthened the new Faith. Bahá'u'lláh was opposed by many Persian and Turkish leaders externally and by some family members internally. The Azalis, followers of Bahá'u'lláh's half-brother Mírzá Yaḥyá, and other Covenant-breakers, had claimed to be Bahá'ís but had then opposed the teachings of the Faith. Eventually these enemies were made into instruments of providence and the emerging global Faith.

9 – Rejection by the People

It is not only religious and civil leaders who reject the Founders, but also the majority of the people who hear Their message. But rejection and banishment spread Their message.

> During their ministries, all the divine educators encounter personal hardship, rejection by the masses, active persecution, and even death at the hands of those who oppose them.[30]

Moses endured the murmurings of His people and wandered in the wilderness to the point of despair, but His experiences became moral object lessons, and eventually the divine law was successfully delivered. Zoroaster was rejected by the village of His birth, and was forced to wander for twelve years, looking for righteous people; but then He was given divine lessons through archangels, and was prepared for His future role as Prophet to the ancient Persians. Krishna escaped persecution by the tyrant King Kamsa, fleeing to a cowherd village where he attracted many devotees. Later He recruited the Pandava brothers as disciples, while other clans and kingdoms rejected Him. Nonetheless, through His ministry during the Mahabharata War, righteousness prevailed anew in ancient India. Buddha and His early disciples were abused and mocked as they traveled from one village to another. But gradually the new Dharma spread over northern India and from there to much of Asia. Christ was rejected and slandered by many Jews, forced to move about from town to town, and was finally crucified. But His Spirit became a palpable force amidst His followers, and the Gospel spread to the Mediterranean and from there to many parts of the world. Muḥammad was branded a charlatan and madman, was forced to flee Mecca, and was pursued aggressively by His fellow tribesmen of the Quraysh. But through exile He unified all of Arabia under new divine law, and His message spread east and west rapidly. Bahá'u'lláh was labelled a heretic and troublemaker, was forced out of Persia, and subsequently endured forty years of exile and persecution. But His message spread throughout the Middle East and India, then to Europe, North America, and the rest of the world.

10 – Sacrificial Suffering

The suffering of the Founders was never in vain, for They were always able to make every trial, no matter how painful, ultimately instructive and redemptive. Amazingly, They achieved their purposes despite the agony inflicted upon Them.

> Suffering and sacrifice have been the lot of all the founders of the great religions. Without exception, they give up personal freedom and comfort. Some leave behind family and friends, others abandon lives of luxury and material riches, and still others sacrifice their very lives for the cause they promote. . . . By providing a living example of detachment and sacrifice, these holy figures have helped us human beings gradually reveal the virtues with which our souls are invested.[31]

Moses suffered a forty-year ordeal, marked by His followers' ingratitude, aggressive complaints, failure of resolve, and regression to idol worship. Yet with divine assistance, He brought them to greater spiritual maturity at the threshold of the Promised Land. Zoroaster's most intense suffering was during His twelve-year search for a significant following and during two holy wars after He became a Royal Prophet. But through His divine mission the Persian Empire, one of the greatest religious civilizations, was created. Krishna failed in diplomatic efforts to prevent the Mahabharata War and, to His frequent despair, was never able to attract His sons to His message. But through His mission, divine law was renewed, righteousness restored, and devotion purified. Buddha endured terrifying experiences during His six-year search for enlightenment and then suffered hurtful words and rejections during His forty-five-year ministry. But He set in motion the Wheel of Dharma that had been halted by moral and spiritual decline. Christ knew His destiny required intense suffering and death on a cross, but He embraced the ultimate sacrifice so that His spirit would be resurrected among His disciples, offering salvation and a new covenant. Muḥammad saw His sufferings as a continuation of the longstanding pattern of persecution against God's Messengers. But He also foresaw the glory of those widespread societies that would embrace His teachings and establish a divinely guided civilization. Bahá'u'lláh, following this same pattern, suffered years of imprisonment and exile. He declared, *"We have accepted to be tried by ills and troubles, that ye may sanctify yourselves from all defilements."*[32]

11 – Symbolic Language as a Test for Believers

The Founders told stories of truth using symbolic language that was meant to be interpreted spiritually. They also told true stories using literal language that was meant to be interpreted concretely and historically. Their most significant messages were spiritual rather than physically explicit, and this served as a test for followers, requiring detachment, purity of heart, and open-mindedness.

> The Scriptures contain passages which qualify the truth of their own doctrines. Recognizing that scripture may be expressed in parables and symbolic language, they teach that spiritual discernment is required for its proper interpretation.[33]

Unfortunately, literalistic understandings, interpretations, and doctrinal schools have become veils that have obscured the originally intended meanings of the scriptures. In Jewish tradition, terms such as *sovereignty, throne,* and *messiah* were interpreted in literal and political ways, keeping many believers from appreciating later revelation. In Zoroastrian tradition, terms such as *fire, pollution,* and *Son of Zoroaster* were interpreted in narrow and concrete ways that obscured later revelation. In Hindu tradition, terms such as *rebirth, caste,* and *avatar* were viewed in literal ways, preventing appreciation of later revelation. In Buddhist tradition, terms such as *sangha, relic,* and *buddha* were interpreted in ways that led to superstition and moral decline. In Christian tradition, phrases such as *body of Christ, return of Christ,* and *Son of Man coming on the clouds of heaven* were interpreted in exclusive ways that closed off understanding of later revelation. In Islamic tradition, phrases such as *seal of the prophets* and *Day of Resurrection* were interpreted in doctrinally rigid ways that functioned as veils against later revelation. A central teaching of Bahá'u'lláh was that symbolic language served repeatedly in religious history as a great test for all who heard a new revelation. *"Wert thou to cleanse the mirror of thy heart from the dust of malice, thou wouldst apprehend the meaning of the symbolic terms revealed by the all-embracing Word of God made manifest in every Dispensation, and wouldst discover the mysteries of divine knowledge."*[34]

12 – Exemplary Women for All Ages: Nurturer and Advocate

Among the immediate followers of each Founder were two especially praiseworthy women—one exemplified a responsive / nurturing role, while the other exemplified an active / assertive role. Taken together, these women provided female role models needed to help bring a greater sense of balance to their patriarchal societies.

> Each of the major world religions has developed, to some extent, a female figure who acts as a role model for women. In the classical formulation of the religion, this has been a role that has emphasized the virtues of comforting and nurturing. This figure has often been the mother or wife of the prophet-founder. . . . But many women have, in the course of each religion's history, and particularly in modern times, preferred an alternative role model, one that takes them out of the home and is more socially active. This has usually been the figure of a female disciple of the prophet-founder of the religion who took an active role in the organizing and promotion of the religion in its early stages.[35]

According to researchers, women occupied roles that were given higher social status than those of men during the time period between the Neolithic Revolution (about 12,000 years ago) and the rise of civilization (about 6000 years ago). But in these last 6000 years, higher social status has been given to roles typically occupied by men. The stories of exemplary women associated with the Founders make us wonder if the Author of Creation were clarifying primordial facts of gender equality to societies which had, due to their developmental limitations, mistakenly placed women in inferior social roles. In today's world, gender equality and interdependence are more obvious, but perhaps in earlier civilization-building stages humanity was not prepared to embrace these realities.

Moses' sister Miriam was mostly remembered for saving the infant Moses by arranging for His royal upbringing through Pharaoh's daughter, and later for praising God in song for liberating her people from Egypt. Deborah was among the greatest of the judges instituted by Moses for leadership during the conquest and settling of the Holy Land; she was also esteemed as a prophetess and poetess. Zoroaster's mother Dughdao was His nurturer and protector, and she was blessed with divine favor, symbolized by the glorious light that shined from her. Zoroaster's daughter Poruchista was a fearless missionary for the early Zoroastrian Faith. Krishna's first and most helpful wife, Rukmini, was the very essence of devotion, faithfulness, and service. Drapaudi, the shared wife of the Pandava brothers, was a courageous heroine who supported the just side in the Mahabharata War and dismantled the warrior caste. Buddha's mother, Mahamaya, though she died soon after His birth, was the most receptive and nurturing woman in Buddhist tradition, because she cared for the Buddha from her heavenly abode, and bested the gods in her understanding and support of the new dharma. The most active and assertive woman in the Buddha's story was Mahaprajapati, His stepmother and aunt, who overcame the Buddha's initial resistance to establishing an order of nuns. Jesus' mother, Mary, has been a highly revered woman in both Christian and Muslim history, honored as a saint, and held up as the ideal of loving devotion and nurturance. Mary Magdalene ministered to Christ in the Galilee, served as an "apostle to the apostles," and was honored as a pioneering representative of women's ministry in the early church. The first wife of Muḥammad, Khadijah, encouraged Him to embrace His role as prophet of the Arabian people, was the first to embrace Islam, and was the mother of Fatimah (the most lauded S̲h̲í'ah Muslim woman). Aisha was Muḥammad's second wife after the death of Khadijah; she was an intelligent, well-educated source of many Islamic traditions, and a matriarch of the early Muslim community. Ṭáhirih, the Báb's only female disciple, was among the most courageous, eloquent, and spiritually gifted women in religious history, championing the new Faith and establishing decisively the cause of women's equality in the new age of humanity's maturity. Bahíyyih K̲h̲ánum, Bahá'u'lláh's daughter, was a very nurturing and supportive figure in the formative decades of the new Faith, cultivating positive relationships with many officials and even heading the Faith on several occasions.

13 – Dying and Ascending Victoriously

The end of the Founders' earthly missions significantly revealed Their station, character, and attainments. Despite powerful opposition to Their ministries, and persecution inflicted on Their cause, They triumphed.

Degrees of longevity and the ways the Founders died appear to vary widely: some lived short lives with dramatic deaths (such as Jesus and the Báb), some lived lives of ordinary length or seemed to be in the middle of unfinished tasks (such as Zoroaster, Krishna, and Muḥammad), and some ended their lives leading their communities in relative tranquility (such as the Buddha and Bahá'u'lláh). But more significantly, all of Them fulfilled Their earthly missions in powerfully memorable ways, and all entered the world of eternity in ways that evoke universal wonder and reverence.

According to scripture, Moses reached, but did not enter, the Promised Land at the age of 120, and the Lord buried His body in an unknown place, perhaps to reduce the prospect of idolatry as His followers established a new civilization. Zoroaster's earthly body was killed at the age of seventy-seven while He was worshipping at a fire temple, but His heavenly spirit guided three great Persian empires enduring 1200 years (550 BCE–650 CE). After giving His final advice to Uddhava, Krishna's mortal body was killed mistakenly by a deer hunter while He was lamenting personal losses alone in the forest at the age of 125, though His eternal spirit sustained an abiding expression of faith in India. Buddha's final advice at the age of eighty emphasized faith in the Buddha, the Dharma, and the Sangha, as well as self-reliance, but His spirit became the light of Asia and attained final release, or parinirvana. At the age of about thirty, Christ's body was crucified, but His spirit was resurrected among the disciples, and was apparent in the many spiritual triumphs of the early Church despite widespread persecution. At the age of sixty-two, Muḥammad's bodily life ended, having achieved Arabian unity, having clarified succession (according to the S͟hí'ah Muslims, but not according to the Sunni Muslims), and having directed the Faith outward toward embracing an Islamic brotherhood. Then His soul made its ascent to the Assembly of Truth.[36] At the age of seventy-five, Bahá'u'lláh made a heavenly ascension, having completed laws for a new world order, unified the Faith, clarified succession, and chosen Mount Carmel as the resting place for the Báb and the world center of the Bahá'í Faith.

14 – Transformative Teaching and Healing

The formal ministries of the Founders included teaching and healing that generated social transformation. Their lives exemplified divine teachings and also empowered Their followers to realize these teachings.

> The religious founders exhibit and proclaim a new image of the human being personified in their sacred biographies. . . .
>
> Most and perhaps all of the major religious traditions detect something fundamentally wrong with the human condition that needs to be set right. The founders bring deliverance from this "out-of-joint"

57

situation. They are the channels through which human beings may be delivered from meaninglessness or evil. . . . Through the founders, meaning is provided, a way through pain and suffering is demonstrated, sleepers are awakened, broken relationships are restored, obedience is commanded and made possible, true human society is revealed, and death is mitigated.[37]

Founders have always trained a special group that religious historian Toynbee has termed the "creative minority." These "chosen ones" were quickened spiritually and transmuted into steadfast souls capable of detachment from material concerns. Unforeseen capacities enabled them to catalyze movements destined to elevate humanity, fostering higher stages of spiritual evolution.

Moses' mission was delivering His people from bondage, giving the law at Sinai, disciplining observance, and bringing them to the Promised Land. He transformed a downtrodden, enslaved people into a "light to the nations." Zoroaster's mission as Royal Prophet lasted for thirty-five years, and it focused on abolishing corrupt practices and instituting new moral concepts, laws, and devotional practices. A small kingdom became the instrument for the development of the vast and noble Persian Empire. Krishna's three-stage mission included the inspiring of devotion, the advising of kings during social disruption, and the establishment of righteousness. Through Krishna, five brothers became the instrument of the moral and spiritual cleansing of India. Buddha taught the Middle Way, the Four Noble Truths, and the Eightfold Path; He developed the sangha (order); and He enlisted the support of kings. Through His guidance, misguided seekers became the instruments of a spiritual movement that would eventually be called the "light of Asia." Christ preached, taught, healed, and empowered many people throughout Palestine, beginning with lowly disciples who built an effective community of love and prophetic witness. Their movement spread rapidly across the Mediterranean, and eventually converted the Roman Empire. Muhammad's mission included warning the Meccans of divine retribution, breaking ties with His tribal heritage, establishing a new system of justice, conducting a holy war against pagan idolaters, initiating peace, and uniting all of Arabia. Initially hostile tribes were transformed into a unified religious civilization that would span from India to Spain. Bahá'u'lláh's mission was to establish world unity through an inclusive, expanded synthesis of all previous teachings—including new ethical and mystical guidance, theological and doctrinal guidance, and social and legal guidance—all of which empowered His followers to model humanity's maturity and the building of an ever-advancing global civilization.

15 – Delivering a Thematic and Complementary Message
The messages of the Founders developed around central themes that have all been complementary to the messages of the other Teachers.

> When considering the great world religions it is striking how each one seems to be centred around one main idea to which all others are subordinated. . . . Indeed, distinguishing epithets have been attached to the religions on this basis, Christianity being referred to as the "religion of love;" Judaism as the "religion of justice;" Islam as the "religion of absolute submission;" Buddhism as the "religion of detachment;" Zoroastrianism as the "religion of purity." . . . The Bahá'í Faith . . . would undoubtedly be the "religion of unity."[38]

Despite the widely varying conditions and settings addressed by the Founders, Their messages became thematically integrated within each tradition, and each message contained special strengths that amplified and enhanced the themes of other Founders. It is as if humanity were being collectively educated and repeatedly invited to learn from people of other faith traditions, discovering moral and spiritual gifts in other homelands.

Moses' central theme was to teach the observance of divine law. A strong emphasis was placed on moral and spiritual accountability to a single authority, and Moses' followers were taught to praise the Author of Creation. Zoroaster's theme was good thoughts, good words, and good deeds, with a strong emphasis on discernment between good and evil, while committing to continuous cultural improvement. Krishna's theme was devotion to the Avatar and selfless action, which emphasizes mystical intimacy with varying representatives and symbols of the divine, so that unity may be discovered in diversity. Buddha's theme was to awaken in compassion for suffering and attain nirvana. Buddha focused on disciplined awareness, which would lead to healing and liberation from the non-essential externals of religion. Christ's theme was salvation and attainment of the kingdom of heaven through sacrificial love. It was a message concerned with unbounded love, inner transformation, and humane public service. Muḥammad's theme was submission to God and the building of a trans-tribal, spiritual nation, which taught self-conquest as a prelude to ever-widening justice. Bahá'u'lláh's theme was unity and the establishment of the new world order. Bahá'u'lláh taught the importance of unity in diversity, personal and societal transformation, and the generating of an ever-advancing global civilization.

16 – Renewing and Embodying Universal Virtues

The Founders taught very similar virtues, which They renewed and embodied fully. Virtues may be described as praiseworthy characteristics or traits; aspects of human excellence; positive capacities of mind, heart, and soul; and divine attributes partly expressible by human beings. Though the virtues are intricately interrelated, three basic kinds may be distinguished based on their domain of application: spiritual, social, and material. The spiritual virtues (such as devotion and reverence) may be viewed as "vertical" in that they mainly concern the relationship of the soul with its Source, whether viewed as deep within or high above. The social virtues (such as compassion and service) may be viewed as "horizontal" in that they mainly concern our relationships with the people around us in circles radiating outward. And the material virtues (such as moderation and generosity) may be viewed as "downward" in that they mainly concern bodily needs, the economic order, and environmental relations. Each time a society is transformed by a Founder's renewal of virtues, a brilliant civilization develops offering humanity inspiring glimpses of an earth modeled on heaven.

> *Universal benefits derive from the grace of the Divine religions, for they lead their true followers to sincerity of intent, to high purpose, to purity and spotless honor, to surpassing kindness and compassion, to the keeping of their covenants when they have covenanted, to concern for the rights of others, to liberality, to justice in every aspect of life, to humanity and philanthropy, to valor and to unflagging efforts in the service of mankind. It is religion, to sum up, which produces all human virtues, and it is these virtues which are the bright candles of civilization.*[39]

Since there are several nearly synonymous terms associated with each virtue, we offer a dual name for each of them, showing some of their referential range. We have selected fifteen virtues to represent the many more taught by each of the Founders. In the chapters highlighting Their teachings, we include virtues that can be interpreted as *spiritual,* such as devotion-faithfulness, gratitude-reverence, self-discipline-obedience, detachment-patience, and wisdom-discernment. We list five *social* virtues, including loving-kindness-compassion, service-responsibility, respect-tolerance, justice-righteousness, and peace-unity. And we mention five *material* virtues, for example trustworthiness-honesty, moderation-balance, generosity-hospitality, creativity-beauty, and earthcare-stewardship. These last five can be considered material virtues because, when acted upon, they bring prosperity to the individuals, as well as collective progress to the economic order.

Even though most virtues can be applied in all three domains—spiritual, social, and material—we can benefit from distinguishing a specific domain or reference area. Appreciating subtle differences among the three types of virtues provides a glimpse of their wide range of application in the building of a new civilization. Yet we must not overlook the highly interdependent and interrelated nature of the virtues, for this is one of their most essential and significant characteristics. Each of the virtues implies several others, if not many more. For example, a loving and compassionate person would also have some qualities of gratitude and reverence, as well as some qualities of trustworthiness and generosity. Each virtue is embedded in an intricate matrix of qualities that help describe persons of praiseworthy character. Any given virtue might be interpreted and applied spiritually, socially, and materially. Therefore these three types must not to be understood rigidly or inflexibly.

Whereas philosophers, sages, and monarchs usually focused on part of one set of virtues, the Founders built a broad foundation upon which all of humanity could contribute their gifts and develop their capacities. They catalyzed new civilizations by renewing wide sets of virtues. Our respect and reverence for the Founders as a whole usually deepens considerably when we discover that They all taught and embodied universal and practical principles that generated great new departures in world history. Here we introduce the virtues pattern briefly, providing examples of one spiritual virtue, one social virtue, and one material virtue taught in each faith.

From the Jewish Faith:
Devotion-Discipline: *"The Lord our God is one Lord; and you shall love the Lord your God with all your heart, and with all your soul, and with all your might."*[40]
Peace-Unity: *"Behold, how good and pleasant it is when brothers dwell in unity!"*[41]

Trustworthiness-Honesty: *"You shall not steal, nor deal falsely, nor lie to one another."*[42]

From the Zoroastrian Faith:
Devotion-Discipline: *"I know that words of prayer which serve a good end are successful before you."*[43]
Peace-Unity: *"May peace triumph over discord."*[44]
Trustworthiness-Honesty: *"May the true-spoken word triumph over the false-spoken word."*[45]

From the Hindu Faith:
Devotion-Discipline: *"The mind is restless and difficult to control. But it can be conquered . . . through regular practice."*[46]
Peace-Unity: *"I look upon all creatures equally; none is less dear to me and none more dear."*[47]
Trustworthiness-Honesty: *"Be self-controlled, sincere, truthful, loving, and full of the desire to serve."*[48]

From the Buddhist Faith:
Devotion-Discipline: *"Carpenters control their timber; and the holy control their soul."*[49]
Peace-Unity: *"Among men who struggle, let us live in peace."*[50]
Trustworthiness-Honesty: *"Just like a beautiful flower . . . are the beautiful fruitful words of the man who speaks and does what he says."*[51]

From the Christian Faith:
Devotion-Discipline: *"Thy will be done, on earth as it is in heaven."*[52]
Peace-Unity: *"Blessed are the peacemakers, for they shall be called sons of God."*[53]
Trustworthiness-Honesty: *"Have a clear conscience toward God and toward men."*[54]

From the Islamic Faith:
Devotion-Discipline: *"Which is the greater war? . . . [the] struggle against the lower self."*[55]
Peace-Unity: *"Hold fast, all together, by the Rope which God (stretches out for you), and be not divided among yourselves."*[56]
Trustworthiness-Honesty: *"Break not your oaths after ye have confirmed them."*[57]

From the Bahá'í Faith:

Devotion-Discipline: *"Possess a pure, kindly and radiant heart."* [58]

Peace-Unity: *"The earth is but one country, and mankind its citizens."* [59]

Trustworthiness-Honesty: *"Commerce is as a heaven, whose sun is trustworthiness."* [60]

17 – Abrogating the Old and Establishing the New: Ritual and Legal Guidance

As divine authorities, the Founders abrogated some rituals, as well as some social and economic laws of the previous dispensation, and then established new ritual and legal guidance. These changes were not arbitrary, but were relevant to the particular developmental capacities of Their followers, and to the cultural context of time and place.

Each major religion has two kinds of teachings: 1) universal principles or virtues; and 2) distinctive social and legal guidelines and ritual practices that were requirements of the age in which they were taught. The first type of guidance was described in the preceding section, and in this section, we introduce the second type.

> At a particular point in their ministries, each of these figures makes a decisive break with the previous, established religion, revealing their true natures as not just reformers of the old religion but as renewers of religion itself. . . .
>
> . . . Following this break with the previous religion, the prophet-founder begins to set out those aspects of his religion that are different from and conflict with the previous religion; for example, the distinctive laws and rituals of his religion.[61]

Moses abolished polytheistic forms of worship that tempted His followers, modified animal sacrifices and fertility rites, and established the Ten Commandments and many other laws addressing ritual practice and social justice. Zoroaster abolished polytheistic forms of worship, animal sacrifices, and magical practices upheld by the magi (priests of Ancient Persia), replacing these with daily prayer facing local fire temples and strong ethical laws. Krishna greatly simplified Vedic ritual and law, made caste practices more flexible, and integrated moral and spiritual guidelines with His teachings on the yogas, which were disciplines of devotion to the Avatar, detached work and service, as well as rigorous meditation techniques. Buddha eliminated the caste system entirely, greatly reduced rituals associated with Brahmanic Hinduism, emphasized self-awareness and compassion for suffering, firmly established the Five Precepts, and outlined a form of welfare society. Christ eliminated the elaborate Mosaic holiness code, including strict Sabbath laws, focusing instead on inner purity, love, and sacrificial service. He established practices of prayer, baptism, communion, and service. Muḥammad abolished polytheistic rituals and exclusivist tribal practices, replacing them with a system of religious law with broad areas of focus: faith and devotional practice, including the Five Pillars; women and family life; as well as social and economic practices. Bahá'u'lláh abrogated Islamic laws of ritual purity, slave-holding, and prohibition of music and usury; then established a legal system emphasizing obligations to God, cultivating virtues and good deeds, community building, and consultative problem-solving at all levels in society.

18 – Human and Divine Qualities: Exemplifying a Dual Station

Each Founder claimed to be human in some respects, and divine in others. They showed super-human qualities, and achieved such heights that They became causes of wonder and controversy.

> The concurrence of humanity and divinity in a single person is a mystery which is described in various ways. . . .
> . . . The orthodox traditions of Islam, Judaism, Theravada Buddhism . . . describe his character in very human terms, in order to avoid any attempt to make him into a god. And yet, mystical and popular strands in many of these religions cherish traditions about the founder's person that recognize in him qualities like unto Ultimate Reality.[62]

> The founders reveal the transcendent through a certain hiddenness or mystery so that there is something unsayable or unfathomable about how they embody the human ideal.[63]

This pattern casts saving light on the conflict and tumult of the world's religious history. The Founders repeatedly claimed to be both human and divine, though humanity has tended to emphasize one side of this dual claim to the exclusion of the other, or to label Their claims as self-contradictory and therefore ignorable. Humanity's rigid interpretations distorted the Founders' stations, weakened the rational basis of religion, and have been a major source of theological and doctrinal confusion and conflict. However, interpreting the Founders as Mediators between divine and human realms could clear much confusion, reduce much conflict, and help to unite the world's communities of faith.

Moses complained at times that His burden was *"too heavy,"* and was described by His followers as *"very meek"*; but the Lord also spoke to Moses face-to-face as a friend and declared that He was *"entrusted with all My house"* and that He *"beholds the form of the Lord."* [64] Zoroaster complained that His first twelve years of preaching yielded so little fruit, and asked for God's guidance frequently; but God and the archangels always responded by providing assurance and visions, making Him a Revealer and manifestation of the divine. Krishna showed many human vulnerabilities including sadness and fear, and allowed Himself to become *"caught in the web of His own* maya [illusion]*"* [65]; but His titles, including the "Supreme Teacher of the World" and the "Soul of All," clearly pointed to His divine station. Buddha admitted to having many ordinary fears, temptations, and pains; but He also denied that He was merely human, and instead claimed to be one with Dharma, and a supreme king Who knew the world of the Creator, and later tradition interpreted Buddha as a manifestation of Absolute Reality (Dharmakaya). [66] Christ was a suffering servant who said while facing the prospect of crucifixion, *"let this cup pass,"* and frequently emphasized His being sent by God; but He also claimed to be the *"light of the world"* and declared *"I and the Father are one."* [67] Muhammad was seen as a humble servant, consulting others regularly, claiming to be *"a man like you"*; but He was also understood as a Universal Revealer, saying, *"Truth has (now) arrived, and Falsehood perished"* and *"Whoever sees me has seen God."* [68] Bahá'u'lláh admitted to experiencing grievous sufferings and described Himself as human; but He also called Himself the "Ancient Beauty" and the "Manifestation of God for this Day."

19 – The Light and the Word

The Light and the Word have been powerful, persistent metaphors for divine guidance, and the Founders made frequent use of them in their teachings. Darkness and deafness were described as spiritual conditions that could be overcome, for the Revealers brought the Light and the Word.

The sacred literature of the world is replete with mentions of the concept of light as the vanquisher of darkness and the source of guidance for humanity. At different times God, the divine educators, the holy books and scriptures, or religion itself have been likened to a light that shines in the darkness of our earthly existence to illuminate the path to salvation and liberation.[69]

In many religions, the excellence of chanting the name(s) of God lies in the mystic syllables which invoke God's purity and sovereign power. . . .
. . . To recite these names is to give a magnificent description of the height, depth, and breadth of divinity.[70]

Religious scriptures are filled with references to light. Jewish scripture teaches: *"The Lord is my light and my salvation"* and *"Thy word is a lamp to my feet, and a light to my path."*[71] Zoroastrian tradition identified light and growth with forces of good; darkness and decay were identified with forces of evil. Hindu scripture declares: *"Dwelling in every heart, it is beyond darkness. It is called the light of lights, the object and goal of knowledge, and knowledge itself."*[72] Buddhist scripture says: *"So long as a Tathagata arises not . . . a Buddha Supreme, there is no shining forth of great light, of great radiance, but gross darkness of bewilderment prevails."*[73] Christian scripture makes the point: *"The light shines in the darkness, and the darkness has not overcome it"* but *"the true light that enlightens every man was coming into the world,"* and Jesus said *"I am the light of the world."*[74] Islamic scripture mentions: *"God is the Light of the heavens and the earth"* and *"He is the God, the Creator, the Maker, the Shaper. To Him belong the Names Most Beautiful."*[75] Bahá'í scripture notes: *"He is a Light which is not followed by darkness and a Truth not overtaken by error"* and Bahá'u'lláh says, *"within thee have I placed the essence of My light."*[76]

20 – Affirming Four Realms: Natural, Human, Revelatory, Divine

The Founders' revelations were meant to be understood in complementary ways—all pointing to four levels of reality: divine, revelatory, human, and natural. They were Mediators between God and the world of humanity. "In the cosmology of most of the world religions, the founder plays a role that places him between the Ultimate Reality and this physical world."[77] This can sometimes be a difficult concept for us to grasp, because we wonder how someone can be human and yet also divine; but the truth is that God and His creation are far beyond our understanding. Focusing too narrowly on our own assumptions can prevent us from seeing greater truths. "Scripture also cautions us from believing that any system of doctrine contains the entirety of truth, for in reality, God's truth is infinite."[78] These points seem especially significant for prospects of interfaith understanding, cooperation, and world peace. When the Founders' teachings about revelation are studied side by side, a common metaphysic of four interacting levels emerges: 1) God, or Ultimate Reality, beyond final human comprehension; 2) the realm of revelatory power and means, the domain of Founders in their divine aspects; 3) the human realm, which includes the immortal soul with powers of discovery and the ability to make choices, with the capability of reflecting higher spiritual reality; and 4) the natural world—made up of mineral, plant, and animal sub-levels.

The Founders were chosen by God, and follow His commands. Moses was told by God, *"I will be your mouth"*[79] and Jewish people have generally understood revelation as God's commands through prophets. Moses was the Revealer and Mediator between God and the chosen people, destined to bring light to the nations. Zoroaster was selected by God and given the charm of speech, enabling Him to proclaim the Sacred Word faithfully. He was the Revealer and Mediator between the Wise Lord and ancient Persians struggling with choices of good and evil in this life. Krishna was understood as Ultimate Reality incarnated—God descended into human form to restore righteousness on earth. He was the Revealer and Mediator between Vishnu the Divine Sustainer and this illusory world. Buddha attained Dharma (Truth, Law) and could thereby elevate humanity with complete understanding of the human condition and the structure of existence. He was the Revealer and Mediator between the Unconditioned Realm and this impermanent and suffering-filled existence. Christ was interpreted as the Word of God become flesh, a unique incarnation of God and as the Revealer and Mediator between the Godhead and powers and principalities of this world. Muḥammad and the early Muslims understood revelation as divine speech recited by Messengers. Muḥammad was the Revealer and Mediator between the Unseen and this realm of the seen. The Bahá'í writings refer to the conditions of existence as threefold— *"the conditions of existence are limited to the conditions of servitude, of prophethood and of Deity"*[80]—and Bahá'u'lláh was a Revealer and Mediator between the Eternal Essence and this material realm.

21 – Promising a Future Savior
and an Age of Spiritual Maturation

Each Founder prophesied the coming of a future Successor who will bring a new dispensation. But there were also scriptural prophecies of an Age that would fulfill all of humanity's deepest longings for peace and justice, a kind of merging together of the earthly and heavenly realms.

> The scriptures of many religions speak of a coming leader who will consummate the fulfillment of the divine will on earth. He will manifest in his person the righteousness and compassion of God, bring about the final defeat of evil, and establish the Kingdom of Heaven on earth.[81]

> The Golden Age that characterizes the rule of the future saviour is . . . described very similarly in the traditions of all religions, although there are, of course, differences that relate to the culture and geography of the area from which the scripture originated. In brief, all the problems that characterized the period before the coming of the saviour are resolved. The physical earth becomes a paradise with plenteous crops and resources sufficient for all. The saviour elevates the moral and spiritual condition of the people. The government becomes just and beneficent.[82]

All of the religions we will be studying contain references to this future savior. God told Moses, *"I will raise up for them a prophet like you from among their brethren,"* a Prophet later referred to as the Messiah ("anointed by God").[83] The Messiah will end Israel's dispersion and humiliation, and usher in Israel's proper recognition in the world. David referred to the Messiah as the "King of Glory" and "Lord of Hosts." Isaiah referred to the Messiah as the "Everlasting Father" and "Prince of Peace." Zoroaster prophesied a series of Spiritual Guides, the most important of whom would be the Saoshyant or Shah-Bahram (World Savior) ushering in a final restoration—the kingdom of heaven on earth. Krishna spoke of His return *"to protect the good, to destroy evil, and to re-establish the Law,"*[84] and the Tenth or the Kalki Avatar would overcome the Age of Decay and establish a new Golden Age for humanity, the greatest of all previous dispensational achievements. Buddha prophesied a Fifth Buddha named Maitreya (Friend) with a vastly wider following, the Buddha of Universal Fellowship, who would once again make progress in religion through the reappearance of disciplined devotees. Christ referred to His Return in many ways. For example, He said, *"I go away, and I will come to you,"*[85] and He also described elaborately the signs of the advent of the future dispensation—the kingdom of heaven on earth. Muḥammad revealed that *"(Jesus) shall be a Sign (for the coming of) the Hour (of Judgment)."* And He also prophesied the Great Announcement, declaring that the Promised One would *"fill the earth with equity and justice."*[86] Bahá'u'lláh claimed to be the Manifestation of God prophesied by the Báb, to be the Promised One of all ages, and also taught that there would be future Manifestations— *"once in about a thousand years shall this City* [the Word of God] *be renewed and readorned."*[87]

22 – Essential Unity of the Revealers through the Ages

Since God or Ultimate Reality is one, and since all Founders share divine qualities as part of Their dual station, They are united in essential purpose— to guide humanity through the ages, fostering spiritual development and unfolding new civilizations.

All the Prophets of God are the Temples of the Cause of God, Who have appeared clothed in divers attire. If thou wilt observe with discriminating eyes, thou wilt behold them all abiding in the same tabernacle, soaring in the same heaven, seated upon the same throne, uttering the same speech, and proclaiming the same Faith. Such is the unity of those Essences of being."[88]

If these holy figures do indeed possess a divine nature, must they not all share in the same quintessential reality? . . . If we find the deeds, words and aims . . . to be in essential harmony, it is probably safe to assume that all do indeed share the same inner reality. . . . The driving motives behind their missions also seem to have been identical—the spiritual-ization of mankind and the improvement of the human condition.[89]

The Founders of the major world religions all claimed to share a station of unity with other Prophets of God. Moses said, *"The Lord, the God of your fathers, the God of Abraham, the God of Isaac, and the God of Jacob, has sent me to you,"* and He also said, *"The Lord your God will raise up for you a prophet like me from among you."*[90] Zoroaster presented Himself as a Prophet in a long line of Prophets, saying there would be three more such Prophets before the final restoration. Krishna said, *"I am born in every age to protect the good, to destroy evil, and to reestablish dharma* [righteousness, the law]*."* [91] Buddha said, *"There is no distinction between any of the Buddhas . . . for all Buddhas are exactly the same as regards Buddha-dhammas* [Their teaching of the Law]*."* [92] Christ said, *"If you believed Moses, you would believe me, for he wrote of me"* and He also said, *"I am the Alpha and the Omega, the beginning and the end."* [93] Muḥammad said, *"We believe in God, and the revelation given to us, and to Abraham, Ismaʿil, Isaac, Jacob, and the tribes, and that given to Moses and Jesus, and that given to (all) Prophets from their Lord: we make no difference between one and another of them."* [94] Bahá'u'lláh said, *"Know thou assuredly that the essence of all the Prophets of God is one and the same."* [95]

23 – Laying Enduring Foundations

The Founders set in place institutional arrangements that bore great fruit in successive generations. Their contributions were generative and foundational, lasting millennia.

> [There is an] imperative inherent in the founder's experience to find expression in thought structures, practice, and organizational forms. . . .
>
> The founder's religious experience and charisma are elements contributing to his authority, and he reveals the truth and the way with an authority from beyond himself. . . . Authority is sometimes viewed as a personal quality of individual leaders, gurus, or spiritual masters. At other times authority is embodied primarily in institutions or scriptures. . . .
>
> . . . They [the Founders] institute the way human life should be transformed to achieve its true purpose. [96]

As we can see from the civilizations that have grown from the world's religions, "the founder's significance lives on in the tradition in its new creative embodiments—not only in oral or written story, but also in art, architecture, theater, dance, and in ritual and festival reenactment." [97]

Moses established a system of elders and judges, and also taught believers to *"set as king over you him whom the Lord your God will choose,"* [98] referring most especially to David. Zoroaster won royal sponsorship of His Faith, reformed the magi, established clear moral guidance, and inspired the great emperors Cyrus and Darius, whose legal, architectural, and administrative attainments astounded the ages. Krishna reduced the power of the gods and the priests, purified and universalized devotional practice, renewed the Eternal Law, and restored the model of righteous kingship that would be implemented during the loftiest periods of the Mauryan and Gupta dynasties. Buddha directed monks outward in compassion and spiritual teaching, clarified the vinaya (discipline), and inspired the future emperor Asoka to observe and enforce the Five Precepts, greatly expanding the Faith. Christ established the Church through His first disciple, Peter, and through His spiritual influence upon Paul, leading eventually to the spiritual conquest of the Roman Empire through the conversion of Emperor Constantine, spreading the Faith from Europe to other lands. Muḥammad's early movement split between those who understood leadership as spiritually designated Imams (the Shí'ah) and those who understood leadership as consensually elected Caliphs (the Sunni). Despite early civil war, Islam developed into a lofty civilization by the ninth century, stretching westward to Spain and eastward to India. Bahá'u'lláh specified more clearly than any previous Founder the institutional arrangements to follow—'Abdu'l-Bahá (His son) became the Center of the Covenant (1892–1921), Shoghi Effendi (His great grandson) became the Guardian (1921–1957), and the Universal House of Justice became the Faith's highest authority from 1963 onward.

24 – Renewing Scriptural Guidance

Scripture is the written form of divine revelation, brought to humanity through the Founders. Though Their spoken words were not usually recorded in Their own generation, believers in each tradition preserved the essence of Their message in written form. Scriptures have always been progressively renewed.

> All the great religions of the world revere sacred scriptures. . . . These sacred scriptures contain essential truths. And they have immeasurably great historical significance, for they have influenced the minds, hearts, and practices of billions of people in the past. They continue to exert tremendous impact in the present. . . . The words of truth in sacred scriptures form the core beliefs of religion and thus, of civilization.[99]

Jewish scriptures are the Torah or the Five Books of Moses, but books of the Prophets and the Writings have also been considered scriptural, along with some later works. Zoroastrian scriptures are the Gathas of Zoroaster, but

other works making up the Avesta are also considered scriptural. The scriptures generated by Krishna and representing the essence of the Hindu Faith
include the Bhagavad Gita, the Uddhava Gita, and the Srimad Bhagavatam;
but the Vedas and the Upanishads are also considered scriptural, along with
some later works. Buddhist scriptures are the Tripitaka containing the most
authentic teachings of Gautama the Buddha; but many later works have
also been considered scriptural. Christian scriptures are the Gospel, which
tells the most authentic stories of Jesus the Christ; but the other writings of
the New Testament have also been considered scriptural. Islamic scriptures
are the Qu'rán, but the Hadith, or the sayings and deeds of the Prophet
Muḥammad, have been very important sources in interpreting the Qu'rán.
The most foundational Bahá'í scriptures are works of Bahá'u'lláh, including
the Kitáb-i-Aqdas (the Most Holy Book) and the Kitáb-i-Íqán (the Book of
Certitude); but other works of the Báb, Bahá'u'lláh, and 'Abdu'l-Bahá are
also considered scriptural.

25 – Generating Civilization Anew

The Founders' teachings include a vision of civilization calling forth ever-
higher fulfillment of humanity's spiritual, social, and material potential.

> The hope for the advent of the millennium, an ideal world, a world
> without evil, a world in which God's sovereignty is fully manifest, is
> present to some degree in every world religion.[100]

Civilization is both an ideal aim on one hand, and a process that can be in
progressive or regressive conditions on the other. Civilization is the ideal aim
of a lofty level of cultural refinement inspired by the Founders. It is also a
widespread process of building upon, or losing sight of, teachings offered by
Founders. As a singular global phenomenon, civilization is an advancing and
degenerating process reflecting the quality of humanity's response to divine
guidance. Civilization at its best would be humanity's creative development
of the three levels of the individual and society: the spiritual, social, and
material realms. Civilization is our highest collective achievement, as well as
the direction of yet greater achievement—all made possible by God's Messengers. Civilization is what the Founders taught humanity to build.

Moses' vision of civilization appeared in teachings about *"a kingdom of
priests and a holy nation,"* later described as *"the city of righteousness"*[101] bring-

ing *shalom*, or peace, prosperity, and tranquility of heart and mind. Zoroaster envisioned a final triumph of good over evil, an enduring peace and prosperity when *"the wolf period goes away, and the sheep period comes"* [102] and the kingdom of heaven on earth will be established. Krishna envisioned an era of widespread refinement and prosperity, when the *"minds of the people will become pure as flawless crystal,"* [103] an age when morality, spirituality, and revering scripture will abound. Buddha envisioned a compassionate, service-oriented society that would be without castes, would be harmonious, and led by righteous rulers modeling the dharma. Christ's vision of civilization was outlined in the beatitudes where qualities such as thirsting for righteousness and purity of heart were blessed; it was also embedded in His prayer that said, *"Thy kingdom come, Thy will be done, on earth as it is in heaven."* [104] Through the Qur'án and the Hadith, Muḥammad offered a large body of guidance for the building of a divinely just society, as implemented in part by the best rulers among the Spanish Umayyads and the Abbasids. Bahá'u'lláh inaugurated a global society with consultative institutions at local, national, and international levels, all designed to generate an *"ever-advancing civilization."* [105]

- 5 -
Moses: Background and Mission

Moses is the Founder, not only of the Jewish Faith, but also of the religious tradition that has dominated the Middle East and the Western world. His revelation casts light on humanity's early understanding of the beginnings of the cosmos, prehistory, the emergence of civilization, as well as the transition from polytheism to monotheism. The mythic and symbolic content of these foundational themes is relatively high, while historic content is relatively low. However, profoundly influential views of morality and basic concepts of divine / human relations are presented by Moses. He was also among the earliest Teachers of the principle that God has continuously offered guidance to humanity, and that Revealers of this guidance have been intimately linked in providential patterns.

1 – Continuity with Previous Dispensations: Ancient Prophets
In our review of the ancient Prophets, Moses, and other Founders, we feel free to draw from the entire body of humanity's scriptures, along with the relevant sciences, aware that the result is an interpretation rather than an objective account. If one God is behind all scriptures, later scriptures can be used to confirm the integrity and essence of earlier ones. Also, if truth is one, there can be no contradiction between true science and true religion, and we should seek interpretations that rely on both sources.

Adam and the Emergence of Religious Civilization
We view Adam as the first Revealer of divine guidance in recorded history. We also see Him as the Founder of religious civilization, which requires the written word. This view seems appropriate in the context of world scriptures taken collectively, along with the sciences relating to humanity's past. Adam was not the first human being ever, but rather the first human being of which there is any significant historical and religious memory. He is the father of

humanity in a culturally relative sense, rather than a biologically absolute sense.

Science offers a convincing picture of human origins in northeastern Africa. Research shows that we began to populate other continents about 60,000 years ago; reaching the Middle East about 55,000 years ago; Central Asia, India, China, and Australia about 50,000 years ago; and Europe about 40,000 years ago. This was the Old Stone Age and the Ice Age, when there may have been competition between Cro-Magnons and Neanderthals. About 15,000 years ago we reached the Americas, and about 11,000 years ago the last Ice Age ended. About 10,000 years ago we learned how to domesticate plants and animals during the Neolithic or Agricultural Revolution. About 8000 years ago Jericho was a Neolithic village of about 2000 people. A thousand years later, Catal Huyuk in Asia Minor was a Neolithic village of about 5000 people. About 6000 years ago, religious civilization was born in Mesopotamia, a milestone related to the story of Adam and Eve. Figures like this "first couple" are found in ancient Middle Eastern and Indian literature. They link prehistory and history, and the Cain and Abel episode contains anxieties that many during the Agricultural Revolution probably experienced related to competition between farmers and shepherds.

In Jewish tradition, Adam's name suggests that He represents man, and though created in the image of God, He was made of earth. He was given power over animals and plants, dominion over the earth, and the ability to name things. All went well in the Garden of Eden until Eve was tempted by a serpent to eat the fruit of the tree of knowledge of good and evil, which they had been forbidden to eat. They became conscious of their nakedness and hid from God, Who evicted them from the garden, condemning them to a toilsome life.[1] This "fall" may be viewed as humanity moving upward in the sense that they were given opportunities for responsible activity and learning. At the time of Adam's grandson, *"men began to call upon the name of the Lord,"*[2] suggesting that monotheism was introduced very early, with a stronger emphasis placed on this teaching in succeeding ages. In Jewish tradition, "Adam was created for the service of the Holy One,"[3] and is depicted as teaching arts and crafts, inventing writing, and composing a book of precepts delivered by God.

In Christian tradition, the sinfulness of Adam and Eve's disobedience has usually been strongly emphasized. Paul identified limitations of the human condition with the sin of Adam and Eve.[4] Though not compatible with Jew-

ish views or with later Islamic interpretation, Augustine's theology of the fall
has been dominant throughout most of Christian history. He depicted Adam
as the prototype of humanity under the old covenant. Adam and Eve's original sin has often been viewed as tainting all humanity thereafter, requiring
the absolute sacrifice of Christ to enable believers to attain even a degree of
salvation.

In Islamic tradition, Adam was created out of clay, and God's spirit was
breathed into Him. He was called *"God's vicegerent on earth"* and has been
considered the first Prophet or Messenger.[5] The names of all things in the
universe were taught to Him, setting Him above angels. All angels prostrated
before Adam, except the rebellious Iblis. Deceived by Iblis, or Satan, who
would *"make them slip"* from their former state, Adam and Eve ate the forbidden fruit.[6] But they repented, and thereafter, humanity needed only occasional new guidance toward the right path. In one Muslim tradition, it is said
that Adam built the foundations of the Kaaba, performing the first worship
there; and according to the Qur'án, God made a covenant with Abraham and
Ismail, thus sanctifying the Kaaba.[7]

In Bahá'í teachings, Adam is considered the first known Manifestation of
God, preceded by others in a preliterate world. Adam and Eve in the Garden
of Eden is a symbolic story with universal messages.[8] Adam is viewed as humanity's heavenly spirit; Eve, as the human soul making choices and subject
to temptation; the serpent, as attachment to the world or sin, as opposed to
the realm of spiritual virtues; and the tree as divine knowledge. Banishment
is seen as human toil in the world of good and evil, and the fall is viewed as
a spiritual descent from paradise to material bondage. The material world is
viewed as an arena of means and opportunities, not as intrinsically evil. This
story offers an outline of key choices, consequences, and opportunities in
our human condition. In the Bahá'í Faith, the search for deeper meanings is
encouraged, and scripture is viewed as having many levels of truth.

Noah and the Flood

About 3000 BCE, there may have been a major flood in the Middle East and
Asia Minor. "Archaeological evidence suggests that traditions of a prehistoric
flood covering the whole earth are heightened versions of local inundations,
e.g. in the Tigris-Euphrates basin."[9] In Genesis, Noah is depicted as a righteous, blameless man who walked with God.[10] Because the earth was corrupt
and violent, God resolved to *"make an end of all flesh,"* except for Noah, His

family, and a breeding pair of each animal species. God's covenant with Noah was later viewed as prohibiting idolatry, blasphemy, murder, adultery, robbery, and eating flesh cut from a living animal. It also created the requirement needed to establish courts of justice. These laws were believed to apply to everyone, not just Jews. The rainbow was the sign of this universal covenant, reminding everyone of God's promise never again to destroy all flesh. Noah was the *"first tiller of the soil"* who *"planted a vineyard."*[11] His sons were depicted as progenitors of subsequent peoples and civilizations—Japheth's line leading to the Persians, Ham's to the Babylonians and Egyptians, and Shem's to the Israelites and Arabs.

In Christian tradition, Noah's universal covenant was referred to twice in Acts, where James said that *"the words of the prophets agree,"* referring to rebuilding the dwelling of David so that all peoples may seek the Lord.[12] Paul preached to the gentiles, mentioning Noah's seven universal laws.[13] In Islamic tradition, Noah's people were warned about the consequences of unrighteous behavior—the *"Penalty of a Grievous Day"*[14]—and the flood seemed more restricted than in other accounts. Noah spoke of God as having created humanity in stages, suggesting that spiritual expectation increases with humanity's maturity. Noah-like figures appeared in other traditions: Yima in Persia,[15] Manu in India,[16] Utnapishtim, who appeared in the ancient Babylonian poem known as the "Epic of Gilgamesh," and in Greek mythology, Prometheus, who gave humanity fire, taught arts to civilization, and showed Deukalion how to escape the flood. These stories suggest that humanity's moral decline leads to destruction but that divine help is always offered.

Hud, Salih, and Ancient Arabia

Islamic and Bahá'í scriptures refer to two Prophets—Hud and Salih—who lived in the third millennium BCE, after Noah and before Abraham. Hud was sent to the people of Ad in central Arabia, while Salih was sent to the people of Thamud in northern Arabia several centuries later. Their missions illustrated the pattern of divine guidance being ignorantly rejected by the people, with dire consequences. Hud was a direct descendant of Noah and may have been the figure called Eber in Genesis 10:24. Hud's teaching was influential among a small group of followers who settled in the Mecca area for perhaps 700 years. Most of those who heard His monotheistic teaching rejected it firmly, and they were destroyed by a ferocious wind.[17] Salih's teachings were influential among a few followers for over a hundred years. Salih was asked by the skeptical people of Thamud in northern Arabia for a sign that He was sent by the one and only God. The divine offering was a she-camel that was not received graciously nor offered water, but rather made lame by the people.[18] This incident symbolized human ignorance vis-à-vis divine guidance and generosity—a spiritual version of "biting the hand that feeds." The people Salih taught were then destroyed by an earthquake.

The Sabaean Prophet and His Faith

In the later half of the third millennium BCE, a Prophet was sent to southern Arabia, a region then called Saba. It had *"two Gardens to the right and to the left,"* which is probably a metaphor for *"Sustenance (provided) by your Lord,"* but the people *"ungratefully rejected Faith."*[19] The Prophet of the Sabaean Faith is not named, but His followers were called a "people of the Book," for they were offered a recorded revelation from God. The Sabaean Prophet's message spread north to Mesopotamia and possibly east to Africa. The Sabaean Faith flourished for a time in Chaldea, so we assume Abraham would have approved of it.

Among the Biblical and Qur'ánic figures who may have been Sabaean was the Queen of Sheba (Bilqis in Qur'ánic commentaries). When she visited Solomon, she asked him thoughtful questions and received inspiring answers. She concluded: *"Blessed be the Lord your God, who has delighted in you and set you on the throne of Israel! Because the Lord loved Israel for ever, he has made you king, that you may execute justice and righteousness."*[20] The Queen of Sheba understood and appreciated monotheistic wisdom. Isaiah referred to Sabaeans as *"men of stature,"*[21] prophesying that they would believe in the one God revealed to Israel. Their original teaching was no doubt compromised over the centuries. Bahá'í teachings refer to the original Sabaeanism as among "nine living revealed religions," including the Jewish, Hindu, Zoroastrian, Buddhist, Christian, Islamic, Bábí, and Bahá'í Faiths.

Some scholars say that Mandeanism, an ancient Gnostic faith with a large body of scripture and a small following still surviving in southern Iraq, may have evolved from Sabaeanism.[22] The major Mandean writings are the *Great Treasure* and the *Book of John.* Adherents of this faith claim that Mandea (Knowledge of Life) was their Founder, and that humanity has been offered redemption through a series of divine Messengers. They also claim that John the Baptist is among their prophets. Like the Essenes and some Christian Gnostics (believers in esoteric knowing) they distinguish between "children of light" and "children of darkness," and look forward to a coming Savior.

Abraham as Father of Many Nations

We find some of the most significant aspects of Moses' background in the period of the Patriarchs—the time of Abraham, Isaac, Jacob, and Joseph. This part of the story begins about 2000 BCE with God's call to Abraham. He was to declare God's oneness, break from His family, from His polytheistic culture, leave Mesopotamia (known as "Ur of the Chaldeans")[23] and migrate to Canaan. Before undertaking this journey of faith, following the pattern of other Founders, He was persecuted by powers and principalities of His day, most notably Nimrod, the Mesopotamian king. But God protected Abraham and promised that His descendants would become a great nation, that the land between the Nile and Euphrates would be theirs, and that through Him *"all the families of the earth shall bless themselves."*[24]

Abraham's God was revered as the one and only Lord, controller of nature, God Almighty, or El Shaddai.[25] Abraham's God was promoted as Judge of all nations, but also Nurturer of all peoples—a personal God Who communicates directly with chosen ones, entering into covenants, or moral and spiritual agreements, with specific peoples. Through Abraham and Sarah came Isaac, Jacob, Joseph, Moses, David, and Jesus—the central figures of the Jewish and Christian Faiths. Through Abraham and Hagar came Ishmael, and a line of descendants leading to Muḥammad. Through Abraham and Keturah came the Persian Zoroastrian heritage as well as the Baháʼí Faith. Abraham's very name means "father of many nations," revealing His essence. God told Abraham, *"Look toward heaven, and number the stars, if you are able to number them. . . . So shall your descendants be."*[26] Abraham was the progenitor of the Israelites, Arabs, and Persians.

In Jewish tradition, Abraham has been revered as the ideal patriarch, the recipient of the covenant of circumcision, the keeper of the oral law even before it had been revealed, and a symbol of all that would happen to Israel. In Christian tradition, He has been revered as an exemplar of the power of faith without law, and the faithful sojourner who *"looked forward to the city which has foundations, whose builder and maker is God."*[27] In Islamic tradition, Abraham has been revered as the restorer, with His son Ishmael, of the original monotheistic worship at the Kaaba, as well as the first Muslim, one obedient to God.

Abraham's legacy of faith was carried by His sons, grandson, and great grandson, Joseph. Isaac's son, Jacob, through a struggle with an angel of God, had his name symbolically changed to Israel, "he who struggles with God."[28] His descendants became known as the Children of Israel. Through Jacob / Israel came twelve sons, each of whom led a tribe. Ten came through Israel and Leah; two through Israel and Rachel.

Joseph and the Children of Israel in Egypt

The jealousy of Joseph's brothers led to his being sold as a slave in Egypt, where he rose to become Pharaoh's vizier. After Joseph interpreted Pharaoh's dreams, Pharaoh said, *"Can we find such a man as this, in whom is the Spirit of God? . . . Since God has shown you all this, there is none so discreet and wise as you are; you shall be over my house . . . only as regards the throne will I be greater than you."*[29] Famine forced Joseph's father, Jacob, to send his sons to Egypt to buy corn. They met Joseph without at first recognizing him. Joseph, a powerful figure in Egypt, forgave his brothers and persuaded Pharaoh to invite them, his father, and their tribes to settle in Egypt. Before Joseph died, he assured his brothers that God would revisit them and bring them to the Promised Land.[30]

The Children of Israel prospered in Egypt for many generations, perhaps several centuries. The Egyptian name for Joseph's people was "Habiru," a term referring to semi-nomadic peoples who worked the caravan routes of the ancient Middle East. Habiru may have meant something like "dusty ones." The Habiru traveled as extended families with their animals, trading with other peoples without staying in one place very long.[31] The Hyksos took control of Egypt in about 1700 BCE and ruled about 150 years. They previously had a lifestyle similar to Abraham's descendants. The Hyksos and Hebrews were ethnically and socioeconomically akin. The early esteem in which Joseph's descendants were held was enhanced under the Hyksos, who treated them well. But the Egyptians resented foreign rulers, and expelled them around 1550 BCE.

Moses' continuity with previous dispensations would later be clarified. God asked Him to say to His people: *"'The Lord, the God of your fathers, the God of Abraham, the God of Isaac, and the God of Jacob, has sent Me to you': this is my name for ever, and thus I am to be remembered throughout all generations."*[32]

2 – Arising to Guide Humanity in the Worst of Times: Pharaoh's Oppression

A few generations later came a Pharaoh who did not know Joseph, and felt threatened by the Hebrews' prosperity. The fortunes of the Children of Israel would change for the worse—at least it seemed this way at first. The next Pharaoh may have been Thutmoses III, who contested the rule of Queen Hatshepsut[33] and built many magnificent temples. In any case, the reigning Pharaoh was afraid that this burgeoning but alien people would become too powerful. He therefore decided to enslave them and weaken them in other ways. But they continued to multiply. In a desperate measure, perhaps around 1500 BCE, Pharaoh ordered that all male Israelite children be put to death. *"And the people of Israel groaned under their bondage, and cried out for help. . . . And God heard their groaning, and God remembered His covenant with Abraham."*[34] Moses now entered the stage of religious history.

3 – Advent Prophesied and Expected: Joseph's Assurance and Soothsayers' Warning

Just before Joseph died, he assured his brothers that *"God will visit you, and bring you up out of this land to the land which He swore to Abraham, to Isaac, and to Jacob."*[35] This seems to have been an anticipation of the rise of Moses and the Exodus. Through the legacy of Abraham and Joseph, the Children of Israel maintained their expectation of returning to the Promised Land. The hope that they may some day bless the nations of the earth was part of their religious and historical consciousness. A deliverer of the stature of Abraham was needed, but how could such a figure arise under conditions of extreme oppression? Before Moses was born, soothsayers warned Pharaoh that a star had risen in heaven, foreshadowing the birth of a child holding the fate of Pharaoh and his people in His hand.[36] Pharaoh had already been fearful of the Hebrews' growth, so he took the soothsayers' prophecy seriously and ordered the slaying of all male newborns within the slave community. Little did he know that the One most feared would grow up in the royal court, enjoying the advantages of the best available Egyptian education.

4 – Auspicious Signs, Birth, and Intimations of Greatness

Moses was born of the house of Levi. His mother was Jochebed, His father Amram, His sister was Miriam, and His brother was Aaron. When Pharaoh ordered all Hebrew newborn males slain, Jochebed hid Him for three months, then made a basket of bulrushes, placing Him among the reeds of the Nile River. His sister Miriam watched, and saw Pharaoh's daughter find Him and take pity because He was crying. Miriam offered to find a nurse from among the Hebrew women, and Pharaoh's daughter accepted this offer. The nurse was none other than Moses' mother.

Moses grew up under the care and protection of Pharaoh's daughter in the royal palace of Egypt, and His caregiver may have become Queen Hatshepsut, according to one researcher.[37] The child was named Moses because He was "drawn out of the water"; but among the Hebrews the name also meant "one who draws out or delivers." For the ancient Hebrews names suggest essential attributes and powers that unfold providentially. As a young man, Moses, though living a privileged life in the Egyptian palace complex, became aware of the great burdens of the Hebrews, with whom He still identified. One day, He saw an Egyptian taskmaster beating a Hebrew slave, and felt indignant. In a fit of righteous indignation, Moses defended the Hebrew by killing the taskmaster.

Moses found two Hebrews quarreling and stepped in to reconcile them. *"Why do you strike your fellow?"* He asked. And the sharp reply was, *"Who made you a prince and a judge over us? Do you mean to kill me as you killed the Egyptian?"* [38] Moses soon realized that His actions would become known to Pharaoh, and indeed, when Pharaoh heard about this incident, he sought to kill Him. Moses learned that it was no simple matter to serve His people under the oppression of His day. Moses then fled from the city out into the pastoral land of Midian, where He was called upon to help the vulnerable. He defended the seven daughters of the priest of Midian, after they were accosted by aggressive nomads. As the daughters told their father, Jethro, *"An Egyptian delivered us out of the hands of the shepherds."* [39]

What early signs of Moses' spiritual station emerge from these events in His young adulthood? Among His significant qualities that would develop and actions that He would take were an acute sense of justice, delivering people from oppression and danger, decisiveness and initiative, strength and courage, responsibility and service, turning to God for discernment in crises, social awareness, and an ability to function well in both city and wilderness.

5 – Divine Commission: The Burning Bush

For several decades Moses maintained a pastoral life in a region settled by Midian, son of Abraham and Keturah, forebear of the Persians. During this time the Hebrews suffered worsening conditions in Egypt. Additional work was given to them in a deliberate attempt to crush their spirit and lock them deeper in bondage. But God saw their plight and remembered His covenant with Abraham. One day Moses was keeping flock in the wilderness near Mount Sinai. A frightful but transforming event occurred: God appeared to Him as a burning bush that was not consumed. *"Put off your shoes"* said the Lord *"for the place on which you are standing is holy ground."*[40] Moses hid His face because divine holiness was widely believed to be a mysterious power that could threaten human life. The Lord told Moses to return to Egypt, confront Pharaoh, and bring His people to *"a land flowing with milk and honey."*[41]

"Who am I that I should go to Pharaoh, and bring the sons of Israel out of Egypt?" asked Moses. God assured Moses of divine assistance, and that Moses *"shall serve God upon this mountain."*[42] Moses, despite being overwhelmed in the moment, could wisely ask what name He should offer for the God Who sent Him. God answered *"I am Who I am."*[43] Moses would say that "I AM" sent Him—the God of His fathers, the God of Abraham, Isaac, and Jacob. Yahweh was a name for God based on the letters YHWH, which stood for the Hebrew phrases "I am Who I am," "I will be What I will be," or "the One Who causes to be." In other words, God described Himself to Moses as the Creator. Moses was told to ask Pharaoh to let the Hebrew slaves go, for they had asked for *"a three days' journey into the wilderness, that we may sacrifice to the Lord our God."*[44] God said Pharaoh would resist, but wonders bringing afflictions to Egypt would force him to let His people go. Moses was promised that He and the Children of Israel would be brought out of affliction to Canaan.

6 – Struggling in Solitude: Doubts about Abilities

Moses' human doubts about His ability to fulfill this divine calling began immediately. He felt certain that people would not believe Him, but God offered Moses a rod and other magical powers, along with mighty signs that would ultimately prove convincing. *"I am not eloquent"* protested Moses again; but God replied that He, the Maker of all mouths, would teach Moses what to speak, and Aaron would also assist Him in speaking to the people. Despite these assurances, Moses carried His doubts in His heart on the long journey back to Egypt. The divine assurances He received were also described in Islamic and Bahá'í scripture. The Bahá'í writings describe Moses' spiritual encounter, *"While returning, Moses entered the holy vale, situate in the wilderness of Sinai, and there beheld the vision of the King of glory from the 'Tree that belongeth neither to the East nor to the West.'"* [45]

7 – Declaration and First Followers: Aaron, the Elders, and Pharaoh

Moses told Aaron *"all the words of the Lord with which He had sent Him."* [46] Moses and Aaron won the support of the elders, *"gathered together all the people of Israel,"* told them God's assurances and showed them the magical powers bestowed upon Moses. *"And the people believed"* and they *"bowed their heads and worshipped."* [47] When Moses came to Pharaoh, He was asked insultingly: *"Art thou not he that committed murder, and became an infidel?"* And Moses replied: *"I did it indeed, and I was one of those who erred. And I fled from you when I feared you, but My Lord hath given Me wisdom, and hath made Me one of His Apostles."* [48]

Even after approaching Pharaoh, Moses continued to express doubts. *"Why didst thou ever send me? For since I came to Pharaoh to speak in thy name, he has done evil to his people, and thou hast not delivered thy people."* [49] But God assured Moses that with a "strong hand" they would be delivered. He was given three kinds of magical powers to help establish His purpose with the people and with Pharaoh: a rod that could turn into a serpent, a hand that could become leprous and heal, and the ability to turn water into blood.

God had told Moses to say to Pharaoh: *"The Lord, the God of the Hebrews, sent me to you, saying, 'Let my people go, that they may serve me in the wilderness; and behold, you have not yet obeyed.'"* [50] God's strong hand and the wonders He promised to Moses were symbolized in the episodes of the ten plagues. These were dramatic negotiations with Pharaoh, establishing that the Lord controlled nature, that He was in direct communication with Moses, that He favored the Hebrews, and that they would be delivered to form a distinct religious nation. The ten plagues sent to the Egyptians by the hand of the Lord included: 1) the Nile turning into blood, 2) frogs, 3) gnats, 4) flies, 5) cattle disease, 6) boils, 7) hail and thunder, 8) locusts, 9) thick darkness, 10) death of the first born. These can be viewed both as natural calamities and divine retribution.

The transformative effect of Moses' dialogue with Pharaoh reached some members of the Egyptian court. Moses' revelation was not directed simply to Hebrews, but must be interpreted more universally in the context of this study. The Qur'án relates that a man in Pharaoh's family asked him regarding Moses: *"Will ye slay a man because he says, 'My Lord is God'?— when he has indeed come to you with Clear (Signs) from your Lord? And if he be a liar, on him is (the sin of) his lie; but, if he is telling the Truth, then will fall on you something of the (calamity) of which he warns you: truly God guides not one who transgresses and lies."* [51] Some Egyptians, including the daughter and wife of Pharaoh, who is called Asiyah in Islamic tradition, were attracted to the new revelation from God. Asiyah has been regarded in both the Islamic and Bahá'í Faiths as among the most spiritually accomplished women in history. In influencing her, Moses was *"armed with the rod of celestial dominion . . . He shone forth from the Sinai of light upon the world. He summoned all the people and kindreds of the earth to the kingdom of eternity, and invited them to partake of the fruit of the tree of faithfulness."* [52]

8 – Overcoming Powerful Opposition: Pharaoh, Priests, Army, Murmurers, and the Golden Calf

Moses confronted Pharaoh in His public declaration and the negotiation of the ten plagues. Demonstrating steadfastness and divine power, Moses overcame the enormous opposition of Pharaoh, leading to the Exodus and the arrival at Mount Sinai. *"The kingdom, wealth and power of Pharaoh and his people, which were the causes of the life of the nation, became, through their opposition, denial and pride, the cause of death, destruction, dispersion, degradation and poverty."* [53] In addition to the external opposition of Pharaoh, his priests and his army, Moses faced two kinds of internal opposition. One was posed by "murmurings" about His ministry by His own people during their forty years of wandering en route to the Promised Land. The other was the making of a "golden calf" as a focus for worship during Moses' forty days on Mount Sinai. These challenges brought forth increasingly authoritative responses, and Moses' power as a Messenger of God came into view.

Murmurings of the People against Moses

The first serious internal opposition to Moses' ministry came in response to the Egyptians' frightening pursuit as the Exodus began. The people said to Moses, *"Is it because there are no graves in Egypt that you have taken us away to die in the wilderness? . . . It would have been better for us to serve the Egyptians than to die in the wilderness."* But Moses replied, *"Fear not, stand firm, and see the salvation of the Lord."*[54] Then came fears about what the people could eat or drink. Finding the water bitter, they asked Moses, *"What shall we drink? . . . and the Lord showed him a tree, and he threw it into the water, and the water became sweet."*[55] Murmuring continued: *"Would that we had died by the hand of the Lord in the land of Egypt, when we sat by the fleshpots and ate bread to the full; for you have brought us out into this wilderness to kill this whole assembly with hunger."* But the Lord again spoke to Moses and said, *"Behold, I will rain bread from heaven for you."*[56] To the people's surprise, God provided "manna," which some scholars believe was an edible honey-dew-like secretion from insects.

Another kind of complaint was that the people already living in the Promised Land were mightier than the people of Israel. This angered God, and Moses again had to step in as advocate for the people. *"All the people of Israel murmured against Moses . . . 'Would that we had died in the land of Egypt! Or would that we had died in the wilderness! Why does the Lord bring us into this land, to fall by the sword?'"*[57] Moses quickly turned to the Lord and said, *"'Pardon the iniquity of this people.' . . . Then the Lord said, 'I have pardoned, according to your word.'"*[58]

The Golden Calf Incident

The most serious opposition to Moses came at Mount Sinai. In Moses' absence due to Him spending time face to face with God on the mountain for forty days and forty nights, the people longed for some visible symbol of divine assistance. This impatience generated the infamous golden calf incident. Moses had gone up to Mount Sinai to speak to God, and after He had been gone for some time, the people began to get restless. They didn't know who to turn to, so Aaron took their gold jewelry, *"and fashioned it with a graving tool, and made a molten calf; and they said, 'These are your gods, O Israel, who brought you up out of the land of Egypt!'"*[59] In a very short time, without Moses there to guide them, the people of Israel had reverted to idol worship.

How did God and Moses respond to these disturbing events? The Lord was angry and said to Moses, *"I have seen this people, and behold, it is a stiff-necked people; now therefore let me alone, that my wrath may burn hot against them and I may consume them."*[60] But Moses asked God not to punish the people of Israel for their mistake. Moses said to the Lord, *"'Turn from thy fierce wrath, and repent of this evil against thy people.' . . . And the Lord repented of the evil which he thought to do to his people."*[61]

But when Moses returned from the mountain and saw everyone dancing and praising the golden calf, His anger was nearly unquenchable. *"And as soon as He came near the camp and saw the calf and the dancing, Moses' anger burned hot, and He threw the tablets out of His hands and broke them at the foot of the mountain. And He took the calf which they had made, and burnt it with fire, and ground it to powder, and scattered it upon the water, and made the people of Israel drink it."*[62] Moses asked the people *"Who is on the Lord's side?"* and He invited the faithful to slay the unfaithful, *"and there fell of the people that day about three thousand men."* Then Moses said to the people, *"You have sinned a great sin. And now I will go up to the Lord; perhaps I can make atonement for your sin."* He asked God to forgive them, or if that were not possible, *"blot me, I pray thee, out of thy book which thou hast written."* But God replied *"Whoever has sinned against me, him will I blot out of my book."*[63]

Pondering this event leaves us in a somber state. We feel a sense of awe and bewilderment, or perhaps a combination of grief and perplexity about our human condition. At times we need strong medicine. The golden calf incident was perhaps the greatest challenge in Moses' ministry, requiring the making of a renewed covenant, while strengthening Moses' stature as a law-giver and deliverer. God is depicted here, as earlier with Abraham, as willing to change in response to Messengers' petitions and Their compassion on behalf of weak and recalcitrant people.

9 – Rejection by the People: More Murmurers

The waves of murmuring against Moses illustrate the pattern in which the Founders are rejected by the people. Yet, through Moses, God offered solutions. After the people followed Moses out of Egypt, they began to complain. *"Why did you bring us up out of Egypt, to kill us and our children and our cattle with thirst?"* So Moses asked the God for help, and the Lord said to Him, *"You shall strike the rock, and water shall come out of it, that the people may drink."*[64] However, there seemed to be a limit to the Lord's patience. *"And the people complained in the hearing of the Lord about their misfortunes; and when the Lord heard it, his anger was kindled, and the fire of the Lord burned among them, and consumed some outlying parts of the camp. Then the people cried to Moses; and Moses prayed to the Lord, and the fire abated."*[65]

At another point in their wandering it was Moses' turn to lose patience. The people said, *"O that we had meat to eat! We remember the fish we ate in Egypt for nothing"* Moses heard the people's weeping and said to the Lord, *"Why hast thou dealt ill with thy servant?". . . And the Lord said to Moses, 'Gather for Me seventy men of the elders of Israel . . . and they shall bear the burden of the people with you.'"* Moses then told the people to consecrate themselves for God, and after having done so, a strong wind brought quail near their camp so that the people had meat to eat.[66] Upon hearing complaints and feeling rejection from His followers, Moses would turn to God for assistance. Like other Messengers, Moses turned every rejection into fruitful lessons that strengthened the foundation of faith, showing humanity how to build a religious civilization.

10 – Sacrificial Suffering: Forty Years Wandering in the Wilderness

In the following passage, Moses recounts His sufferings at the hands of a stubborn, impatient people who succumb to idol worship. Their failure is of such magnitude that it forces Moses to return to Mount Sinai and endure another forty days and nights of anguish before God reveals the Ten Commandments a second time. *"And I looked, and behold, you had sinned against the Lord your God; you had made yourselves a molten calf; you had turned aside quickly from the way which the Lord had commanded you. So I took hold of the two tables, and cast them out of my two hands, and broke them before your eyes. Then I lay prostrate before the Lord as before, forty days and forty nights; I neither ate bread nor drank water, because of all the sin which you had committed."* And Moses continued, *"And I prayed to the Lord, 'O Lord God, destroy not thy people and thy heritage, whom thou hast redeemed through Thy greatness.'"*[67] Repeatedly throughout His forty-year ordeal in the wilderness, Moses bears the wrath of God on behalf of an ungrateful people, showing the weakness and failure of all humanity. These sacrifices of Moses inspired and educated a faithful minority of His followers in succeeding generations. His anguish, then, was not in vain. The foundation of religious civilization was reestablished through sacrificial labors, and it would be built upon by successive Founders.

11 – Symbolic Language as a Test for Believers

As with all scriptures, symbolism abounds in the books of Moses, as well as in the books amplifying His revelation later. The burning bush, the ten plagues, the parting of the sea, the pillar of light, the breaking of tablets, the devouring fire on the mountain—all these were used to convey significant processes that could not be conveyed with ordinary language. This is not to suggest that they have no historical content whatever, but rather to emphasize their primary role in evoking moral commitment and spiritual discernment.

When Isaiah was called by God, symbolic language was used—language that may have been outwardly confusing, but was inwardly illuminating. God asked Isaiah to say to the people: *"Hear and hear, but do not understand; see and see, but do not perceive."*[68] This may be interpreted as a divine assignment to help the people distinguish between their previous beliefs and new spiritual meanings, to give them "new ears and eyes." Immediately after this, God commanded Isaiah: *"Make the heart of this people fat, and their ears heavy, and shut their eyes; lest they see with their eyes, and hear with their ears, and understand with their hearts, and turn and be healed."*[69] Through this enigmatic statement, Isaiah was assigned to offer new spiritual messages leading "old ears" and "old eyes" to become dysfunctional, so they would be forced to perceive anew—thus awakening them, turning them around, and correcting rigid misconceptions.

The divine calling of Jeremiah was similarly obscure and illuminating. God said: *"I have set you this day over nations and over kingdoms, to pluck up and to break down, to destroy and to overthrow, to build and to plant."*[70] Jeremiah was being told that he would be instrumental in a spiritual revolution, where the old would be torn down and the new would be built. Immediately after this, God offered Jeremiah a lesson on symbolism. He asked Jeremiah what he saw, and Jeremiah answered: *"I see a boiling pot, facing away from the north."* And then God explained the meaning of his perception: *"Out of the north evil shall break forth upon all the inhabitants of the land."*[71] Jeremiah's perception of a boiling pot was used by God to illustrate that its hot contents—an outpouring of destruction—would flow from the north. Like Isaiah, Jeremiah was taught to prophesy with symbolic language.

Moses promised a Prophet like Him would one day arise from among His people. At first, the term Prophet was correctly understood as pointing to a Revealer of divine law—a figure like Noah, Abraham, or Moses. But the term *messiah*, especially after David's united kingdom, became strongly linked with political sovereignty. The expectation of a returned David-like ruler became most intense when Israel came under Roman domination in the decades before Jesus. Terms related to burgeoning messianic expectation, such as sovereignty, kingship, and throne, were interpreted literally or politically, rather than symbolically or spiritually. They became veils obscuring the significance of Jesus, Muḥammad, and Bahá'u'lláh. New eyes and ears were needed to recognize Their station.

12 – Exemplary Women:
Miriam the Nurturer, Deborah the Advocate

Miriam was the older sister of Moses and Aaron, and it was she who watched when His mother placed the infant Moses in a basket at the river's edge, hoping to escape Pharaoh's wrath while inviting divine protection. Miriam saw that it was the Pharaoh's daughter who found Him, and then in consultation with the Pharaoh's daughter, Miriam arranged for Moses' mother to be His nurse. We might assume that Miriam remained in contact with the Pharaoh's daughter as her brother grew up, seeing that she took care of Him and rejoicing that she adopted Him as her son. Miriam was also the one who led the celebration when the Exodus proved successful. When the Hebrews escaped the avenging Egyptians with God's help, she led the people in singing a victory song she composed. An excerpt from her song in Exodus 15 reveals her poetic talent, showing an acute sense of destiny and refined faithfulness.

> *I will sing to the Lord, for he has triumphed gloriously;*
> *the horse and the rider he has thrown into the sea.*
> *The Lord is my strength and my song,*
> *And he has become my salvation; this is my God, and I will praise him,*
> *My father's God, and I will exalt him.*

If Miriam was a model of sensitivity and nurturance, Deborah was a model of assertiveness. Deborah served as a judge, military commander, prophetess, and poet during the conquest of the Promised Land. In Judges 4 and 5, she was depicted as a strong, confident leader, implementing divine will decisively. She masterminded victory in the war of liberation from the oppression of King Jabin of Canaan. Deborah's may have been Israel's last campaign against the Canaanites. *"Hear, O kings; give ear, O princes; to the Lord I will sing, I will make melody to the Lord, the God of Israel. . . . My heart goes out to the commanders of Israel who offered themselves willingly among the people. Bless the Lord."*[72]

13 – Dying and Ascending Victoriously: Final Blessings and the Lord's Burial

Moses saw the Promised Land, but was not allowed to enter. His final address to His followers was a beautiful blessing of the tribes and all the faithful in His posterity, which may be interpreted as including the Christian Faith, the Islamic Faith, and the Bahá'í Faith. God said to Moses: *"'This is the land which I swore to Abraham. . . . I have let you see it with your eyes, but you shall not go over there.' So Moses the servant of the Lord died there in Moab, according to the word of the Lord, and he buried him in the valley . . . but no man knows the place of his burial to this day."*[73] He knew God face to face and fulfilled a mighty mission: saving the Hebrews from Egypt, delivering divine law, renewing their identity as Children of Israel, leading them to the Promised Land, and shaping them into a spiritual nation fit to reclaim the dwelling place of Abraham. How fitting that God gave Moses a private burial, which can be seen as honoring Their intimate bond and removing temptations to idolize His grave.

- 6 -
Moses: Teaching and Legacy

14 – Transformative Teaching and Healing: Exodus and Sinai

Moses' transformative mission included delivering His people from bondage, healing their spiritual wounds, convincing them that they had been chosen as partners in a divine covenant, teaching them how to develop as a religious nation, delivering the divine law, establishing a system of judges, reinterpreting cultic-devotional life through the ark and tabernacle, as well as preparing them to enter the Promised Land. We now touch on some of the highlights of this great drama.

The Exodus

According to biblical researcher James W. Jack, the Exodus may have taken place as early as 1500 BCE, and this date seems more likely than the traditional date of 1300 BCE, given the needed spacing of developments between Moses and David. In any case, the Exodus involved a "mixed multitude" of Hebrews, other slaves, and some converted Egyptians, totaling perhaps 10,000 people. It was a political deliverance and a spiritual liberation, having economic aspects as well. *"The people of Israel had also done as Moses told them, for they had asked of the Egyptians jewelry of silver and of gold, and clothing; and the Lord had given the people favor in the sight of the Egyptians, so that they let them have what they asked."*[1]

Even though Pharaoh finally heeded Moses' demand to let His people go, the sight of their victorious departure "hardened his heart," and changing his mind, he ordered his soldiers into action. *"The Egyptians pursued them, all Pharaoh's horses and chariots and his horsemen and his army, and they overtook them."* But Moses said, *"Fear not, stand firm, and see the salvation of the Lord."* God said to Moses, *"Lift up your rod, and stretch out your hand over the sea and divide it, that the people of Israel may go on dry land through the sea."*[2] And then

God drove the waters back by blowing *"a strong east wind all night, and made the sea dry land, and the waters were divided."* After the Hebrews were safely across the "sea of reeds," *"the waters returned and covered the chariots and the horsemen and all the host of Pharaoh . . . and the people feared the Lord; and they believed in the Lord and in his servant Moses."* [3]

Renewal and Reinterpretation

The tenth plague marked a reinterpreted festival of Passover. God said: *"It is the Lord's Passover. For I will pass through the land of Egypt that night, and I will smite all the first-born in the land of Egypt. . . . This day shall be for you a memorial day, and you shall keep it as a feast to the Lord."* [4] The original Passover ritual had been for nomadic shepherds, and involved sprinkling the blood of a sheep or goat on family property to ward off evil powers. This provided protection, especially for vulnerable newborns. Moses reinterpreted this ritual as a memorial of the Lord's deliverance. There had also been an ancient feast of unleavened bread associated with the harvest festival. But on the eve of the Exodus, Moses commanded the people to eat roasted lamb, bitter herbs, and unleavened bread *"in haste."* [5] This new interpretation historicized a long-standing pastoral ritual. Moses gave two nomadic spring festivals historic and spiritual import.

A third tradition given new depth was the Sabbath. Moses reminded the people that God rested on the seventh day of creation. Moses commanded weekly rest and renewal, and then extended the Sabbath to "manservants and maidservants," reminding the people that they too had once been slaves in Egypt. [6] "The traditions about the sabbath as redefined by Moses thus combine the divine and the human, the cosmic and the historical, the cultic and the ethical, the ritual and the humanitarian." [7]

Scholars conclude that Moses gave existing traditions new significance, combining cultic and ethical ordinances. There were rarely complete breaks from the past, but rather, symbolic changes giving past events and practices an expanded, more spiritual meaning. Collective salvation was to be remembered always, and the people must remain worthy of divine beneficence. Reinterpretation and renewal were intrinsic to Moses' teaching and ministry. He "rediscovered and reinterpreted his own relationship with his people and his ancestors; he rediscovered and reinterpreted the meaning of Yahweh; and . . . he was to recast and revitalize traditional bodies of law." [8]

Mount Sinai and Delivery of the Law

Through Moses, God promised Israel: *"I will redeem you. . . . I will take you for my people, and I will be your God."* [9] The desert years introduced them to dynamics of freedom and responsibility, but as they approached Mount Sinai, soul-stirring experiences even greater than the Exodus awaited them. The people looked up: *"there were thunders and lightnings, and a thick cloud upon the mountain, and a very loud trumpet blast, so that all the people in the camp trembled. Then Moses brought the people out of the camp to meet God. . . . And Mount Sinai was wrapped in smoke, because the Lord descended upon it in fire . . . and the whole mountain quaked greatly."* [10] Then God told Moses: *"Come up to me on the mountain, and wait there; and I will give you the tables of stone, with the law and the commandment, which I have written for their instruction."* [11]

This is when Moses received the Ten Commandments, which provided foundational moral principles in a brief, memorable, and easily transmitted form capable of surviving intact over a vast length of time. The Ten Commandments taught the Children of Israel that they should not have any other gods but God; that they should not create graven images; that they should not take the Lord's name in vain; that they should remember the Sabbath day and keep it holy; that they should honor their parents; that they should not kill, commit adultery, steal, bear false witness, or covet their neighbor.[12] The Decalogue taught monotheism—recognition that Divine Reality is one, authoritative and unknowable—as well as reverence for God, necessity of worship, family unity, social justice, and inner purity.

After teaching the Law on stone tablets, as well as other legal and ritual guidelines, Moses read the Book of the Covenant *"in the hearing of the people; and they said, 'All that the Lord has spoken we will do, and we will be obedient.' And Moses took the blood* [of oxen] *and threw it upon the people, and said, 'Behold the blood of the covenant which the Lord has made with you in accordance with all these words.'"* [13] The Ten Commandments had a categorical tone, prescribing foundational and essential duties to God and humanity. They were minimal restraints enabling the people to establish a universal religious civilization. They preserved and protected the basics: holiness, family life, property, honesty, life itself, and removal of ill-intent. An important principle that today would be called "equal justice for all" was also established. In that day it required *"one law for the sojourner and for the native"* [14] and that one should *"hear the small and the great alike."*[15] And the people agreed to the covenant saying, *"All that the Lord has spoken we will do, and we will be obedient."*[16]

The Ark and Tabernacle: Portable Religion

The Ark of the Covenant was a container, made by God's command through Moses, for carrying the tablets of the covenant during the Hebrews' wilderness travels. Such an institutional device provided for a more portable religion. The Book of Exodus provides details on constructing the Ark of the Covenant, along with a proper table, lamp and lampstand, tabernacle or tent sanctuary, curtain, veil, altar, court, priestly vestments, etc. The ordination of priests was also described, *"You shall take the anointing oil, and pour it on his head and anoint him."*[17] Anointing became associated with the One promised by Moses, a divine but earthly king, the messiah. The top part of the ark was understood as a symbolic "footstool of God"—a portable and visible reminder of the invisible divine presence. The Lord said to Moses: *"There I will meet with you, and from above the mercy seat, from between the two cherubim that are upon the ark of the testimony, I will speak with you."*[18] He also said, *"I will consecrate the tent of meeting and the altar. . . . I will dwell among the people of Israel, and will be their God."*[19]

A striking development that went along with these changes was that God could be with them even when they left Mount Sinai. A portable religion was a more universal religion. A divine "cloud" guided the people by day, and divine "fire" comforted them by night. *"The glory of the Lord filled the tabernacle. Throughout all their journeys, whenever the cloud was taken up from over the tabernacle, the people of Israel would go onward . . . and fire was in it by night, in the sight of all the house of Israel."*[20] Moses later looked back on His mission with the people of Israel declaring that, despite their past and future breaches of the covenant, they would ultimately triumph. *"The Lord your God has multiplied you, and behold, you are this day as the stars of heaven for multitude. May the Lord . . . make you a thousand times as many as you are, and bless you, as He has promised you!"*[21]

15 – Delivering a Thematic and Complementary Message: Observing the Covenant of Divine Law

The message to humanity that comes to us through Moses is a set of spiritual, social, and material virtues that have the power to undergird a lofty religious civilization. Some details of these three sets of teachings are presented in other sections. Here we focus on Moses' central theme, which was to observe the covenant of divine law. This theme is consistent with, but complementary to, all other messages of the Prophets before and after Him. It cast fresh light on God's nature and His manner of guiding humanity.

The Nature of God

In Moses' revelation God was presented as the one and only Creator, He Who creates what comes into existence. Despite this remote and transcendent quality, God works through certain groups of people at specific times and places, and speaks intimately with selected Prophets. Through special Messengers and other prophetic voices, God initiates covenants or binding moral and spiritual agreements—with expectations and promises, along with appropriate rewards and punishments.

Previously, God was known by various names, including *El Elyon,* or the Highest God, and *El Shaddai,* or God Almighty. Now through Moses, He was being presented as the Lord—suggesting authority, sovereignty, majesty, and ultimately benevolent and redemptive purposes. God is depicted as able to control the unfolding of events, miraculously when necessary, all to establish His power and clarify His message. He is able and willing to deliver and save a "chosen people." He requires worship, sacrifice, service, and observance. In Moses' dispensation, cultic practices and moral injunctions were more distinct from each other than in other dispensations (such as Buddha's or Christ's). Moses presented God as both judging and forgiving, and even able to repent or be changed by a Messenger's advocacy on behalf of the people. An instructive summary of divine qualities was provided in Exodus 34:6–7. *"The Lord, the Lord, a God merciful and gracious, slow to anger, and abounding in steadfast love and faithfulness, keeping steadfast love for thousands, forgiving iniquity and transgression and sin, but Who will by no means clear the guilty, visiting the iniquity of the fathers upon the children and the children's children, to the third and fourth generation."*

A commonly held view in the West is stated by David Daiches as follows: "The God of nature, of history and of the moral order dwelling invisibly on high and making the most exacting demands on the people he adopted as peculiarly his own—there is nothing like this in the traditions of any other ancient people."[22] However, our study shows that the ancient Persians and Hindus had comparable views of God. It is better to view the Founders' themes as progressive and complementary rather than unique.

Covenant Renewal

An important covenant renewal was offered in Exodus 34:10–13. This development bridged the years of wandering to the years of conquest. God said to Moses: *"Behold, I make a covenant. Before all your people I will do marvels, such as have not been wrought in all the earth or in any nation. . . . Observe what I command you this day. Behold, I will drive out before you the Amorites, the Canaanites . . . You shall tear down their altars."* Morally objectionable practices of the Canaanites were child sacrifice, sacred prostitution, and black magic. By saying that their altars needed to be torn down, God was reminding Moses and His followers of the importance of following Him—the one and only God.

The rewards for observing the covenant were peace and prosperity, while the corresponding punishments for disobedience were impoverishment, defeat, and domination by other nations. God said: *"I will have regard for you and make you fruitful and multiply you, and will confirm my covenant with you. . . . I will walk among you, and I will be your God, and you shall be my people. . . . But if you will not hearken to me . . . I will set my face against you, and you shall be smitten before your enemies; those who hate you shall rule over you."*[23] Though many of the rules at that time may sound harsh to modern ears, we must remember that executive forces in the current sense were lacking for the ancient Israelites. Therefore, very strong language was needed to guide their behavior. Nonetheless, there were also more soothing scriptural passages, and this benediction was common: *"The Lord bless you and keep you: The Lord make his face to shine upon you, and be gracious to you: The Lord lift up his countenance upon you, and give you peace."*[24]

The lovely word *shalom,* a common greeting in Jewish traditions, means peace, but with very prized nuances. It is renewal, prosperity, and well-being, deepened by a sense of spiritual completeness, wholeness, and harmony. Shalom is peaceful obedience in covenantal relation, and is a vision of a universal peace between God and humanity—the very loftiest goal of Jewish life.

Covenantal Dynamics

Both the exaltation and the dangers of covenantal dynamics are revealed in key passages in the Book of Numbers, in the context of Canaan's conquest. *"The glory of the Lord appeared at the tent of meeting to all the people of Israel. And the Lord said to Moses, 'How long will this people despise me? . . . I will strike them with the pestilence and disinherit them, and I will make of you a nation greater and mightier than they.'"*[25] God was threatening to bring Moses to a different people—new "chosen ones"—who would be more receptive to His message. But later, after Moses' pleading with God, the Lord spoke words that seem to have implications in the distant future, as well as immediate significance. *"I have pardoned, according to your word, but truly, as I live, and as all the earth shall be filled with the glory of the Lord, none of the men who have seen my glory and my signs . . . shall see the land which I swore to their fathers."* [26]

Later, God speaks through Balaam, a Babylonian diviner, revealing further aspects of covenantal dynamics, including images of future dispensations. Balaam said, *"The Lord their God is with them, and the shout of a King is among them,"* and later he said, *"A star shall come forth out of Jacob, and a scepter shall rise out of Israel."* [27] These hope-giving words look ahead at least to David, if not also to the exalted kingships and dispensations of Jesus, Muḥammad, and Bahá'u'lláh.

The Second Law: Deuteronomy

The covenantal theme was deepened and expanded in Deuteronomy, a name meaning "second law." This book is thought to be a later interpretation of Moses' teachings, and to contain aspects of His message not emphasized or understood in His own day. A distinctive teaching of Deuteronomy is that worship should be centralized, and the central sanctuary became the temple in Jerusalem. In Moses' second farewell addresses, He said: *"You shall walk in all the way which the Lord your God has commanded you, that you may live, and that it may go well with you."* [28] Israel showed understanding of its divine blessings and historical role, saying: *"Behold, the Lord our God has shown us His glory and greatness. . . . For who is there of all flesh, that has heard the voice of the living God speaking out of the midst of fire, as we have, and has lived?"* [29]

The first commandment, rendered in positive, inspiring form, was used continuously for devotional purposes in the famous *shema,* which meant "hear." *"Hear, O Israel: The Lord our God is one Lord; and thou shall love the Lord your God with all your heart, and with all your soul, and with all your might."* [30] Other important covenantal passages in Deuteronomy refer to the importance of the faithful keeping their covenant with God, and being steadfast in their love for Him and in their obedience to His commandments. It also reminds believers how they must *"walk in His ways"* through their fear, love, and service to God. [31]

The importance of centralized worship as an advance in the covenantal relationship, while looking ahead to establishing Jerusalem as the holy city, is accented in this passage. *"You shall not do according to all that we are doing here this day, every man doing whatever is right in his own eyes. . . . But when you go over the Jordan, and live in the land which the Lord your God gives you to inherit . . . then to the place that the Lord your God will choose, to make His name dwell there, thither you shall bring all that I command thee. . . . And you shall rejoice before the Lord your God."*[32]

Covenantal Blessings and Warnings

The conclusion of Moses' second address in Deuteronomy contained a prophetic passage of blessings and warnings. It seems to apply not only to Israel in an ethno-specific sense, but to all who sincerely try to be faithful to God. *"And if you obey the voice of the Lord your God, being careful to do all his commandments which I command you this day, the Lord your God will set you high above all the nations of the earth. And all these blessings shall come upon you and overtake you, if you obey the voice of the Lord your God."*[33] But later it goes on to say, *"But if you will not obey the voice of the Lord your God then all these curses shall come upon you and overtake you."*[34]

Later in this address came a passage appearing to anticipate the exile and Diaspora. *"Because you did not serve the Lord your God with joyfulness and gladness of heart, by reason of the abundance of all things, therefore you shall serve your enemies whom the Lord will send against you."*[35] But the possibility of renewed commitment was left open. *"I have set before you life and death, blessing and curse; therefore choose life, that you and your descendants may live, loving the Lord your God."*[36]

16 – Renewing and Embodying Universal Virtues

A renewed body of universal guidelines for character development was taught by each of the Founders. They taught virtues, those praiseworthy qualities or heavenly attributes that are partly attainable by human beings. The Founders taught through both words and deeds, embodying in Their ministry inspiring models of living. Virtues are a vast common ground for understanding and cooperation across traditional boundaries. They are excellent mirrors to our souls, revealing both strengths and weaknesses. They disclose our prejudices and attachments, as well as our highest aspirations. Whether we identify with one religion or another, or with no religion at all, virtuous conduct is universally lauded. Societies built on such teachings become great religious civilizations.

What virtue-teachings are associated with Moses' dispensation? Here we pause in our narrative and overview of early Jewish theological concepts to provide some brief examples of fifteen virtues that guided the formation of Jewish religious civilization. For comparative purposes, we will use the same virtues, sorted into three basic types—spiritual, social, and material—in describing the messages of all the Founders in this study.

Spiritual Virtues in the Mosaic Revelation

Devotion-Faithfulness: *"Try me and know my thoughts! And see if there be any wicked way in me, and lead me in the way everlasting."*[37]

Gratitude-Reverence: *"O Lord, how manifold are thy works! In wisdom hast thou made them all."*[38]

Self-discipline-Obedience: *"He who is slow to anger is better than the mighty, and he who rules his spirit is better than he who takes a city."*[39]

Detachment-Patience: *"The Lord is my shepherd, I shall not want."*[40]

Wisdom-Discernment: *"The fear of the Lord is the beginning of wisdom; a good understanding have all those who practice it."*[41]

Social Virtues in the Mosaic Revelation

Loving-kindness-Compassion: *"Love your neighbor as yourself."*[42]

Service-Responsibility: *"He has showed you, O man, what is good; and what does the Lord require of you but to do justice, and to love kindness, and to walk humbly with your God?"*[43]

Respect-Tolerance: *"Have we not all one father? Has not one God created us? Why then are we faithless to one another, profaning the covenant of our fathers?"*[44]

Justice-Righteousness: *"You shall not be partial in judgment; you shall hear the small and the great alike; you shall not be afraid of the face of man, for the judgment is God's."*[45]

Peace-Unity: *"They shall beat their swords into plowshares, and their spears into pruning hooks; nation shall not lift up sword against nation, neither shall they study war any more."*[46]

Material Virtues in the Mosaic Revelation

Trustworthiness-Honesty: *"You shall not bear false witness against your neighbor."*[47]

Moderation-Balance: *"He who oppresses the poor to increase his own wealth, or gives to the rich, will only come to want."*[48]

101

Generosity-Hospitality: *"Do not withhold good from those to whom it is due, when it is in your power to do it."*[49]

Creativity-Beauty: *"Make a joyful noise to God, all the earth; sing the glory of his name; give to him glorious praise!"*[50]

Earthcare-Stewardship: *"Have dominion . . . over every living thing that moves upon the earth."*[51]

17 – Abrogating the Old and Establishing the New: Ritual and Legal Guidance

Each Founder offered two basic kinds of guidance—moral and spiritual principles on one hand, and ritual practices and sociolegal norms on the other. Prophets not only reaffirm and renew virtues that are abiding and universal. They also abrogate or modify practices related to specific social and historical conditions of Their day.

Ever since the journeys of Abraham, the tribes of Israel had been surrounded by polytheistic cultures. It was impossible for them to escape the influence of the Babylonians, Egyptians, and Canaanites. Among the major tasks of Moses as a divine Teacher, then, was to reinterpret and carry forward what was still useful from the societies His people had encountered. Scholars have noticed some similarities between Moses' ritual and legal guidance on one hand, and Hammurabi's Code, Hittite covenants between kings and vassals, and Egyptian ethical injunctions on the other. By looking at this through a historical context, we can appreciate that it was reasonable and prudent for the Founders to build upon familiar and practical forms while introducing new guidance. The Messengers of God, acting as Teachers of humanity, speak in a language that Their students, the people to whom They came, can understand. We now touch briefly on some of the new cultic and legal guidelines Moses offered the people during their transformative wandering in the wilderness.

The Holiness Code is a mixture of ethical and ritual injunctions, and its central exposition is in Leviticus, chapters 17 to 26. Peace offerings or covenantal meals that celebrate binding ritual practices, both between fellow observers and between the people and God, are described. Guilt offerings requiring restitution and sacrifices for offenses against one's fellows and God are also described. Laws about cleanliness, purification, and diseases are included, as well as the ritual for the Day of Atonement. There are passages on forbidden food, pollution, infection, contagious diseases, and taking vengeance. Laws against magic, sorcery, witchcraft, sacred prostitution, self-mutilation, incest, sodomy, bestiality, sacrificing children, defrauding, tale-bearing, and corrupt judging can be found. The code addressed the slaughter of animals, sexual relations, spiritual attitudes, priestly functions, and sacred feasts. It included laws about three annual festivals and ethical injunctions on liberating slaves in the jubilee year. This code upheld the famous "eye for an eye" rule, which, given the retaliatory practices of the day, was a step toward justice, for it contained the principle of proportional force. Under David, Israel came closer than ever before (or since) to living by this elaborate system of religious law.

18 – Human and Divine Qualities: Exemplifying a Dual Station

Each Founder can be justifiably interpreted as both human and divine. His life illustrates an historic and limited nature, as well as a universal and transcendent nature. In the beginning of His ministry, Moses' human qualities were obvious; but as events unfolded, His divinity emerged.

Moses' Human Station

At first, Moses felt unfit to be a Messenger of God, claiming that He was *"not eloquent . . . slow of speech and of tongue."* [52] He often felt overwhelmed with the demands placed upon Him, and in a very human manner, He accepted Jethro's advice on delegating responsibility. Once, Moses came to despair in dealing with the "stiff-necked" Israelites, even wishing to be killed by God rather than having to deal with the people alone. He complained to God about His troubles, *"I am not able to carry all this people alone, the burden is too heavy for me."* [53] His humanness was very evident to his followers, for they perceived Him as humble and ordinary. *"The man Moses was very meek, more than all men that were on the face of the earth."* [54]

Moses' Divine Station

At first, Moses used Aaron as His spokesman, but gradually Moses grew beyond His dependence on Aaron and began to bring divine messages to the people Himself. The power of divine speech was bestowed upon Moses. *"I will be with your mouth and with his mouth* [Aaron], *and will teach you what you shall do."* [55] There were references to Moses as clearly above the people in spiritual station. The people said to Him: *"You speak to us, and we will hear; but let not God speak to us, lest we die."* [56] The people also said: *"The Lord used to speak to Moses face to face, as a man speaks to his friend,"* and that *"Moses . . . the Lord knew face to face."*[57] God had also said, *"Moses alone shall come near to the Lord."*[58] Some references even suggested that Moses was closer to God than to the people. After returning from Mount Sinai, it was said of Moses that, *"the skin of His face shone because he had been talking with God. And when Aaron and all the people of Israel saw Moses . . . they were afraid to come near him."*[59] So Moses' divine station became very clear to all who witnessed His ministry and felt its effects in succeeding centuries.

19 – The Light and the Word

In many scriptural passages of the Mosaic revelation, God is light overcoming darkness, and His Word penetrates the people's ignorance, showing them the correct path to walk. Some passages, especially those from Isaiah, seem to be prophetic references to future revelations and dispensations.

I have given you as a covenant to the people, a light to the nations, to open the eyes that are blind.[60]

Arise, shine; for your light has come, and the glory of the Lord has risen upon you. . . . And nations shall come to your light, and kings to the brightness of your rising.[61]

The Lord will be your everlasting light, and your God will be your glory.[62]

20 – Affirming Four Realms: Natural, Human, Revelatory, Divine

An exciting and hopeful discovery in interfaith relations is that all major scriptural traditions offer a similar map of reality. In very comparable ways, they proclaim the same basic metaphysical big picture with four distinguishable levels. But because sincere multi-scriptural study is rare, and because the key terms for each faith tradition arise from different cultural and historical settings, this common metaphysical ground is not often glimpsed. Among the benefits of a study like ours is an invitation to behold the unified reality to which most of the symbols and parables point.

According to the world's scriptures collectively, our human condition is described as both in and above the material world. Below us and around us is the realm of nature and matter, in which we discover three major sub-levels: matter, plants, and animals. We have reasoning, discerning souls capable of directing themselves in both material and spiritual directions. Above us is the revelatory world of the spirit, always made accessible to us by Divine Educators. And above Them is a realm even They cannot fully penetrate—the infinite divine realm. This makes for four intricate and interrelating levels of reality: the natural, the human, the revelatory, and the divine. How did the Mosaic revelation depict these four realms?

The Natural Realm

In Genesis and Psalms, we find a cosmology reasonably consistent with a scientific worldview. A creative power was at work in the beginning. *"Let there be light. . . . Let there be a firmament in the midst of the waters. . . . Let the waters under the heavens be gathered into one place, and let dry land appear."*[63] The Psalms described creation by saying, *"The heavens are telling the glory of God; and the firmament proclaims his handiwork."*[64] After the physical cosmos was created, life began on earth. First came the plant kingdom: *"The earth brought forth vegetation, plants yielding seeds according to their own kinds."*[65] The Book of Genesis also says, *"And out of the ground the Lord God made to grow every tree."*[66] Then came the animal kingdom: *"Let the waters bring forth swarms of living creatures, and let birds fly above the earth. . . . Let the earth bring forth living creatures according to their kinds."*[67] Such conditions on earth being established, the way was prepared for the emergence of human life.

The Human Realm

Human beings were created by God. We were given special powers, for better and for worse. *"Let us make man in our image, after our likeness; and let them have dominion over . . . all the earth."*[68] God gave humanity dignified roles, along with moral responsibility. *"Thou hast made him* [humanity] *little less than God, and dost crown him with glory and honor. Thou hast given him dominion over the works of thy hands; thou hast put all things under his feet."*[69] We were given the power to discern truth: *"Come now, let us reason together, says the Lord."*[70] Against God's advice, and succumbing to temptation, humanity ate of the tree of the knowledge of good and evil and the *"eyes of both* [Adam and Eve] *were opened, and they knew that they were naked; and they sewed fig leaves together and made themselves aprons."*[71] Consequences ensued: *"Cursed is the ground because of you; in toil you shall eat of it all the days of your life. . . . In the sweat of your face you shall eat bread till you return to the ground."*[72] But we accepted the conditions of human life. *"O Lord, thou art our Father; we are the clay, and thou art our potter; we are all the work of thy hand.*[73] We knew that *"affliction does not come from the dust, nor does trouble sprout from the ground; but man is born to trouble as the sparks fly upward,"* [74] and we learned from our mistakes. The soul breathed into each of us is immortal. *"God will ransom my soul from the power of Sheol; for he will receive me,"* and it shall exist with God for all eternity: *"Surely goodness and mercy shall follow me all the days of my life; and I shall dwell in the house of the Lord for ever."* [75]

The Revelatory Realm

Higher than the human realm was the spiritual world of the Holy Spirit, or heavenly wisdom, which is mediated by Prophets and offered to humanity. Moses' concept of revelation was a set of covenantal commands through Messengers like Himself, assisted by prophetic figures like David and Isaiah. *"I will raise up for them a prophet like you [Moses] from among their brethren; and I will put my words in his mouth, and he shall speak to them all that I command him."* [76] Wisdom was understood as a power in the revelatory realm. Humanity was able to receive it, but not produce it. *"But where shall wisdom be found? And where is the place of understanding? Man does not know the way to it, and it is not found in the land of the living. . . . God understands the way to it, and he knows its place. For he looks to the ends of the earth, and sees everything under the heavens."* [77] The caring or personal aspects of God were also shown as coming from the revelatory realm. *"He kept him as the apple of his eye. Like an eagle that . . . flutters over its young, spreading out its wings, catching them, bearing them on its pinions."* [78] It is also described that God helps those in need, *"The Lord lifts up those who are bowed down,"* and that His love flows over everything, *"The Lord is good to all, and his compassion is over all He has made."* [79] Finally, the Word of God has creative and transformative power, affecting all parts of creation—past, present, and future. *"The counsel of the Lord stands for ever, the thoughts of his heart to all generations."* [80]

The Divine Realm

Even higher than the revelatory realm is the transcendent realm of divine mystery. God said to Moses: *"You cannot see my face; for man shall not see me and live."* [81] Other passages depict God as far beyond human grasp.

Great is the Lord, and greatly to be praised, and his greatness is unsearchable.[82]

I am the first and I am the last; besides me there is no god.[83]

For my thoughts are not your thoughts, neither are your ways my ways, says the Lord. For as the heavens are higher than the earth, so are my ways higher than your ways, and my thoughts than your thoughts.[84]

Can you find out the deep things of God? Can you find out the limit of the Almighty? It is higher than heaven. . . . Its measure is longer than the earth, and broader than the sea.[85]

21 – Promising a Future Savior and a New Golden Age: The Messiah and the Everlasting Dominion

Moses prophesied a successor, a *"prophet like me."* [86] He could not have been referring to figures like Nathan, David, or Isaiah, because—as significant as these figures were—they expressed Moses' revelation, and were not "like Moses" Who inaugurated a completely new dispensation. After Samuel (the judge and prophet who anointed David), the term "messiah" was used variously in different historical periods. According to Christian, Muslim, and Bahá'í interpretations, David prophesied the coming of the Messiah in these words: *"Lift up your heads, O gates! and be lifted up, O ancient doors! that the King of glory may come in. Who is this King of glory? The Lord of hosts, he is the King of glory!"* [87] In traditional Jewish interpretation, *messiah* at first referred to dedicated kings, high priests, and individuals with truly divine missions. "After the Exile, the prophetic vision of God's kingdom was associated with the ingathering of Israel under an anointed scion of the House of David. During the period of Roman rule, the expectation of a messiah who would deliver the Jewish people gained prominence."[88]

Isaiah's famous prophecies are interpreted differently by each of the Abrahamic traditions. Jews expect a David-like liberator; Christians claim these prophecies all referred to Jesus; Muslims say they refer primarily to Muḥammad; and Bahá'ís believe they refer in part to Christ and Muḥammad, but most fully to Bahá'u'lláh. *"For to us a child is born, to us a son is given; and the government will be upon his shoulder, and his name will be called 'Wonderful Counselor, Mighty God, Everlasting Father, Prince of Peace.' Of the increase of his government and of peace there will be no end."* [89] The Book of Isaiah also says, *"There shall come forth a shoot from the stump of Jesse, and a branch shall grow out of his roots. And the Spirit of the Lord shall rest upon him, the spirit of wisdom and understanding, the spirit of counsel and might, the spirit of knowledge and the fear of the Lord."*[90] And in another prophecy it says, *"I am coming to gather all nations and tongues; and they shall come and see my glory, and I will set a sign among them."*[91]

The following prophecies by Isaiah and Daniel refer to a spiritual golden age or *"new heavens and a new earth"*[92] that would be greater than any yet attained—a fulfillment of all previous divine promises in an "everlasting dominion." These famous passages are also interpreted quite differently. Christians claim they refer to the Return of Christ; Muslims claim they refer to the era brought by the Mahdi (rightly guided one); Bahá'ís claim they refer to the current age initiated by Bahá'u'lláh. One passage states, *"He shall judge between the nations, and shall decide for many peoples; and they shall beat their swords into plowshares, and their spears into pruning hooks; nation shall not lift up sword against nation, neither shall they learn war any more."*[93] Another passage says, *"With the clouds of heaven there came one like a son of man. . . . And to him was given dominion and glory and kingdom, that all peoples, nations, and languages should serve him; his dominion is an everlasting dominion."*[94]

22 – Essential Unity of the Revealers through the Ages

In His final blessing, Moses offered a panoramic vision of divine vigilance, past and future, applying not only to His tradition, but also those to come. This was a vision of divine oneness, dramatically asserting essential unity among all revealed religions. *"The Lord came from Sinai, and dawned from Se'ir upon us; he shone forth from Mount Paran, he came from the ten thousands of holy ones, with flaming fire at his right hand."*[95] From the perspective of global religious history, this might be viewed as referring to the Jewish Faith (Sinai), the Christian Faith (Se'ir or Syria), the Islamic Faith (Mount Paran or Arabia), and the Bahá'í Faith ("thousands of holy ones"). If Moses was indeed a Revealer, He had access to all knowledge—past and future—and could evoke at will the essential markers and symbols of distant spiritual developments. *"There is none like God, O Jesh'urun* [upright one], *who rides through the heavens to your help, and in his majesty through the skies. The eternal God is your dwelling place, and underneath are the everlasting arms."*[96] According to Moses, the everlasting arms of God would carry the faithful among the multitude of nations generated by Abraham. After long declines, and under conditions of severe oppression, the eternal God would enter our temporal realm of history and carry us forward again.

23 – Laying Enduring Foundations: Judges and Elders, the Conquest of Canaan, and David's Anointed Kingship

Judges and Elders

When Moses' father-in-law, Jethro the Midian priest, noticed how heavy the demands upon Moses were becoming, he suggested that Moses *"Choose able men from all the people, such as fear God, men who are trustworthy . . . and place such men over the people as rulers of thousands, of hundreds, of fifties, and of tens. And let them judge the people at all times; every great matter they shall bring to you, but any small matter they shall decide themselves."*[97] Moses respected Jethro's wisdom and implemented this advice. Later, when Moses felt especially burdened by the people's waywardness, God stepped in to establish the institution of the elders. *"Gather for me seventy men of the elders of Israel . . . and I will take some of the spirit which is upon you and put it upon them; and they shall bear the burden of the people with you."*[98] Their role was to help in governing the community and administering the law, so as to lead the people of Israel to nationhood. The elders may have been the historical basis for the Sanhedrin, an assembly of legal decision-makers functioning in the first century BCE.

The Conquest of Canaan

The concept of the Promised Land was born when the Lord said to Abraham, *"To your descendants I give this land, from the river of Egypt to the great river, the river Euphrates."*[99] We note that this is a larger piece of land than modern Israel. Jewish people have interpreted this promise as applying only to them, but the descendants of Abraham were a multitude of nations including the Children of Israel, Arabs, Persians, and perhaps other faithful peoples.

In preparation for Moses' passing, there was need to address succession. Who would lead the Israelites in regaining the Promised Land? God said to Moses: *"Take Joshua . . . and you shall commission him in their sight. You shall invest him with some of your authority, that all the congregation of the people of Israel may obey."*[100] Then the Lord spoke to Joshua: *"Be strong and of good courage; for you shall bring the children of Israel into the land which I swore to give them: I will be with you."*[101] Under the leadership of Moses' successor, Joshua—and other figures such as Deborah, Gideon, and Samuel—the peoples of Canaan were partially conquered. There is debate about how long this process took. In any case, the Israelites took halting steps toward nationhood. Their various transitions—from highly individualistic and semi-nomadic tribes, to slaves in Egypt, to wanderers in the wilderness learning obedience to divine law, to more cooperative and settled villagers tilling the land—were all very difficult. Yet, considerable progress was made. It was later revealed: *"In Joshua's time there were thirty-one governments in the hands of the Israelites, and in every noble human attribute—learning, stability, determination, courage, honor, generosity—this people came to surpass all the nations of the earth."*[102] Theirs was a lofty model of an advanced civilization.

David's Anointed Kingship

A scriptural teaching on the institution of kingship that David exemplified for Israelites was offered in Deuteronomy. The Lord said through Moses: *"Set as king over you him whom the Lord your God will choose. One from among thy brethren you shall set as king over you. . . . He must not multiply horses for himself. . . . And he shall not multiply wives for himself, lest his heart turn away; nor shall he greatly multiply for himself silver and gold. And when he sits on the throne of his kingdom, he shall write for himself in a book a copy of this law . . . that he may learn to fear the Lord his God, be keeping all the words of this law and these statutes, and doing them; that his heart may not be lifted up above his brethren."*[103]

During the century before David established a united kingdom centered in Jerusalem, there was development from semi-autonomous tribal chieftains toward a more monarchic society. Threats from the Philistines, especially, created pressure on the Israelites to unite under Saul, Israel's first king. But Saul served somewhat frantically as a kind of emergency dictator. He banished the young David, whom he feared as a potential rival. Upon Saul's death, the southern tribes of Judah were ready to accept David's reign from Hebron in about 1000 BCE.

The Lord said to the prophet-judge Samuel: *"Arise, anoint him* [David]; *for this is he.' . . . And the Spirit of the Lord came mightily upon David from that day forward."*[104] David confirmed his divine sanction by killing Goliath. He ruled Judah alone before establishing a truly united kingdom by successfully bonding Judah with the northern tribes. King David's reign lasted forty years. He completed the conquest of the Philistines, overcame pockets of Canaanite resistance, established a capital at Jerusalem, transferred the Ark of the Covenant there, making it the religious and political center, and wrote much of the Psalms—in sum an inspired, creative testimony of divine guidance and sacred history. Though David was not depicted as sinless, he was praised for being repentant and God-fearing, able to combine deep devotion with administrative duty. His piety and righteousness was also praised in the Qur'án: *"We* [God] *strengthened his kingdom, and gave him wisdom and sound judgment."*[105]

The United Kingdom

Through most of Jewish history, David's achievement was celebrated as a magnificent arrival point, a trumpet-blast of destiny, demonstrating a goodly portion of God's promises fulfilled. His reign showed the children of Abraham and Moses transformed from nomadic warriors into rulers of a divinely-guided kingdom, and it has provided memories and hopes that have sustained many for three millennia. Solomon, David's son, peacefully succeeded him as king. After building a splendid palace, Solomon completed an even more impressive Temple compound that integrated religious and royal functions. Among his brilliant innovations was dividing the nation into twelve districts. Sacred wisdom traditions were written down in this golden age, and Solomon established a widespread reputation as wise, just, and concerned with the needs of all classes of people.

24 – Renewing Scriptural Guidance:
Torah, Prophets, and Writings

Mosaic scripture is all the canonical Hebrew scriptures—the Law or *Torah*, the Prophets or *Nebi'im*, and the Writings or *Ketuvim*. This amounts to the traditional thirty-nine books of the Hebrew Bible. But the sacred literature that seems most clearly under Moses' spiritual authority and power includes, besides the Torah, the books of Psalms, Isaiah, Ezekiel, and Daniel. Within the Hebrew Bible taken as a whole, we can discern progressive revelation—the self-disclosure of God becomes more developed and sophisticated as humanity matures through great challenges and trials, and as we advance in our capacity to receive divine guidance.

25 – Generating Civilization Anew:
Righteous City, Holy Nation, and Shalom

Near the end of the Books of Moses came the stunning Song of Moses. It placed the drama of ancient Israel in cosmic perspective by repeating the covenantal theme and by placing emphasis on hope. There are passages from Deuteronomy 32 that are especially universal and seem to be an early version of the teaching of progressive revelation, God's continuing renewal of revelation after humanity's periodic spiritual declines. *"May my teaching drop as the rain, my speech distil as the dew, as the gentle rain upon the tender grass, and as the showers upon the herb. For I will proclaim the name of the Lord. Ascribe greatness to Our God! The Rock, His work is perfect; for all His ways are justice. A God of faithfulness and without iniquity, just and right is He. . . . You were unmindful of the Rock that begot you, and you forgot the God who gave you birth. . . . For the Lord will vindicate his people and have compassion on his servants, when he sees that their power is gone."*

Moses' teachings were described as rain for humanity, a heavenly nourishment that descended from the Lord. God was the Rock, the solid foundation of these teachings, their Eternal Source. But too often we forget the Rock of our collective salvation. This passage in Deuteronomy could be an early allusion to progressive revelation. This interpretation is supported by the reference to God's compassion when He sees that the people's power is gone. God renews revelatory guidance for a society in decline. The Song of Moses is a promise of new birth and the return of divine guidance at the end of each dispensation when religious civilization decays. Hope is the theme of this process of decline and renewal.

What vision of civilization sustained the people of Israel through the centuries? In the tumultuous course of world history, the revelation of divine guidance generated civilization anew. When Moses' teaching was embraced with increasing fullness in successive generations, the emerging society truly served as a "light to the nations." The people of Israel were given a noble and lofty aim—a vision of civilization more advanced spiritually, socially, and materially than anything the world had seen. Implementing the Covenant and Holiness Code made them, at their best, a *"kingdom of priests and a holy nation."*[106] David and Solomon fulfilled this vision in part by uniting separate tribes, establishing the righteous city of Jerusalem, and generating a widely lauded civilization. At its height, Israel surpassed her contemporaries—Egypt and Babylonia—in the splendor of wisdom, effective social and administrative order, a magnificent palace and temple complex, as well as prosperity and peace. Persia, Greece, and Rome were to learn much from her brilliance.

The Hebrew word *shalom* has deeper significance than generally known. It is far more than a friendly greeting and an offer of good wishes. It conjures images of deep peace, a condition that can only arrive through widely shared faithfulness to divine guidance. It is tranquility of heart and mind, abiding spiritual contentment, yet also creative activity directed to health and prosperity of people everywhere. It evokes a rainbow vision of unity in diversity, of harmony and friendship beneath a canopy of divine love.

Israel's prophetic literature sustained her through many trials and failures. We close this chapter with some of these images of longing and hope.

Let justice roll down like waters, and righteousness like an ever-flowing stream.[107]

You shall be called the city of righteousness, the faithful city.[108]

Every valley shall be lifted up, and every mountain and hill be made low; the uneven ground shall become level, and the rough places a plain. And the glory of the Lord shall be revealed, and all flesh shall see it together, for the mouth of the Lord has spoken.[109]

Zoroaster: Background and Mission

Who was Zoroaster? What Faith did He generate? Is this Faith significant in the history of civilizations? These questions arise because Zoroaster is less well known than most of the Founders in this study. Though there may be only an estimated 200,000 Zoroastrians today, there are excellent reasons to study their Faith. Zoroastrianism, or the "Good Religion," was the leading Faith of three great Persian empires: the Achaemenid, the Parthian, and the Sasanian. These eras extended twelve centuries from 550 BCE to 650 CE, rivaling the glory of Greece and the grandeur of Rome.

Zoroaster lived about 1000 BCE in what is today called Afghanistan, Iran, and Iraq. His teachings include a lofty monotheism and an advanced ethical code, with well-developed doctrines on the future. These teachings influenced and linked with the development of Jewish, Greek, Christian, and Islamic thought. The Zoroastrian Faith has all the markings of a genuine revelation. Some historians suggest that if the Greeks had not halted the Persian advance in 480 BCE, all of Europe might have become Zoroastrian. Sophisticated teachings on divine unity, the struggle of good against evil, spiritual and demonic attributes, heeding the conscience, building prosperous communities, caring for the earth, immortality of the soul, future saviors, establishing a heavenly kingdom, and the ultimate triumph of good were all taught by Zoroaster.

The Persian name for Zoroaster was Zarathustra, and was probably a title meaning "eternal light." His primary name for God was Ahura Mazda, meaning the Wise Lord, the Creator of heaven and earth. The West has inherited the Greek name Zoroaster, and that is the name we will use throughout this work. The scriptural tradition that built up around Zoroaster was called the Avesta. However, the most authentic part of the Avesta was the Gathas, which were made up of Zoroaster's hymns and prayers.

1 – Continuity with Previous Dispensations: Cosmic Beginnings, Divine Agencies, Sage-Kings, and Prophets of Ancient Persia

Some time between Abraham's covenant with God and Moses' exodus from Egypt, the Aryans or Indo-Europeans entered Iran, which means "land of the Aryans." This land came to be called Persia, and the people who developed the most influential civilization there were the Persians. They were preceded by Sumerians, Elamites, and other Mesopotamians. Some of their tribes may have been contemporaries of Babylonians, Assyrians, and Medes.

The Persians' early religion showed many similarities with Vedic religion, probably because of common Aryan influence. It included worship of a sun god called Mithra, a sky god called Ahura, an earth goddess called Anahita, as well as deities of fire, thunder, rain, and seas. Their language was also similar to ancient Sanskrit.

Zoroastrian cosmogony, an account of the birth and fulfillment of the cosmic process, was developed late in the Zoroastrian dispensation, and so may not accurately represent Zoroaster's teaching. However, this cosmogony provides us with a Zoroastrian view of time and timelessness, and gives us a glimpse of how Zoroaster's background and advent have been understood. Four periods were envisioned of 3000 years each.[1]

1) In the beginning, there was a Timeless Time, a spiritual and non-tangible creation, during which choice was offered to God's twins. One twin chose goodness and creativity (the Holy Spirit), and the other twin chose evil and destruction (the Destructive Spirit). God was above in the light, while His adversary was below in the dark, and they did not interact.

2) After 3000 years, preliminary physical and tangible dimensions came into being. Its creative possibilities were tolerated by the Destructive Spirit for another 3000 years. God was gradually generating the spiritual and material world. It would serve as a trap for the Destroyer, who would one day be overcome through a Future Savior and His faithful followers.

3) Then the Destroyer attacked the Creator, and so the Creator arranged a pact with him to limit their struggle in time and space. First,

the spiritual realm became differentiated as seven beneficent spirits and its *fravashis* (eternal souls), who were given assignments as well as choices about their roles in the struggle of good against evil. Then the physical universe was established as a field of contest between good and evil, and as a trap for the Destroyer. At this time the sky was made of stone crystal. Other stages of creation followed, such as water, earth, plant life, animal life, and humanity. Gayomart was the primeval man, followed by a sequence of archetypal kings and saviors. But the material world and humanity became "mixed," or contaminated with destructive aggression, because the Destroyer attracted his archdemons, each corresponding to one of the beneficent spirits. In this third period, the Destroyer dominated the material world, but was unable to escape from it, having been trapped by the Creator. Thereby the Destroyer began to generate his own demise.

4) Then a special Savior was selected, Zoroaster, to initiate a process of divine / human cooperation by which the Destroyer would be gradually overcome. In the first thousand years of this period, Zoroaster's teachings begin to uplift humanity. In this current 3000-year period, three figures, known as "Sons of Zoroaster," guide humanity in its battle with the Destroyer. The first two Sons of Zoroaster do battle and guide humanity for a thousand years each. Finally, the Saoshyant, the Future Savior, will bring the final triumph of good over evil, the end of the age, a restoration of the world, and the establishment of the kingdom of heaven on earth.

This is a brief account of Zoroastrian cosmogony and cosmology, and now we must briefly outline the corresponding mythic genealogy, accounting for the emergence and sequence of sage-kings and prophets ensuring humanity's fulfillment. The sequence of mythic and spiritual events helps explain why the ancient Persians felt it necessary for a Prophet like Zoroaster to arrive when He did. When the fravashis (eternal souls) were created, Zoroaster was there in the divine court, ready to serve God at His command. The time was not yet ripe for Him to descend to earth. But in the third period of time, the Destroyer began to dominate humanity and the earth. The need for a Savior was voiced and prophesied by Yima, the archetypal king, and later by an ox who proclaimed that a revelation of truth would soon shatter the reign of tyranny.

The approximate order of savior figures in Zoroastrian tradition seems to be: Mashya and Mashyoi, brother and sister of humanity, who were born pure in thought, word, and deed, but soon forgot the Creator's gifts to them and were corrupted; Haoshangha, the first lawgiver; Yima, the ideal king, who (like Noah) saved life on earth from complete destruction; Spitama of the fifth generation; Haechataspa of the tenth generation; King Manuschir from the thirtieth generation; Zoroaster, Who came around the forty-fifth generation, Whose family name was Spitama; the first Son of Zoroaster (one millennium later); the second Son of Zoroaster (another millennium later); the third Son of Zoroaster, the Saoshyant (three millennia after Zoroaster). This mytho-historical background parallels that of Moses in the biblical account, suggesting that Zoroaster's birth was expected as an integral part of God's plan.

2 – Arising to Guide Humanity in the Worst of Times: Ancient Persia's Violence and Corruption

In the early Zoroastrian literature, several different terms were applied to the priests who conducted rituals, sacrifices, and ceremonies. These titles included magi, athravans, zaotars, and karapans. It seems unclear whether these terms applied to various priestly roles, to classes, or to ethnic groups. In any case, the term "magi" has been the most historically enduring name for the Persian priests who preceded and opposed Zoroaster. But later, the magi also accepted, promoted, modified, corrupted, and renewed Zoroastrian teachings down through the centuries, beginning about 1000 BCE—our provisional date for the advent of Zoroaster.

Zoroaster's people were suffering from frequent violent raids of warrior nomads. Hordes of raiders swept over struggling villages that were plowing their fields and grazing their cattle, "leaving smouldering homesteads in their trail and bodies of helpless peasants."[2] It was an age of lawless plunder and killing; and because the kings, princes, and priests could not protect villagers from their deplorable condition, there were renewed cries for a Savior. In the actions of the "blood thirsty wicked," Zoroaster would eventually see the operation of evil forces, both within and beyond humanity. He would later use the term *daevas* to refer to the evil forces that motivated the hostile and cruel invaders. He would also identify daeva-worship with false religious teachings, especially the corrupt manipulations, hardened dogmas, and superstitious rituals of priests. Zoroaster eventually opposed all unjust force, animal sacrifices, ancestor worship, polytheistic beliefs, and any use of intoxicating drinks in religious rites. He found the clergy's misuse of their knowledge and power abhorrent, and sought to transform their understanding and influence into service of the one God, Ahura Mazda, Lord of Wisdom.

3 – Advent Prophesied and Expected: Cry for a Savior Intensifies, Voiced by the Soul of Creation

The need for, and the rising of, periodic sage-kings and prophets were well-established patterns in the ancient Persian worldview. Life was understood as a struggle between good and evil forces, both within the soul and out in the larger world of tribes and cities. But in this fourth 3000-year period, the incredible depths of atrocities would occasion greater heights of spiritual progress. God would send a series of decisive Revealers of righteousness Who would help humanity advance and eventually vanquish evil.

Zoroaster's setting was so full of religious abuse, senseless violence, and plundering of croplands that cries for help transcended the merely human realm. The soul of the earthly creation, a spiritual being perhaps like Gaia in the Greek pantheon, cried out to God for a righteous deliverer.[3] When the Soul of Creation saw that Zoroaster was the heavenly choice for the next Savior, she was at first very disappointed with her Maker's decision. She viewed Zoroaster as unfit for an undertaking of this magnitude. To rescue the earth from injustice would require, she lamented, one of considerably greater nobility, fame, and power. But God informed her that spiritual power, not worldly status, was needed for the task. She admitted that God knew best, and requested Him to grant the prophet-designate the mental and spiritual power to fulfill his mission. Thereupon God granted Him the charm of speech as well. The prophet was a charismatic person with intelligence, the power of persuasion, and eloquence. Thus Zoroaster became an incarnation of perfection in this world.

4 – Auspicious Signs, Birth, and Intimations of Greatness: Divine Mother, Humble Father, and Early Threats Miraculously Overcome

Proposed dates for the birth of Zoroaster vary from the sixth to the seventeenth century BCE, but the weight of contemporary scholarship seems to point to about 1000 BCE. The place of His birth has been less controversial, most researchers agreeing on eastern Afghanistan. Tradition held that Zoroaster's father, Porushaspa, lived in a village near Lake Chaychast as a poor but pious man. He had prayed to Haoma for a worthy son who would bear the family name of Spitama. His mother, Dughdao, was from the religious city of Ragha, the daughter of a pious and noble family who faithfully obeyed the magi. When Dughdao was born, a glorious light shined from her that both amazed and frightened those who witnessed it. Later, when bitter winters, pestilence, and invasions plagued her people, some of them blamed their troubles on the girl's sorceries. Under great community pressure, her father sent young Dughdao away to the home of Porushaspa, and they soon married.

One day Porushaspa asked his young (and still virgin) wife to milk two virgin cows that had miraculously begun to give milk. Tradition held that Zoroaster's personality had been placed in that milk by heavenly decree, and that Porushaspa mixed this milk with the juice of a sacred plant containing the fravashi (eternal soul) of Zoroaster. Husband and wife then drank the holy mixture. In this way Zoroaster's personality and eternal soul combined with the glorious light that had shone from Dughdao since her birth, and Zoroaster was conceived in her womb.

But demons were eager to slay this child of promise, even before He was born. They afflicted Dughdao with an illness so dreadful, that in desperation she turned to the famous wizard Storko for help. But a heavenly voice forbade her to accept the wizard's help, and instead gave her medical advice that brought a quick cure. "For three days and nights before the expected birth, the whole village was so lit by the mysterious light in Dughdao that the villagers ran away, saying that the birth of this Child betokened some strange misfortune for Porushaspa and his village. . . . And so, in a holy hour, the Child was born; Vohumanah himself [the archangel of Good Thought] at once entered the infant mind. . . . The Babe laughed aloud instead of wailing as do all the children of men. . . . All Nature, even trees and waters, rejoiced, and demons fled away as a bright light shone out upon the world."[4]

Even at a very young age, Zoroaster showed great piety and was able to expound on lofty religious themes. So His father thought that the chief of the local wizards, Durasrobo, should come to see his wondrous child. However, the chief wizard was a friend of demons, and immediately tried to crush Zoroaster's tender head. But a throbbing headache suddenly prevented him. Durasrobo persisted in his warnings to Porushaspa about the bewitching powers of his dangerous son, and eventually persuaded him that, for the good of the village and region, Zoroaster must die.

They placed Him on some firewood and set the pile ablaze, but it would not burn. Dughdao found her son sitting unafraid on the firewood and took Him home. But Durasrobo and Porushaspa made three more attempts on His life before Porushaspa recognized that his son was receiving divine protection, and must be allowed to grow up and fulfill His mission. Durasrobo and Porushaspa encouraged oxen to trample Zoroaster to death, but one stood over and protected Him. The same pattern was repeated with horses. Finally, they killed the young of a mother wolf to make her fierce, then placed Zoroaster in her den, but the wolf paid no heed. Finally, after this third failure, Porushaspa gave up his attempts to kill his son.

The young Zoroaster was later sent to the class of a famous teacher, Aganakes. One day, He was playing with his classmates when Durasrobo and another evil wizard appeared and tried to cast a spell on Him, but the spell had no effect on Him. Later, the wizards offered to consecrate the milk at Porushaspa's home, but the young Zoroaster said firmly, *"In this house I alone consecrate the milk!"* [5] And He poured it out on the ground. Durasrobo was enraged, cursed Zoroaster and left the house, but on his ride home fell from his horse and died.

In His early youth, Zoroaster clearly enunciated the principle of moral and spiritual dualism that He would greatly develop later. *"When I looked upwards I saw that our souls that go up to the sky will go up to the best existence. When I looked downwards I saw the demon and the fiend, the wizard and the witch, become buried below in the earth and fall paralyzed back to hell."* [6] At the age of fifteen, Zoroaster and His four brothers were discussing how the family property might be divided, when He announced that His choice was the *kusti,* the sacred girdle. He then put it on with vows and prayers, saying He would pursue a religious career.

Zoroaster was soon thereafter trained as a priest who specialized in the writing of learned religious poetry. He praised those who sought truth, and believed they attained eternal happiness. He once asked wise men for good advice, and they told Him to feed the poor, feed cattle, feed the fire, pour haoma juice in water, and worship daevas, which were understood as deities by the people, but as demons by Zoroaster. He became known as a kind and compassionate young man who helped the elderly, fed the poor, and made sure animals were well treated.

His parents arranged for His marriage, but His understanding of truth required that He know what kind of wife they had in mind. He asked to see the face of His proposed bride before marrying her, but they refused. Zoroaster then declared that He would not marry her. At age twenty, He left home without His parents' permission, asking people *"Who most seeks righteousness and feeds the poor?"* [7] This inquiry led Him to help a young Turanian who gave away daily a huge cauldron of bread, milk, and other necessities to the poor.

Throughout His twenties, Zoroaster sought to go beyond the spiritual wisdom of the sages of His day. Through prayer, meditation, and contemplation of the higher realms, He aimed to realize the most profound truths that could be found. This implicit and explicit criticism of the religion of His day left Him cast out by kinsfolk, rejected by priestly colleagues, and often refused hospitality while traveling. Much of the time He lived in solitary communion with God, living in a cave that He had painted to represent the earth and the planets, lit up by a glorious fire, all the while surviving on the bounty of the good earth, the occasional generosity of herdsmen and villagers, as well as divine grace.

5 – Divine Commission:
Led by an Archangel to God's Heavenly Court

At the age of thirty, Zoroaster left His cave, crossed the Caspian Sea, and reached Iran in time for a spring festival. It was an occasion of great rejoicing, to which many people flocked from all directions and great distances. While still in a solitary place, He saw a vision in which "a mighty crowd of people came to him out of the demon-haunted North, and at their head his cousin Maidhyomaonha led the way. Then he understood that he should teach multitudes, and that his cousin would first accept him as the spiritual guide for life." [8] It would indeed come to pass that Zoroaster's first convert, when He had reached the age of forty, was His cousin Maidhyoimah, and that He would teach multitudes, but not without great resistance beforehand.

On the day of a great festival, He went out to wade in a sacred river. On the far side, He saw a glorious vision of the archangel Vohu Manah (Good Thought) dressed in a robe of light, carrying a radiant staff. *"Who are you? What do you seek in life?"* asked the archangel. *"I want only to know and do God's will,"* answered Zoroaster. [9] The archangel also queried about the deepest desire of Zoroaster's heart, and was assured that the would-be Prophet sought only righteousness.

Vohu Manah told Zoroaster to lay aside the vesture of His material body, and then led Him to mount to the presence of Ahura Mazda, the Wise Lord. "Then Zarathustra [Zoroaster] saw God Himself, surrounded by the Heavenly Court of Angels and Archangels. So great was the glory of this vision that Zarathustra noted his shadow was dimmed out by its supernal light. He prostrated in humble adoration, and then sat respectfully to one side, while God taught him the essence of the Faith, and through visions outlined its future history. Having then gladly passed through the ordeal of fire, he accepted the task of being God's Prophet to Iran, to destroy evil, to comfort the good and warn the wicked, to teach the way of Righteousness."[10]

6 – Struggling in Solitude: Doubts and Temptations, Heavenly Assistance and Revelatory Visions

After His divine call, Zoroaster immediately began to preach with zeal the law of righteousness that was commanded by the one God, Ahura Mazda, and warned against daeva worship. But He had no visible success. Very discouraged, He was visited by severe temptation from the evil spirit, who bade Him to renounce this new religion of Mazda worship. "But Zarathustra answered him: *'No! I shall never renounce the good religion . . . not though life, limb, and soul should part asunder.'"*[11]

At one point, the Prophet asked God where He should go that might be more fruitful. He was advised to make a humbler beginning closer to home. He had left home long before without receiving parental permission. Perhaps His failure was due to the lack of their holy blessing, so He resolved to mend this breach. We do not know if He went back to the village where He was born, and found His aged parents waiting for their long lost son. But we do know that He was rewarded in His own homeland. God favored Him with six more revelations, which taught Him the religion in all its fullness.[12]

Over the twelve years of wandering and preaching that followed His divine call, six archangels appeared to Zoroaster in visions and expanded His revelatory message. These included: Vohu Manah (Good Thought), Asha (Righteousness), Khsathra (Virtuous Power or Majestic Dominion), Armaiti (Loving Devotion), Haurvatat (Individual Wholeness), and Ameretat (Collective Salvation and Immortality). We will explore these figures and teachings in upcoming sections, but here we simply note that they were understood as personifications of divine attributes, as well as human spiritual capacities that could be chosen for development, rather than succumbing to the opposite demonic capacities, such as bad thought, deception, oppression, false religion, brokenness, and decay.

During this long period of testing and revelatory learning, Zoroaster had other visions. They were revelations about heaven and hell, the judgment bridge, the nature of the soul and conscience, the foundations of the cosmos, humanity's earliest days, heroes and demons of the past, as well as future saviors and the ultimate triumph of good over evil. Despite all His faithful teaching of this guidance over twelve years, Zoroaster had won no converts besides Maidhyoimah, His cousin.

7 – Declaration and First Followers: Vishtaspa and His Royal Court

More than a decade elapsed from Zoroaster's first public declaration of His message from God to the royal conversion that brought Him fully onto the stage of world history. In His early forties, Zoroaster complained bitterly to God of His failure to accomplish the divine mission He had been assigned. Where, He wondered, was the body of followers who could implement His teachings? God consoled Him with the promise that soon, many would gather around Him.

Zoroaster was sent by the Holy Spirit to the court of an Aryan king named Vishtaspa in Balkh (eastern Iran). Vishtaspa seems to have been an honest, simple, and sincere monarch who was dominated by the priests surrounding him. These priests, called *karapans*, were very preoccupied with magical procedures to keep the crops growing, the marauding nomads at a distance, and other demonic forces at bay. The karapans had so much influence on Vishtaspa that even though the king was at first very impressed with Zoroaster's teachings and spiritual powers as demonstrated before the entire court, they managed to have Him cast into prison, for they saw Him as a threat to their status.

A great turning point in religious history came when Vishtaspa's favorite black horse fell very ill, and Zoroaster promised to cure the horse if the king and his court would judge Him fairly. With the support of the queen, Hutaosa, and an archangelic vision that the whole court witnessed, their conversion to the Faith of Zoroaster was complete. Among the most important early followers beside the king and queen were Jamaspa, the king's minister; Zarir, the king's brother; Spentodata, the king's son who later became a great hero of the Faith; and Frashaoshtra, Jamaspa's brother and another leading minister of the king.

8 – Overcoming Powerful Opposition:
Wizards, Magi, and Turanians

We have seen that early in His life, Zoroaster was opposed by wizards who felt threatened by His righteousness and striving after the good. We have seen that in His twenties, during His arduous quest for truth, both kinsfolk and strangers refused Him hospitality. We have seen that in His thirties, after His divine call, the magi and other priestly classes rejected His message, because it included a critique of their polytheistic beliefs, magical practices, and their capitalizing on the people's superstitions. After He converted Vishtaspa's court, he became a Royal Prophet, and was opposed in two holy wars by Turanian rulers and armies.

Some observers have surmised that these wars may not have been completely unprovoked. It is quite probable that while Zoroaster was singing psalms and hymns to God in His temples, His supporters went far beyond His wishes in their interpretation of His warning not to help the wicked. Their use of force may have sparked violence in reply.[13] It was also reported that some of the royal preachers who failed to persuade by the tongue, may have resorted to the sword.

The first holy war took place when Zoroaster was fifty-nine years old. One of the strongest Turanian chieftains, Arejataspa, refused to pay the tribute asked by Vishtaspa, and also rejected the Faith. In fact, Arejataspa went so far as to demand that Vishtaspa renounce the Faith within two months or face invasion from the north. When Vishtaspa sent back a sharply negative reply, both sides prepared for war. All of the major Turanian tribes became united in their desire to overthrow the Faith. The first battle took place on the Oxus River near the boundary of the two kingdoms, and at first the fighting went against the Persian / Zoroastrian cause. But a few weeks later, Spentodata rose to heroic heights in battle. The Turanians were defeated, Arejataspa was driven away, his capital was captured, and a Zoroastrian fire temple was erected there. Zoroaster's Faith and Cause had survived its first threat.

9 – Rejection by the People

Like other founding Prophets, Zoroaster suffered rejection and banishment. He had been rejected by His family and tribe, by the common people, as well as by the religious and civil leaders. He cried out: *"To what land shall I flee? Where bend my steps? I am thrust out from family and tribe; I have no favor from the village to which I would belong, nor from the wicked rulers of the country: How then, O Lord, shall I obtain thy favor?"*[14] Zoroaster also wondered when the new friends of God would appear and spread the new Faith. When would the rotting mass of lies dissolve by which priests dupe their devotees, and the wicked rulers persuade the masses, to carry out their ill intent?[15]

For the first two years after His divine call, Zoroaster preached to the most powerful, rich, and learned in the land, but they consistently closed their ears and hearts to the basic truths He offered: that there was only one God, that we have to make the choice between right or wrong, and that we must accept the resulting future of joy or anguish after death that our decisions would entail. Kings, rich men, scholars, and priests all preferred their own wealth and power to any promise of reward for virtue that might come to them in an intangible hereafter.

Zoroaster was rejected because He challenged the popular daeva worship, and because He wielded no army, nor even a retinue of followers and servants. Perhaps His greatest temptation was to compromise with the prevailing evils, and to buy some power at the cost of divine loyalty and integrity. Rebuffed at every turn, the Prophet turned to God for comfort in His failure; and God assured Him that heaven awaited the faithful, while hell awaited the arrogant. Zoroaster was to be an instrument of the providential plan, and His efforts would bear great fruit.

10 – Sacrificial Suffering

Though rejection by His homeland was perhaps the deepest source of His own suffering, Zoroaster was not unprepared for the consequences of His divine calling. He had foreseen His own suffering and testing at the very beginning of His ministry, along with the salvation it would bring to a portion of humanity. He even asked to be tested so that the power of the new Faith could be shown, the brave separated from the cowardly, and the faithful distinguished from the faithless. He said, *"As the holy one I recognized thee, O Wise Lord, When he came to me as Good Mind, When first I was instructed in your word. Suffering among men will be caused to me by my zeal to carry out that which you tell me is the greatest good."* [16]

11 – Symbolic Language as a Test for Believers

Among the many issues that have divided the religious world throughout recorded human history is the interpretation of scriptural language. How are the key terms and images of revelation to be understood? The spiritually awake and alert have been able to hear and see deeper and more universal meanings in the words of their Prophet, while those invested in the religious status quo or in material comforts of the day have tended to make more rigid and literalistic interpretations.

A key term in the Zoroastrian revelation is "fire." Should the ceremonial blaze in the temple be worshiped for itself, or for the larger realities to which it points? Is devotional fire the private possession of one tradition only, or does it reflect the power and light of God, Who offers guidance and nurturance to all people in all times and places? Zoroaster as a Prophet of God emphasized moral and spiritual significances, rather than narrow or exclusive practices. The fire referred to in the following verse offers a choice to befriend God through authentic worship, as well as a choice to oppose God through idolatry. *"Thy fire, O Lord, mighty through Righteousness, swift and powerful—we would that it may be a resplendent support for him who exalts it; but for the enemy, O Wise One, according to the powers of thy hand, the clear showing of his trespasses!"* [17]

This scriptural passage offers the distinction between the act of exalting fire properly, as done by the Prophet Himself and His followers who receive resplendent support, and the act of trespassing fire, as done by the false priests, magicians, and nomadic invaders. Fire is presented both as a choice and a judgment. Depending on its interpretation and implementation, fire can lift its users to the highest righteousness, or degrade them into destructive practices.

Other troublesome terms in Zoroastrian history have included "king" and "pollution." Some Persian kings and high priests made themselves the highest authority, forgetting the higher kingship of Zoroaster as Prophet, and the yet higher kingship of Ahura Mazda, Creator of heaven and earth. Many Zoroastrians throughout history, taking a literalistic path, have understood rotting corpses as the worst sources of pollution, forgetting that evil deeds and breaches of righteousness are far more polluting in the larger scheme of things.

Perhaps the most seriously misunderstood term in Zoroastrian history is "Son of Zoroaster." As we will see later in the section on future Saviors, Zoroaster prophesied both spiritual declines and renewals. At the end of one decline would come the first Son of Zoroaster; at the end of the second decline would come the second Son of Zoroaster; and at the end of the third decline would come the third Son of Zoroaster, Who would bring the final restoration and the kingdom of heaven on earth. Sons of Zoroaster, then, referred to major Prophets acting as agents of God's providential plan. However, under the influence of self-regarding high priests, Sons of Zoroaster were usually interpreted as referring to traditional Zoroastrians rather than to successive Revealers having the same spiritual station as the Prophet of the Wise Lord. From this attached, clergy-centered perspective, which appears to be a narrowing and distortion of Zoroaster's actual teaching, the significance of Jesus, Muḥammad, and Bahá'u'lláh were missed by most Zoroastrians down through the ages. Provincial and sectarian outlooks inevitably blind the followers of one scriptural tradition from recognizing a new revelation from God.

The hypothesis of progressive revelation leads to a more universal perspective on humanity's religious heritage, viewing this heritage as one continuous story. If the same one and only God offers successive revelations that are adapted to humanity's historical and cultural capacities, then all of the divine Teachers must be embraced in the order that They appear. To the degree that we can remain alert to broad patterns in humanity's spiritual evolution, bringing a pure heart and an open mind to the study of religion, we can pass spiritual tests and see through the veils of hardened tradition.

12 – Exemplary Women:
Dughdao the Nurturer, Poruchista the Advocate

The most nurturing and receptive woman in the story of Zoroaster was Dughdao, Zoroaster's mother. Tradition held that from her own birth onward, a glorious light shined from her, suggesting divine favor and destiny. As a young child she was suspected of sorceries and blamed for the troubles of her people, but she bore these false accusations patiently. As a young woman, Dughdao was obedient to her older husband, and his directives led to her giving birth as a virgin to Zoroaster. She rescued Zoroaster from some of the malicious plots of the chief wizard, and she tolerated her husband's occasional buckling to pressure from the wizards. She seems to have realized the divine destiny of her son, as well as her own providential role in His preparations.

Perhaps the most active and assertive woman in the story of Zoroaster was Poruchista, Zoroaster's daughter. She was His daughter by His third wife, Huovi, who was His first female disciple. Poruchista married Jamaspa, the leading male disciple of Zoroaster, and her contributions to the spread of the Faith, as a consultant to Jamaspa and a fearless missionary in her own right, were comparable to her husband's. She was a fearless missionary for the Zoroastrian Faith, and among its most powerful and effective first-generation leaders. In the Gathas, women appear to be treated on an equal footing with men.[18]

13 – Dying and Ascending Victoriously: At the Fire Temple, Having Purified Devotion and Law

Spentodata, the hero of the first holy war, had been placed in prison during the latter part of the peaceful period which followed, because his jealous brother, Kavarazem, had filled their father, King Vishtaspa, with doubts about the hero's motives and suitability to be next king. Zoroaster had reached the age of seventy-seven. Vishtaspa was temporarily away from his capital at Balkh, and Spentodata was still in prison when Arejataspa, the vengeful Turanian leader, returned to attack with his newly-gathered armies.

In this second holy war, as in the first, the enemies of the Good Religion were at first successful. They had fought their way into Balkh itself, and even broke into the fire temple. The Prophet was at worship with many of His priests. The famous tenth-century CE Iranian poet, Firdawsi, author of the esteemed *Shanameh* (Book of Kings), described the scene movingly. "The army thereupon entered Balkh, and the world became darkened with rapine and murder. They advanced towards the Temple of Fire, and to the Palace and glorious Hall of Gold. They burned the Zendavesta entire, and they set fire to the edifice and the Palace alike. There were eighty priests, whose tongues ceased not to repeat the Name of God; all these they slew in the very presence of the Fire and put an end to their life of devotion. By the blood of these was extinguished the Fire of Zarathushtra. . . . They have crushed the head of the Master and of all the priests."[19] Other traditions claimed that Turbaratur killed the Prophet by sword, and that as the Holy One fell,

He threw His rosary at His slayer, emitting a fire which killed the Turanian invader.

News of the great tragedy reached King Vishtaspa, who immediately arose to the military defense of his kingdom. In one battle, he lost one of his sons. He then released his hero son, Spentodata, from prison, and after much imploring persuaded him to fight to save Persia and the Good Religion. In the final battle of the second holy war, Vishtaspa and Spentodata defeated Arejataspa. There were reports of a mountain landslide that helped to assure them of victory. This seemingly miraculous event was interpreted as divine favor.

The king sent out written religious appeals to the rulers of the world known to him. Many heeded his word about Zoroaster's teaching and the Good Religion. According to some traditions, in less than a generation, the Faith was being taught in all of the seven regions of the known world at that time. The heavy mantle of Zoroaster fell on the learned and capable minister, who later became a priest, Jamaspa. It was said that Jamaspa wrote 1200 chapters of dictation from the spoken words of Zoroaster. The kingdom of Seistan became an especially strong center of the Faith, with the high priest Saena leading a hundred student priests. Spentodata tried to convert a neighboring king, Rustem, but lost his life in battle. Zoroaster's daughters—Poruchista, Freni, and Thriti—all became prominent teachers of the Faith.

Those who carefully assess the place of Zoroaster in religious history soon realize that His was a super-human achievement. Alone, with only gentle divine assurances and spiritual visions, He persisted and ultimately prevailed against unconquerable obstacles. He established monotheism and purified the devotional tradition in a land that had been intransigently polytheistic and magical in belief and practice. He established a lofty ethical code in a region of plunder and random violence. He elevated the love of learning and refinement where there had been only superstition and degradation. He offered profound philosophical and theological understandings that would instruct some of the greatest minds ever, including Plato and Aristotle, and would influence several great world religions. And He taught the spiritual principles and moral ideals that could unite hostile tribes and regions into one of the highest civilizations in the history of humanity.

- 8 -
Zoroaster: Teaching and Legacy

14 – Transformative Teaching and Healing:
The Royal Prophet and His Promotion of the Faith

We described the twelve years following Zoroaster's divine call as His period of struggling in solitude, rather than His mission. These years of unheeded preaching, humble perseverance, and new revelations prepared the way for His mission, which began after Vishtaspa's court converted to the new Faith. The court's acceptance helps explain the later rise of the Persian Empire and the glorious reigns of Cyrus and Darius. Zoroaster's mission extended for thirty-five years, from the commissioning of His first followers at age forty-two, to the time of His death at age seventy-seven. Zoroaster's thirty-five-year mission was divided into two seventeen-year periods with a holy war between them and another following them. We described the first war in the section on opposition; the second was integral to Zoroaster's death and ascension.

The Royal Prophet

After Vishtaspa and his court embraced the Prophet's teachings, Zoroaster enjoyed a position of great honor and influence. He was free to spread the Good Religion throughout the kingdom, taking up this mission with zeal. As high priest in Balkh He established many fire temples. "Vishtaspa transferred the ancient Fire said to have been lit by King Yima . . . in the far south-west of the Empire, and the 'Glory-given Fire' to Kabul in the East. But in those early days there was probably very little ritual in these temples, and as Herodotus knew the religion of the people it was mostly carried out in the open air on hill-tops and beside the rivers."[1]

Family life now became possible for Zoroaster, and tradition mentions three wives. By His first wife He had three daughters—Poruchista, Freni, and Thriti—and all three made great contributions to the Faith. He also had a son, Isadvastra, who became the father of Ururvija, the zealous missionary. His second wife gave Him two more sons. This family development enabled the Faith to spread across regions and generations.

At the age of forty-nine, the Prophet healed a blind man during a missionary journey to the Median Empire. "He put the juice of a certain herb into the man's eyes, and the cure was very rapid. Certainly Zarathushtra realised the value of his knowledge of 'magic' and science, and a large part of the later Nasks [traditional writings] were devoted to such socially useful knowledge."[2] This story offers a glimpse of how religious and scientific knowledge were once integrated. Reality is an interconnected whole, but at various times in history, revelation and reason have become artificially separated.

Promotion of the Faith

After the first holy war Zoroaster consolidated His position in the kingdom with another royal marriage, to Huovi, His third wife, the daughter of a noted court minister, Frashaoshtra. To the other noted minister, Jamaspa, Zoroaster gave His daughter, Poruchista. Huovi's brothers became loyal friends of the Prophet, further expanding the Faith and deepening the peace in the region. Under the Prophet's direction, fire temples were built all over the kingdom, with the fires themselves serving as points of adoration for daily prayer. Temples were built as far east as the western edge of India. Jamaspa's former teacher, a brahmin sage from India, once questioned the Prophet rigorously. Finding the answers comprehensive and illuminating, he retuned to India and spread the Faith there.

One tradition of the Good Religion held that Spentodata, the heroic son of King Vishtaspa, was sent out on missionary journeys to Anatolia and India with copies of the Avesta. Spentodata's impressive military and religious achievements made him the intended inheritor of the kingdom, but on the jealous advice of Vishtaspa's other son, Kavarazem, Spentodata was imprisoned. King Vishtaspa himself was also directly involved in early missionary work of the Faith. He converted another monarch, Parshad the Bull, who had resisted Zoroaster forty years earlier. Seistan became a stronghold of the Faith. Another tradition held that Zoroaster "dictated the whole of the twenty-one books of the Avesta scriptures, and Jamaspa wrote them down on twelve thousand ox-hides in letters of gold. . . . King Vishtaspa took the two original manuscripts of these holy books, and placed one in the Royal Library at Istakhr, or Persepolis, where it remained until burned by Alexander . . . in BC 330, and the other in the treasury of Shapigan at Samarqand."³

According to Bahá'í writings, Zoroaster *"held converse with some of the Prophets of Israel."*⁴ This suggests that Zoroaster's missionary journey paralleled Abraham's and included the Western Holy Land. It also helps explain how the Zoroastrian Faith would one day stretch from India to Turkey. Some scholars who believe that Zoroaster lived from 660 to 583 BCE speculate that He brought the Faith to Babylon, converting the city from sorcery. But the spiritual conquest of the Babylonian Empire was probably due to faithful Zoroastrians in Cyrus' day, nearly a half millennium after Zoroaster's earthly mission.

15 – Delivering a Thematic and Complementary Message: Good Thoughts, Good Words, and Good Deeds

Zoroaster's teachings were integrated and comprehensive. The theme weaving His concepts together was "good thoughts, good words, good deeds." These principles were seen as the most basic expectation of God for humanity's individual and social advance. Their order was significant. A human being's moral growth, or conquest of evil, was seen as beginning with a good thought that eventually manifested itself as a good word, and finally emerged as a good deed. In this way, bad thoughts, words, and deeds could be systematically overcome. We now touch briefly on the major beliefs of Zoroastrian tradition. We say tradition rather than teachings of Zoroaster Himself, because it is unclear how far the Good Religion may have veered away from His original teachings. In any case, this body of guidance is a theological and ethical system that served as the foundation and basis of an advanced civilization that also enriched Judaism, Christianity, and Islam.

God: Ahura Mazda

Ahura Mazda, the Lord of Wisdom, is understood as the one and only Creator of all things, Who from the beginning has always offered genuine choice. He is therefore not responsible for the evil choices and agencies of humanity. God's creation is a continuing emanation from Himself as an infinite source. He is the essence of being and wisdom. His energy is the Holy Spirit, and He has six cardinal epithets or primary attributes, known as the Beneficent Spirits that are described below. God sends Prophets to humanity periodically to restore righteousness.

Choice, Free Will, and Responsibility

All beings have degrees of choice, and human beings have a completely free will in moral and spiritual matters. So we are responsible for our thoughts, words, and deeds individually. We are also responsible for justice in society collectively.

Good vs Evil: The Struggle against Angra Mainyu and Temptation

Angra Mainyu—known as the Evil Spirit, the Adversary, and the Destroyer—rebelled against God and contaminated creation, the world, and the human condition. Human beings are called to struggle with God against evil, both in the world and within their souls, strengthening the Good Religion. Zoroaster taught of the Spirits Twain, Good and Evil, who came together at creation's dawn. The Holy Spirit is depicted as in dialogue with the Evil Spirit, saying in effect: Between us, neither thoughts, nor wills, nor words, nor teachings, nor beliefs, nor deeds are in accord; for our inner selves and souls are far apart indeed.[5]

Creation: Cosmos and World

The spiritual realm preceded the material realm. The cosmos and the world are understood as intrinsically good, despite having been mixed with destructive tendencies. Therefore, the cosmos has become a field of contest between creative and integrative forces on one hand, and disruptive and decaying forces on the other.

Caring for the Earth and Its Creatures

The earth, its elements, and its life forms are intrinsically good, and must be cared for responsibly. Animal husbandry and agriculture are especially important in the Zoroastrian system, and these require humanity to avoid polluting the soil, air, and water. These practices lead to prosperity and the conquest of evil.

Devotion, Prayer, and the Symbol of Fire

Regular adoration and gratitude to God, as shown through prayers, chants, and ceremonies at fire temples, are expected of believers. Ritual fire is seen as a symbol of divine presence, power, wisdom, and purity. The prayers are usually in the ancient Avestan language that was used by Zoroaster. Zoroastrians are expected to pray three times daily facing the nearest fire temple.

Human Nature: Soul and Conscience

Human nature consists of parts or agencies that are engaged in the constant challenge of generating good thoughts, good words, and good deeds. Our inner agencies include the body, the vital spirit, the personality, the reason, the conscience, the soul, the destiny, and the fravasi or eternal soul. The fravasi is that part of us that preexisted our birth, consented to join creation, and, collectively as humanity, was the chief creation of God.

Prophets and Saviors

Because of the strength of the evil forces in creation, God sends humanity certain prophetic figures and saviors at regular intervals. Zoroaster was an especially decisive Prophet in the process of salvation and humanity's collective struggle with evil. The Saoshyant, or Future Savior, will be another especially significant Figure, because He will usher in the final triumph or restoration.

The Holy Spirit and the Beneficent Spirits

The Holy (or Creative) Spirit is God's way of developing creation. It enables growth and progress, in both a qualitative and quantitative sense. "It is the self-realizing quality or activity of *Ahura Mazda*; it is the self-generating energy that leads to the creation and evolution of the universe."[6] The Holy Spirit is a cardinal attribute of God, working closely with six beneficent spirits. These spirits are seen as moral and spiritual forces sometimes personified as archangels, but are also viewed as moral and spiritual capacities operating in the soul. The Holy Spirit was called Spenta Mainyu, and the beneficent spirits were called Amesha Spentas. These made up the seven primary powers, and have been called the divine heptad. "Although they are seven, they are one thought, one word and one deed; they are father and children; they are source and rays of light; and they present plurality in oneness."[7] The beneficent spirits were defined as: 1) Good Thought: Vohu Manah, representing wisdom, sublime mind, high purpose, purity, and contentment; 2) Righteousness: Asha, representing justice, divine and natural law, moral order, and fair judgment; 3) Virtuous Power: Khsathra, representing helping the poor, divine majesty, dominion, and the kingdom of God on earth; 4) Devoted Love: Armaiti, representing faithful obedience, worship, devotion, selfless service, piety, and harmony; 5) Perfection: Haurvatat, representing wholeness, fulfillment, health, prosperity, excellence, integrity, and individual salvation; 6) Eternal Salvation: Ameretat, representing immortality, progressive growth, and collective salvation. Opposing these beneficent spirits are six evil spirits, believed to assist Angra Mainyu in working destruction within the human heart and in the world. These are: Bad Thought (or wrath), The Lie (or deceptive temptation), Vicious Power (or oppression), Bad Faith (or blasphemy), Imperfection (or brokenness), and Eternal Condemnation (or decay). But their eventual defeat in the final restoration is assured by the Wise Lord.

The Afterlife: Heaven and Hell

Consequences of choices in this life will be faced in the next life, because our souls are immortal, and because divine righteousness always prevails. This is called the principle of yield, meaning our choices yield consequences for good and evil. We are judged in the afterlife for thoughts, words, and deeds enacted in this life. By this means, we receive proper reward and punishment. Heaven is called the "best existence" and hell is called the "worst existence." But all souls will be restored to original purity with God at the final restoration.

The Final Restoration: Frasokereti

Good ultimately triumphs over evil. "The promised final victory of goodness pours hope and happiness into the hearts of all who work for the happiness of others."[8] At the end of the fourth cosmic period (3000 years after Zoroaster) God, the Holy Spirit, the beneficent spirits, and righteous human beings will, with the guidance of the Future Savior, overcome evil. All will receive final judgment and restoration, thereby establishing the kingdom of heaven on earth.

16 – Renewing and Embodying Universal Virtues

Zoroaster renewed the loftiest teachings that had been offered to the world. He placed special emphasis on ethical responsibility and discernment between what is higher and lower, better and worse, constructive and destructive. Zoroaster's thoughts, words, and deeds point out to humanity the path of righteousness. We now provide a sample of Zoroastrian virtue teachings, using our three major themes, fifteen virtues in all, and offering an example of each virtue. Not all quotes are directly from Zoroaster, just as not all biblical books were taught directly by Moses and Jesus, but they all convey the Founders' teachings.

Spiritual Virtues in the Zoroastrian Revelation

Devotion-Faithfulness: *"We will make offering unto thee with worship, O Lord, and to the Right, that you may achieve through Good Mind the destiny of all creatures in the Dominion."* [9]

Gratitude-Reverence: *"Those who shall give hearing and reverence shall attain unto Perfection and Immortality by the deeds of good spirit of the Lord of Wisdom!"* [10]

Self-discipline-Obedience: *"Toward the wicked man and the righteous one and him in whom right and wrong meet shall the Judge act in upright manner, according to the laws of the present existence."* [11]

Detachment-Patience: *"O Wise One with Right and Good Mind, Give me this sign: the entire remaking of this existence, that a greater joy may be mine in your worship and praise."* [12]

Wisdom-Discernment: *"Take counsel with thy reason, and wisely carry out the holiest deeds of Devotion!"* [13]

Social Virtues in the Zoroastrian Revelation

Loving-kindness-Compassion: *"May love triumph over contempt."* [14]

Service-Responsibility: *"Do not put off for tomorrow any good work you can do today."* [15]

Respect-Tolerance: *"Listen to all that you hear and do not repeat it at random. . . . Do not mock at anyone."* [16]

Justice-Righteousness: *"Do not do unto others what would not be good for yourself."* [17]

Peace-Unity: *"May peace triumph over discord."* [18]

Material Virtues in the Zoroastrian Revelation

Trustworthiness-Honesty: *"Do not break a promise, not that which you contracted with a non-Zoroastrian nor that with a co-religionist. Both are valid."* [19]

Moderation-Balance: *"The Religion of omniscience (is) like a mighty tree with one trunk, two great boughs. . . . And the one trunk is the Mean, the two great boughs are action and abstention."* [20]

Generosity-Hospitality: *"Holy is the man of devotion; through thoughts and words and deed, and through his conscience he increases Righteousness."* [21]

Creativity-Beauty: *"Be zealous in pursuit of culture (frahang), for culture is an adornment in prosperity, a protection in distress, a ready helper in calamity, and becomes a habit in adversity."* [22]

Earthcare-Stewardship: *"Till the earth and do good, for all men live and are nourished by the tilling of Spandamart, the Earth."*[23]

17 – Abrogating the Old and Establishing the New: Ritual and Legal Guidance

All Founders claimed authority to abrogate previous ritual and legal guidance, and to establish new religious practices and social norms for Their day. In responding to the corruption and rampant violence of His times, Zoroaster made clear advances over polytheistic cults and the "might makes right" practices of Iran's tribes 3000 years ago. Like Moses, Zoroaster reinterpreted the traditional practices and beliefs of His age, while developing them in a highly ethical direction. A fire deity associated with coveted earthly possessions was replaced by symbolic fire in local temples. Popular gods or daevas associated with raiding and military conquest were reinterpreted as devils, who were transcended by one Creator assisted by spirits of righteousness, justice, truth, and devotion. Plundering and pillaging were replaced by defense of the weak, by an ethic of good purposes and deeds, as well as by a reinvigorated agricultural ethic.

Ox sacrifice was forbidden and replaced by animal husbandry and a generation of community prosperity. *"The ordinance of sprinkling the water of the cattle, for the welfare of the ox, and the milk for the welfare of men desiring food, this has the Wise Lord, the Holy One, fashioned by his decree, in accord with Righteousness."*[24] In one elegant procedural change, where Zoroaster abolished ritual slaughter and established animal rights, wasteful practices were replaced by domestic harmony between humans and animals.

Zoroaster dramatically altered the role of the magi or priests in His day. Before His revelation, the ancient Persian priests generally engaged in appeasing the gods through chants and animal sacrifices. They often capitalized on the fears of the people—whether those fears were related to agricultural productivity, home and village security, or physical and spiritual health—by demanding special payment for rituals conducted on their behalf. Soon after the Zoroastrian revelation, priests were devoted to preserving the spiritual purity of leaders and ordinary families, inspiring them to righteous conduct, and encouraging the growth of prosperous cities.

In addition to leading prayers at fire temples, magi conducted initiations, weddings, and funerals, and also provided education on legal, theological, historical, medical, and scientific matters. At their best, they were very high-minded and socially conscientious. In cooperation with righteous kings such as Cyrus, Darius, and Anushirvan, they contributed admirably to the heights of Persian civilization. But of course, as with the clergy in other traditions, the magi regressed and reformed in their practices many times down through the ages—sometimes distorting the message of their Founder, and at other times regaining the essentials of the Good Religion.

18 – Human and Divine Qualities: Exemplifying a Dual Station

Among the greatest controversies in humanity's religious history has been the status of the Founders. Who and what were They in the larger scheme of things? Their eloquence and charisma, Their comprehension of ultimate reality and of the human condition, Their spiritual and ethical authority, and Their impact on succeeding centuries and millennia raise questions about Their status. They seem to be both human and divine, having a dual station, as it appears for Zoroaster.

Zoroaster's Human Station

In the disappointment that Zoroaster suffered in His first twelve years of teaching, in His pleading for God's assistance, as well as in His struggles after becoming a Royal Prophet, Zoroastrians find evidence that He was a natural man who attained moral and spiritual perfection through sincere questing and obedience to God. His complaints were signs of mere humanness. Zoroaster asked, *"What help shall my soul expect from anyone, in whom am I to put my trust as a protector for my cattle?"* [25] Zoroaster complained of His alienation from His family and tribe, *"I am thrust out from family and tribe; I have no favour from the village to which I would belong, nor from the wicked rulers of the country: How then, O Lord, shall I obtain thy favour?"* [26] But Zoroaster also declared a special role in the drama of existence. He referred to Himself as *"the prophet and sworn friend of Righteousness."* He went on to say, *"I will harness for you, O Wise One with Righteousness, by the spur of your praise the swiftest steeds."* [27] He also swore never to renounce the good law of God's worshippers, though His body and soul be burst asunder.

Zoroaster's Divine Station

Most Zoroastrians through the ages have seen their Prophet as an Ameshaspand—a human form of the divine power that was observable in, for example, Vohu Manah (Good Thought), Asha (Righteousness), and Khsathra

(Majestic Dominion). From this vantage, Zoroaster was far more than merely human, because He aspired to make His voice identical to God's voice, and succeeded in this cosmic mission. He claimed to bring humanity immortality and the dominion of integrity, which has been translated as eternal life and truth.[28] Zoroaster declared Himself an instrument of revelation. *"To whom will help come through the Good Mind? To me, for I am chosen for the revelation by thee, O Lord."*[29] He rose up with Vohu Manah's assistance to see God and to commune with Him frequently. The divine heptad, the Holy Spirit and the beneficent spirits, taught Him the Lord's wisdom for humanity. Zoroaster was selected for a kind of equality with the seven primary spiritual attributes, and in this sense was beyond human as a direct bearer of divine revelation. These are not merely mortal powers. He was revered as a Mediator between humanity and God. "Among orthodox Parsis [contemporary Zoroastrians in India] He is often seen as . . . a manifestation of the divine, almost as an avatara [incarnation of God]."[30]

19 – The Light and the Word

In the Zoroastrian revelation light is a frequently used metaphor for the divine guidance and creative forces opposing the darkness of the evil spirit. Zoroaster asked God rhetorically: What artificer made light and darkness? In the Zoroastrian writings, the Word brings the cosmos into being, and through Prophets, shows the way to humanity. The Word was understood as operative before the earth came into being, even before all of God's good creation. God through His Holy Word declared in the beginning that His light would stream through all the lights on high, revealing the law of truth. God includes among His primary names Understanding, Knowledge, All-Seeing, and All-Wise. Zoroaster taught righteousness so that humanity could be perfected and see the light. He assured His early followers that they would model constant illumination, and establish a realm of radiance and abundance.[31]

20 – Affirming Four Realms: Natural, Human, Revelatory, Divine

All major scriptural traditions offer a map of reality and present a big picture that is comparable, if not essentially the same. The Founders all convey a metaphysic of four interacting levels of reality. Sentient, choosing creatures occupy the human realm, and are expected to care for the natural realm below. They are progressively guided by the revelatory realm above, which the

Messengers reveal through Their words and deeds. But the Founders Themselves are sent by God, the Divine Mystery, Who represents the highest of all possible realms. How did Zoroaster depict these levels?

The Natural Realm

Zoroaster taught that the natural realm was divinely created. God fashioned the cosmos, including the sky, water, earth, plants, animals, human beings, and the lights of the heavens. The physical creation is good and bountiful, but also permeated with choice, which allows for a struggle against evil for the best existence. Through His questioning of existence, Zoroaster demonstrates that God is the Creator of all. *"Who is the first begetter, father of the Cosmic Law? Who assigned orbit to the sun and the stars? Who causes the moon to wax and again to wane? Who other than Thee?"*[32] All natural things precious to the eye, such as the sparkling dawn of the days, are meant to evoke divine praise.[33]

The Human Realm

In Zoroastrian teaching, humans are endowed with a fravasi—an eternal soul that preexisted our birth and is part of God's original creation. Human nature is distinguished above the natural realm by its ability to choose. We are responsible for discerning better and higher things, for joining creative forces, and for avoiding evil temptation. We must bring justice and prosperity to the community and beautify the earth. We also must oppose injustice, all in preparation for the final restoration. With a clear mind, we are to discern good and evil and better and worse, and we must apply this awareness to our thoughts, words, and deeds.[34] Different deeds and words lift up the mind or lower it, and our choices have consequences for our eternal destinies.[35] After death, individual souls encounter what is known as the "Bridge of the Separator." The record of each soul is judged according to its balance of good and bad deeds. If souls have made mostly good choices, they go to heaven, which is known as the best existence, paradise, and the house of song. If they have made mostly bad choices, they go to hell, which is known as the worst existence, the abode of anguish, and the house of lies. If human lives have been marginal, their souls go to *hamistigan*, the region of the mixed. Each person crosses the bridge of judgment, becoming yoked to his or her deeds through reward and punishment, until the final restoration.[36]

The Revelatory Realm

How did Zoroaster describe His revelation? We saw that Moses viewed His revelation as God's commands through Prophets. We will see that Krishna presented His revelation as ultimate reality incarnated; Buddha as Dharma attained; Christ as the Word made flesh; and Muḥammad as divine speech recited. Bahá'u'lláh presented His revelation as progressive, and as the initiation of a new cycle of fulfillment for humanity. These views of revelation are complementary, rather than contradictory or mutually exclusive. Zoroaster viewed His revelation in a mode consistent with other Founders. He described His teachings as the Sacred Word proclaimed. God declared Zoroaster as One who hearkened to divine commands. For His Creator and for truth, He was willing to announce a divine message, so the Wise Lord bestowed upon Him the charm of speech.[37] The Sacred Word would be proclaimed, and would offer salvation to those who had gone astray.[38]

Zoroastrians believe that Zoroaster saw God in a spiritual sense, felt conscious of His presence, heard His words, and conveyed His divine message to humanity directly through the Gathas. This is a two-way process of choice and accountability: Zoroaster and God chose each other, were faithful to each other, and together revealed a body of saving wisdom for humanity. Zoroaster was given the gift of attractive speech so that despite powerful resistance from kings, priests, and the wealthy, a critical mass would receive saving wisdom by the tongue, not by the sword.

Zoroaster's revelation is also depicted as coming to Him through the divine heptad, which includes Ahura Mazda (the Wise Lord) and His six benevolent spirits. These seven forces may be conceived of in the abstract as divine attributes that can be reflected in the human soul, or they can be personified as archangels whose voices we can hear and whose leadership we can follow. In any case, they are spiritual powers opposing evil and destructive forces in the world and in the soul. Collectively, they make for an intriguing and sophisticated system of theological understanding. In Yasna 45, Zoroaster preached to a large crowd, summarizing the benevolent spirits as *"things which are best in this existence."* They promote justice and prosperity in this life, and lead to eternal life in the house of song. They build the good life in this dispensation and help overcome false gods, preparing the way for the Future Savior and the establishment of the kingdom of heaven on earth.

A contemporary Zoroastrian scholar speaks for most Zoroastrians down through the ages by describing the revelation of Zoroaster as rational, practical, and universal. "The Gathas are rational. Holy reason is a constant thread running throughout the Gathas. Sublime Mind (or Wisdom) is the first mentioned quality of God. . . . The prophet invites his audience to listen to his sermons and weigh them with their good minds and reasoning. He insists upon their making their choice rationally. . . . The Gathas are practical. They teach mankind to lead an active life based on good thoughts, good words, and good deeds for the happiness of all and for the progress and renovation of the world. The rules of morality make up the main body of the Gathas. They direct man's life in a most simple and practical manner. . . . The Gathas are universal. According to the Gathas, their message contains the highest truths for all mankind. Zoroaster preaches for everybody without distinction of race, color, or sex. His aim is the universal uplift of truth, the promotion of love, harmonization of mind and heart, the self-realization of man."[39]

Notes of universality were struck throughout the Avesta, where there are passages that say in effect, that which is good for everyone is good for oneself. What we hold good for ourselves, we should honor for all. Only universal law is true law. For Zoroastrians, revelation has long been understood as the Sacred Word proclaimed for all of humanity, the divine law for all discerning souls.[40]

The Divine Realm

Zoroaster gave divine nature many titles, including the First and the Last, the Most Adorable One, the Father of Good Thought, the Creator of the Eternal Law of Righteousness, and the Lord Judge.[41] God is also described as the Supreme Benevolent Providence, the Primeval Cause of all creation, and the Perfectly Just Who renders fair recompense for all actions until the last day of creation.[42] God is to be evoked as the Holy Judge of actions, the Lord of Truth, and the Revealer of Mysteries and Plans through Prophets.[43]

The Zoroastrian conception of God has also been summarized in this way. "He is the Absolute, the All-Perfect, the Spirit of Spirits, the Essence of Being, the First Cause, the Creator, the Sustainer, the Source of Goodness, the Sublime Wisdom, the Nature of Truth, the Quintessence of Justice, the Boundless Constructive Power, the Eternal Law, the Unchangeable, the Ultimate Reality, and the only Adorable One to be worshipped." God is also described as "beyond time and space, though time and space are with and in him. All creations exist in the presence of God. Cosmos does not veil God. . . . It is an expression of God's creativity." And finally, God is explained as the manifestation of His attributes, "Ahura Mazda is ineffable and appears to man only in his attributes. According to the Gathas he is Intelligence, Righteousness-with-Justice, Tranquility-with-Love, Divine Might, Perfection, and Eternity. He is the Light of Lights, and all goodness emanates from him. His attributes are etherealized moral concepts expressed in pure abstractions."[44]

Zoroastrian beliefs about God and religion are quite similar to many Westerner's beliefs about God. To summarize, "Zoroastrianism believes in one creator-sustainer of the universe; he is omniscient, omnipresent, and omnipotent; he is the only one worthy of worship; he is without beginning and end, unchanging and eternal. . . . He created man as his coworker with faculties to discern between right and wrong and to work for the advancement of the universe; he revealed his eternal law to the prophet Zoroaster in the *Gathas*; he proclaimed the law of consequences and the reality of the life hereafter; and he prescribed true happiness . . . for the righteous."[45]

21 – Promising a Future Savior and a New Golden Age: The Saoshyant and the Final Restoration

The Soashyant is a very significant theme, addressing many of the deepest longings of humanity down through the ages. The Saoshyant has been understood as that prophesied Figure who will bring about humanity's reunion with God and the long-awaited triumph over evil. He has played the same role for Zoroastrians as the Messiah has for Jews, the Kalki Avatar for Hindus, the Maitreya Buddha for Buddhists, the Return of Christ for Christians, and the Mahdi or Promised One for Muslims.

For Bahá'ís, Bahá'u'lláh is the Saoshyant, and has ushered in the final restoration. Zoroastrian evidence for this Bahá'í claim includes these two points: 1) It was taught that the Saoshyant would be immediately preceded by the Hushidar Boomit, meaning the "Gate of Knowledge from this land" (referring to Persia). Bahá'u'lláh was preceded immediately by a Prophet called the Báb, meaning the "Gate of God," and the Báb was born in Persia. 2) Another title for the future Savior was Shah Bahram Varjavand, meaning the Invincible Bringer of the Glory of God. The name Bahá'u'lláh means the "Glory of God," and He brought teachings on world unity.

As with other prophetic visions in the major world religions, the Saoshyant was seen as coming in a future age of darkness, or an iron age preceding a new golden age. This would be a time when evil, injustice, and suffering reach unprecedented depths, and people everywhere cry out for one final Savior to eliminate all evils and establish heaven on earth. In the last times there will be only one in a myriad who believes in the Good Religion, and even he will not observe it correctly, though it be a duty.[46] There will be a dispersion of sovereignty from Iran, the ancient birthplace of the Zoroastrian Faith, bringing deep disturbances of just law, scattering the valiant, and exterminating good works. This will be the age mingled with iron, and among humanity's darkest hours.[47]

However, some three millennia after Zoroaster, the Saoshyant will work with the Holy Spirit and righteous people throughout the world, together ushering in universal salvation, and not merely a new religious dispensation. It will be a consummation of the age-old vision of peace and justice. This process will restore the entire world, and has been called the final restoration (*frasokereti*). Final judgment and purification of all the souls who have ever lived will take place, and good will triumph over evil.

In one place Zoroaster referred to a future Savior who will be the friend, brother, and father of all the world.[48] In another place He pointed to a series of spiritual Guides Who bring advancement in righteousness. *"When, O Wise One, shall the wills of the future saviors come forth, the dawns of the days when, through powerful judgment, the world shall uphold Righteousness?"*[49] In other places Zoroaster referred to these spiritual Guides as "Sons of Zoroaster," and since They were to appear about a millennium apart, They may have been prophecies of Christ, Muḥammad, and Bahá'u'lláh. Zoroaster asked about the timing, powers, and attainments of the future Saviors. When bloody tyrants, following falsehood, rush in from every side, who will stand erect and upright, firm in wisdom's love? God's answer was revealed: *"Those are the future saviors of the peoples Who through Good Mind strive in their deeds to carry out the judgment which thou hast decreed, O Wise One, as righteousness. For they were created the foes of Fury."*[50]

In another verse, Zoroaster referred to the final purification in a divine fire, in which the False One, or Evil Spirit, will be completely overcome, and the Truthful One, or Saoshyant, will succeed in attaining final good for all. *"Both parties, True and False, are put to test, O Mazda, by blazing Fire Divine; this Fiery Test lays bare their inmost Souls, as the award to each one indicates; complete frustration shall the False One find, the blessing full the Truthful One shall reap."*[51]

Jamaspa, Zoroaster's leading disciple and the chief minister of His royal kingdom, once asked Zoroaster when He would return for the final triumph of light over darkness. Zoroaster's reply seemed to refer to our current age with its modern technological conveniences. He said He would return when lamps will be lit without candles by merely touching the walls, when carriages will be driven without horses, and when men shall fly like birds, then the time will be ripe for His return and the advent of the future Savior.[52]

The future Savior will come forth in full glory, and will be entrusted with the seat of supreme authority. His teachings will be considered the true explanation of all moral and spiritual matters. He will drive away all covetousness and hatred, and restore the countries of ancient Persia. The period of the wolf will end, and the period of the sheep will begin.[53]

How will the final restoration actually feel? In some Zoroastrian prophecies we are offered glimpses of humanity's spiritual maturation. The whole of humankind will be firmly and enduringly linked in mutual love. Dark spirits will utterly despair of ever being able to harm the world again, and fear will be no more. Humanity will become one voice and will give praise to one God. There will be universal joy for the whole of creation.[54]

22 – Essential Unity of the Revealers through the Ages

Zoroaster understood His teachings were not His own, but rather, were given to Him by God through spiritual intermediaries. He also understood that the very first of these spirits—the Holy Spirit or the Word—had inspired all the Prophets of the past. The Holy Spirit would also inspire all the future Saviors of humanity that Zoroaster prophesied. This means that all of the Prophets, past and future, are united under God, conveying the Word to humanity in the form of scriptural guidance. The Revealers are essentially one in bringing divine guidance to our world.

Zoroaster had said that the Word was before God's good creation. The Word is the power by which all the Prophets and Founders have access to divine knowledge and power. It is the source of the Prophets' station of unity, as contrasted with Their various historical settings, which gave Them each a station of distinction as well. The Revealers had dual stations, and by virtue of their shared station of unity, They were one in service to God and humanity, proclaiming the sacred Word.

Additional evidence that Zoroaster understood Himself as one with the future Saviors is His use of the term *Sons of Zoroaster*. This term shows how intimate He felt with those Figures Who were to follow Him in the struggle for the good. They would be His Sons, and They would all share a family relationship as regards Their divine role. The future Saviors would be the "return of Zoroaster," just as Moses had promised a "Prophet like me," and just as Krishna had promised to return in each age to restore righteousness. The first Son of Zoroaster appears to have been Jesus; the second, Muḥammad; and the third, Bahá'u'lláh.

Zoroaster prophesied, *"A child shall be conceived in the womb of a virgin. . . . He shall be like a tree with beautiful foliage and laden with fruit, standing in parched land; and the inhabitants of that land shall be gathered together to uproot it from the earth, but shall not be able. Then they will take Him and will crucify Him."* But this will only serve to strengthen His message, as the prophecy goes on to describe, *"from the depth, He will be exalted to the height. . . . His light shall surpass that of the sun."* And it goes on to say that the magi will be the first to recognize Him, *"You will be the first to perceive the coming of that great King. . . . And when that star rises of which I have spoken, let ambassadors bearing offerings be sent by you . . . for He is the King of kings, and all kings receive their crowns from Him. He and I are one."* [55] He also gave a time frame for when this future savior would arrive, *"When a thousand two hundred and some years have passed from the inception of the religion of the Arabian and the overthrow of the Kingdom of Írán and the degradation of the followers of My religion, a descendant of the Iranian kings will be raised up as a Prophet."* [56]

The first of the above prophecies supports the adoration of the magi story of Christian tradition. The second suggests links between Zoroaster, Muḥammad, and Bahá'u'lláh. If these prophecies are authentically Zoroastrian, it is further evidence of the essential unity of the Revealers.

23 – Laying Enduring Foundations: Fire Temples, Jamaspa, Cyrus, Darius, and Tolerant Empires

From Jamaspa to Cyrus the Great

The hypothesis that Zoroaster lived about 1000 BCE is based on linguistic and conceptual similarities between the Gathas and some of the Vedic literature in India. But because a great deal of valuable Zoroastrian literature and records were lost in the tumultuous 1000 years between 300 BCE and 700 CE, materials which might have explained or cast light on chronological developments, we are somewhat in the dark about what happened between

Zoroaster's death and the rise of Cyrus the Great. We can be reasonably sure that Jamaspa and Vishtaspa spread the Faith through what is today called Afghanistan, Iran, and Iraq; and their efforts led to the building up of a religious civilization strong enough to compete with and eventually replace the Medes. Many fire temples were built and several royal libraries were established. But we do not yet know to what degree the magi taught Zoroaster's Word authentically; nor do we know the ways they might have influenced the late Assyrians, Babylonians, and Medes; nor do we know the way interactions with these cultures may have influenced the magi. With the rise of Cyrus the Great, however, the records became more enduring and trustworthy.

The Achaemenid Empire: 550–330 BCE

In 559 BCE, Cyrus became ruler of part of the Median Empire. In 550 BCE, he made the old Median Empire the center of what became the Persian Empire, in which Zoroastrianism enjoyed the status of being the official state religion, though Cyrus was tolerant of other religions. He called his empire the Achaemenid, after his revered ancestor Achaemenes. He took control of Western Asia Minor after defeating Croesus of Lydia about 545 BCE. In 538 BCE, Cyrus conquered Babylon, and freed the Jews in captivity, encouraging them to rebuild the Temple that had been destroyed by the Babylonians. The Achaemenids held sway from northern India to the edges of Greece and Egypt. Cyrus set up an efficient system of local rulers (*satraps*), an effective communications network, roads, and a postal system of horseback riders. A strong legal system assured a high degree of justice, and nations besides the Jews considered Persian rule beneficial.

Darius the Great became emperor in 522 BCE, expanding and consolidating the empire, and bringing Achaemenid Persia to its height. As an administrator and financier, Darius was brilliant, emphasizing regular, equitable taxes, accurate weights and measures, and cautious monetary policies. Religious tolerance continued to enable regional harmony and loyalty to the emperor. Martial traditions, artistic and technical skill, and the learned and high-minded magi all contributed to obedience, cooperation, and productivity. Darius chose Susa as his capital, bringing in materials, workers, and artisans from all over the empire to rebuild the city, erecting a magnificent stone and brick palace as well as new fire temples. At Persepolis, he generated another set of ambitious building projects.

Xerxes followed Darius as emperor, putting down revolts in Babylonia and Egypt, and waging several long and destructive wars against Greece. Researchers have noted that, during these years "world history hung in the balance. . . . Xerxes invaded Greece, and perhaps only the disaster of Salamis prevented Zoroaster's faith from becoming a major religion of the Western world."[57] The Achaemenids became distracted by Greek rebellions and drifted into a decline.

Greek Influence: 330–247 BCE

In 334 BCE, Alexander of Macedon, who was referred to as the "Accursed" in Zoroastrian texts, began to move across the Persian Empire, conquering Susa and Persepolis, killing some magi and replacing the last Achaemenid king in 330 BCE. He destroyed cultural centers, and replaced them with Greek-style architecture. Hellenistic influence impacted Persian culture directly for almost 100 years. The Seleucid monarchs built Greek-style cities and encouraged immigration.

The Parthian Empire: 247 BCE–224 CE

But the Seleucids could not stem the tide of rebellion that arose in the eastern provinces, starting in 247 BCE, when a new Persian dynasty, the Parthians, began to reassert local control. By the mid-second century BCE, a Parthian warrior-king had subdued most of the empire and occupied the Seleucid capital. Greek influences were partly accepted and partly rejected by the Parthians. Much of their energy was devoted to fending off eastward incursions by the Romans. Parthian religion digressed toward polytheism to a much greater degree than was the case for Achaemenid and Sasanian religion. Among the cults of the Parthians was that of Mithra, a deity in the old Indo-Iranian pantheon who retained an honored position in Zoroastrian tradition.[58] Mithraism spread into parts of the Roman Empire. It claimed to have been founded by Zoroaster, and became known as the Persian Mysteries.

The Sasanian Empire: 224–652 CE

In 224 CE, the weakened Parthians fell to the Sasanians, a vigorous people from Persia's heartland who justified their takeover as a reassertion of legitimate Zoroastrian rule. The new king Ardashir replaced Parthian feudalism with a centralized administration. His son, Shapur I, extended the empire to include all of modern Iran as well as parts of Iraq, Afghanistan, Pakistan, and Arabia. He managed to defend the empire against a series of Roman invasions, establishing the Sasanian Empire as the strongest power of late classical antiquity.

The Sasanian Empire was described as follows: "The Sasanian era was perhaps the time of greatest courtly splendour in Iran, with lavish royal patronage of great temples, with magnificent palaces decorated with mosaics, furnished with superb utensils, many of which have survived the ravages of history and enable scholars to reconstruct much of Sasanian magnificence. The monarchs threw their considerable power behind the official priesthood (magi), so Church and State were spoken of as 'brothers, born of one womb and never to be divided.' Once the authority of the chief priests had been declared, deviance from their teaching became not only heresy, but treason. . . . The Sasanian period is the only era in Zoroastrian history where there is clear evidence of oppression of other religions."[59] However, the oppressiveness of Sasanian rule may have had more to do with Zurvanism, a heretical view that reflected the Greek emphasis on fate. In Zurvanism, time was the father of choice, and so the ultimate controller of all things, even seemingly above Ahura Mazda, thus challenging belief in the essential goodness of the world.

Another challenge for Sasanian Zoroastrianism was the rise of Manichaeism, founded by Mani (216–276 CE). Mani claimed to be the last "apostle of light" with "saving knowledge" after Zoroaster, Buddha, and Jesus. He taught that matter is evil and opposed to the light of God; our human task therefore is to free the particles of light trapped in matter, delivering them back to their original state. Within Manichaeism, there were two classes of believers: the elect and the auditors. The elect were distinguished from auditors, who supported them. Shapur I patronized this faith, which prospered until 274 CE when Kartir, an influential high priest, convinced Bahram I to execute Mani. Through the efforts of Kartir, Zoroastrianism became the undisputed state religion, but how closely this resembled Zoroaster's original teaching is debated. Fire temples were expanded, Avestan scriptures collected, and an extensive theological literature generated. To this day, the official Zoroastrian religious calendar refers back to 632 CE when Yazdegird III, the last Sasanian king, took the throne.

The peak of Sasanian power and authority was reached under Khosrau I (531–579 CE), who was also called Anushirvan the Generous and Just. Religion and government came into mutually beneficial relations, and the peoples who lived under Sasanian rule at this time felt that they were treated very fairly. Even Muḥammad, who was born in 570 in Arabia, would later say that he was "born in the time of a just king," referring to Anushirvan. But soon after his reign, the Persian and Byzantine Empires exhausted each other with border disputes, so that by 652 CE, the new Islamic Empire eclipsed them in power. After the Islamic conquest of the entire Middle East, Zoroastrians became a persecuted minority, limited mostly to the cities of Yazd and Kerman in Iran. After the tenth century CE, they would also reside in Bombay, India, where they became an influential minority known as Parsees. Today there are also small communities of Zoroastrians in England, the United States, and Canada.

24 – Renewing Scriptural Guidance: The Avesta

The holy books of Zoroastrianism are called the Avesta, which means "the injunction" (of Zoroaster). About three-quarters of the original material has been lost due to invasions and persecutions over three millennia. Fortunately, there are still some summaries of much of the missing material. Among the twenty-one books of the Avesta is the Yasna, which contains the Gathas of Zoroaster. The Gathas consist of Zoroaster's poems and hymns of praise to Ahura Mazda, and which describe a complete body of moral and spiritual teaching. When we read the Gathas, we can be reasonably certain we are hearing the voice of the historical Zoroaster. Other books of the Avesta include the Vendidad, which contain some Genesis-like material and laws, and the Yasht, which contain Zoroastrian epic literature. But Zoroastrians also use the Pahlavi texts of the Sasanian Empire—the Bundahisn, a collection on cosmology, and the Dinkard, a body of lore and accumulated beliefs. In modern religious practice, Zoroastrians use the Khorda Avesta (little Avesta), a collection of daily prayers.

25 – Generating Civilization Anew: The Kingdom of Heaven on Earth

What vision of civilization has sustained Zoroastrians throughout the last three millennia? It was a vision concrete and powerful enough to sustain three lofty empires stretching 1200 years. Zoroaster gave us a glimpse of the kingdom of heaven on earth. When Prophets succeed in gathering a sizeable portion of humanity (including kings) under divine law, then a lofty civilization arises in which there is a high degree of justice, rationality, and prosperity—in the full moral, economic, and artistic sense of the word prosperity. There is also a high degree of peace. As the Zoroastrian writings say, the wolf period goes away, and the sheep period comes.[60] Full implementation of divine law in the final triumph yields the kingdom of heaven on earth—a co-creation of God, the Saoshyant, and obedient humanity.

Insights on the Zoroastrian vision of civilization can be gained by examining the concept of the *good dominion*. This refers to a majestic sociopolitical realm in which God's Word is operative in the world because humanity has embraced and implemented the latest Prophet's teaching. Heavenly gifts drop like gentle rain upon the earth, and they can be graciously received and cultivated by humanity. Humanity has been taught to beautify the earth, the Good Shepherd or Divine Protector will foster all life through righteous law. Perhaps the future Savior, most especially, will help creation on its upward march. This upward march will be enhanced by a teaching campaign. Divine light will dawn on the truthful and the truth-seeking—those who expound and receive the Holy Word.[61]

Good and just kings like Vishtaspa can help lead us all into the light of a global civilization. Builders of civilization serve humanity better by acts of service than by words, and they are of one mind in granting blessings unto all of humankind.[62] A divinely guided global civilization will feature faithfulness linked with good rule, vice weakened and virtue strengthened, the common people well, and a world that is prosperous as a whole, which will lead to creation rejoicing.[63] This is not an end, but a great turning point. "That event will mark the end of one stage and the start of a new one in the history of mankind. The turning point is the culmination of a long process of gradual progress—both quantitative and qualitative—toward perfection. . . . It is characterized by universal harmony, goodness, and happiness. . . . It is the end of disharmony, contradiction, struggle, and discomfort; it proclaims the consummation of accord, peace, and love."[64]

Krishna: Background and Mission

To appreciate the reverence shown for Krishna in India over the last 3000 years, we need a basic overview of the religious heritage of India. This requires identifying the prominent features of what has been called Hinduism. We also need an outline of major beliefs and practices in the centuries preceding Krishna—the role of manus or semi-divine patriarchs, the four ages, the basic shape of Vedic religion, the belief in many gods and One Ultimate Reality, as well as the nature and role of Avatars, including Krishna's predecessor, Rama. Who was Krishna? Why is He still among the most exalted Figures in India's glorious past? How does He compare with other Founders? What is His background?

Key Features of India's Religious Heritage

We find great variety in the religious beliefs and practices that grew in India over the last four millennia. However, there were enough common features among the majority of the population to identify the world religion that has been termed Hinduism. Here are ten common features.

(1) Brahman or Ultimate Reality is both personal and impersonal and appears in many forms; (2) it is accessible through a variety of paths (*margas*): knowledge (*jnana yoga*), devotion (*bhakti yoga*), and action (*karma yoga*); and (3) it is realized by those sages who have attained union or communion with that Reality. (4) On the other hand, creation and the phenomena of worldly life are temporal and partial; they conceal the total Truth and its realization. (5) Hindus further hold the doctrine of *karma*, which says that each thought, word, and action brings appropriate recompense, thereby upholding the moral government and ultimate justice of the cosmos; and (6) the doctrine of reincarnation, understood as a dreary round of continued suffering or a continuous

series of fresh opportunities to improve one's lot. Inequality of endowment and fortune is explained as the working out of karma and not as
the result of some discrimination by God. Hindus also uphold (7) the
authority of the Vedas; (8) the traditions of family and social life, with
its four stages of student, householder, spiritual seeker, and ascetic who
renounces all for the sake of spiritual progress and the welfare of all; (9)
the four goals of life: righteousness (*dharma*), worldly success (*artha*),
pleasure (*kama*), and spiritual freedom (*moksha*); and (10) the validity
and viability of the ideal social order and its attendant duties, which
have degenerated into the caste system.[1]

Other religions have emerged from India such as Jainism, Buddhism, and
Sikhism, all of which protested against and changed some of these features,
thereby distinguishing themselves from Hindu tradition.

1 – Continuity with Previous Dispensations: Manus and Eons, Vedic Religion, Divinities and One Ultimate Reality, Avatars and Renewing Righteousness

Continuity means there is a lineage of revered figures understood as revealing
in a progressive way a body of ancient guidance. The Veda was the earliest
body of sacred knowledge in India, and its oral form may date back to 3000
BCE. The Veda is believed to have been heard by many un-named sages,
whose poetic utterances, ritual guidance, and mythic explanations conveyed
an eternal body of truth. Vedic religion, or Brahmanism, provides the background from which all the beliefs and practices of what would later be called
Hinduism developed.

Manus, Eons, and Ages

Vedic literature referred to Manu as the semi-divine lawgiver who initiated this
eon or manu-cycle, and we are now in the seventh eon, with seven more eons to
come in this Day of Brahma. A Day of Brahma was viewed as a visible universe,
after which follows a Night of Brahma, an invisible period of pure potentiality,
followed by a new visible universe. Each eon, or world cycle, is made up of four
ages—golden, silver, bronze, and iron—with each age decreasing in length
by a quarter. The Iron or Dark Age (Kali Yuga) is said to have begun with the
death of Krishna. The term manu means a thinking being or man, able to
reflect divine guidance for a new eon. In the Hindu myth of the flood, it was

Manu who (like Noah) constructed a boat and sailed to the Himalayas and became the progenitor of a renewed human race. One set of laws is prescribed for the Golden Age, another set for the following Silver Age, a third for the Bronze Age, and a fourth for the Iron Age.[2] Manus initiated both eons and the four ages within each eon. The series of semi-divine patriarchs seems to merge with the series of Avatars or divine manifestations, including Rama and Krishna. Such figures rescue humanity on a periodic basis from spiritual decay and moral darkness. Hinduism depicts humanity as in need of Founders to renew divine law periodically, in order to regenerate civilization.

Vedic Religion and the Caste System

Between 1500 and 1000 BCE, a religious system developed drawing from its Aryan and Dravidian origins. Veda is a wide-ranging Sanskrit term referring to sacred knowledge that is held as the basis of true belief and appropriate practice. Veda is sacred knowledge heard or seen by holy ones in direct contact with the Eternal Realm. Priests and other holy people then orally transmitted spiritual truths and practices to generations of priestly devotees. Vedic literature includes invocations of praise to deities, descriptions of proper ritual, cosmological and metaphysical discourses, and a vast body of social and religious laws.

The priestly caste, known as brahmins, became the dominant or highest caste, developing an ever more elaborate system of devotional and sacrificial rituals that only they could perform and interpret. Other castes—such as rulers and warriors, householders and merchants, craftsmen and laborers—had no direct access to Vedic religion or Brahmanism. In turn, priests were viewed as indispensable bridges between human and divine realms. The corruption that developed within Brahmanism was among the issues addressed by Krishna and Buddha.

Many Gods and One Ultimate Reality: Brahman-Atman

Among the stumbling-blocks for Westerners who study Eastern religion is the belief in many deities. Vedic literature refers to Indra (god of war and storm), Varuna (god of waters and a moral overseer), Agni (god of fire and intermediary between heaven and earth), Ganga (river goddess), Parvati (mountain goddess), Kali (devouring goddess), and many others.

However, Krishna and Buddha, while not eliminating the gods, reduced their importance and transcended their power, as we will see. For most Hin-

155

dus today, worship of deities is a unified process. Diverse devotional practices are simply different ways of glorifying one Divine Reality. The gods and goddesses are widely understood as functions or expressions of Brahman-Atman, the Ultimate Reality both within and beyond us, *"The One Being sages call by many names."* [3]

God as Creator, Sustainer, and Transformer: The Trimurti

Hindus think of God as infinite, far beyond the qualities and aspects that we can normally understand. Yet three types of infinitude are ascribed to God: infinite being (*sat*), infinite knowledge (*chid*), and infinite joy (*ananda*). The Hindu Godhead is Brahman-Atman, which has three major expressions or functions: God as Creator (Brahma), Sustainer (Vishnu), and Transformer (Shiva). All deities of the Hindu pantheon are viewed as under the sovereignty of the trimurti, the three major expressions of divine activity. Most Hindu believers, by family tradition, are aligned intimately with either Vishnu or Shiva. Vishnu is the divine form that is most similar to God as conceived in the other world religions.

Avatars of Vishnu, the Divine Sustainer

Vishnu as Sustainer is the aspect of God that hears and responds to the people's needs. In this sense, Vishnu presents God as personally and continually available. When the Dharma (the law of righteousness, or cosmic and moral order) is violated significantly by humanity, Vishnu takes form as an Avatar, a human manifestation of divine power. He descends to earth to reestablish justice and inspire humanity anew. For Hindus, there have been nine Avatars, the last three include Rama, Krishna, and Buddha. Kalki is viewed as the tenth and future Avatar Who is to initiate the Golden Age of a new world cycle. Hinduism affirms belief in a series of Divine Educators who, despite extremely desperate conditions during Their time on earth, uplift the people who hear Their message, and carry humanity and civilization forward and upward.

Rama and the "Ramayana"

Krishna probably lived some time between 1400 and 1100 BCE, and His predecessor by perhaps 500 years was Rama, the eldest son of the king of Kosala, who ruled from the capital city of Ayodha. Rama's story is told in the *Ramayana*, one of the two greatest Indian epics, along with the *Mahabharata*, telling the story of Krishna and the transition to Hindu Faith and civilization.

The *Ramayana* exalted the virtues and obligations of family life as superior to claims of political rule and economic wealth. Rama and Sita were held up as exemplars of courage, faithfulness, moral nobility, and spiritual dignity. A human prince developed miraculous powers, became a divine incarnation, liberated his devotees, and reestablished righteous rule and the observance of divine law. Vishnu promised to repeat this pattern when necessary for humanity's salvation. It was widely believed that Rama, Krishna, and Buddha were sons of Manu, and part of the Solar Dynasty that featured prominently in northern India. This dynasty was said to be linked to the ancient Vedic sun god Surya, but more significantly to Vishnu, the Divine Sustainer. Krishna claimed to have renewed the teaching of Their common lineage.[4] As an Avatar, Krishna knew and embodied the Eternal Law (*Sanatana Dharma*). Like Abraham, Moses, and Christ in the West, the Avatars of the East were considered both spiritually and genealogically related.[5]

2 – Arising to Guide Humanity in the Worst of Times: Tyrant Kings Oppressing Northern India

Just as Moses was central in the drama of ancient Israel, as well as the Revealer and re-interpreter of what came before Him, Krishna was central in the drama of ancient India, reforming Vedic religion and giving it a deeply devotional focus that generated a new civilization. The story of Krishna is embedded in the eighteen-volume collection known as *Mahabharata*, the epic describing the build up to a great war that probably occurred between 1400 and 1100 BCE. This influential body of myth, history, and divine guidance contains the Bhagavad Gita, a spiritual classic that describes Krishna's advice to His disciple Arjuna, purifying and redirecting Brahmanic religion.

Like other scriptures, the *Mahabharata* contains both mythic and historic material. It offers both symbolic stories of truth and true stories that contribute to our factual understanding of humanity's religious unfolding. We are challenged to discern which kind of story is meant to be taken as concrete reporting, and which kind as painting a picture of higher realms. Like the Bible, the *Mahabharata*, provides a broad cosmological background, then focuses upon particular persons and places. In this epic story, two large and accomplished clans, the Pandavas and the Kauravas, and their interactions over several generations become a drama of good against evil. But also like the Bible, it is a body of moral and spiritual ambiguities, testing both the acting participants and the readers of the story.

Now Krishna entered the arena of world history. More than 3000 years ago, the tyrant King Kamsa ruled all of northern India from his capital city Mathura. No other tribal chief dared to murmur a word against him, for Kamsa was widely known for his horrific oppression. Conditions were morally intolerable due to a reign of terror unparalleled up to that day. The earth was groaning under the weight of iniquities. The people lived in constant fear, hoping for another Liberator, a bringer of divine bounties. The climate of expectation intensified, and they longed for another Avatar, like Rama, who could restore righteousness.

3 – Advent Prophesied and Expected: A Heavenly Voice Declares that Evil Will be Overcome and Righteousness Restored

Like Moses, Buddha, and all other Founders, Krishna was heralded, suggesting that His coming into the world was not accidental but part of a redemptive scheme for humanity. God arranged for a divine announcement that conditions on earth had not escaped His glance, that times were about to change, and that salvation was at hand.

During the wedding of Kamsa's sister Devaki to Vasudeva, a heavenly voice prophesied to Kamsa that Devaki's eighth child (Krishna) would kill Kamsa and deliver his land from wickedness. In response to this prophecy, Kamsa initiated a campaign of suppression of all neighboring tribes, with the backing of his father-in-law, the also cruel King Jarasandha of Magadha. Panic ensued, bringing an exodus out of the cities in an attempt to escape Kamsa's wrath. Turning directly to Devaki and Vasudeva, Kamsa ordered that all six of their children be smashed on a rock before their horrified eyes. Their only consolation was the prophecy that their eighth child would save the people. Kamsa then put the couple in a dungeon, had them bound on two separate pillars and guarded, so that no more births were possible for them. The prayers of the people rose to heaven in a constant stream, and God heard those prayers.

4 – Auspicious Signs, Birth, and Intimations of Greatness: Prince Born in a Dungeon, Raised by Cowherds, Slaying Demons, Besting Gods, Enchanting by Flute

To accent divine agency and sanction, the birth of Saviors has been accompanied by heavenly and earthly signs, and Their early lives show beyond-human capacities. Krishna's birth was no exception to this. A bright conjunction of stars—along with blossoming lotuses, crooning birds, and noble souls more acutely awake—heralded the Avatar's birth.

The Lord entered the mind of Vasudeva, who became aware that new light was shining within him, and this redemptive spirit was transmitted from Vasudeva to Devaki. Thus did she conceive the Lord Krishna through her husband. At the moment of Krishna's birth, the dungeon was filled with light. Krishna, as an infant, gave His mother a vision of His divine form, and conveyed to His father His need to go to Gokula, the home of the cowherd chief Nanda, whose wife had just given birth to a baby girl. Krishna was to grow up there, and Nanda's infant daughter would replace Him in the dungeon. With divine aid, all these miraculous changes took place.

When King Kamsa realized that Devaki's eighth child (Krishna) had escaped him, he ordered a massacre of all baby boys and holy men in the region. But this spree of atrocities failed again to eliminate Krishna, who had gone to Gokula, and would one day defeat Kamsa and redirect the course of history. Kamsa sent a series of demons to find and kill Krishna, but these efforts all failed. The scene then shifted to Gokula, the cowherd village where Yashoda and Nanda, Krishna's foster parents, would nurture Him through childhood and youth. They asked a sage to perform a purification and naming ceremony, through which He was named Krishna, meaning the beautiful dark One who attracts the hearts of all. The sage prophesied that those who came in contact with Him would belong to Him forever; those who persecuted Him would be persecuted; those who loved Him would be loved; and numerous would be the holy names bestowed upon Him.

The story of Krishna's childhood and youth in Gokula were embellished with tales of charming mischief, miraculous defenses against demons, completing an increasing number of daily chores and responsibilities, being taught what He already knew, as well as arousing desires among women without alienating them from their husbands. These stories carried the universal message that God could enter into the human condition thoroughly, occupy all human roles, and most especially, be cared for, nurtured, and taught in a way parallel to the way adults care for, nurture, and educate children and youth. The message was that humanity could "parent God" as well as be parented by God.

There were several early signs of Krishna's divine status. A bright stellar conjunction was reported at a time when those of noble character awakened. Yashoda, His foster mother, saw the whole universe in His mouth. He allowed Himself to be bound by Yashoda's rope, and to be controlled to a degree by those who loved Him, though He was boundless in power. Krishna bested the gods at their various functions. Even Brahma and Indra showed Him reverence, perhaps symbolizing the eclipse of polytheism as a dominant view in India.

Enchanting by Flute

With His sublime flute-playing in the forests, Krishna enchanted animals, humans, and gods. Stories of the handsome young Krishna luring girls and married women into the moonlit forests with His enchanting flute, and engaging them in amorous dalliances, have been inspiring to people of India, but suspicious to peoples of the Middle East and West. India has viewed Krishna's youthful activity as a spiritual mission, and it is our task to understand and appreciate the Indian view. Krishna said to young married women: *"O you pure ones, your duties must be first to your husbands and children. Go back to your homes and live in their service. You need not come to me. For if you only meditate on me, you will gain salvation."* [6] It is said that those who meditate on the divine love of Lord Krishna, and on the affectionate relationship between Him and the shepherd girls, become free from sensuality.

Taming the Sky God, Indra

Young Krishna criticized sacrifices made to Indra, king of the gods, who was said to be responsible for thunder, lightning, and rain. Even after He was told that pastoral villages must appease Indra to have regular rain for their fields and animals, Krishna replied that such things had more to do with effort and karma than Vedic sacrifices. Indra became angry, and the villages were about to be swept away in a mighty flood, when Krishna uprooted a mighty mountain and held it aloft to protect the people. Indra saw a new star rising in his place.

The Divine Lover and Radha

Krishna's favorite playmate in His youth was Radha. She was described as sweet and beguiling, willful and contrary, but filled with adoration for her Lord. Later, she was revered as the Divine Mother. As soon as her ego would assert itself, Krishna disappeared, along with her pride. Whatever was needed for the spiritual growth of His lovers, Krishna would do. Tradition made Radha the primary consort of Krishna, describing them as eternally embraced in heaven.

Teaching the Virtue of Detachment

Krishna taught devotees to be less attached to Him in the possessive sense. He explained that He was as celibate as a certain sage was abstemious in his eating habits. Krishna arranged for them to see this sage enjoying a sumptuous feast to show them that he, like Krishna, was at all times spiritually motivated, though he could enjoy sensual things for the sake of widening bonds of fellowship and love. Krishna taught that we must be detached from sensual possessiveness, and attached to love, righteousness, and divine will.

5 – Divine Commission: Sage Narada's Disclosure, Festival of the Bow, Krishna's Rising to Defeat Kamsa

Just as the human side of Moses would have preferred to maintain His peaceful pastoral life in Midian, the human side of Krishna would have preferred to maintain His enjoyable life on the forested banks of the Yamuna River. But renewal of Dharma required Krishna's boundless spiritual capacities to be exercised elsewhere. It was prophesied that Krishna would kill King Kamsa and liberate the people of Mathura. The time to fulfill this prophecy had come.

The feats we have described eventually made Krishna's existence known to Narada, the sage advisor to Kamsa. Narada facilitated the divine process by informing Kamsa of Krishna's activities and location, leading to Kamsa's eventual demise. This rise of Krishna to defeat Kamsa, a move from country to city, may be viewed as His divine call to restore righteousness, beginning in Kamsa's stronghold of Mathura. Kamsa invited Krishna to the widely announced Festival of the Bow, having concocted several plans for killing Him—with an elephant, with famous wrestlers, or with his own sword. But all these plans by Krishna's demonic uncle Kamsa failed.

Krishna's parting from the people of His youth was one that would last the rest of their lives, for a new phase of His life was beginning, a time when He would occupy the lofty role of king-maker. Nanda tried to warn his foster son of Kamsa's intentions, but Krishna simply said the king's formal commands must be obeyed. In Mathura, Krishna broke the bow, making all witnesses tremble, including Kamsa. He also killed the elephant and defeated the wrestlers sent by Kamsa. Finally, Kamsa himself tried to kill Krishna with his sword, but Krishna caught hold of his hair, threw him to the ground, stepped lightly on his chest, and the evil king's soul melted into the aura surrounding Krishna. Kamsa's subjects applauded their evil king's death.

Even those who had not yet accepted Krishna's divine status and mission held him to be a hero who restored the people's freedom and hope by removing their tyrant king. Krishna said to His parents when He freed them from prison, where they had been during the whole of Krishna's youth. *"O Father! O Mother! It behooves you to pardon us for not serving you at a time when you needed us most. . . . A man is not able to redeem, even in a hundred years of life, the debt he owes to the parents who gave birth to and nourished the body, which is the basis for the achievement of all objects in life, including liberation."* [7] Krishna's parents were greatly comforted. Faith in their son's divine station had sustained them through more than two decades of imprisonment. Now Krishna's true mission could begin; but first, a test.

6 – Struggling in Solitude: Doubt, Temptation, Bound by Love

Stories of Founders show Them conquering self before embarking on the spiritual conquest of the world. There is a decisive transition from a time when Their human qualities are quite visible, to a time when their divine qualities begin to dominate the story. In Mathura, Krishna heard about the misery of his foster parents, and also about the deep longing of the community he had left back in Gokula. They missed Him terribly, and He missed them. He was tempted to go back to them, because His greatest weakness was love for those who loved Him, but returning could halt the divine plan. Krishna doubted His own ability to explain, face to face, His new calling to His childhood home and community.

Krishna needed help with this transition. He therefore sent Uddhava—His cousin, friend, and disciple, who would later serve as His prime minister—to deliver a message of love and explanation to Gokula. The prospect of delivering this message Himself felt quite beyond Krishna's emotional capacities at this point in the unfolding of sacred events. Many were the times when Krishna was tempted to save Himself and others from the pain of their karmic bondage, but as a divine agent, such temptation had to be overcome. Uddhava was a man of great learning. Krishna entrusted him with a letter of compassion for the people He left behind in Gokula. Uddhava was sent on this mission for several reasons. Krishna doubted His own ability to overcome the temptation to return to the beloved community that had nurtured Him. The people were in deep need of His compassion, and also, Uddhava needed a lesson in the pure and selfless love that the cowherds and milkmaids could teach him.

Nanda, Krishna's foster father, asked Uddhava, "Does Krishna still remember the people of Gokula? . . . Every spot here is filled with memories relating to Him." Uddhava responded by saying that Krishna "is not your son alone. He is the child of all. He is the father of all. He is the mother of all. He is the soul of all."[8] Krishna's letter elaborated on this by telling the people of His community, *"Your grief is My grief and your joy My joy. For love such as yours there can be no end. I, who am boundless, have been bound by your love. Blessed are you among women, for your names will ever be remembered by the world to come. When I am far away physically, meditate on Me, and thus you will be able to commune with Me."*[9]

7 – Declaration and First Followers: Arjuna, Yudishthira, and the Pandavas

Founders often declare Their divine mission privately to a small group of disciples, and later make a more public announcement. Krishna was destined to restore righteousness in the land, to renew the ancient and eternal law of God. His instruments for these divine tasks, His first followers and disciples, were the Pandavas—the good side of the Kuru dynasty, who would oppose the evil side of the Kurus, namely the Kauravas led by Duryodhana. This struggle between the Pandavas and the Kauravas was the central plot line of the *Mahabharata*, one of the great classics of Indian literature, in which Krishna plays the central role.

The Pandavas, the five sons of Pandu and Kunti, were trained by Krishna as His primary divine instruments. In order of age they were Yudhishthira, Bhima, Arjuna, Nakula, and Sahadeva. Duryodhana tried to kill the Pandavas by inviting them to a flammable palace during a festival and then setting it on fire. But the Pandavas escaped and lived in the forest for several years, developing virtues under Krishna's guidance.

The Pandava brothers emerged from the forest for a competition. Arjuna won an archery contest, and the prize was a beautiful bride named Draupadi. With Krishna's help, they were able to retain their prize bride, despite armed resistance from neighboring princes. When the Pandava brothers returned to the forest, their mother Kunti awaited them. They told her that they brought home a wonderful treasure. She reminded them that they must share this treasure equally. But then she saw the prize bride, Draupadi, and was in deep dismay. But her word was sacred to her sons, and so Drapaudi married all the Pandava brothers together.

Several events might be considered public announcements of Krishna's divine station and mission. Two of these were His victory over Shiva (god of transformation), and His conference with the sages in Dwaraka. Krishna once went on a mission to rescue His grandson, and this led to a battle with a powerful thousand-armed form of the god Shiva. Krishna cut off his arms one by one like the branches of a tree. "The Lord's victory over Shiva is the culmination of His victories over the ancient gods. . . . Thus, the superiority of Krishna over the ancient *Vedic* gods was established. . . . In the *Kali Yuga*, or Iron Age, in which we are living now, the path of *bhakti*, or devotion, is advocated and the main propagator of this path is Lord Krishna Himself."[10]

A large group of sages once went to Dwaraka to glimpse their Lord. Krishna praised these sages and holy men as more worthy of praise and worship than images, pilgrimage sites, and spiritual austerities. This statement was an abrogation of some forms of Vedic worship and sacrifice. Then, to set an example, Krishna bowed down to the sages, who had given their all in quest of the Supreme. They replied by saying, "Today, by meeting You who are the goal of all pious men, we have attained the fulfillment of our lives. . . . You are the highest excellence that one can attain. . . . You are the Supreme Being and the Lord of all."[11]

8 – Overcoming Powerful Opposition: Kamsa, Jarasandha, and Duryodhana

The transformation brought about by Founders always evoked powerful opposition on the part of leaders who felt threatened by Their impact. The ability to overcome such enemies is a major proof of Their beyond-human station. Krishna's predecessor, Rama, had been opposed by a demonic king named Ravana; Moses had been opposed by Pharaoh; Zoroaster by Arejataspa. Forces for good offer distinct choices, thus allowing the emergence and clarification of what constitutes evil or ungodly practices. Stories of Saviors and Avatars always show forces of righteousness overcoming the forces of corruption.

There were several waves of opposition against Krishna, and He not only defeated these enemies, but transformed their characters to a higher spiritual plane. The first opposition that Krishna faced was King Kamsa of Mathura, who tried to kill Krishna because of the prophecy that Krishna would defeat him. Another wave of opposition came from King Jarasandha of Magadha, who attempted many times to crush Krishna and the Yadavas. Another came from Shishupala, Rukmini's one-time suitor, who tried to stir up the princes against Krishna and Yudhishthira for revenge. Further opposition came from King Salva, who attacked Krishna's capital with a fearsome aerial weapon, because he had been Shishupala's friend and had vowed to rid the world of Krishna and the Yadavas. The most extensive opposition came from Duryodhana, which culminated in the Mahabharata War. The final wave of opposition came from Ashvattama, just after the War, when this arch-enemy attempted to eliminate the Pandava line.

In addition to all this political or civil opposition, there was spiritual opposition as well. Durvasa, a brahmin sage, cursed Krishna in a jealous rage. Paundraka, a foolish king, made the counter-claim that he, rather than Krishna, was the true Avatar for the age. There were also stories about different kinds of demons rising up against Krishna, perhaps symbolizing enraged ancestors who resented developments initiated by the Avatar and His loyal Pandavas. But through a variety of means, all of the opposition to Krishna was overcome, and righteous kings replaced tyrants.

9 – Rejection by the People

Not only leaders oppose Founders, but ordinary people as well, usually preferring comfortable tradition to the challenge of new revelatory guidance. Krishna lamented the small number of His followers compared to the large number who had been offered His new Dharma. Despite His mighty deeds of righteousness and His ministry, surprisingly few recognized the truth of His teachings or the loftiness of His station. *"One person in many thousands may seek perfection, yet of these only a few reach the goal and come to realize me."* [12] Even Krishna's many sons, who had seen and heard Him many times, were more interested in earthly pleasures and secular ventures than ethical principles or spiritual disciplines. Like Zoroaster, Krishna was turned away by many kinsfolk and villagers that He encountered in His travels. But the Cause of God was not thwarted by public rejection. It would succeed through a small group of chosen ones.

10 – Sacrificial Suffering

Divine Educators share our human condition, and so They too experience hardship and pain. But in Their case, the suffering is completely redemptive in that humanity's spiritual progress is assured. The drama of Their suffering gives posterity deep lessons to ponder over for centuries and millennia. God's mercy is repeatedly offered to us, even though we persecute His Saviors. When will we learn to receive revelatory guidance more gratefully?

We saw earlier how Krishna could not face directly the emotional agony of parting from his rural childhood home when He had to depart for a campaign against the tyrant King Kamsa. Later, Krishna accepted the curse of Gandhari, who was the revered mother of the Kaurava clan, for His allowing so much loss of innocent life in the War. These were cases of redemptive suffering, for through them, righteousness replaced oppression. Perhaps the single most painful episode in Krishna's life came just before His earthly end. Though He had offered much spiritual care to His sons, they rejected it all, preferring to waste their time in useless pursuits. None of them would carry their father's spiritual legacy forward. In fact, their curse of the holy men brought disaster to their people, as we will see.

11 – Symbolic Language as a Test for Believers

Scriptures of the world's major religions warn their readers that challenging spiritual truths are contained in their mysterious symbols and images. Scriptures insist that devotees purify their hearts, proceed with humility, and not interpret the messages too literally or rigidly. The symbolic language of scripture, therefore, serves as a spiritual test, helping to distinguish those who are truly awake and receptive from those who are attached and invested in narrow beliefs and practices. Among the most important dangers scriptures attempt to prevent are: 1) that poor interpretations do not harden into idolatrous veils that block essential truths of the revelation, and 2) that traditional views do not prevent people from recognizing the prophesied Successor when He appears.

Krishna's revelation is no exception to this pattern. He knew that impure desires, hardened dogmas, and rigid rituals had caused religious decline in the past, and would do so in the future. He gave an early warning about this problem. *"The Word is measured in four quarters. The wise who possess insight know these four divisions. Three quarters, concealed in secret, cause no movement. The fourth is the quarter that is spoken by men."* [13] This suggests that the majority of scripture is veiled from ordinary understanding and speech, though the discerning are aware of the deeper meanings and broader picture offered by scripture.

Other passages in Hindu scripture reinforce this message. *"There are ignorant people who speak flowery words and take delight in the letter of the law, say-*

ing that there is nothing else. Their hearts are full of selfish desires . . . and the aim of all their activities is pleasure and power." [14] Another passage uses metaphors to describe our inability to understand the full meaning of scripture, *"Just as a fire is covered by smoke and a mirror is obscured by dust, just as the embryo rests deep within the womb, knowledge is hidden by selfish desire."* [15] These verses suggest that clinging to the letter masks selfishness and investment in the status quo. True understanding, though offered in scripture, can be obscured by the impure motives of religious leaders.

Passages from later Hindu scriptures reinforce Krishna's teachings on the spiritual dangers of attachment to the letter. *"The ignorant think that Brahman is known, but the wise know him to be beyond knowledge."* [16] True divine knowledge is above humanity's understanding, *"The eye cannot see it; the mind cannot grasp it. The deathless Self has neither caste nor race. . . . Sages say this Self is infinite in the great and in the small, everlasting and changeless, the source of life."* [17] We should not become too attached to our own ideas, but be willing to search for divine knowledge everywhere, *"Like the bee, gathering honey from different flowers, the wise man accepts the essence of different scriptures and sees only the good in all religions."* [18] These verses advocate humility before God or the Ultimate Reality, which transcends any particular doctrine.

Concepts which proved especially troublesome in Hindu tradition after Krishna include *Avatar, caste,* and *rebirth.* These terms were misinterpreted, and led to spiritual blindness and degradation. An Avatar was originally understood to be a descent of God in human form to restore righteousness and the Dharma (path of truth) when religion and morals had fallen to the lowest degree. Avatars appeared at intervals of about 500 to 1000 years, and Rama had been Krishna's predecessor. An Avatar, then, is the Indian equivalent of a Prophet of God. But Krishna's significance and authority began to erode markedly by Buddha's time, and this erosion posed obstacles to the proper recognition of Buddha's station. After the fall of the Gupta Dynasty in the early sixth century CE, the perceived station of the Avatar and the Buddha diminished to the point where sages and even sculptures were declared avatars and buddhas. It was also thought that ordinary people could become avatars by a process of divine infilling. These are breakdowns of moral and spiritual authority, contributing to social decline.

The original notion of caste was a functional ideal of social order. Differentiation of social roles and statuses was an effective method of societal development some 4000 years ago. It brought useful measures of harmony and prosperity to ancient India. And as caste was redefined by Krishna, with flexibility and virtues emphasized, it remained functional for perhaps another 500 years. But by Buddha's time the caste system had become socially crippling and religiously corrupt. A rigid code of conduct based strictly on birth lineage, stage of life, and narrowly defined duties all served to maintain brahmin control, while preventing innovation, learning, and individual excellence. In areas where Buddha's egalitarian and spiritual emphasis was influential, these problems were less evident. After a few centuries of classical refinement under the Guptas, the worst aspects of the caste system returned to Indian society, and it declined sharply.

Another troublesome term in the history of Indian religion has been *rebirth*. Krishna taught about rebirth as a spiritual process whereby our spiritual nature continues to develop after the death of our bodies. The soul was understood to be eternal, but also subject to causal influence, which is known as karma. Souls were said to endure in many different states and conditions, while suffering and enjoying consequences of their moral choices, and as related to their degree of receptivity to spiritual principles and practices. "Life and death" and "heaven and hell" were taught as relative terms describing various degrees of vitality and progress of the soul. For Krishna, the soul was defined as a spiritual rather than a physical reality. If He used a term like "womb" to describe the soul's new condition, this was a metaphor for a change of developmental level. We conclude that He did not teach the doctrine of physical reincarnation, though this conclusion has been widely rejected in Hindu tradition.

At the hands of the brahmins and the multitudes who came after Krishna, true intangibles were made false tangibles, figurative language was interpreted literally, and spiritual images and metaphors were reduced to concrete, visual hopes and threats. Scriptural teachings about rebirth were understood in terms of physical reincarnation—the misfortune of the soul returning to this world and inhabiting the bodies of animals and humans. Since the vast majority of people do not even claim to remember past lives, punishment based on them would be profoundly unfair. It seems that the belief in reincarnation could not be true in a world ruled by Dharma.

Belief in physical reincarnation was a response to the sense that one earthly lifetime was insufficient to overcome spiritual defects. Many assumed that since Avatars return, so do ordinary mortals. Combined with belief in physical reincarnation were ever more rigid notions of caste and karma. There could be no upward mobility in a lifetime, nor should conditions among the lower castes be ameliorated, because this would interfere with paying karmic debts. Such beliefs supported the status quo, preventing any real social or spiritual progress. Indian society declined steadily, and was quite weak before the Muslims arrived.

Symbolic language, then, poses a great challenge to religious leaders and adherents. When a religious civilization remains faithful to the spirit of its Founder's teachings, it grows in creative ways. But when authoritative teachings become veiled by selfish desires, vested interests, hardened doctrines, and rigid practices, then spiritual decay begins. If no significant reform movements reverse this process of decay, it only accelerates.

12 – Exemplary Women for All Ages: Rukmini the Nurturer, Draupadi the Advocate

It is deeply instructive that, despite the patriarchy of religious traditions throughout recorded history, stories of Founders reveal dignified and exemplary roles for women. Though the last 6000 years have favored males and male roles, revelation itself paints a more egalitarian picture. The most nurturing and receptive woman in Krishna's story was Rukmini, the princess of Vidarbha, lovely in body and soul, who became Krishna's first and most helpful wife. She was devoted to Krishna from the age of five, and had vowed to marry none other. When her father arranged her betrothal to another prince, she vowed to end her life after a long vigil unless Krishna rescued her, which He was able to do just in time. As Krishna's wife, she always attended with perfect faithfulness to His needs, to the needs of His sons, and even to the needs of Radha, Krishna's most famous wife, who was elevated many centuries later to the status of divine consort. It was Rukmini who came to best represent the virtues of humility, nurturance, and receptiveness for the Faith.

The most assertive woman in Krishna's story was Drapaudi, the wife of the Pandava brothers. She was indeed the heroine of the *Mahabharata*. She was shared equally in a polyandrous marriage, showing how unified the Pandava kingship was. A heavenly voice had announced that she would bring the decline of the warrior caste. In the middle of the Mahabharata epic, Draupadi was dragged into the gambling hall of Duryodhana half un-dressed. Hearing that she had been declared a slave, she asked if Yudishthira had gambled himself away before possessing her, and declared that if this was the case, he had lost his rights to gamble away anyone else. This brilliant self-defense led to the gambling match's nullification and to the Pandava exile. Duryodhana tried to disrobe and humiliate her, but in desperation she cried out for Krishna, wondering how He could forsake her. Miraculously, despite the attempted disrobing, yard after yard of clothing preserved her dignity. Drapaudi and the Pandavas, through devotion to Krishna, helped overcome the Kauravas, a feat which weakened the status of the military. Over time Drapaudi became a great model of female courage and will power.

13 – Dying and Ascending Victoriously: Final Advice and Death of the Deathless

The final years of Krishna's life on earth were spent giving advice to those nearest and dearest. His later messages seem especially universal. *"We are all potentially divine, children of infinity, and it is possible for each one of us to work out our own salvation at our own pace. In the beginningless and endless school of mortal existence, no one is ever expelled. . . . Whether he or she is high or low on the scale of evolution is immaterial. What matters is that each one should try to perfect himself or herself and in this very affirmation and sincerity lies the victory."* [19] Krishna tried to teach His followers to see beyond Him, and to see divine qualities everywhere. *"He who sees the One in the many and the many as coming from the One is the seer, the man of true knowledge."* He went on to say, *"Everything moving and unmoving, should be looked upon as manifestations of the divine, not merely Me. . . . Expand your vision so that it embraces the whole world. If you see the divinity in Me, your son, then look upon all men and women as your sons and daughters and thus recognize that they are also divine. . . . See the unity underlying the diversity and you will come to recognize the entire universe as nothing but an extension of your own self. The spark of divinity that glows in the core of your being blazes in the heart of all creation."* [20]

Just before Krishna's final address to Uddhava, as He was preparing to leave this world, there was celestial recognition. *"Now Brahma descended to the city of Dvaraka where the Radiant One, Krishna, could be found."* Other divine beings descended, including Shiva, Indra, the celestial musicians, and the ancient ones who first saw the Vedas. Together these hosts from the heavens entered the city, gazing upon the Beloved, the Avatar, Krishna, singing His praises, calling Him Beloved Protector, Excellent One, Resplendent One, Infinite One, and Supreme Spirit. They said, *"You took human birth because we beseeched you to relieve the burden of the earth. This you have done to perfection. You have placed the laws of virtuous living in the hands of the trustworthy and the righteous. And you have allowed your glory to be heard by all. . . . Nothing remains to be accomplished by you.*" [21]

But Krishna had a few needful things remaining—the fulfillment of the sages' curse, and His final advice to Uddhava as friend, prime minister, immediate successor, and bearer of His message to the world. *"This famous Yadu line made proud by their many victories, is making a bid to seize all that they see. But just as the shore stops the ocean wave, I have stopped their ambition. I cannot leave before their destruction is complete or they will surely overrun the earth."* [22]

The Uddhava Gita, the scripture containing Krishna's farewell messages and summations, included several important topics, and completed His teaching. He taught that there were twenty-four teachers: earth, trees, air, sky, water, fire, moon, sun, and many more. He spoke at length about the human soul and the divine soul, and how love and devotion is their proper relation, and that love transcends in importance philosophy, study, austerity, and renunciation. He warned Uddhava not to encourage use of miraculous powers, for they distract from spiritual growth. He taught that the basic dharma for all persons, whatever caste or creed, was doing what is beneficial for all. Krishna taught anew the death of the body and immortality of the soul, as well as the three yogas of knowledge, devotion, and action—integrating them under the umbrella of divine love. He added details on the three forces (*gunas*) of evolution: 1) purity or harmony, 2) activity or restlessness, 3) lethargy or inertia. He reminded posterity that chanting divine names was a higher form of spiritual discipline than Vedic rituals, such as immersion in the Ganges River.

Having answered Uddhava's questions, Krishna completed what He set out to do. In Dwaraka, revelry at frivolous feasts began to take the place of devotion and selfless service. Individual fights grew into violently opposed factions. "Kith and kin stood ranged against each other. Son killed sire and sire killed son. The Yadavas, having reached the day of their doom, rushed upon death like moths to the flame. . . . The Lord alone stood calmly in the midst of the fray and watched in silence as His deluded kinsmen destroyed one another." [23]

Krishna told women of His household that Arjuna would take them to Hastinapura where they would recover and thrive under Yudhishthira's rule. He retired to the forests to lament and await fulfillment of the dark prophecy.

A deer hunter mistook Krishna's foot for the face of a deer, and shot the fateful arrow. The soon-to-ascend Avatar comforted His grieving slayer. Krishna's final words were to His charioteer, Daruka. *"I am the Divine Charioteer seated in the heart of every human being. Follow the* Bhagavata Dharma [Law] *which I have expounded. Knowing the whole universe to be but an expression of My* maya [fleeting processes], *leave the reins of your life in My hands and remain at peace."* [24]

- 10 -
Krishna: Teaching and Legacy

14 – Transformative Teaching and Healing: Inspiring Devotion, Advising Kings, Establishing Righteousness

Humanity's Saviors arise at times when inner spiritual life has become degraded, and when outer social order is in disarray. Violence and oppression abound. To this context They bring healing transformation, empowering followers to attain astounding heights of sacrificial love, wisdom, and justice. Out of the ruins of a society groveling in depravity, They generate a lofty new civilization. Powerful spiritual forces are released. Extraordinary developments unfold. Such superhuman feats by Avatars and Founders cannot be explained by sociopsychological or political factors alone. The God hypothesis seems essential.

Krishna occupied many roles in His life and ministry of 125 years, including poor cowherd, friend, hermit, lover, witness, devotee, servant, prince, husband, father, counselor, teacher, unifier, ruler, ambassador, king-maker, charioteer, military leader, revealer, and object of worship. His early, middle, and later years were described respectively as focused on inspiring devotion, advising kings, and establishing righteousness. We described His youthful years as a time when He replaced Vedic gods and became the central focus of loving devotion, establishing a new religious paradigm that would serve as the basis of a new kind of civilization. We turn now to His middle and later years, focused on advising kings and establishing righteousness.

Struggling with King Jarasandha and Moving to Dwaraka
King Jarasandha of Magadha was a powerful tyrant king who swore to destroy the Yadavas, Krishna's tribal people. When Krishna heard that Jarasandha was making specific plans for an invasion, He mobilized the ill-prepared people of Mathura to repel the attack. Jarasandha attacked

over a dozen times, but each time was repulsed, though Krishna knew that they could not hope to hold out much longer. When Mathura was besieged by Jarasandha for the eighteenth time, Krishna and his brother Balarama lured Jarasandha out into the nearby hills and set the fields afire, thus avoiding disaster. Then He led the Yadavas to move their capital to the island of Dwaraka, where they built a magnificent city with beautiful palaces, mansions, parks, and temples.

Abducting Rukmini and Krishna's First Marital Alliance

Rukmini, the beautiful and noble daughter of a nearby king, vowed at a very young age that she would marry none other than the Prince of the Yadavas, Krishna. But the king arranged for Rukmini to be married to Shishupala before informing either her or Dwaraka. A brahman informed Krishna of her resolve that she would rather die than marry anyone other than Him. Though neighboring kings and their entourages had arrived for her wedding to Shishupala, earlier Rukmini had written a desperate note to Krishna, threatening to fast unto death unless Krishna consented to be her husband. Just in time, Krishna arrived at her palace, lifted her up to His seat, and abducted her to the wild cheers of multitudes of citizens. Dwaraka awaited the arrival of the royal couple, and their wedding was conducted on a grand scale. Jarasandha and Shishupala vowed revenge.

Protecting and Training the Pandavas

Stories of Krishna's teaching ministry with the Pandavas, His disciples, are too numerous to be summarized here. But examples with two of the Pandava brothers illustrate this pattern. Krishna encouraged Yudhishthira to develop his great powers of righteous leadership, and to transcend his weakness for gambling, through which he lost his kingdom and was thrown into years of exile, so that he could reemerge after the Mahabharata War as the universal king or emperor of India. Krishna encouraged Arjuna to balance his warrior skills by spending years in renunciation. Krishna taught Arjuna the timeless message of renunciation and selflessness, which was recorded in the Bhagavad Gita, just as the Mahabharata War began. Krishna's skillful charioteering and counsel led the Pandavas to victory, though they were greatly outnumbered by the Kauravas. Krishna also gave Arjuna refresher lessons when his spiritual learning had been forgotten. Through these and numerous other means, Krishna protected and trained the Pandavas, equipping them to be the unifiers of the tribes and cities of India.

The Divine Husband, His Wives and Sons

Krishna was said to be the perfect husband to countless wives, and the perfect father to countless sons. Though His wives were depicted as completely devoted to Him, His sons were depicted as disinclined to spiritual matters, never seeking out any guidance from their father. In these stories, Krishna never forced advice or direction on unreceptive souls. Though some of these stories of Krishna's family life may strain our credulity, it is more important to learn their basic lesson than to separate history from myth. The Founders' lives were greater than the merely factual and mythical. Krishna's family life showed Him capable of miraculous feats if they were in service of love and righteousness, if they fulfilled the divine plan, and if they did not interfere with karma—the unfolding of events based on previous choices. As an Avatar His powers were limitless in some respects, finite and karma-bound in others. Though it may be impossible for an earthly man to keep so many family members happy, or to instruct so many in the eternal law, with divine aid this is possible.

Unifying the Tribes against King Jarasandha

Though Ugrasena was king of the tribes, which were united and strengthened during Krishna's ministry, most citizens and officials looked to Krishna as the wielder of real power. Under His guidance many loosely knit tribes became a mighty kingdom, the equal of Jarasandha's. Krishna advised many assemblies before most of their final deliberations. One day at Dwaraka, when Krishna was speaking to an assembly, an unknown person entered and pleaded for Krishna's help in releasing the many kings who were rotting in the dungeons of Jarasandha, including some twenty thousand such defeated rulers in one fortress.[1] Later, the sage Narada arrived, saying he had advised Yudhishthira to perform the rajasuya sacrifice, where he would declare himself the world emperor, but Yudhishthira requested Krishna's approval and blessing before assuming the title of emperor. Krishna consulted Uddhava, his friend and prime minister, as well as the Yadava chiefs, and concluded that Jarasandha should be defeated first, the many kings freed, and then plans made to elevate Yudhishthira.

Elevating Yudhishthira and Defeating Jarasandha

Yudhishthira asked Krishna face to face whether the Lord thought him worthy to conduct the stupendously important and bold rajasuya sacrifice. Krishna assured His righteous disciple that he was indeed worthy of such a lofty role, if the tyrannical king Jarasandha could be defeated, and all the captured kings freed to declare their loyalty to Yudhishthira. Krishna outlined a plan to send out emissaries to all ruling kings, except Jarasandha, asking for the vassal fee to show their support for Yudhishthira's rule as emperor. The other four Pandava brothers were the emissaries sent in all four directions. They sought and won universal loyalty because Yudhishthira was respected by all but the ungodly.

Now only Jarasandha remained. Krishna suggested that He, Arjuna, and Bhima (his physically powerful brother) should go to Jarasandha's capital and challenge him to a duel. Jarasandha, who was a powerful warrior himself, accepted the challenge, and fought a mighty battle with Bhima that went on for days. Krishna reminded Bhima of Jarasandha's physical weak point. The two grappled with each other for their lives, but Bhima, armed with Krishna's advice, was finally able to kill Jarasandha, thus ending the tyranny. Kings that had been captured and imprisoned were freed, finally allowing plans for the rajasuya to move forward.

After elaborate preparations under Krishna's supervision, the rajasuya ceremony was a magnificent success. All the foremost kings, sages, and brahmins of India were present with lavish accompaniment. Krishna deliberately misinterpreted Yudhishthira's comment that His feet should be washed, by proceeding to wash the feet of all guests, as well as clearing the leaf plates upon which people ate. The final act in the ceremony was the worship of the noblest man present, and Krishna was chosen for this honor. "By His grace alone all these rituals have become fruitful and mankind can attain the fourfold goals of *dharma* [justice], *artha* [worldly success], *kama* [pleasure or enjoyment], and *moksha* [liberation]. . . . The Lord is the root from which this variegated tree of the world has sprouted. . . . Krishna shines as the sun in the midst of His own rays."[2]

Yudhishthira's Lost Kingdom and the Pandavas' Exile

After the Pandava brothers emerged from the forest and won their beautiful bride Draupadi, they were still resented by their evil cousin Duryodhana of the Kauravas. The Pandavas and Kauravas were each given half the kingdom of their elders, though the Pandavas' half was considered less desirable. However, the Pandavas cleared the wilderness and developed the land with zeal and skill, and without complaint; and they built a fine city, crowning their eldest brother Yudhishthira as king.

But the jealous and scheming Duryodhana exploited Yudhishthira's weakness for gambling, cheating him of his kingdom. The Pandavas were forced into exile for thirteen years, during which Krishna saw to their spiritual training. They practiced austere disciplines and undertook heroic deeds, ever growing in wisdom, strength, and humility. After the exile period officially ended, the envious and manipulative Duryodhana refused to return any of the Pandavas' rightful land. Because of Duryodhana's intense greed, and despite Krishna's diplomatic peace mission, the great Mahabharata War became inevitable. Krishna led His chosen Pandavas to an extremely costly victory in this continental struggle.

> The entire life of the Pandavas is a great example to all devotees. They were most dear to Krishna, yet we find their lives to be filled with hardships. At one moment they were taken to the pinnacle of glory at the *Rajasuya*, when the whole of Bharatavarsha [India] rose up to acclaim them as emperors, and the next moment they were branded as slaves. . . . What is the lesson to be learned? God's ways are mysterious. He is not interested in our material prospects or our physical problems. The sole aim of the divine is to fulfill the cosmic purpose of our achieving unity with Him, and for that no means are neglected.[3]

Krishna's Noble Peace Mission Fails

At a council meeting for the Pandavas, their friends, and allies, Krishna proposed a course fair and acceptable to both Pandavas and Kauravas. Each side should be given half the kingdom and live in peace and harmony. Krishna said, *"Peace is always preferable to war, because in a war neither party really wins. Only suffering results. Thousands of women become widows."*[4] But Duryodhana's reply was defiant: "Let them achieve on the battlefield what they could not regain by gambling and can certainly not regain by negotiation." Krishna "did His best to make Duryodhana listen to reason . . . but when he refused to do so, it became apparent that the course of *dharma* was at cross-purposes with that of peace. Therefore, war became a necessity."[5] Krishna was equally related to both sides, and offered his Yadava army to one side and Himself to the other. Arjuna was given first choice, and unhesitatingly chose Krishna, while Duryodhana was equally happy to accept the Yadava army. Yudhishthira was completely torn between his love of peace and the requirements of justice, but he abided by Krishna's decision.

Krishna decided to make one final face-to-face appeal to Duryodhana, and the dialogue can be summarized as follows. Krishna tried to reason that the elders desired peace. Why wasn't Duryodhana willing to obey them? Why rush headlong into the destruction of so many? Duryodhana replied that the Pandavas had gambled away their kingdom voluntarily. Completion of their exile entitled them to live only as the king's subjects. Krishna warned Duryodhana not to mistake the Pandavas' love of peace for weakness. If they were denied their due, they would surely declare war, leading to loss of lives, poverty, famine, and suffering. Krishna said that everyone would curse the cause of the war, and Duryodhana would bear the brunt of their curses. But Duryodhana refused to bow down to anyone. Krishna then tried to negotiate in order to avoid war. He claimed that for peace, Yudhishthira was willing to settle for a small piece of land. Duryodhana was unwilling to negotiate. He refused to give the Pandavas anything. After realizing that Duryodhana could not be swayed, Krishna was direct and told him what was to come. He told Duryodhana that he had taken all the Pandavas' possessions in an unfair game of dice. He had humiliated their wife Drapaudi, and he had tried to burn them to death. Now he was trying to cheat them of their rightful heritage. Krishna warned that he would be forced to return it all, after he was defeated on the battlefield. In response to Krishna's warning, Duryodhana marched out of the assembly.

Krishna asked the Kauravas to bind up Duryodhana and make peace with the Pandavas. They summoned Duryodhana back into the assembly. Krishna asked him to swear by striking a pillar that he was ready for war. Duryodhana said it was below his dignity to negotiate with a lowly cowherd who was pleading on behalf of men who had been living in the forest like wild animals. Nothing could alter Duryodhana's evil path.

Declaration of War and Preparations

Both sides declared war, and the battlefield would be Kurukshetra (near today's New Delhi), inherited from the dynastic ancestors of both the Pandavas and Kauravas. King Kuru, progenitor of the dynasty, had prayed that all who died on that field would attain heaven. Commanders of the two armies met to decide on the rules of battle, for it was to be a war of righteousness, a just war. They decided that there would only be fighting from sunrise to sunset, none were to be attacked from the rear, those who surrendered were to be spared, and all duels would be between equals only, as well as other rules that were deemed to be in keeping with Dharma. But during the actual conduct of the war, most of these rules were abandoned.

Arjuna's Charioteer in the Mahabharata War

The Bhagavad Gita is Krishna's moral and spiritual advice to Arjuna just as the War began. Krishna's role as charioteer has been interpreted in many different ways through the ages. Arjuna sitting in the chariot, with Krishna holding a firm rein over four prancing white horses, is an allegory of our con-flicted human life. The chariot represents the body; Arjuna, the embodied soul, seated within; Krishna, the cosmic soul, who has ever been his companion, but whom he has not yet recognized as the Supreme; the four horses, our four mental faculties—mind, intellect, ego, and super-consciousness. Arjuna faced a violent crisis that seemed incompatible with his moral and spiritual aspirations. But he had the wisdom to recognize his helplessness without Krishna, to whom he handed over the reins of his life as the divine charioteer.

The Bhagavad Gita does not always look on human nature and the natural world as good and beautiful. Sometimes the sacred text describes grimness and disturbing dimensions of the social and physical environment. It seems to suggest that unless we have the courage to face existence as it is, we will never be able to arrive at a solution to its conflicting demands. A central theme of the Bhagavad Gita is reconciling, or bringing unity, between the inner, highest spiritual truth in ourselves, the practical exigencies of our lives, and the cosmic order or Dharma.[6]

The Pandavas' Tragic Victory and Gandhari's Curse

The Mahabharata War lasted eighteen days, and ended with the death of Duryodhana. The Pandavas won an empire at the cost of their sons. Krishna took on the dreaded task of comforting the parents of the Kauravas. Soon after this, as if both sides had not suffered enough, Ashvatthama, the son of the teacher of many of the Pandavas and Kauravas, enacted a diabolical plan for revenge against the Pandavas. Ashvatthama slipped into their tents by night and killed many, including some of the field generals, as well as Draupadi's sons. There was complete pandemonium as news of the midnight massacre spread. Ashvatthama was captured and condemned to centuries of banishment. A procession of royal women of both the Pandavas and Kauravas came to mourn their dead, as prophesied by Krishna. One woman who knew of Krishna's superhuman powers, Gandhari, asked Him: "Where are they now, my splendid sons who were like burning meteors? . . . O Krishna, my whole body is afire with grief." In her sorrow and anger she went on to curse Krishna, saying, "I pronounce this curse upon You and Your race: You shall become the slayer of Your own kinsmen thirty-six years from now. After having brought about the destruction of Your sons and kinsmen, You Yourself shall perish alone in the wilderness." Krishna humbly accepted her curse, saying *"Blessed are you, O Mother, for you have aided Me in the completion of My task. . . . With folded hands I gladly accept your curse!"* [7]

Righteous Cities: Hastinapura, Mithila, and Dwaraka

Yudhishthira's palace in Hastinapura, with Krishna's occasional help, became an abode of happiness led by an ideal emperor, reminding all citizens of stories about the wondrous days of Rama and His magnificent realm. Mithila, already famed for its rule by philosopher-kings, shined even more brightly, and its citizens thronged along decorated streets to have a glimpse of Krishna when He visited or even passed through. Kings and brahmins fell at Krishna's feet with devotion, ruling with a deep sense of love and knowledge. Krishna's own hometown, Dwaraka, was filled with abundance and enjoyed a status and prosperity hitherto unheard of throughout the land, with over three decades of splendor. Krishna's parents had nearly forgotten their son's divine birth and status, due to extended intimacy and familiarity. His father, however, asked for spiritual instruction and was made to rediscover his son's divinity. Krishna's mother shared her longing to have a glimpse of her six sons who were born before Krishna's advent, and He granted her wish. He also spent more time giving spiritual instruction, for His time on earth was ending.

The Curse of the Sages

However, years of prosperity eventually led to an inevitable decline. "Slowly, like a canker growing within a perfect rose, affluence was taking its inevitable toll. The high principles of physical fitness and spiritual brilliance which had characterized the previous generation were giving way to moral laxness and physical weakness. Krishna's own sons were no exception to this. No leniency would the Lord show to any just because they happened to have blood relationship with Him. The whole of creation was related to Him. The Lord knew that the Yadavas could not be checked by any other power and that He Himself would have to amputate the putrid arm. The time was ripe for the fruition of Gandhari's curse." To fulfill conditions of the curse, and to facilitate the unfolding of karmic developments, Krishna invited sages to visit Dwaraka. The men who had gathered to meet the sages were disrespectful and sarcastic with their questions, and so the sages pronounced, "An iron pestle . . . will be the instrumental cause of the destruction of your entire race." The men laughed off this announcement, but very soon one of Krishna's sons began writhing, and an iron pestle came out of his stomach. In terror, the men ran to the king with this story, and he directed a blacksmith to pulverize the iron pestle. The iron filings washed into the sea, having ill effects on fish and grass, and eventually on the livelihood of the people. Rumors of disturbing happenings circulated, and a nameless terror took hold of the people as greed, lust, and anger accelerated. Krishna alone knew the meaning of these events, and watched unmoved.[8]

15 – Delivering a Thematic and Complementary Message: Devotion to God through the Avatar and Selfless Action in the World

In this study we affirm that messages of Founders are not contradictory, but rather, complementary. The same twenty-five patterns apply to each and all of Their ministries. Each Teacher adds guidance to previous teachings under a new and integrated theme so as to assure humanity's progress. Their differences are due to changing cultural and historical condition, as well as humanity's developing capacities, requiring modified ritual and legal guidance. But Their spiritual teachings and virtues are essentially one, as They are agents of the same providential plan. The theme of Krishna's message is devotion to the Avatar and selfless action in the world. This theme weaves together all of Krishna's advice to Arjuna in the Bhagavad Gita, as well as His teachings that are recorded elsewhere. We have already touched on Krishna's teachings about God, the three primary forms of divine expression, dharma and karma, stations or castes, and the shift from Vedic ritual sacrifices to love-oriented devotional practices. We will now briefly review these teachings, adding comments on Krishna's views of samsara and moksha, the three major yogas, as well as the stages and aims of life.

God as Brahman-Atman

Krishna taught that God or Ultimate Reality is both beyond and within each part of the universe, including human experience. God is the absolute or supreme reality, representing infinite being, consciousness, and joy. This supreme reality creates, sustains, and transforms all lesser forms of reality. In its sustaining mode, Brahman-Atman takes the form of a personal God that can be embraced, worshiped, and symbolized in many ways. Some of Krishna's revelation was transmitted through the wisdom of other figures in the *Mahabharata,* just as some of Moses' revelation was transmitted through David and Isaiah; and some of Christ's teachings through Matthew and Paul. Yudishthira asked about the proper way of worshipping the Supreme Being, and Bhishma, the great grandfather of the Pandavas and Kauravas, answered in a way that revealed that Krishna is one with the Dharma and the Atman, or universal self, within all beings. "By meditating on Him and His manifold names, one can transcend all sorrow. He is the greatest source of energy, the highest penance, the Eternal Brahman. Surrender your heart and soul to Him, for He is the Lord of past, present, and future." Bhishma also said, "Follow the Truth always. Strive for it in thought, word, and deed. Practice self-denial. Be compassionate. Attain knowledge of the Supreme Brahman. This is the *dharma* of all *dharmas.* Know that where Krishna, the Universal Self, dwells, there *dharma* will ever be. And where *dharma* is, victory will inevitably follow."[9]

The Trimurti: Three Major Expressions of Divine Power

Krishna taught that there are three inter-related expressions of God's activity: the creative power (Brahma), the sustaining power (Vishnu, who occasionally descends or incarnates as an Avatar to renew dharma and save humanity), and the destroying or transforming power (Shiva). Krishna emphasized the sustaining and nurturing power of God, and His own role as Avatar, embodying and teaching divine love and devotion.

Dharma and Karma: Order and Consequences

Krishna taught that Dharma is the moral and spiritual order of the universe. It was revealed in the Vedas, but was now being revealed anew through Him. Dharma was being given a new form through Krishna's emphasis on love-oriented devotional practice, and ethically-oriented, or detached, action and service. Karma, or the law of action and consequences, had been focused on ritual sacrifices before Krishna's time. But He emphasized that the restraints and residues of karma could be overcome through loving devotion to the Avatar and detached action in the world. *"All creatures get their just deserts. The wheel of Time turns slowly, but in the end it encompasses the destruction of all things. . . . Each thing is created for a purpose. The moment that purpose is achieved, it will perish. . . . This is the case even with Me. I have created Myself on this earth for a purpose. It is not yet over. But the moment it is fulfilled, I will also die."* [10] Krishna encouraged followers to not sit idly, but to take action, especially for the cause of justice. *"As long as Duryodhana does not try to embody his evil thoughts into action, there is hope for him. But on the other hand, it is not correct for us to sit idly and tolerate adharma* [injustice]*."* [11]

Samsara and Moksha: Transient World and Attaining Release
Samsara meant that not only the world, but also heavens and hells were transient and ultimately unsatisfactory. However, Krishna placed the emphasis on transcendence, or salvation, through loving devotion to the Avatar, and detached action in the world. Release or liberation (*moksha*) from the transience of existence was now most readily available through surrender and detached love. Kunti, the mother of the Pandava brothers, said in a prayer to Krishna: "I thank You for not having given me comforts, I thank You for not having given me any wealth, for due to that I have realized that You are my only treasure. You alone are the wealth of those who have no other wealth. I do not care for kingdom or glory, but only to have Your blessed vision all my life." [12]

The Trimarga: Three Major Disciplines (Love, Work, and Knowledge)
Among the most remarkable features of the Bhagavad Gita is that it synthesizes and dignifies all three main paths of spiritual discipline, known as *yoga*, or yoking oneself to God. If Krishna had not redefined and synthesized the yogas, they may have become three separate religions. But in His hands they are all honored, dignified, and inter-related. Though Krishna emphasized the path of love and devotion (*bhakti yoga*), He showed its intimate relationship to the path of detached work (*karma yoga*) and the path of meditative knowledge (*jnana yoga*). People have differing temperaments that make them lean toward one of these three paths, and to reject the others. But Krishna commended and blended all three, showing how love, detached work, and spiritual wisdom are complementary and mutually beneficial processes. A fourth yoga has been called *raja yoga*, and it integrates some of the practices

of the three main yogas. Krishna described the yogas, *"At the beginning of time I declared two paths for the pure heart:* jnana yoga, *the contemplative path of spiritual wisdom, and* karma yoga, *the active path of selfless service."* He went on to describe raja yoga, *"Little by little, through patience and repeated effort, the mind will become stilled in the Self."* And He described bhakti yoga, *"To those steadfast in love and devotion I give spiritual wisdom, so that they may come to me."* [13]

Krishna taught that love, service, and wisdom are intimately connected. *"How noble are the trees. They live entirely for the sake of others. . . . People take shelter beneath them, and finally they give up their very lives to provide man with fuel. Man's life in this world is meaningful only to the extent that his energies, wealth, and intelligence are utilized for the good of others."* [14] Krishna expounded on the importance of love: *"Among those who love others, even if it is unrequited, there are two kinds—those who are by nature kind and loving and those like parents, who love their children without expecting reciprocation."* [15] Krishna also spoke of the need to be detached from this world: *"Clouds in the sky are scattered here and there by the wind. So also the Creator brings together and separates human beings. We have been parted physically from each other, but you are ever in my mind. Do not think your devotion to Me will go unrewarded, for it will enable you to cut the coils of mortal life and attain union with Me, who am the Infinite source of Bliss."* [16]

Four Stages, Aims, and Stations of Life

In ancient India the four stages (*asramas*) of life were described as: 1) the youthful learning years, 2) the house-holding years, 3) the service in retirement years, and 4) the free and wandering years. These were somewhat correlated with the four sequential aims (*purusartha*) of life: 1) sensual pleasure, 2) worldly success, 3) dutiful service, and 4) spiritual release. These stages and aims varied somewhat among the four stations (*varnas*) or castes: 1) brahmins or seers and teachers, 2) kshatriyas or rulers and warriors, 3) vaishyas or artisans and producers, and 4) shudras or laborers. Krishna supported this system but allowed more flexibility, giving priority to loving devotion and detached action.

16 – Renewing and Embodying Universal Virtues

As an Avatar, Krishna had been here before in the sense that His divine station is eternal, and had descended to restore righteousness many times over the ages. Each time of descent or incarnation, Dharma, or divine qualities, are taught anew. Krishna taught that, *"The divine qualities lead to freedom."* [17] These virtues, when observed by people in any and all stations of life, foster ever-widening benevolence. Krishna adapted this body of guidance to the situation in ancient India, as it transitioned from Vedic Brahmanism to the Faith decisively shaped by Him, which was later called Krishna Devotion.

Spiritual Virtues in Krishna's Revelation

Devotion-Faithfulness: *"Fill your mind with me; love me; serve me; worship me always. Seeking me in your heart, you will at last be united with me."* [18]

Gratitude-Reverence: *"Make every act an offering to me; regard me as your only protector."* [19]

Self-Discipline-Obedience: *"Those who overcome the impulses of lust and anger which arise in the body are made whole and live in joy."* [20]

Detachment-Patience: *"Perform work in this world . . . without selfish attachments, and alike in success and defeat."* [21]

Wisdom-Discernment: *"They live in wisdom who see themselves in all and all in them."* [22]

Social Virtues in Krishna's Revelation

Loving-kindness-Compassion: *"That one I love who is incapable of ill will, who is friendly and compassionate."* [23]

Service-Responsibility: *"Strive constantly to serve the welfare of the world. . . . Do your work with the welfare of others always in mind."* [24]

Respect-Tolerance: *"All those who take refuge in me, whatever their birth, race, sex, or caste, will attain the supreme goal; this realization can be attained even by those whom society scorns."* [25]

Justice-Righteousness: *"One should not behave towards others in a way which is disagreeable to oneself. This is the essence of morality."* [26]

Peace-Unity: *"All the scriptures lead to me; I am their author and their wisdom."* [27]

Material Virtues in Krishna's Revelation

Trustworthiness-Honesty: *"Be self-controlled, sincere, truthful, loving, and full of desire to serve."* [28]

Moderation-Balance: *"Those who eat too much or too little, who sleep too much or sleep too little, will not succeed in meditation. But those who are temperate in eating and sleeping, work and recreation, will come to the end of sorrow through meditation."* [29]

Generosity-Hospitality: *"Giving simply because it is right to give, without thought of return, at a proper time, in proper circumstances, and to a worthy person, is sattvic* [pure] *giving."* [30]

Creativity-Beauty: *"'Through selfless service, you will always be fruitful and find the fulfillment of your desires': this is the promise of the Creator."* [31]

Earthcare-Stewardship: *"Under my watchful eye the laws of nature take their course. Thus is the world set in motion; thus the animate and the inanimate are created."* [32]

17 – Abrogating the Old and Establishing the New: Ritual and Legal Guidance

Like Moses and Zoroaster, Krishna claimed to have the authority to modify and abrogate rituals and laws. In Krishna's case, this claim is especially powerful, because the rituals and laws were understood by the ancient Indians to be based on Dharma—the natural and moral order of the universe. Only a Figure like Krishna, an Avatar of God, could successfully change rituals and laws that had previously been foundational to ancient Indian society. What modification and abrogation did Krishna deem necessary in the decades preceding and following the Mahabharata War? How did His followers respond to these changes in the centuries that followed? In some respects, Krishna transformed Vedic rituals, but in other respects, He replaced them with devotional practices focused directly on Himself as a divine and loving presence.

There are a number of verses that show a transition from Vedic sacrifices to a more spiritually pure devotional practice. Krishna explains that while sacrifice is important, it is the thought behind it that makes the difference. *"The sattvic* [pure] *perform sacrifices with their entire mind fixed on the purpose of the sacrifice. Without thought of reward, they follow the teachings of the scriptures."* [33] Krishna also clarified that spiritual wisdom and understanding should be emphasized over rituals. *"Better indeed is knowledge than mechanical practice. Better than knowledge is meditation. But better still is surrender of attachment to results, because there follows immediate peace."* [34] These verses suggest that Vedic practices might have been effective if the motivation of the worshiper had been purified.

Below are verses showing a new love-oriented (*bhakti*) form of worship distinctive to Krishna's dispensation, and they may remind Christians of their worship forms. They show a shift from inner-focused detachment over to emotionally warmer and more outer-focused giving exercises. *"Whatever I am offered in devotion with a pure heart—a leaf, a flower, fruit, or water—I partake of that love offering. Whatever you do, make it an offering to me. . . . In this way you will be freed from the bondage of karma."* [35] Krishna, trying to show that outdated ritual practices were no longer necessary, explained that belief in Him was the new form of ritual practice. He said, *"I am the ritual and the sacrifice; I am true medicine. . . . I am the offering and the fire which consumes it, and He to whom it is offered."* [36]

Krishna became a central focus in the major festivals of the Hindu Faith including Holi (a spring harvest festival); Divali (a fall festival of lights and prosperity); Krishnajayanti (a summer celebration of Krishna's birth); daily darshans (ritual viewings of Krishna) that became popular among many Hindus; as well as elaborate ritual dramas about Krishna's life that express divine play (*lila*) as an uplifting, creative, and saving feature of life.

In terms of economic guidance, before Krishna's time, the ideal seemed to be a static economy, based on stable observance of dharma-based caste duties. After Krishna, the door was opened to greater social mobility and economic innovation, for He declared that all His devotees—whatever their birth, race, sex, or caste—could achieve the highest realization, even those scorned by society.[37] He renewed expectations that kings must be just and prefer peace to war, that the wealthy must be generous, that the strong must help the weak, and that all should contribute to social well-being.

18 – Human and Divine Qualities: Exemplifying a Dual Station

The world's major faith traditions differ widely in the degree of divinity conferred upon their Founders. Yet a comparative and open-minded study of scriptural stories shows evidence of Their dual station. They were human in some respects and divine in other respects, making it reasonable to interpret Them as Intermediaries between God and humanity.

Krishna's Human Station

As a child, Krishna was annoyed to find his foster mother occasionally missing when He was hungry. At times He shed tears of disappointment. There were also moments described when His lips trembled with fury, and that He feared His step-mother's punishments. As a young adult, He perspired from efforts to help people, saluted elders with humility, trembled when He thought that His father might be killed by King Salva; and He once said, *"You have discovered my weak point—that the only thing that can bind Me is the power of love."*[38] Arjuna also referred to Krishna's "gentle human form" in the Bhagavad Gita.

After the War, tears came to Krishna's eyes when He realized that Arjuna would soon discover his son's death. Later, Krishna's eyes filled with tears when He saw parents grieving for their lost sons. Finally, He was mortally struck in His heel by a deer hunter while lamenting the loss of family members. Some have wondered "why He allows Himself to get caught in the web of His own creation?" The answer is that "the Supreme Actor has to forget His true nature and allow Himself to be caught in the web of His own *maya* [illusive play] if He is to completely and satisfyingly enact the different roles."[39] Krishna was in the world and subject to karmic laws, but unlike mere mortals, He also shaped and transcended the world.

Krishna's Divine Station
As with the other Founders, stories of Krishna show trans-human powers. He is depicted as a Supreme Being—eternal, infinite, and self-manifesting. Many titles were given to Him, including Supreme Teacher of the World, Resplendent One, and Soul of All. He transcended the gods, and helped prepare humanity to dispense with them. The Bhagavata Purana declares that Krishna is God Himself.[40] As an Avatar, Krishna is viewed as God in human form, Who came to earth to reestablish righteousness. Krishna's most well-known incident of divine self-manifestation was to Arjuna in the Bhagavad Gita, where He was seen and described as a million divine forms—an unlimited variety of shapes and colors, numberless faces, decorated with heavenly jewels and beautiful garments, displaying unending miracles, the source of all wonders, as bright as a thousand suns rising together.

19 – The Light and the Word
As in other scriptural traditions, images of light and praises of the Word abound in Krishna's revelation. Krishna explains that revelation is like the light of the sun, *"The light of this knowledge shines like the sun, revealing the supreme Brahman."*[41] He also says that He Himself is the source of light and wisdom, *"I light the lamp of wisdom and dispel all darkness," "I am the silence of the unknown and the wisdom of the wise,"* and *"I am the sacred word and the sound heard in air."*[42] Through meditation and self-awareness, we too can become sources of light, *"As the sun lights up the world, the Self dwelling in the field is the source of all light in the field,"* and He says, *"Repeating in this state the*

divine Name, the syllable Om *that represents the changeless Brahman, you will go forth from the body and attain the supreme goal."*[43]

20 – Affirming Four Realms: Divine, Revelatory, Human, Natural

Hinduism contains some of the most elaborate and complex teachings on cosmology (or levels of reality) in the world's faith traditions. These teachings include areas that in the West are called cosmogony (or theory of origins), metaphysics, natural and revealed theology, epistemology, psychology, spiritual practice, holistic health, devotional literature, and rituals. Not all of this material can be described as consistent, however, for diverging perspectives live side by side. But Krishna integrated and synthesized the teachings that preceded Him. He also reinterpreted the major metaphysical and psychospiritual systems of His day, bringing consistency to them, adding new guidance, and uniting the many well-developed perspectives and practices of ancient India. Whereas Hinduism as a whole is not uniform, the teachings of Krishna are integrated and coherent, as we would expect from a Teacher with divine knowledge.

The Natural Realm

Prakriti is described as primordial matter, nature, a field of evolutionary energy. It traverses the natural, the human, and that part of the revelatory realm containing spiritual beings lower than Avatars. Prakriti is said to display three forces or tendencies (*gunas*): a) harmony and refinement (*sattva*), b) activity and passion (*rajas*), and c) passivity and dullness (*tamas*). Krishna explained, *"Knowledge of the Absolute is sattvic. Knowledge of duality is rajasic. The absence of knowledge is tamasic. . . . The forest is sattvic, the city is rajasic and the gambling dens are tamasic."*[44] Prakriti is set into evolutionary motion by its relation to *purusha* (spirit or consciousness). *"Prakriti is the agent, cause, and effect of every action, but it is Purusha that seems to experience pleasure and pain. Purusha, resting in prakriti, witnesses the play of the gunas born of prakriti."*[45] The relationship between purusha and prakriti is described as a lame man with good sight being carried by a blind man with strong legs. The natural realm, then, is a restless and creative interaction between matter and spirit; and as a whole, it is created by Brahma, the creative power of God. The natural realm and the human realm together are said to be the "abode of embodied beings" always undergoing a process of change. *"Everything that takes form, whether visible or invisible, will have an origin, and as it is trans-formed will become the next thing—like earthen clay transforming into a cup: the state in which it is a cup has only a relative reality."*[46] The gross elements of the natural realm are space, air, fire, water, and earth. The subtle elements are form, touch, sound, smell, and taste. Living things in the natural realm contain individual living selves, known as *jivas*. Animals and humans possess sense capacities and action capacities.

The Human Realm

The human being is said to have an individual soul or *jivatman*. We have a mind capacity, called *manas*, that engages in thinking, imagining, remembering, and more, along with the special action capacity of speech. We have unique access to the Atman, or universal self, dwelling within. Because the universal self dwells within each human being, we have the capacity to learn about higher realms of reality and to make moral and spiritual progress in response to renewed dharma (truth). Prakriti operates at the human level. *"When sattva predominates, the light of wisdom shines through every gate of the body. When rajas predominates, a person runs about pursuing selfish and greedy ends, driven by restlessness and desire. When tamas is dominant a person lives in darkness—slothful, confused, and easily infatuated."*[47] The varieties and challenges in the human condition are described in terms of ever-changing combinations of these three gunas (forces or tendencies). We are caught up in samsara—the contingencies of worldly existence, and the cycle of birth, death, and rebirth, which is best interpreted figuratively. We can make progress toward moksha, or release from the struggles of evolutionary existence. Especially through devotion to the Avatar and selfless action, we can rise above earthly existence and grow closer to God. As Krishna said, *"Adore me, make every act an offering to me, and you shall come to me."*[48]

The Revelatory Realm

As an Avatar, Krishna is viewed as Ultimate Reality in manifest and human form. The Bhagavata Purana describes Krishna as God Himself.[49] His deeds and words are understood as a message from God to humanity. They reveal divine love and grace, and provide spiritual wisdom and means of redemption. This revelation was meant not only for people of Krishna's day, but also for the worship and contemplation of posterity. Krishna taught that those who listen to the story of His life sanctify themselves. His story, along with

190

stories of other Avatars and Buddhas, has been embraced as a divine saga by Hindus. Contemporary, universally-minded Hindus believe that Krishna "is the expression of the redeeming love of God for man which manifests itself in different ages and in different lands, bringing spiritual enlightenment and bliss into the otherwise dreary life of humanity." It is also believed that Krishna "appears human and is yet divine. This has to be, for the object of the *avatar* is to show that a human birth with all its limitations can still be the means for a divine birth."[50]

That love of God manifests in many ages and lands is our central thesis. The revelatory realm also contains dharma, the Word or Truth, perhaps identical to mahat, or cosmic intelligence. Krishna explained that although this physical world may change, the spiritual world is eternal. *"The mountains of the Himalayas may shift their site, the earth may split into a thousand fragments, and the firmament itself with its myriad stars may fall down, but My words will never be futile."*[51] The revelatory realm also contains what have been called gods, goddesses, and spiritual beings, which can be understood as graspable attributes, aspects, and names of divine reality.

The Divine Realm

The highest of all realms is even higher than Brahma (the Creator), Vishnu (the Sustainer and the Avatars), and Shiva (the Transformer)—as exalted as these divine expressions may be. In Krishna's teaching, Brahman is the highest reality, the ultimate source from which all lower levels of reality emanate. It is beyond God in any form that can be revealed, the Absolute, the Godhead that contains all potential, both manifest and un-manifest. Krishna's teachings support the oscillating universe theory. Krishna said the universe has a day and a night, which we can take to mean alternating periods of being manifest and un-manifest, actual and potential. *"When the day of Brahma dawns, forms are brought forth from the Un-manifest; when the night of Brahma comes, these forms merge in the Formless again."*[52]

Brahman is far beyond human grasp, and we are dependent on Avatars, Revealers, and the Sacred Word to develop any intimation of It. Krishna, when describing Himself, said, *"I am infinite time, and the sustainer whose face is seen everywhere. . . . I am the goodness of the virtuous. . . . I am the silence of the unknown and the wisdom of the wise. . . . Wherever you find strength, or beauty, or spiritual power, you may be sure that these have sprung from a spark of my essence."*[53]

21 – Promising a Future Savior and a New Golden Age: The Kalki Avatar and the Universal Golden Age

The longing for a Messiah-like figure, a Savior, an Avatar, is one of the most powerful themes in the world's religious history. Those who are sensitive to the needs of their own times, viewing them in historical perspective, can discern a serious decline, and the need for renewed moral and spiritual guidance. A closely related theme is the vision of a golden age ushered in by the Savior. Krishna explained both His own advent and that of His Successors. *"Whenever dharma declines and the purpose of life is forgotten, I manifest myself on earth. I am born in every age to protect the good, to destroy evil, and to reestablish dharma."* [54] He also gives several descriptions of the conditions to come at the end of the dark or iron age (believed to be the current age). Krishna's devotees have expected Him to descend again as Kalki, the tenth Avatar, perhaps 2500 years after the Buddha, Who was the ninth. Kalki was expected to be the future punisher of evil-doers, the restorer of justice, and the One who would usher in a new Golden Age (*Krta Yuga*).

The end times are described in the Bhagavata Purana and the Vishnu Purana. They say that confusion will abound regarding the nature of true religion. Scriptures will be ignored and even condemned, and vows and duties will not be observed. Material wealth will be the only accepted criterion of status, and clothing, rather than character or excellence, will be the only sign of success. Force and violence will determine whose views would prevail. Marriage will be determined by sexual attraction, rather than social suitability, and family bonds will break down. Dishonesty and greed will abound in the marketplaces and ruling assemblies, unskilled people will occupy high positions, and anxiety and fear will oppress people everywhere.

During these end times the Kalki Avatar will arise to establish a new Golden Age for humanity. His mission will be to *"show the way, the truth, and the life to humanity. Such an incarnation is an avatar, an embodiment of God on earth."* [55] What will the Golden Age be like? *"The minds of the people will become pure as flawless crystal, and they will be as if awakened at the conclusion of a night. And these men, the residue of mankind, will thus be transformed . . . And these offspring will follow the ways of the Krta Age."* [56] The Krta or Golden Age will be characterized by unprecedented excellence, harmony, and peace.

22 – Essential Unity of the Revealers through the Ages

If all of the Avatars, past and future, are divine, then They are essentially one, even though They appear in different bodies and in different cultural settings. This is a difficult truth to grasp, and it mystified Arjuna, Krishna's disciple. When Krishna said that He had "told the secret" of the eternal dharma to His predecessor Vivasvat, it sounded very strange to Arjuna. How could a secret be passed on to one who lived before? But its truth becomes apparent if we realize that there is essential unity among all the Revealers through the ages, because They are all agents of the same, and the only, God. Just as Christ could say "before Abraham was, I am," Krishna could say that, before the Manus of past ages, He knew the eternal law of God.

Krishna tried to explain the paradox that He was both in the world and engaged in its activities, and beyond the world and aware of future developments. *"I take birth in various forms, constantly changing myself, in order to protect Virtue and to establish it. . . . In every cycle I have to repair the causeway of Virtue, and I am born in diverse forms, out of my desire to do good to my creatures."* [57] Krishna was speaking as the One God Who guides the world at intervals, reestablishing virtue, coming in the forms of Avatars and Buddhas.

23 – Laying Enduring Foundations: Shaping Kingship and Purifying Devotion

Because They are greater than human, Founders establish institutions that last much longer than the institutions invented and arranged by mortal leaders, no matter how much authority is bestowed upon them. Krishna guided Yudhishthira as a model of the universal king. *"The king should always bear himself toward his subjects as a mother toward the child of her womb. As the mother, disregarding those objects that are most cherished by her, seeks the good of her child alone, even so should kings conduct themselves."* [58] Compassion and righteousness must guide the universal king in ruling the people. This standard directly influenced the Mauryan Dynasty (323–184 BCE) and the Gupta Dynasty (350–540 CE).

Some of the traditions that grew from Krishna's ministry were mentioned above under ritual and legal guidance. Here we add only a few brief points. Krishna, like the other early Divine Educators, reduced the power of the gods, as well as the rigidity and complexity of rituals. He mitigated the dominance of the priesthood and introduced flexibility into caste law, while tempering the influence of speculative abstraction. He also unified the yogas and the philosophy of prakriti and purusha (nature and spirit) under a devotional or love-oriented theme, strengthening the practice of warm reverence for parents, religious teachers, and holy ones.

In Krishna's later years, both kings and brahmins washed His feet, and He passed this quality of reverence on to the holy ones and sages who would carry on his devotional tradition, saying, *"Know that I am ever present in the holy ones, the sages. They are My reflections and therefore they should be adored with the same faith with which you adore Me. That indeed is My true worship, not the worship of images with costly offerings."* [59]

24 – Renewing Scriptural Guidance: The Bhagavad Gita and the Uddhava Gita

The Bhagavad Gita and the Uddhava Gita contain the essence of Krishna's teachings. Though the Mahabharata as a whole is not considered scripture by Krishna's devotees, it contains much of the sacred story of their Lord, and so is essential for devotional life. The Vishnu Purana, the Bhagavata Purana, and the Harivamsa are scriptures completing the life and lessons of Krishna. Other Hindu scriptures seen as foundational are the four Vedas: Rig Veda, Sama Veda, Yajur Veda, and Atharva Veda, as well as the principal Upanishads. Most Hindus, however, consider Krishna's teaching and story to be of more saving power than the older Vedic literature.

25 – Generating Civilization Anew: A New Golden Age with Minds Awake and Pure

What is the ideal civilization envisioned by devotees of Krishna? Though there have been many social visions among Hindus, Krishna's teachings offer a coherent vision, one that was partly realized in the Mauryan and Gupta Empires. The Kalki Avatar was envisioned as a world Savior who will overcome the very foundations of evil and darkness, bringing about a world civilization. His Golden Age will not be for a single region or society or even an empire, but for the whole world. Its brightness will be in stark contrast to the decline and depravity of the Dark Age, which many Hindus say is ending in our own day.

With minds awakened and pure as crystal, morality, spirituality, and reverence for scripture will abound. Differentiated roles and duties of global society will be embraced dutifully. Prosperity will come to all lands. Knowledge and wisdom will be widespread. New arts will flower, beautifying the world. Krishna said, *"Wherever you find strength, or beauty, or spiritual power, you may be sure that these have sprung from a spark of my essence."* [60] He also described how to achieve spiritual refinement, *"Control of the mind and control of the senses, tolerance and perception, practicing the austerities inherent in one's duty, truthfulness and compassion, mindfulness and contentment, generosity and dispassion, shame for wrongs done, faith accompanied by charity, modesty and simplicity, and turning one's vision inward to the Self. . . . These are the effects of sattva* [spiritual refinement]." [61] This is a glimpse of the civilization envisioned in Krishna's revelation.

- 11 -
Buddha: Background and Mission

To understand and appreciate how Siddhartha Gautama became one of the most celebrated and influential Figures in history, and indeed became the "Light of Asia," we must look at several important aspects of His context and background. Just as before the rise of other great Teachers, there was a decline of the previous faith tradition. Krishna's great devotional synthesis had broken down, and religion in India had slipped back into rigid ritualism and intense theological dispute. There was growing restlessness in the face of corruption, institutional instability, and violence. There was an intensifying need for One to arise and renew the ancient, abiding truths. Another Savior was needed to re-inspire and redirect the people. Siddhartha Gautama rose to this call.

1 – Continuity with Previous Dispensations: Former Avatars and Buddhas, Hindu Decline, and Spiritual Revolt

As we have seen, divinely guided Teachers do not appear out of the blue. They have Predecessors and are part of a revered lineage of saving Figures of great antiquity, arising at times of historic need. They are understood as integral to the dharmic order guiding humanity. The expectation of periodic Enlightened Ones was especially pronounced in ancient India, as we saw in the story of Krishna. The Indian context of expectation needs special emphasis in the case of Buddha because many Westerners today have become fascinated with Buddhism, and tend to believe He was free of cultural, historical, and even religious influences. Westerners sometimes interpret Him in an abstract, impersonal way that distorts His historical setting and His deep spiritual significance. Buddha said: *"I have seen an ancient Path, an ancient road traversed by the rightly enlightened ones of former times."* [1]

197

Former Avatars, Buddhas, and Tathagatas

For at least a thousand years before Buddha's time, people in India were familiar with the concept of the Samma Sambuddha—the Teacher of Supreme Enlightenment who appears on earth when the knowledge of the Dharma or Path fades. The perfectly Enlightened One came as a welcome member of a series of Enlightened Ones who came throughout the ages. He was equivalent to an Avatar as understood centuries earlier in Krishna's day. Buddhism inherited a periodic understanding of the religious past. "Numerous 'Buddhas' appear successively at suitable intervals. Buddhism sees itself not as the record of the sayings of one man who lived in Northern India about 500 BC. His teachings are represented as the uniform result of an often repeated irruption of spiritual reality into this world."[2]

It was said that Enlightened Ones caused the wheel of Dharma to revolve, and They brought salvation to a whole era. Though omniscient, They clarified paths of good and evil, offering practical means of attaining release from the fetters of this material world, for these are the deeper needs of finite human beings, and they were especially acute in Buddha's day.

Jatakas were stories about previous Buddhas, and how "our" Buddha (Gautama) related to them. These stories reinforced the idea that Buddha was not the only one of His kind. The Jatakas spoke of twenty-four Buddhas or Tathagatas (Those Who have fully arrived), the last few of whom were said to be in our present eon. The earliest known Buddha of the series was Dipankara, the Kindler of Lights, believed to have spoken of a future Buddha, *"perfect in knowledge and conduct, well-gone, a world-knower, unsurpassed, a leader of men to be tamed, a teacher of gods and men."* He *"will turn the wheel of the highest Dharma, preside over a harmoniously united body of Disciples, and both gods and men will listen . . . and believe."* And that one day He would become *"the weal and happiness of the many, out of compassion for the world."*[3]

The very same phrases and ideas were repeated in later passages, including some of Buddha's own succession prophecies about Maitreya (Kindness). Gautama spoke of past and future Buddhas: *"In this auspicious eon three leaders have there been: Kakusandha, Konagamana and the leader Kassapa too. I am now the perfect Buddha; and there will be Maitreya too before this same auspicious eon runs to the end of its years."*[4] He clearly prophesied a future Buddha Who would come after Him: *"There will arise in the world an Exalted One named Metteyya. He will be . . . Fully Awakened, abounding in wisdom and goodness, happy, with knowledge of the worlds . . . a Buddha, even as I am now."*[5] Buddhas do not arise until righteousness declines to an alarming degree, and humanity falls into deep spiritual degradation. Leaders are corrupt and multitudes reel in despair. What was India like before Buddha arose?

Vedic and Hindu Decline

People of ancient India, like the ancient Chinese and Middle Eastern peoples, believed there was once a golden age when the boundary between heaven and earth, the rift between human and divine, had been gloriously absent. Bounty, prosperity, and peace prevailed. Whether or not such a mythic background had any historic basis, there were widespread beliefs that periodic renewal was necessary to bring back the ancient path of harmony and righteousness.

Vedic Brahmanism maintained the four-level caste system that included brahmin priests; kshatriya rulers and warriors; vaishya farmers, stockbreeders, and merchants; and shudra laborers or slaves. Priests gave this system sacred significance, making it difficult to alter. Despite Krishna's universal moral and spiritual teachings and inclusive practices, memory and aspiration faded over the centuries. Priests established an ever tighter grip on the rituals, writings, and caste laws, thus keeping themselves in power. Caste expectations stifled any creative social or spiritual movement. This deeply conservative orientation inevitably brought social and spiritual decline.

Spiritual-Intellectual Revolt: The Upanishads

Between 800 and 700 BCE, spiritual and intellectual experimentation sprung up in northwestern India. Sages transmitted to those who "sat near" esoteric teachings on the connections between the deep self or soul (atman) and the divine ground of all reality (Brahman). These insights were rebellious, because they suggested that salvation did not depend on ritual sacrifices or incantations; but rather, salvation was available within. Absolute and eternal reality abounds within, and could be accessed with a new knowledge yoga (jnana). The ultimate discovery was formulated as *"That thou art!"* meaning, that which we can find deep within ourselves is ultimately identical to Supreme Reality. Unbeknown to ordinary awareness, we abide in eternity. Admittedly, this realization was not easily graspable by the multitudes who remained absorbed in the dualities and false contradictions of worldly existence. Yet proper meditative exercises, along with guided study with advanced souls could bring liberation—liberation both from the Vedic priests and their rituals on one hand, and from the all-too-earthly caste system on the other.

2 – Arising to Guide Humanity in the Worst of Times: Spiritual Restlessness, Political Oppression, and Economic Exploitation in Northern India

Despite the creative revolt against the ritual domination of brahmin priests, most people were left spiritually adrift. Multitudes were disenchanted with the rigidities of Brahmanic Hinduism, but alternatives were not yet deemed satisfactory. The old securities were breaking down, but a widespread spiritual solution was not yet in view. Economic and technological advances brought greater power to a few, but the vast majority feared the prospects in this life and the next. It was a time filled with anxiety.

A number of religious and philosophical historians have pointed out that humanity seems to have undergone a major change-of-consciousness between 800 and 200 BCE, through the influence of such foundational figures as Zoroaster, Isaiah, Confucius, Mahavira, Buddha, Socrates, and Plato. Before these pivotal centuries, humanity took its place in the cosmic and social order for granted, and lived without radical questioning of the way things were. Beliefs and traditions were more stable, and the notion of the choice-making individual, who is both restless and capable of mastering his fate, had not fully emerged.

Karl Jaspers, a twentieth century philosopher and cultural historian, called this period centered about 2500 years ago the Axial Age. Writers who developed this theme maintained that our basic conceptions of history, the world, and civilization began during this crucial 600-year period. Four very different areas of the world—China, India, Persia, and the Eastern Mediterranean—established similar foundational notions: that we must not rely on traditions of ancestors without question; that scripture should not be for a private elite, but for everyone; that the highest principles and realities can be found within; that human life contains a great deal of disruption, tragedy, and pain; that self-conscious ethics and spiritual discipline are more likely to lead to progress than are appeasing the gods or using magical techniques; and that God or the Ultimate Realm demands compassion and justice, more than ritual sacrifice. Who introduced these new perspectives?

Zoroaster taught Persians a strong ethical monotheism, distinguishing good and evil sharply, and depicting the soul as free and responsible for aligning itself with powers of goodness and light. Isaiah challenged the mythical certainties of the ancients, warning Israel that God judges her through domination by enemies. Confucius made the highest ideals of the Chinese ancients a matter of conscious selection and cultivation, rather than unconscious tradition. Mahavira, the founder of Jainism (perhaps an older contemporary of Buddha), taught asceticism as a means of heroically transcending human impurities. Buddha, as we will soon see, was an exemplar of the highest Axial Age principles, emphasizing self-conscious compassion and the spiritual transcendence of suffering. Socrates and Plato challenged ancient Greek traditions, while pointing to ethical and spiritual universals discernible by the mind. Axial Age teachings share strong family resemblances, as if humanity were undergoing a sea-change.

Economic Exploitation and Religious Ferment in the Ganges Plain

What was the immediate social and cultural context addressed by Buddha? In the middle of the first millennium BCE, northeastern India was in a period of intense religious ferment, accelerated by the rise of urban commercial centers and the breakdown of old political systems. "Power was passing from the old partnership of King and Temple to the merchants. . . . The market economy also undermined the status quo: merchants could no longer defer obediently to the priests and aristocracy. . . . A new urban class was coming into being, and it was powerful, thrusting, ambitious and determined to take its destiny into its own hands. It was clearly in tune with the newly emerging spiritual ethos."[6]

What was this new spiritual ethos? In response to the breakdown of the old spiritual ways, to the urban transition, and to the resulting confusion and anomie, many felt the frailty and pain of human life quite acutely. Young men longed for "homelessness"—a taking to the open road, a spiritual renunciation in search of new and better paths to inner peace and social harmony. These wandering monks were not perceived as drop-outs from society. On the contrary, royalty, merchants, and wealthy householders vied for the privilege of feeding them. The homeless seekers were spiritual pioneers, offering hope for bewildered masses. Monks were seen as a productive response to spiritual crisis.

All castes were mingling, and so the caste-system was weakening, and there was also intense discussion of new social and spiritual ideas. The cities became more exciting and threatening places that offered trade, gambling, theater, dancing, prostitution, drinking, and a wide-ranging arena of spiritual experimentation. Kingdoms were being transformed into efficient bureaucracies with armies that were more loyal to their kings than to their ethnic tribes and clans. Planned violence was a frequent tool for controlling trade routes and amassing wealth. Ritual sacrifices seemed increasingly irrelevant, but abandoning them left spiritual voids that were growing wider and left people searching for answers. The metaphysical approach of the Upanishads could not satisfy the spiritual hungers of people on the Ganges Plain. The times were calling desperately for a Buddha.

3 – Advent Prophesied and Expected: Heavenly and Earthly Events Prepare the Way

All the Teachers in our study were specifically predicted and expected, illustrating Their spiritual significance and pivotal role in the unfolding of humanity's development. Higher levels of reality were involved in Their advent, marking dramatically the stories carried through the ages in scriptures. Buddhists believe that before His birth, Buddha was in Tusita Heaven, a sort of staging ground for His descent into this world.[7] He was born into a royal family, to King Suddhodana and Queen Mahamaya, that could trace its lineage back to the first king who ruled at the beginning of the current cycle of time.

Soon after Gautama was born, His father, king of the Sakyas, summoned fortune-tellers to cast light on his son's future. They said that if He embraced the world, He would become a world ruler, but if He renounced the world, He would become a world redeemer. Asita, the great seer, came to the palace of the ruler of the Sakyas, thirsting for true Dharma. In wonderment he looked upon the infant Buddha. To the king he said: "He is born who shall discover the extinction of birth, which is so hard to win. Uninterested in worldly affairs he will give up his kingdom. By strenuous efforts he will win that which is truly real . . . and remove the darkness of delusion from this world. The world is carried away in distress on the flooded river of suffering. . . . Across this river he will ferry the world. . . . He shall proclaim the path which leads to salvation, as to travellers who have lost their way."[8]

4 – Auspicious Signs, Birth, and Intimations of Greatness: A Heavenly Elephant and Insight under a Rose-Apple Tree

Stories of the Teachers include heavenly signs, viewed astronomically or spiritually, that mark Their births. As we have seen, divine interventions were part of the birth stories of Moses, Zoroaster, and Krishna. Such stories describe supernatural or paranormal circumstances surrounding Their births. Buddha's birth is no exception. Buddha's father, Suddhodana, the king of the Sakyas, was pure in conduct, and beloved of the Sakyas. He had a wife, beautiful and steadfast, who was called the Great Maya (Mahamaya) from her resemblance to the goddess Maya. One day she conceived the fruit of her womb, but without any defilement. Just before her conception she had a dream. A white elephant seemed to enter her body. She bore in her womb the glory of the dynasty. Pure herself, she longed to withdraw into the pure forest, so she set her heart on going to Lumbini, a delightful grove. And a son was born to the queen, for the benefit of the world. He came out of her side, without causing her any pain, and He appeared like one descended from the sky, born in full awareness. Instantly He walked seven steps, and spoke these words full of meaning for the future: *"For enlightenment I was born, for the good of all that lives."* [9]

Legends grew around Buddha's birth. It was said that "the worlds were flooded with light at his birth. The blind so longed to see his glory that they received their sight; the deaf and dumb conversed in ecstasy of the things that were to come. Crooked became straight; the lame walked. Prisoners were freed from their chains and the fires of hell were quenched. . . . Only Mara, the Evil One, did not rejoice." [10]

Because of Asita's prophecy, the king took great pains to shield his son from discomfort and any evidence of life's frailties, for he wanted his son to embrace the world and become a universal monarch, rather than renounce the world and become a monk. So His upbringing was luxurious, surrounded with pleasure and bounty at every turn. At the contest for His bride, Yasodhara, a neighboring princess, who was said to be majestic, dignified, and graceful, Gautama's evil-minded cousin, Devadatta, tried to prevent others from taking part in the competition by killing an elephant and leaving it blocking the city gate. Gautama removed the elephant easily, bested all comers in the contest, and won the bride. [11]

Among the clearest early signs of the message and mission that Gautama later developed were His experiences, which may have occurred during His late teen years, of fleeing into the forest and meditating under a rose-apple tree. [12] This time spent in the forest as a teen is a story of discovery foreshadowing what Gautama would rediscover later in His six-year search after leaving home. It was an early version of the new Dharma He would teach and exemplify after His enlightenment.

Even amidst the allurement of the finest opportunities for sensuous enjoyment, the young Prince felt no contentment. In the hope that a visit to the forest might bring Him some peace, He left the palace with the king's consent. In the countryside He saw the soil being ploughed, and the land was littered with tiny creatures who had been injured or killed from the plough's shears. This sight grieved the Prince as deeply as if He had witnessed the slaughter of His own kinsmen. He reflected on the generation and passing of all things. In a solitary spot at the foot of a rose-apple tree, His mind became stable and concentrated. When he had achieved mental stability, He was suddenly freed from all desire for objects or cares of any kind, and felt a sense of the highest rapture and joy. When He thus gained insight into the realities of disease, old age, and death in this world, He lost at the same moment all self-intoxication. All doubt and lassitude disappeared, sensuous excitements could no longer influence Him, and His mind was free of any contempt for others.

5 – Divine Commission: Reflection on Nirvana, Four Passing Sights, Celestial Messenger, and the Great "Going Forth"

Several stories in Buddhist literature can be interpreted as a divine call—a providential indication that palace life was a barrier to spiritual insight, and that a great mission to help humanity transcend suffering awaited beyond the gates. In His restless youth, Gautama seemed to forget His true identity and destiny, but there were several powerful reminders.

Once, a beautiful Sakya maiden, Kisagotami, was taken with the Prince's lovely appearance. "Blissful is the mother, and blissful is the father of one such as this, and blissful is the woman with a husband like him."[13] Buddha was deeply affected when He first heard of the concept of nirvana, "When he heard the sound of the word Nirvana, he listened with rapt attention . . . [and] meditated on it." In gratitude to Kisagotami for inspiring Him, He gave her a costly string of pearls as a "teacher's fee." Back at the palace, the young women of Gautama's harem entertained Him with seductive songs, but in His own mind, the gods had placed litanies of verses praising detachment. Eventually, Gautama fell asleep, as did the harem. Later, He woke up and found the women slumbering and snoring, laying in "immodest attitudes," their beauty and attractiveness gone. Gautama was filled with disgust and nausea, and thought of the women as "ignorant ones," and "like fish caught in a net."[14]

The most well-known portrayal of Gautama's call is called the "Four Passing Sights." Though His father had given strict orders that the whole court should shield the Prince from all contact with sickness, decrepitude, and death, the gods arranged for His spiritual education. One day, Gautama saw an old man for the first time. The man was broken-toothed, gray-haired, bent over, and trembling, and Gautama learned the reality of old age. Another day, He encountered a body racked with a painful sickness, lying on the roadside, and He learned the reality of disease. A third day, He came upon a corpse, and learned the reality of death. Finally, He saw a monk with a shaven head, yellow robe, and a begging bowl, and He learned the reality of spiritual withdrawal from the world. These experiences symbolized the future Buddha's realization that life's fulfillment was not to be found in the material realm. After seeing these four sights, Gautama wondered, *"Life is subject to age and death. Where is the realm of life in which there is neither age nor death?"* [15]

The story most like the divine call of the other Founders is Gautama's encounter with a celestial messenger. Once while the Prince was meditating on questions of suffering, He beheld a venerable figure, a holy man, who told the future Buddha, "Troubled at the thought of old age, disease and death, I have left my home to seek the path of salvation. . . . Everything changes, and there is no permanency; only the words of Buddhas are immutable. . . . I have retired into an unfrequented dell to live in solitude. . . . I devote myself to the one thing needful." Gautama asked, *"Can peace be gained in this world of unrest?"* The celestial messenger spoke of correlatives: heat and cold, good and evil, bliss and suffering—each member implies the other. If a lost man does not find the road, it is not the fault of the road; if a sick man does not avail himself of a physician, it is not the fault of the physician; or if a spiritually blind man does not seek the help of a Spiritual Guide, it is not the fault of the Guide.

The Prince was delighted with these noble words, and said, *"Thou bringest good tidings, for now I know that my purpose will be accomplished."* The messenger encouraged the Prince to act quickly, for no time could be inopportune for waking the world. With great joy, Gautama declared, *"Now is the time to sever all ties that would prevent me from attaining perfect enlightenment."* The celestial messenger replied, "Thou art the Tathagata [the fully arrived one]." The messenger also called Him the King of Truth, and told Him not to forsake the straight path of righteousness, but that He should let heavenly wisdom guide His steps. He told Buddha that He would be the One to "enlighten the world and save mankind from perdition." Gautama was filled with resolve. *"I have awakened to the truth and I am resolved to accomplish my purpose. . . . I will go out from my home to seek the way of salvation. . . . Verily, I shall become a Buddha."* [16]

6 – Struggling in Solitude: Six Years in the Forest, Testing the Teachings of Brahmins, Withstanding Temptation, Enlightenment under the Bodhi Tree

After leaving home, Gautama shaved His head, put on a monk's robe, and went in search of several leading brahmin teachers. In light of His earlier experiences, the next six years appear to be preparation for His future mission. It was a time of self-purification and testing, as He learned about attractive but limited paths of merely human questing.

First, He studied with Arada Kalama, but He soon saw the limitations of his approach, and quickly mastered all that he could teach. Second, He studied with Udraka Ramaputra, and though He reached a higher stage of meditative awareness, was still not satisfied that this path led to tranquility and nirvana. Third, He joined a band of ascetics and practiced austerities. In His desire for solitude, He emaciated His body for six years, and carried out a number of strict methods of fasting. Though His body began to waste away, His glory and majesty remained unimpaired, and He often brought joy to those who met Him. After a time, however, it became clear that this kind of excessive self-torture wore out His body without any useful result. After some time, He reasoned as follows: *"This is not the Dharma which leads to . . . emancipation. That method which some time ago I found under the rose-apple tree, that was more certain in its results."* [17]

Enlightenment

Gautama's decision not to continue with the ascetic path was, more positively, a decision to pursue what became known as the Middle Way between austerity (as in the forest) and indulgence (as in the palace). It was also a decision to resume the path begun under the rose-apple tree—a disciplined path of compassionate contemplation. In preparation for His first meal, He went into the Nairanjana River to bathe. Nandabala, the daughter of the overseer of the cowherds, happened to pass by and she begged Him to accept some milk-rice from her. This meal allowed Him to gain the strength He needed to win enlightenment. He walked over to the Bodhi Tree and made a vow to win enlightenment. He said, *"I shall not change this My position so long as I have not done what I set out to do!"* [18]

Buddha described His enlightenment in this way. *"When the real nature of things becomes clear to the ardent, meditating Brahmana, then all his doubts fade away, since he has understood the cessation of causation."* [19] Upon achieving enlightenment He viewed all of karmic history, the entire range of right and wrong views, the multitudes of beings and their inability to escape death, the Four Noble Truths, and impermanence.

The story of Mara, the Tempter, illustrates other aspects of Buddha's enlightenment. Mara attacked in the form of desire, parading three voluptuous women with their tempting retinues. When the Buddha-to-be remained unmoved, the Tempter switched his guise to the lord of death. His powerful hosts assailed the aspirant with hurricanes, torrential rains, and showers of flaming rocks, but the weapons found no target to strike and turned into flower petals. When, in final desperation, Mara challenged His right to do what He was doing, Gautama touched the earth, whereupon the earth responded, thundering, "I bear you witness." Gautama's meditation deepened through watch after watch until His mind pierced at last the bubble of the universe. The Great Awakening had arrived. Gautama's being was transformed and He emerged the Buddha. The event was of cosmic import. All created things filled the morning air with their rejoicings, but Mara was waiting with one last temptation. Who could be expected to understand? How could speech-defying revelation be translated into words? Why not slip at once into nirvana? But Buddha answered, *"There will be some who will understand,"* and Mara was banished. [20]

Buddha spoke "doubt-dispelling utterances." He talked about overcoming cravings, *"Having cut off craving, I have rid myself of defilement. The dried up asravas [impurities] do not flow. The road of craving has been cut off, and is no longer there. This then is the end of suffering."* [21] He taught that by mastering our cravings, we can achieve enlightenment, *"Now I have seen thee, house-builder: never more shalt thou build this house. The rafters of sins are broken. The ridge-pole of ignorance is destroyed. The fever of craving is past: for my mortal mind is gone to the joy of the immortal Nirvana."* [22]

7 – Declaration and First Followers: Two Merchants, Five Monks, First Sermon

After enlightenment, Buddha reflected for a time on His mission. *"I now desire to turn the wheel of the excellent law . . . to give light to those enshrouded in darkness, and to open the gate of Immortality."* [23] Then two merchants passed by, offering food, and Buddha thanked them with a few words of Dharma. As a result of these good tidings they became His first lay disciples. In Benares at the deer park, Buddha met His former companions, the five ascetic monks he had befriended during His period of austerities. At first they were repelled by Him because He had gained weight and seemed to have lost His discipline. But natural and spiritual attraction led them to hear His story and message, and they became the first sangha, or Buddhist religious order. Buddha clarified His new status with them. *"Do not call the Tathagata by His name nor address Him as 'friend', for He is the Buddha, the Holy One. The Buddha looks with a kind heart equally on all living beings, and they therefore call Him 'Father.'"* [24] The first sermon was about the Middle Way between asceticism and self-indulgence, the Four Noble Truths, the Eightfold Path, as well as the doctrines of no-self, impermanence, and interdependent origination, all of which will be explored in the next chapter. The Buddhist view of these lessons is that they set in motion, once again, the Wheel of Dharma, with all its saving-power for humanity.

8 – Overcoming Powerful Opposition: Brahmins, Devadatta, and Ajatasattu

Great Teachers and Revealers always evoke jealousy and hatred from those who feel threatened by Their influence and by the devotion shown to them by the multitudes. This pattern of opposition is usually both external and internal. It comes from religious and civil leaders who experience the impact of the Founder's mission, as well as from supposed followers who want more recognition and authority than they are granted. In Buddha's case, external opposition came from brahmins and a prince, while internal opposition came from a disenchanted monk.

Many brahmins resented the prestige Buddha gained, and resorted to false rumors to tarnish His name. The sangha was even accused of murdering a female ascetic. Observing this pattern of false accusation, Buddha said: *"Some recluses and brahmins are vain and empty liars, and misrepresent me contrary to facts . . . saying 'The recluse Gotama is a conjurer and he knows a conjuring technique by means of which he lures away the followers of other sects.'"* [25] It has been plausibly suggested that the reason Buddhism almost disappeared from its Indian homeland in 1000 CE was because, over the centuries, many brahmins maliciously depicted it as an atheistic belief system. Such a depiction distorts Buddha's true teaching about Ultimate Reality, as we will see.

There was also internal opposition from Devadatta, Buddha's cousin and rival from the days of their youth, who was an ambitious man of ability and deceptiveness.[26] Though he joined the sangha, he was never devoted to his Master. When Buddha was asked by other monks why Devadatta opposed Him, Buddha suggested this pattern was very old indeed. About eight years before Buddha's death, Devadatta became very focused on his own power base, and utterly resented Buddha's hold over the sangha. He sought Prince Ajatasattu, King Bimbisara's son, to win his support, and succeeded in forming a strong alliance with him. Devadatta soon approached Buddha, and proposed to Him in front of the monks, that he become His successor. Buddha rejected this idea, explaining that the Dharma and the discipline were sufficient to guide the spiritual, social, and material life of the sangha. Devadatta was furious and vowed vengeance.

Devadatta approached Ajatasattu again, proposing that the prince kill his father, Bimbisara, while Devadatta kill the Buddha. Their initial attempts failed, but later, Ajatasattu arrested his father and starved him to death. Now Ajatasattu was king and backed Devadatta's treacherous plans. Devadatta's malevolent attempts failed, and Ajatasattu became a lay follower of Buddha. Then Devadatta tried to bring about a schism by forming a separate community of monks that adopted a more stringent discipline. Buddha sent Sariputta and Moggallana to persuade them to return, and they succeeded in reuniting the sangha. After this, Devadatta became seriously ill and died several months later.

9 – Rejection by the People

It was not only religious and civil leaders who opposed Buddha's mission. Townspeople also showed resentment over His growing influence. They spread criticism about Buddha and the sangha, saying: *"The recluse Gotama gets along by making [us] childless, the recluse Gotama gets along by making [us] widows, the recluse Gotama gets along by breaking up families . . . Who now will be led away by him?"*[27] In some cases the rejection was part of organized plots.

In this town there was one who resented him and who bribed wicked men to circulate false stories about him. Under these circumstances it was difficult for his disciples to get sufficient food from their begging, and there was much abuse.

Ananda said to Sakyamuni, "We had better not stay in a town like this. There are other and better towns to go to. We had better leave this town."

The Blessed One replied, "Suppose the next town is like this, what shall we do then?"

"Then we move to another."

The Blessed One said, "No, Ananda, there will be no end in that way. We had better remain here and bear the abuse patiently until it ceases, and then we move to another place. . . . The Enlightened One is not controlled by these external things."[28]

Each rejection of the early Buddhist community ultimately made it stronger and helped spread the new Dharma.

10 – Sacrificial Suffering

The two most severe periods of suffering endured by Buddha seem to have been the inner turmoil He experienced in the palace-complex before He left for the homeless life, and then the fear and horror He felt after going forth into the forest to experiment with austere spiritual practices. Deepening awareness of sickness, aging, and death, along with the transience of all ordinary human fulfillments, brought Gautama profound anxieties and spiritual restlessness. These experiences readied Him for the divine call brought by the celestial messenger.

Then out in the forest, Gautama undertook a six-year demonstration of austerity that showed that humanly designed techniques cannot bring deep inner peace to the individual, much less salvation for humanity. "He ate so little—six grains of rice a day during one of his fasts—that 'when I thought I would touch the skin of my stomach I actually took hold of my spine.' He would clench his teeth and press his tongue to his palate until 'sweat flowed from my armpits.' He would hold his breath until it felt 'as if a strap were being twisted around my head.' In the end he grew so weak that he fell into a faint; and if companions had not been around to feed him some warm rice gruel, he could easily have died."[29]

But even after His enlightenment and during His teaching ministry, comments made by ungrateful villagers could still bring sadness. *"I will endure words that hurt in silent peace as the strong elephant endures in battle arrows sent by the bow."* [30] What was gained by the suffering endured by Buddha? He distinguished with crystal clarity the fleeting material realm from the abiding spiritual realm. He showed the futility of priestly practices and ascetic austerities. He attained nirvana and revealed a new Dharma with saving power.

He renewed and modeled universal virtues, and inspired the multitudes. He also established the sangha, a socially transformative and civilizing power in world history.

11 – Symbolic Language as a Test for Believers

Veneration of Buddha was not an obstacle to moral and spiritual growth, if this meant revering and practicing the truth that He revealed. But as in other faith traditions, terms and practices associated with Buddha, with the sangha, and with Buddhist relics would later harden into rigid dogmas and stifling rituals. Symbolic or figurative terms were taken literally, and practices developed in culture-bound ways that removed devotees far from the original teaching. These all-too-human tendencies were tests of the purity of the Buddhist Faith, and when these tests were failed, certain beliefs and practices became idolatrous veils between devotees and the truth.

Buddha knew this pattern of rigidifying teachings, and taking too literally what had been said, had crippled humanity's spiritual development in the past, and would cripple His followers in the future. In reference to this He said, *"In the unessential they imagine the essential, in the essential they see the unessential—they who entertain such wrong thoughts never realize the essence. What is essential they regard as essential, what is unessential they regard as unessential—they who entertain such right thoughts realize the essence."* [31] What is referred to as essential here is the Dharma or Truth in its purest form, while the unessential is a set of doctrines and practices violating the spirit of the truth. Of course, sorting the essential from the unessential is a challenge of interpretation, but Buddha provided considerable guidance on this.

Buddha often shared stories to illustrate his teachings, and the parable of the arrow directs attention away from metaphysical speculation toward service. "A man has been struck by a poisoned arrow and a physician has been brought to the scene. But before the man will allow the physician to remove the arrow he wants to know: who shot the arrow, to what clan he belongs, what wood the bow and the arrow shaft were made from, what kind of feathers were used on the arrow, and what kind of tip the arrow had (on which the poison had been smeared). Just as this man would die, said the Buddha, before his questions were answered, so also a person wishing to know the nature of the Absolute in words will die before the Buddha would be able to elucidate it to him." [32]

The parable of the blind men and the elephant also directs attention away from metaphysical and theological speculation, emphasizing the need to appreciate various perspectives and contributions. Blind men would describe an elephant in very different ways, depending on what part of the elephant they were touching. They should listen to each other to learn the larger truth. This extended metaphor is a powerful encouragement to openness of mind and heart, which will help us to overcome prejudicial views and attachments to creeds and positions.

Another warning focused on intellectual pride, which Buddha understood to lead directly to moral impurity. Those that become well-versed in numerous doctrinal works often become proud of their knowledge, and digress in their morals to the point where they cannot save others by their learning. Some Buddhist intellectuals taught with diverse analogies, techniques, and innovative doctrines that were believed to be justified if they led to higher awareness. But it is easy to see how such diversification led to abuse, disunity, and confusion. In extreme cases, almost anyone might be deemed a buddha, thus clouding the exalted station of the true Buddha and the sanctity of His guidance.

Buddha wished to be remembered after His body died, and in His day this meant cremation and a burial mound. Relics of Buddha's cremation were taken to Kusinagari. Later, many claims were made that cuttings and seeds of trees grown from the original Bodhi Tree had been dispersed to many other places where impressive stupas or ceremonial monuments were built. Some stupas or pagodas were built for their own sake, and included statues of Buddha and remains of Buddhist saints. Though at their best, these sites evoke true reverence for Buddha's mission and teaching, some associated practices became idolatrous.

Buddha wanted the spirit of His words and acts to be revered and practiced. He warned against human tendencies to establish hardened dogmas, superstitious beliefs, and empty rituals. But these obstructive habits did indeed develop over the centuries as Buddhism, in its increasingly dilute and diverse forms, moved across Asia. When genuine Teachers and Revealers did appear for humanity after Buddha, Their light could not penetrate the veils fabricated in Buddha's name.

12 – Exemplary Women for All Ages: Mahamaya the Nurturer, Mahaprajapati the Advocate

The most nurturing and receptive woman in Buddha's story was Queen Mahamaya, His mother, who died only a week after giving birth to Him, being unable to bear the joy she felt over His future promise. However, according to tradition, she vigilantly attended to Him from heaven. During Gautama's period of austerities, she feared He would die, and began to lament the world's loss and her own affliction. Her great caring roused Him from stupor, and led Him to the decision to resume eating. Mahamaya also offered the most receptive heart to her Son's sermons in the heavenly realm, besting even the gods in her appreciation and understanding. He felt unable to thank her enough for her heavenly kindness. It was said that soon after Buddha's death, she descended to earth to mourn, whereupon He sat up in the coffin to comfort her.

The most active and assertive woman in Buddha's story was Mahapraja-pati, His step-mother and aunt, who raised Him at the palace in Kapilavastu. When He taught at the Sakya court, Mahaprajapati wished to become a nun, even before the order had been initiated. A few years later, she insisted that an order of nuns be established. When Buddha refused, she and her companions shaved their heads, put on robes, and asked again. When He refused yet again, she asked Ananda, His attendant, to make the case for them. Finally, Buddha consented, and Mahaprajapati became the first leader of the Buddhist order of nuns. "For a variety of reasons not yet well known, the order of Buddhist nuns did not fare equally well in all regions where Buddhism became established. In India, after several prosperous centuries, it faded into obscurity. . . . However the order became quite powerful in China and remained a significant force in Chinese Buddhism until the Mao-ist revolution."[33]

13 – Dying and Ascending Victoriously: Last Journey, Final Advice, and Parinirvana

There were key developments in Buddha's last journey, His final advice, and parinirvana, meaning last death, complete extinction, or final rest. This stage of His life included "suffering and the end of suffering," an apt summary of the Buddhist Faith. He turned His thoughts to the sangha's future without Him. The sangha would prosper through: 1) regular assemblies, 2) meeting in harmony, 3) maintaining training rules, 4) honoring superiors, 5) rising above worldly desires, 6) remaining devoted to forest hermitages, and 7) preserving mindfulness. He distinguished different group levels of attainment with a river-crossing analogy: 1) the wisest had already reached the other shore, 2) monks were swimming competently on their own, 3) lay followers were finding a bridge or boarding a raft, and 4) brahmins were not even trying to cross. He also revealed a teaching known as the "Mirror of Dharma." With an unwavering three-fold faith in the Buddha, the Dharma, and the sangha, spiritual practitioners could see as clearly as in a mirror that they were destined for enlightenment.

In the last year of His life, Buddha became very ill. Ananda, His personal attendant, asked about His plans for a successor. Buddha was surprised by this question, reminding him that He had not been a "closed fist" teacher that held certain teachings and directives secret. None of the monks had been or would be given special authority, and all had access to the Buddha, the Dharma, and the sangha so each could be his own refuge. But Mara, the Evil One, appeared, encouraging Buddha to pass immediately into parinirvana. Buddha replied that there was a little more teaching to do, and He would enter parinirvana in exactly three months. The Buddha offered guidelines for determining the authenticity of claims about doctrine. Judgment should be suspended until claims could be compared to established discourses and the disciplinary code, and those claims that diverged from this standard must be discarded.

A blacksmith, Cunda, served Buddha His last meal, whereupon He became very sick, enduring His condition without complaint. He thanked Cunda for the meal, assuring him of its merit, asking him not to blame himself. Ananda expressed profound grief that he was losing his Beloved Lord, and that he had not yet attained enlightenment. Buddha praised him for many services, remarkable qualities, and reminded him of the teaching of impermanence. Ananda asked how they should pay homage to His body, and He asked that His remains be treated as those of a universal king.

All the nearby monks assembled for a final discourse. Buddha explained that after He was gone, the Dharma and discipline would assure each faithful one salvation. He empowered the sangha to modify certain secondary rules after a time, if this helped maintain harmony. He specified four places of pilgrimage, which commemorated His birth, enlightenment, first sermon, and parinirvana. And He clarified that the monks were to interact with nuns and laywomen mindfully. Then Buddha asked, three times, if there were remaining questions or uncertainties, and there were none. Wise sayings from his farewell have echoed through the ages: *"Be lamps unto yourselves. Betake yourselves to no external refuge. Hold fast as a refuge to the Truth. Work out your own salvation with diligence."*[34] Then Buddha passed into parinirvana.

- 12 -
Buddha: Teaching and Legacy

14 – Transformative Teaching and Healing:
Early Spiritual Victories, Supportive Royalty,
Leading Disciples, and Return Home

As was the case with Zoroaster and Krishna, the teachings offered by Buddha empowered His followers to show great courage, compassion, and eloquence in spreading the Faith for a new era. From their original homeland, Buddhists carried good tidings in all four directions. Buddhist scriptures place relatively more emphasis on Buddha's quest, enlightenment, and message, and relatively less emphasis on His forty-five-years of teaching, healing, and sangha development. He traveled with His monks and taught ways to transcend suffering. He showed compassion, comforted the distressed, healed the sick, trained monks, counseled paupers and kings, advocated social and legal reform, and always worked toward expanding the new Faith.

Early Spiritual Victories

Yasa, the son of a guild master and harem owner, became disgusted with the sensual life; but he was invited by Buddha to overcome his distress. He soon converted to the new teaching, along with his parents and another prominent family. Also, fifty of Yasa's friends converted to the Faith. The teaching campaigns of Buddha's first sixty monks were very successful, not only attracting lay disciples, but also new recruits to the sangha. In a similar incident, Buddha met thirty friends who had been socializing in a woodland. A courtesan among them stole some of their belongings, and they were in pursuit of her when Buddha asked, *"Which is better for you, that you seek for a woman or that you seek for the self?"* [1] As a result of their ensuing dialogue, thirty new monks were added to the sangha. Buddha commanded all the monks: *"Go forward for the benefit of many people . . .*

215

out of compassion for the world, for the good, welfare and happiness of gods and men. May no two of you go the same way!"[2]

Buddha once used miraculous powers to get the attention of a respected Hindu leader, Kasyapa; but what shook him profoundly was Buddha's informing him that he was not enlightened, nor could he ever be on his current path. This led to Kasyapa's conversion, along with 500 of his Hindu followers. Buddha's famous Fire Sermon was instrumental in this mass conversion, which attracted the attention of some kings. *"Everything is burning. . . . The eye is burning . . . the ear, the nose, the tongue, the body, and the mind are burning. . . . With what are they burning? With the fire of passion, with the fire of hatred, with the fire of delusion. They are burning because of birth, old age, disease, death. . . . They are burning because of suffering."*[3] This sermon was described as reducing the three fires of greed, hatred, and delusion, which was meant as an ironic and spiritual critique of the holy fires of the old Vedic system.[4]

King Bimbisara and King Pasenadi: Supportive Royalty

King Bimbisara of Magadha invited Buddha to his court. He was very impressed with Buddha's far-reaching influence, and after a sermon, he converted as a lay disciple. Bimbisara offered Buddha a bamboo grove, called Venuvana, as a retreat site. This large gift was accepted graciously, setting a precedent for royal support to the growing Faith. King Pasenadi of Kosala got word of Buddha's teaching, and invited Him to his court. He had heard that those who tried to confound Him ended up as disciples, and that Buddha reformed and converted a murderer who had terrorized Pasenadi. The king was so stunned by the order's discipline—the love, affection, and respectful silence showed by monks for their Teacher—that he said, *"Would that my son might have such calm."*[5] Bimbisara and Pasenadi frequently sought Buddha's advice, and were among the Buddhist kings with explicit programs of social and political reform.

Sariputta and Moggallana: Leading Disciples

Sariputta and Moggallana were friends who, in their youth, agreed to follow any teacher who could bring them liberation. Sariputta found the Buddha first by hearing someone quoting Him, saying, *"The Tathagata has explained the cause of those elements of reality that arise from a cause, and he . . . has also spoken of their cessation."*[6] Sariputta grasped this teaching immediately,

216

and became serene enough for Moggallana to notice a difference in his appearance. When Buddha first saw them, He said they would become His chief disciples and would do great things for the sangha. Sariputta became a model for Theravadin Buddhists because of his wisdom, moral discipline, and attention to institutional details. Moggallana was more intuitive and mystical, with prowess in visiting heaven, and became a model for Mahayana Buddhists.

Return Home: Mass Conversion of the Sakyas in Kapilavastu
At His father's request, Buddha returned to His home town of Kapilavastu, reuniting with King Suddhodana; His step-mother, Mahaprajapati; His wife and son, Yasodhara and Rahula; His half-brother, Nanda; His cousins, Ananda and Devadatta; as well as many other relatives, ministers of the court, and servants. When His father asked about Buddha's humble robe, his Son replied: *"The Buddhas who have been and who shall be, of these am I and what they did, I do."*[7] All who heard His teaching in Kapilavastu became lay disciples and monks. But social equilibrium was temporarily upset. A nearby brahmin villager observed, "The wanderer Gautama is coming. His band is like a hailstorm that decimates the crops. Those of you who are parents are without a doubt going to be deprived of your sons!"[8] In response, Suddhodana established the rule that in families with several sons, only one could join the sangha. The king also extracted a promise from his Son that henceforth no one would be ordained without parental consent.

There was a memorable dialogue between Buddha's wife, Yasodhara, and her servant, about her feelings toward the returned Prince. *"I am sad because the Lord Buddha . . . no longer loves me. . . . I can accept being abandoned, but the Buddha should have sympathy for his son."* The servant then reminds her of her husband's former affection and thoughtfulness, how He sometimes shared in the housework. *"My husband has not even greeted me"* she complained. Later, she said directly to Buddha, *"O my Lord, I pay my respects to you. I am unlucky and ashamed before you. . . . You abandoned me and our child without any compassion."* However, both she and her son joined the order.[9]

Settling Down: Rules and Contentions
Buddha and the sangha spent the annual three-month rainy season at retreats, attending to matters of the order. For the first twenty years, they moved about to various retreats, but for most of the last twenty-five years of Buddha's

ministry, though they still traveled, they adopted a permanent home at the Jetavana Monastery in Sravasti. Rules that developed at monastic settings aimed at promoting harmony and consensus, and were ritually reaffirmed at intervals. Once, a dispute arose between a monk who left waste water in the bathroom, and another who said this was an offense to be confessed. The first monk said he was unaware of the rule; the second said ignorance of rules was no excuse. Factions formed around these views, and matters escalated into a major conflict. Buddha said both factions were at fault and should mend their ways, but His suggestions were refused several times, so He left the area without telling anyone. Villagers noticed He was gone, blamed the monks and stopped feeding them. Hungry and ashamed, the monks sought their Master, begging His forgiveness and return. Then they reconciled themselves.[10]

15 – Delivering a Thematic and Complementary Message: Awakening in Compassion for Suffering and Attaining Nirvana

The theme connecting all of Buddha's main teachings is a practical one, which we can describe as awakening in compassion for suffering and attaining nirvana. This theme complemented Krishna's emphasis on devotion to the Avatar and selfless action, but was more adapted to the anxieties and capacities of northern India six centuries later. Buddha's message focused on reducing ones' own and others' suffering, overcoming fear of death, and enabling humanity to transcend the temporal world, thereby attaining eternity.

The Four Noble Truths

Buddha's most central teachings were presented in His first sermon in Deer Park to his five fellow seekers in the forest. The Four Noble Truths were recorded in the "Sutra of the Foundation of the Kingdom of Righteousness," a title that sounds Zoroastrian; and indeed, Buddha's message was a deepening of the earlier emphasis on good thoughts, words, and deeds. How can we gain masterly self-control? What are the most essential truths of our human condition? How can we transcend the limitations of this painful existence, for ourselves and all sentient beings? Buddha answered by describing the Four Noble Truths.

1. Suffering (*dukkha*): Human life as typically lived is full of suffering, pain, disease, dislocation, and feeling awry. There are six main forms

of our suffering: a) the trauma of birth, b) sickness, c) aging or decrepitude, d) the phobia of death, e) being separated from our loves, and f) being tied to our hates. Buddha was called a Spiritual Physician, and His First Truth is like a physician's identification of symptoms.

2. Craving (*tanha*): The primary cause of our suffering is our craving or egoistic desire to benefit at others' expense. The more we crave, the more we shut ourselves off from the sources of our physical, moral, and spiritual well-being. This is the diagnosis.

3. Overcoming Suffering by Overcoming Craving: Suffering can indeed be overcome, because craving can be overcome. This hope-giving truth serves as the prognosis.

4. Steps on the Path by which Suffering is Overcome: Eight sequential exercises of wisdom, moral conduct, and spiritual discipline lead to the end of suffering. This is the prescription.[11]

The Eightfold Path

Buddha spoke broadly of two ways of living: wandering or taking a path. An essential preliminary to taking a path was right association—the idea that we need to spend time with those principled enough to choose a path. The path included three kinds of steps, with eight steps in total.

Wisdom Steps included right views and intent: 1) Right Views: discerning the essential reasonableness and correctness of the Four Noble Truths as a guide to transcend the human condition; 2) Right Intent: aligning the heart properly and seeking Enlightenment. Moral Steps were right speech, conduct, and livelihood: 3) Right Speech: confining our speech to truth-seeking and relationship-improving; 4) Right Conduct: studying our motives and actions, and observing the Five Precepts (no killing, stealing, lying, sexual misconduct, or substance abuse); 5) Right Livelihood: joining a spiritual order or working only at life-promoting trades. Spiritual Steps were right effort, mindfulness, and concentration: 6) Right Effort: developing the virtues of perseverance, compassion, and detachment; 7) Right Mindfulness: continuous and un-distracted introspection; and 8) Right Concentration: rigorous and regenerative meditation to eliminate the three poisons of delusion, craving, and hostility.

The Doctrine of No-Self

Buddha maintained that the human ego, though it seems the most real and important aspect of our experience, is ultimately insubstantial or fleeting. He analyzed the components of the self as including body, sensations, thoughts, feelings, and consciousness. He concluded that these were all insubstantial, un-abiding, temporary realities. It was also said that He denied the existence of the soul as traditionally understood in Hindu traditions. Buddha interpreted reincarnation as an influence that survives death, comparable to molds that leave imprints elsewhere, or to flames that light other wicks and so endure after the original flame is blown out. The transience of things was seen as paramount.

However, this no-self doctrine has been controversial, because it appears inconsistent with other important Buddhist teachings, and it seems to contradict the teachings of other Founders. Without a self or a soul, who or what could receive His teaching? Who or what abided in other realms—past and future, or heavens and hells? Could His teaching on the absence of a soul be more of a strategy for reducing the ego than a substantive doctrine?

Several of Buddha's discourses had the theme that a person who loves the self should not harm the self of others. What could such teachings mean if there is no self? He also said, *"In days gone by this mind of mine used to stray wherever selfish desire or lust or pleasure would lead it. Today this mind does not stray and is under the harmony of control, even as a wild elephant is controlled by the trainer."* [12] If there was no self or soul, who noticed the mind straying, and then brought it under control? He also taught, *"Guard well your mind. Uplift yourself from your lower self, even as an elephant draws himself out of a muddy swamp."* [13] Who could guard the mind, and lift the lower self? Buddha affirmed an inner agency that can benefit from His teaching—a higher self that monitors, harmonizes, and elevates the relatively insubstantial lower self.

The Doctrine of Impermanence

Buddha taught that what we call physical and mental existence is impermanent, ever-changing, ending in one form and transforming into another. This suggests that processes and events are more basic descriptions of our experience than so-called permanent substances. The skandhas or components of human life (bodies, sensations, thoughts, feelings, consciousness) are like strands that inevitably come loose. Possessions are only temporarily ours; we cannot take them with us into future realms. Death leaves unfulfilled desires or forces that continue elsewhere. Expiring flames do not really go out, but rather return to pure energy. Individual awareness will be eclipsed in the light of total awareness, as raindrops are absorbed by the ocean into which they fall.

The Doctrine of Interdependent Origination

Buddha taught that physical and mental realities—twelve basic forms of them—mutually give rise to one another, in a complex process called interdependent origination. It is a philosophical and spiritual elaboration of the idea that things both cause, and are caused by, one another. Here is how the doctrine was presented in one scriptural passage:

> *On [1] ignorance depends [2] kamma; on kamma depends [3] consciousness; on consciousness depends [4] name and form; on name and form depends [5] the sense organs; on the sense organs depend [6] contact; on contact depends [7] sensation; on sensation depends [8] desire; on desire depends [9] attachment; on attachment depends [10] existence; on existence depends [11] birth; on birth depends [12] dukkha: old age and death, sorrow, lamentation, misery, grief and despair.*[14]

In more contemporary terms, the same idea is explained as follows: "The last idea or impulse of a dying human being . . . has been conditioned by all the *kamma* of his or her life. This 'consciousness' becomes the germ of a new 'name and form' in the womb of its mother. The personality of this embryo is conditioned by the quality of the dying 'consciousness' of its predecessor. Once the fetus is linked with this 'consciousness,' a new life cycle can begin. The embryo develops sense organs and, after its birth, these make 'contact' with the external world. This sensual contact gives rise to 'sensations' or feelings, which lead to 'desire,' the most powerful cause of *dukkha*. Desire leads to 'attachments' which prevent our liberation and enlightenment, and which doom us to a new 'existence,' a new birth and further sorrow, sickness, grief and death."[15]

Nirvana: The Goal of Human Life

Buddha spoke of nirvana as the goal of human life, the extinguishing of craving, the transcending of the boundaries of the ego, a sense of abundant life and awareness, and the end of our journey. Though He considered it

221

ultimately undescribable, He provided His listeners with metaphors that point to some of its aspects. It was like the other shore, beyond the realm of death, the home of the pure, the land unknown, the sky of liberation, and the breaking of all fetters. It offered the secure refuge, eternal joy, and peace. If it did not exist, there would be no hope of escaping the suffering built into the nature of existence. Since it does exist, our moral and spiritual striving can bear abiding fruit.

Did Buddha Affirm the Divine Realm?

Many Buddhists claim they do not believe in God, assuming that God means a personal Creator Who is distinct from what He created. Some add that Buddhism is unique among religions in rejecting God. But as this study shows, all the major religions offer impersonal and transcendent concepts of the divine, while some offer personal concepts as well. It is true that Buddha considered theological speculation to be unedifying, and taught that the character of unconditioned nirvana could not be delineated without misrepresenting it. However, there are many indications that Buddha affirmed an impersonal, transcendent reality beyond the gods—an Unconditioned Absolute out of which the conditioned universe continually arises. In Buddhist tradition, creation is seen as ongoing rather than having occurred all at once in the distant past. *"There is, monks, an unborn, a not-become, a not-made, a not-compounded. If, monks, there were not this unborn, not-become, not-made, not-compounded, there would not here be an escape from the born, the become, the made, the compounded. But because there is an unborn, a not-become, a not-made, a not-compounded, therefore there is and escape from the born, the become, the made, the compounded."* [16]

He taught that Dharma or the eternal law is the truth taught by Teachers through the ages. He taught that Buddhas, or the Truly Awakened Ones, abide forever in eternity. Also, much of His description of nirvana can be viewed as affirming the divine realm, for nirvana can be understood as the highest good, the glorious, the supreme vision, the supreme perfection, and an infinite void without beginning or end. Also, much of what He affirmed about Himself implies a realm from which He drew His powers and wisdom, and toward which He directed humanity.

Profitable and Unprofitable States of Mind

Buddha distinguished between profitable or skillful states of mind, and unprofitable or unskillful states of mind. In particular, He encouraged the cultivation of compassion, alertness, calmness, and confidence. Each of these lofty attitudes or virtues help to banish unprofitable opposites such as hatred, indolence, anxiety, and uncertainty.[17]

Was Buddha's Emphasis Individual or Social?

Among the controversies within Buddhism down through the ages has been the question of to whom Buddha's teachings were directed—to individuals or to multitudes. Early Theravadin Buddhists emphasized individuals, whereas later Mahayana Buddhists emphasized the wider social context, if not all humanity and all sentient beings. But there is evidence that social virtues were emphasized in both early and later Buddhism. Here are some of Buddha's fairly well-known social teachings, sprinkled throughout the Dhammapada. "*We are here in this world to live in harmony," "Among those who hate, let us live in love. . . . Hate is conquered by love," "How can there be laughter, how can there be pleasure, when the whole world is burning," "The followers of Buddha Gautama . . . find joy in love for all beings," "It is sweet to have friends in need; and to share enjoyment is sweet," "follow the path of Nirvana . . . the path of infinite joy."*

Among Buddha's most quoted teachings is this passage.

May all beings be happy and secure, may their hearts be wholesome! Whatever living beings there be: feeble or strong, tall, stout or medium, short, small or large, without exception; seen or unseen, those dwelling far or near, those who are born or those yet unborn—may all beings be happy!

Let none deceive another, nor despise any person whatsoever in any place. Let him not wish any harm to another out of anger or ill-will. Just as a mother would protect her only child at the risk of her own life, even so, let him cultivate a boundless heart towards all beings.[18]

16 – Renewing and Embodying Universal Virtues

Virtues are our human ability to reflect divine guidance as mediated by a Revealer. Buddha emphasized awareness of and compassion for suffering in ever wider circles of experience and relationship. "*Walk on the right path. He who follows the right path has joy in this world and in the world beyond."*[19] The Five Precepts are part of right action in the Eightfold Path, and these are expected of lay Buddhists. Buddhists are to refrain from: 1) taking life, 2) taking what is not given, 3) sexual misconduct, 4) falsehood, and 5) abusive substances. The Ten Perfections have been expected of Buddhist monks over the last 2500 years: 1) generosity, 2) ethics or morality (discipline, purity), 3) patience, 4) effort, 5) concentration or courage (fearlessness in the face of obstacles), 6) intuitive wisdom, 7) skillful means or tact, 8) aspiration, 9) powerful compassion, and 10) serene wisdom.[20] Here are some Buddhist teachings on the fifteen virtues we are emphasizing.

Spiritual Virtues in the Buddhist Revelation

Devotion-Faithfulness: *"The man who arises in faith, who ever remembers his high purposes, whose work is pure . . . that man shall rise in glory."* [21]

Gratitude-Reverence: *"The worthy person is grateful and mindful of benefits done to him."* [22]

Self-discipline-Obedience: *"Even as rain breaks not through a well-thatched house, passions break not through a well-guarded mind."* [23]

Detachment-Patience: *"Good men, at all times, surrender in truth all attachments. The holy spend not idle words on things of desire. When pleasure or pain comes to them, the wise feel above pleasure and pain."* [24]

Wisdom-Discernment: *"Among the blind multitudes shines pure the light of wisdom of the student who follows the Buddha, the One who is truly awake."* [25]

Social Virtues in the Buddhist Revelation

Loving-kindness-Compassion: *"As a mother with her own life guards the life of her own child, let all-embracing thoughts for all that lives be thine."* [26]

Service-Responsibility: *"How does a person rain down everywhere? He gives to all, be they recluses and brahmins or wretched, needy beggars; he is a giver of food and drink, clothing . . . lodging and lights."* [27]

Respect-Tolerance: *"Think not of the faults of others, of what they have done or not done. Think rather of your own sins, of the things you have done or not done."* [28]

Justice-Righteousness: *"He who for the sake of happiness does not hurt others who also want happiness, shall hereafter find happiness."* [29]

Peace-Unity: *"Better than a thousand useless words is one single word that gives peace."* [30]

Material Virtues in the Buddhist Revelation

Trustworthiness-Honesty: *"A wise man calmly considers what is right and what is wrong, and faces different opinions with truth, non-violence and peace. This man is guarded by truth, and is a guardian of truth."* [31]

Moderation-Balance: *"He who lives not for pleasures, and whose soul is in self-*

harmony, who eats or fasts with moderation, and has faith and the power of virtue—this man is not moved by temptations, as a great rock is not shaken by the wind." [32]

Generosity-Hospitality: *"Noble men find joy in generosity, and this gives them joy in higher worlds."* [33]

Creativity-Beauty: *"A good all-round education, appreciation of the arts, a highly trained discipline and pleasant speech; this is the highest blessing."* [34]

Earthcare-Stewardship: *"As the bee takes the essence of a flower and flies away without destroying its beauty and perfume, so let the sage wander in this life."* [35]

17 – Abrogating the Old and Establishing the New: Ritual and Legal Guidance

Buddha's Predecessor, Krishna, purified and synthesized the Vedic traditions that preceded Him. The decline of Brahmanic Hinduism was severe half a millennium later in Buddha's time. In a similar manner to Krishna, Buddha abrogated previous social and ritual guidelines. He abolished the caste system, eliminated or reduced priestly rituals, turned spiritual attention inward, moral attention outward, while also establishing a very egalitarian socioeconomic system.

There is clear evidence of Buddha's attempt to abrogate the caste system. "The Buddha gave new, spiritual definitions to Hindu racial and caste terms like aryian and brahmin."[36] He viewed aryans not as a light-skinned race from the north, but as those noble souls who were able to follow the new Dharma. He viewed brahmins not as members of a privileged class, but as morally and spiritually upright wherever they happened to live. *"I call not a man a Brahmin because he was born from a certain family or mother, for he may be proud, and he may be wealthy. The man who is free from possessions and free from desires—him I call a Brahmin."* [37] Buddha considered such titles, names, and races merely worldly conventions to be transcended in a new social order.

Buddha redefined priestly rituals in His day. To an anxious brahmin priest preparing for a complex ritual sacrifice, Buddha said: *"Consider the man who honors his father and mother—this is called the fire of the venerable. . . . Consider . . . the man who honors his sons, womenfolk, slaves, messengers, workmen—this is called the fire of the householder. . . . Consider . . . those recluses and godly men who abstain from pride and indolence, who bear things patiently and meekly, each taming self, each calming self, each cooling self—this is called the fire of the gift-worthy."* [38] Buddha explained that these elaborate rituals are not what will truly purify one's inner being. *"All the various penances performed for immortality, neither incantations, oblations, sacrifices, nor observing seasonal feasts will cleanse a man who has not overcome his doubt."* [39] It is one's inner purity that is most important. *"Not by sacred water is one pure, although many folk bathe in it. In whom is truth and dhamma, he is pure; he is a brahmin."* [40]

The order of monks and nuns established by Buddha was responsible for the pursuit of individual enlightenment and the collective salvation of humanity. This entailed meditation and study, teaching the Dharma, conducting rituals, reciting sacred texts, offering social services, and advising political leaders. Public rituals were essential in Indian life. [41] It is unclear to what extent Buddha Himself was the actual initiator of these rituals. Some of these practices probably emerged within the sangha as it adapted to many different cultural settings in Asia, or as it regressed to older Hindu practices.

Initiating a new Buddhist believer was called *abhiseka*, which meant anointing with water, and it may have been an adaptation of the coronation ceremony of ancient kings. The initiate is sprinkled with water by a monk, symbolizing the transfer of spiritual wisdom and awareness of the Dharma. This ritual involves vow-taking and sometimes the beginning of more advanced instruction. The bimonthly new moon and full moon observances were called *uposatha*, and were a time of fasting. This observance entails, in addition to fasting, public confession on the part of sangha members for any breach of the disciplinary code, and they remind all participants of Buddha's birth, enlightenment, and parinirvana (final release). Healing and blessing rites were called *paritta*, which meant protection. Care and compassion were given official, public form through these ceremonies. Through them, gratitude was expressed that both spirits and natural elements can conform to human needs and aspirations.

Another merit-making activity was the pilgrimage to Buddhist monuments. "The wise know the virtues of the Buddha to be such that, given equal purity of mind, the same fruit will be won either by reverencing the Seer during his worldly existence or by doing obeisance to his relics after the Parinirvana." [42] In northeastern India, Buddhist devotees have shown reverence for Buddha in Kapilavastu, commemorating His birth; in Bodhgaya, where He attained enlightenment; in Sarnath, where He gave His first sermon; in Vaisali, where He made His decision to leave the world; in Rajaghra, where the conversion of King Bimbisara took place; in Sravasti and Samkasya, known for where

His most impressive miracles took place; and in Kusinagari, the city of His parinirvana (final release). In Sri Lanka, special sites include Anuradhapura, where Bodhi Tree cuttings were planted; and the sacred mountain of Adam's Peak, where Buddha's "footprint" is celebrated.[43]

Buddha directed moral attention outward to the disadvantaged, and established an egalitarian socioeconomic system that differed radically from anything that India had experienced before. He instructed lay followers to save for emergencies, look after their dependents, give alms to monks and the needy, avoid debt, and invest money carefully.[44] *"Throughout your kingdom let no wrongdoing prevail. And whosoever in your kingdom is poor, to him let wealth be given."*[45]

Buddha spoke to King Bimbisara, and proposed that a noble man possesses power, wealth, and religion, and enjoys them with discretion and wisdom. He taught that a kind man makes good use of wealth, and is rightly said to possess great treasure; but the miser who hoards up riches will have no profit. Buddha hoped that Bimbisara's kingdom would enjoy peace and prosperity, with wisdom shed upon his rule like the noon-day sun.[46] Buddha went further than Krishna in dismantling the caste system and establishing a welfare state, not because He had a higher spiritual station, but because revelation is progressive, and by 500 BCE, people of India developed the spiritual capacity to heed more advanced social teachings.

18 – Human and Divine Qualities: Exemplifying a Dual Station

As we saw with Krishna, scriptural evidence could be found for Buddha's human and divine station. Though Krishna's divine station became increasingly dominant down through the centuries, the stories of His humanness could not be eliminated. Perhaps in reaction to the deifying of Krishna, early Buddhists emphasized Buddha's humanness, saying He attained enlightenment and nirvana through His own unaided efforts. However, there is much evidence that Buddha claimed and exemplified a divine station as well. So again, as with all Founders, it makes sense to ascribe a dual station to Buddha. Buddha was neither merely human nor identical to Divine Reality. He occupied an intermediate spiritual station, showing both sets of qualities.

Buddha's Human Station

Indications of Gautama's humanness include the sensual delights He occasionally succumbed to in the palace, the restlessness He felt before leaving home, the fear He felt in the forest, His long and difficult search for an effective path to enlightenment, His wasting away during the period of austerities, His occasional digestive problems, headaches, and injuries, His continually feeling the sorrows and joys of others, and the discomforts of His final journey when He likened His aging body to an old cart held together with straps. Yet there were attempts to deify Him in His lifetime, which He rejected.

Buddha's Divine Station

Buddha also claimed that He was not merely human. *"Not by mere morals or rituals, by much learning or high concentration . . . can I reach that joy of freedom which is not reached by those of the world."*[47] He referred to Himself as a king, *"I am a supreme king. So let your doubts about me cease. I am the holy one beyond compare. I rejoice free from fear."*[48] But He said that His royalty did not come from the world, but from God, *"I am the Lord's own son, born of his mouth, born of Dhamma, formed by Dhamma, heir to Dhamma."*[49] *"He who sees the Norm [Dharma], he sees me; he who sees me, he sees the Norm [Dharma]."*[50] *"This dharma, which the Tathagata has fully known or demonstrated—it cannot be grasped, it cannot be talked about. . . . And why? Because an Absolute exalts the Holy Persons."*[51] Buddhists have perceived a transcendent pattern discernible in the life of the Tathagata. In Mahayana Buddhism, emphasis on the ultimate status of Buddha has been explicit. The Tathagata's earthly life was but a manifestation of a transcendent, unchanging, eternal body of truth—the Dharmakaya. His life events served as teaching models for humanity's benefit.

19 – The Light and the Word

Like Krishna and Zoroaster before Him and Christ after Him, Buddha was a light in the darkness of the human condition. His Dharma was the saving Word that had become fainter in the centuries that led to His arising. There are some scriptural passages that lift up these roles of illumination. *"So long as the rightly awakened ones arise not in the world, the sophists [learned] get no light, nor do their followers, and those of wrong views cannot be released from Ill."*[52] Buddha explains that His coming is like a light for the world, *"When a Bodhisattva [Buddha] descends from heaven, there appears in this world an immeasurable, splendid light surpassing the glory of the most powerful glow. And whatever dark spaces lie beyond the world's end will be illuminated by this light."*[53]

20 – Affirming Four Levels of Reality: Natural, Human, Revelatory, Divine

Among the ironies of Buddhist history is that, even though Buddha warned about the dangers of speculative metaphysics, we find a great deal of complex philosophical exposition in Mahayana Buddhism. Just as Moses' revelation developed over a millennium, so did Buddha's, and we cannot ignore either the early or later Buddhist scriptures. What basic metaphysical picture does the Buddhist revelation offer? Can it be compared with the levels we call natural, human, revelatory, and divine?

There are three major realms (*dhatu*) in the most common Buddhist cosmology, but we cannot be certain that all these views accurately portray Buddha's teachings. The highest realm has been called the Formless Realm (*Arupya-Dhatu*), characterized as infinite mind and space. Below this was placed the Form Realm (*Rupa-Dhatu*), characterized as heavens or exalted meditative states. And below this realm was placed the Realm of Desire (*Kama-Dhatu*), characterized as containing gods, human beings, ghosts, animals, plants, and elemental forces. These realms appear consistent with the metaphysical map offered by the Founders as a whole.[54]

The Natural Realm

For Buddhists, the natural world is an impermanent set of processes, rather than a system of stable substances. All that we said above regarding the doctrines of impermanence and interdependent origination applies here. Nature is the Realm of Desire—without spiritual power, and lower than humanity's higher capacities. It includes unenlightened human beings, animals, plants, and elements. *"The world exists because of causal actions; all things are produced by causal actions and all beings are governed and bound by causal actions. They are fixed like the rolling wheel of a cart, fixed by the pin of its axle shaft."* [55] As we noted earlier, Buddha taught that all physical realities are impermanent and transitory; but human beings have the capacity to transcend the bondage of physical realities.

The Human Realm

For Buddhists, human beings are part of the Realm of Desire, but have the spiritual capacity to transcend this realm through obedience to the path of truth that has been taught and renewed by the Buddhas. The power or capacity by which we heed Their guidance is the inner observer or conscious agent. What we said above regarding the doctrine of no-self would apply here. Though Buddha clarified the insubstantial nature of ordinary selfhood, He used the term soul many times and described its need for purification and release. *"Only a man himself can be master of himself. . . . Any wrong or evil a man does, is born in himself and is caused by himself."*[56] He talked about how important it was to maintain the goodness of one's soul, *"Let no man endanger his duty, the good of his soul, for the good of another, however great. When he has seen the good of his soul, let him follow it with earnestness."*[57]

The Revelatory Realm

For Buddhists, the term Dharma is the nearest equivalent to what other faith traditions call the revelatory Word. Buddhists have variously interpreted the Dharma as righteousness, truth, law, the structure of existence, the renewal of an ancient path, and a heavenly descent of infinite wisdom and power. Buddha affirmed, *"He who sees the Norm* [Dharma]*, he sees me; he who sees me, he sees the Norm* [Dharma]*."*[58] The term Realm of Form corresponds closely with what we call the revelatory realm, and in Buddhist thought includes or is described as the abode of the Pure Ones or Buddhas, celestial beings, the heavens, advanced meditative states and nirvana, the land unknown, the home of the pure, and eternal joy and peace.

The Buddha's preferred title, the Tathagata, means One Who has come to the Truth (Thus-Come), a Path-Maker or a Way-Shower, One Who is traceless, trackless, or transcendent. *"The Tathagata is the victor unvanquished, the absolute seer, self-controlled."*[59] Buddha explained that His divine station transcended His physical body. *"Those only who do not believe, call Me Gotama, but you call me the Buddha, the Blessed One, the Teacher. And this is right, for I have in this life entered Nirvana. . . . This body of mine is Gotama's body and it will be dissolved in due time. . . . The Buddha will not die; the Buddha will continue to live in the holy body of the law."*[60]

The Divine Realm

For Buddhists, the term Formless Realm refers to what we have called the divine realm, including concepts of infinite mind and space. Most Buddhists would also consider Dharmakaya, or Truth Body, to be equivalent to the Formless Realm, because Dharmakaya also means Ultimate Reality. These terms can all be interpreted as impersonal, transcendent concepts of the divine. *"What is meant by the eternally-abiding reality? The ancient road of reality*

. . . has been here all the time, like gold, silver, or pearl preserved in the mine. The Dharmadhatu *(Absolute Truth) abides forever, whether the Tathagata appears in the world or not. As the Tathagata eternally abides so does the Reason of all things. Reality forever abides, reality keeps its order, like the roads in an ancient city.*"[61] Dharma is described as part of an absolute, infinite realm, and Buddha likens Himself to this idea of Dharma. *"Attaining the absolute Dharma-body is [attaining] the absolute One Vehicle. . . . The Tathagata is identical with the Dharma-body. . . . The Absolute is unlimited and unceasing.*"[62]

21 – Promising a Future Savior and a New Golden Age: Maitreya, City of Righteousness, Pure Land

Just as the Mosaic revelation referred to a coming Messiah and the Everlasting Dominion, and the Hindu revelation referred to the Kalki Avatar and the New Golden Age, the Buddhist revelation referred to Maitreya and the Pure Land of the Western Paradise. Such promises have given believers great hope through the ages, declaring that Saviors are sent to humanity at appropriate intervals, and that eventually a time of enduring fairness and peace will come.

Buddha was called the fourth Buddha of this eon, and He spoke of the fifth Who would come. *"There will arise in the world an Exalted One named Metteya. He will be . . . Fully Awakened, abounding in wisdom and goodness, happy, with knowledge of the worlds, unsurpassed as a guide to mortals willing to be led, a teacher for gods and men, an Exalted One, a Buddha, even as I am now. He, by himself, will thoroughly know and see, as it were face to face, this universe, with its worlds of the spirits. . . . The Law, lovely in its origin, lovely in its progress, lovely in its consummation, will he proclaim, both in the spirit and in the letter; the higher life will he make known, in all its fulness and in all its purity, even as I do now.*"[63]

Contemporary studies of Buddhism describe this expectation of the coming of a future Buddha: "As the years pass, the impulse of the teaching of the Buddha Shakyamuni gradually exhausts itself, and attention shifts to Maitreya, the coming Buddha. . . . His name is derived from *mitra*, "friend." . . . At present, many Buddhists look forward to his coming. In South Asia these eschatological hopes are little stressed, whereas in Central Asia they are a source of great religious fervour. To be born in Maitreya's presence is the greatest wish of many Tibetans and Mongols, and the inscription 'Come, Maitreya, come!' on the rocks of numerous mountains testifies to their longing."[64]

Another account suggests that the new Buddha's following will be much greater than the fourth's. He will have a heavenly voice that reaches far, and instead of hundreds of followers in His lifetime, He will be able to attract a retinue of about 84,000 persons whom He will instruct. Under Maitreya's guidance, hundreds of thousands will enter upon a religious life, and the earth will become crowded with revered exemplars of faith who transcend their moral faults. They will no longer regard things as merely their own, for they will be providers and servants of the whole world. The new Buddha will teach a new law and a new order that will discipline and empower hundreds of millions.[65]

What type of world will be brought about by the Buddha to come? One image was the City of Righteousness, and another the Pure Land of the Western Paradise. These descriptions might remind us of the Christian description of the New Jerusalem, and they might be interpreted as visions of heaven on earth.

When the city is built, and stands complete and perfect he goes away to another land. And in time the city becomes rich and prosperous, peaceful and happy, free from plague and calamity, and filled with people of all classes and professions and of all lands. . . . All these folk coming to live in the new city and finding it so well planned, faultless, perfect and beautiful, exclaim: 'Skilled indeed must be the builder of this city!'

So the Lord . . . in his infinite goodness . . . when he had achieved the highest powers of Buddhahood and had conquered Mara and his hosts . . . built the City of Righteousness.

The Lord's City of Righteousness has virtue for its ramparts, fear of sin for its moat, knowledge for its gates, zeal for its turrets, faith for its pillars, concentration for its watchman, wisdom for its palaces. . . .

. . . Whoever wishes to be free from age and death . . . enters the glorious city of Nirvana, stainless and undefiled, pure and white, unaging, deathless, secure and calm and happy, and his mind is emancipated as a perfected being.[66]

Some Buddhist traditions refer to a king, Amitabha, who achieved Buddhahood on the condition that he receive at death all who sincerely call upon his name, carrying them to his Western Paradise to pursue the quest of perfection. This future world, called the Western Paradise during the first millennium of Buddha's dispensation, was viewed as the coming world system of the Lord Amitabha. It was viewed as a distant era that would be prosperous, comfortable, fertile, delightful, and filled with spiritually advanced souls. It was envisioned as a world with many gardens, rich in a great variety of flowers and fruits, adorned with jewel trees, and frequented by flocks of beautiful birds singing sweet songs. There will be great rivers in that new day, and their sound will be as pleasant as that of musical instruments—clear, harmonious, touching the heart, and none will ever tire of hearing this natural melody. In this pure land there will be transformed conceptions of fire, sun, moon, planets, stars, and constellations. All of humanity will regain enlightenment upon hearing the name of the Lord. They will be of one mind, unified in their thought and aspiration, raising their hearts to Him with resolve and serene faith.[67]

22 – Essential Unity of the Revealers through the Ages

If the divine realm is one, and if Founders share a divine station, then They must be united in purpose: to guide humanity over centuries and millennia toward ever-higher spiritual, social, and material attainment. "These great spiritual luminaries, the divine teachers, the Buddhas, are no more different from each other than the sun of today is from the sun of yesterday or the sun of tomorrow. There are no yesterdays, todays and tomorrows on the sun. . . . The conditions of our world obscure only our view of the sun, they can neither touch nor effect its reality and power, for the sun is ever shining."[68] Buddha referred to His essential unity with former Buddhas. *"There is no distinction between any of the Buddhas."*[69] He spoke of *"an ancient Path, an ancient road traversed by the Rightly Enlightened Ones of former times."*[70] He also promised future Buddhas, especially Maitreya or Amitabha, the knower of the worlds, Who will make known the higher life in all its fullness and purity. He will bring humanity to new heights of spiritual and creative unfoldment. So Buddha, like other Teachers, and in perfect unity with Them, adapted His message to optimize humanity's progress.

23 – Laying Enduring Foundations: Sangha Discipline, Asoka, Theravada and Mahayana Schools, and Asian Expansion

Like other Founders, Buddha made institutional arrangements that endured much longer and had a more transformative impact on society than those made by ordinary mortals. A few major developments are listed here.

Buddha's Great Commission

Buddha commissioned His first sixty monks to spread the Dharma in all directions for the benefit of many people, out of compassion for the world. Buddhism was not conceived as a private discovery, but rather as a message and method of salvation for all of humanity. So it had to be spread as widely as possible. Now we look briefly at how, when, and where it spread.

The Sangha's Confession of Faith

In the Buddha's day, the monks were expected to come together every six years to recite a common confession of faith. This was an effective way to transform disparate groups of monks into a sangha (order). The confession went as follows, *"Refraining from all that is harmful, attaining what is skillful, and purifying one's own mind; this is what the Buddhas teach. Forbearance and patience are the highest of all austerities; and the Buddhas declare that Nibbana* [Nirvana] *is the supreme value. Nobody who hurts another has truly 'Gone Forth' from the home life. Nobody who injures others is a true monk. No faultfinding, no harming, restraint, knowing the rules regarding food, the single bed and chair, application in the higher perception derived from meditation—this is what the Awakened Ones teach."* [71] After the Buddha's death, this recitation was made more elaborate, and was repeated every two weeks.

Early Buddhist Councils

A generation or two after the Buddha's death, a recollecting process was necessary to establish Buddhism as a religion. His teachings, the stories of His life, His expectations of the order, and His relics, or symbolic remains, had to be gathered, authenticated, and distributed properly. These tasks were the main agenda at the first four Buddhist Councils. The First Council was held about 483 BCE in Rajaghra. The Second was held about 383 BCE in Vaisali, and it focused on monastic discipline. The Third was held about 346 BCE in Pataliputra and it focused on some doctrinal differences that were emerging. This was the first sign of the Theravada / Mahayana split that would take place two or three centuries later. The Fourth was held about 252 BCE in Pataliputra during Asoka's reign, and it focused on identifying heretical beliefs. The fifth was held about 90 CE in Kashmir or Ghandara during Kanishka's reign, and it established a new monastic discipline.

Asoka: The Emperor Who Made Buddhism a World Religion

Asoka ruled India for forty years (272–232 BCE) and was among the greatest religiously-motivated monarchs in history. He became the archetypal Buddhist king, having worked tirelessly toward establishing a dharma realm—a civilization based on Buddhist virtues of righteousness, compassion, toleration, and service. Hindus, Buddhist, Jains, and skeptics were all included as "children of the king" with the right to live happily and attain heaven. Through a system of dharma officers, he spread Buddhism in three directions: northwest toward Central Asia, south toward Sri Lanka, and east toward Southeast Asia. At least thirty-two of his famous rock and pillar edicts have been found, in which he shared some of his Buddhist beliefs for all to see. He exhorted people to have "few sins and many good deeds, of kindness, liberality, truthfulness and purity." He described the level of sacrifice one needs to have for their beliefs, "This world and the next are hard to gain without great devotion to dharma, great self-awareness, great obedience, great care, great effort: through my instruction, reverence and love for dharma increase each day." He also recognized that his impact went beyond his kingdom, but affected the whole world, "I am not satisfied with fulfilling the obligations of the state, for I reckon my work to be for the welfare of the whole world. . . . I do all I can, to clear my debt to all beings."[72]

The Apocryphal Journeys

As a way of legitimizing the authenticity of the Buddhist Faith in areas removed from the Ganges Plain, elaborate stories about Buddha's visits to other areas were developed. These visits were said to take place in the Northwest, including what is today called Pakistan, Afghanistan, and Central Asia; Southern India and Sri Lanka; and Southeast Asia, including what is today called Burma or Myanmar. In these stories, indigenous deities are tolerated, but given Buddhist sponsorship, which was an important principle for centuries of Buddhist growth and intercultural relations.

Early Buddhist Art and Story: Mutually Influential

Scholars have noticed that the interpretation of Buddhist stories influenced Buddhist sculpture and painting, and in turn, the artistic interpretations of events in the Buddha's life influenced how stories and traditions developed. The same patterns of mutual influence have also been found between Buddhist rituals and ceremonies and Buddhist stories, as well as between pilgrimage sites and the stories associated with them.[73]

Theravada and Mahayana: Two Major Schools

Theravada Buddhism, known as the way of the elders, claims to be the religion of the historical Buddha. Today it is found in Sri Lanka, Burma (Myanmar), Thailand, Cambodia, and Indonesia. It emphasizes self-effort (more than grace), wisdom (more than compassion), monastic orders (more than lay practice), the arhat who remains in nirvana after death (more than the bodhisattva who returns to the world), the Buddha as a saintly teacher (more than as savior), minimal rituals metaphysics, and meditation (more than petitionary prayer). The earliest Buddhist texts we have support the Theravada interpretation. Mahayana Buddhism, known as the great vehicle, claims to be the spirit of all Buddhas in and beyond the world. Today it is found in China, Tibet, Mongolia, Japan, and Korea. It emphasizes grace (more than self-effort), compassion (more than wisdom), lay adaptations (more than monastic commitment), the socially-oriented bodhisattva (more than the individualistic arhat), the Buddha as a savior (more than a saint or teacher), elaborate rituals, metaphysics, and petitionary chants (more than meditation). The way the Buddha lived supports Mahayana interpretation.

Spread of Buddhism in Asia

Buddhism spread to northeastern and southern India, Sri Lanka, and Burma about 250 BCE; to Central Asia about 150 BCE; to China about 50 CE; to Cambodia about 150 CE; to Vietnam about 250 CE; to Malaysia, Indonesia, and Korea about 370 CE; to Thailand and Japan about 550 CE; to Tibet about 740 CE; and to Mongolia about 1250 CE. But by 1200 CE, it almost disappeared in India, though it had often been confluent with the Hindu Faith as in Gupta times.[74]

24 – Renewing Scriptural Guidance: The Tripitaka

The most reliable and authentic of early Buddhist scriptures are called the Tripitaka (three baskets). The first of these three collections is called the Sutta Pitaka, and its four most important sections are the Digha Nikaya (spiritual discourses), the Majjhima Nikaya (sermons and stories), the Samyutta Nikaya (the Eightfold Path and the components of personality), and the Khuddaka-Nikaya (epigrams and maxims, including the very well-loved Dhammapada). The second basket is called the Vinaya Pitaka (the Book of Monastic Discipline) and it codifies the rules of the order or sangha. The third basket is called the Abhidhamma Pitaka (the Book of Philosophical Discourses). But we must remember that, just as there is more Jewish scripture than the recorded words of Moses, and more Christian scripture than the recorded words of Christ, there is also more Buddhist scripture than the recorded words of Buddha. Other influential texts include: Treatise on the Awakening of Faith, Perfection of Wisdom, Diamond Sutra, Pure Land Sutras, Root Verses on the Middle Way, Lotus Sutra, and Guide to the Bodhisattva's Way of Life.

25 – Generating Civilization Anew: Compassionate and Service-Oriented Society

What vision of civilization sustained various Buddhist societies over the last twenty-five centuries? There were a range of views, but Buddha's social teachings offer a unified vision, and established an advanced spiritual civilization, which envisioned a caste-less society that was compassionate and service-oriented. *"The people will all feel equal, and will be of one mind, mutually expressing pleasure upon meeting their fellows."*[75] Buddha saw poverty as a cause of immorality and crime, and taught that the economy must be forever improving.

Buddha envisioned righteous rulers who would command: *"You shall slay no living thing. You shall not take what has not been given. You shall not act wrongly, touching bodily desires. You shall speak no lie. You shall drink no maddening drink."*[76] A righteous ruler could lead to the happiness of all, *"The whole land dwells in happiness if the ruler lives aright."*[77] Buddha taught that a king should be willing to make sacrifices on behalf of the people, *"A king should abandon his own precious life, but not the jewel of Righteousness, whereby the world is gladdened."*[78] Just as Buddha made the kings Bimbisara and Pasenadi His partners in social reform, spiritual principles and civil rule must become closely integrated.

The sangha was a blueprint for a whole new social order, and a model for republican governments, proceeding in a highly consultative manner, similar to what took place under Asoka. Guidance of the wise and learned was to be heeded on all the issues facing leaders and civil servants. Taxes were to be moderate, punishments mild, elders honored, women and children protected and nurtured, and the entire economy geared toward peace and prosperity for all.

- 13 -
Christ: Background and Mission

Jesus Christ is the most familiar Founder to most Westerners, and He is revered by almost a third of humanity as the "only Son of God." However, this familiarity and standard interpretation bring some obstacles to His being embraced as among a series of spiritually comparable Figures. The diverse range of beliefs about Christ make it more difficult to appraise Him as part of a providential plan in which other Founders play equally significant roles. This means, in approaching Him afresh, we are competing with a vast number of claims from various sects, along with their conflicting doctrines and interpretations. Yet peace between the religions requires such a reappraisal, and so we venture forth toward a more universal view.

1 – Continuity with Previous Dispensations:
Israel's Trials, Prophecies, and Messianic Expectations

Christians understand their Faith to be a continuation and fulfillment of Moses' dispensation. That is why they published and distributed the Hebrew Scriptures along with the New Testament, and not just the latter alone. Jesus Himself affirmed this sense of continuity and fulfillment. To the Jewish leaders of His day He taught, *"Do not think that I shall accuse you to the Father; it is Moses who accuses you, on whom you set your hopes. If you believed Moses, you would believe me, for he wrote of me."* [1] This was a declaration that, in order to follow Moses sincerely, Jews were required to follow the One Who Moses said would succeed Him.

Jesus also spoke to Jewish leaders about continuity. He said, *"Think not that I have come to abolish the law and the prophets; I have come not to abolish them but to fulfil them."* [2] Here the emphasis was on perfecting and completing the process that was given decisive shape by Moses. The Christian revelation that was generated after Jesus' own teaching and ministry would also emphasize continuity with, and fulfillment of, the Mosaic revelation. *"In*

239

many and various ways God spoke of old to our fathers by the prophets; but in these last days he has spoken to us by a Son."[3] This suggests that the same God taught through several means down through the ages—patriarchs, lawgivers, prophets, and now a Son. The background of Jesus' story includes major developments in the history of Israel after David. We touch briefly on this span of over 900 years. Such an overview will help us appreciate the challenging conditions Christ faced, and the new forces He set in motion.

Divided Kingdom (922–721 BCE)

Succession problems began immediately upon Solomon's death when his son Rehoboam increased the people's taxes and workloads. A protestor, Jeroboam, led the ten northern tribes in rebellion against Rehoboam. Jeroboam established a capital at Shechem and established shrines centered on the worship of golden calves. This conflict became two states in political and military opposition—Israel in the north, Judah in the south.

Fall of Northern Kingdom, Assyrian Domination (721–587 BCE)

Assyria captured the capital city of Samaria in 721 BCE, ending the Kingdom of Israel (northern tribes) and scattering the Ten Lost Tribes into historical oblivion. However, Judah (southern tribes) had more dynastic stability and survived, but precariously, due to the ever-present threat of Assyrian oppression. Judah claimed to be faithful to the House of David. But the Babylonians destroyed Jerusalem and its Temple in 587 BCE, deporting the Jewish people to Babylon, thus ending the Kingdom of Judah also, and beginning a half century of exile.

Prophetic Warnings, Messianic Prophecies (circa 740–540 BCE)

Israel and Judah were warned—especially by Isaiah, Jeremiah, and Ezekiel—that foreign oppression and suffering would result from their weakened faith and disobedience to the covenant. Their increasing attachment to morally shallow and worldly ways would bring dispersion, if not annihilation. But Israel and Judah were also told of the fulfillment of divine promises in future dispensations, providing other covenantal opportunities and judgments.

Isaiah gave a frightening warning to Jerusalem, and its fulfillment began in 721 when Assyrians swept down from the north: *"Behold, the Lord will hurl you away violently, O you strong man. He will seize firm hold on you, and whirl you round and round, throw you like a ball into a wide land."*[4] But Isaiah also made dramatic announcements that contributed to intensifying messianic expectation through the centuries: *"O house of David! . . . The Lord himself will give you a sign. Behold, a young woman shall conceive and bear a son."*[5] And Isaiah prophesied that this child would lead the people, *"For to us a child is born, to us a son is given; and the government will be upon his shoulder, and his name will be called 'Wonderful Counselor, Mighty God, Everlasting Father, Prince of Peace.' Of the increase of his government and of peace there will be no end."*[6] Later, Christians became convinced that this pointed directly to Christ. Muslims and Bahá'ís would claim that it also pointed to later dispensations.

Jeremiah warned Judah that, like the northern tribes of Israel, their days were numbered. Warning of a future threat, he said, *"Lift up your eyes and see those who come from the north."*[7] But Jeremiah also offered a vision of the messianic age: *"Behold, the days are coming, says the Lord, when I will make a new covenant with the house of Israel and the house of Judah."*[8] This was another important prophecy that was interpreted differently in succeeding dispensations.

Ezekiel anticipated the Babylonian captivity, giving this prophecy specifically to the prince in Jerusalem: *"I will bring him to Babylon in the land of the Chaldeans, yet he shall not see it; and he shall die there."*[9] The prophecy also spoke of the fate of the prince's subjects, *"And they shall know that I am the Lord, when I disperse them among the nations and scatter them through the countries."*[10] But Ezekiel also prophesied God's bountiful promises: *"I will make a covenant of peace with them; it shall be an everlasting covenant with them; and I will bless them and multiply them, and I will set my sanctuary in the midst of them for evermore."*[11] These prophecies supported the opposing messianic views that developed among early first century Christians and Jews.

Daniel shared a prophecy or vision he had of four beasts. Christians interpreted the symbolic beasts as Babylonians, Medes, Persians, and Greeks. But others saw in this imagery a more long-term sequence such as Jews, Greco-Romans, Christians, and Muslims. In Daniel's vision he saw *"One like a son of man. . . . And to him was given dominion and glory and kingdom, that all peoples, nations, and languages should serve him; his dominion is an everlasting dominion."*[12] Christians interpreted the son of man as Jesus; Muslims believed the reference was to Muḥammad; and Bahá'ís have claimed that this figure best represents Bahá'u'lláh.

Babylonian Captivity and Exile (587–538 BCE)

Though it lasted only two generations, the Babylonian captivity had a powerful impact on Jewish self-understanding and aspirations, generating an
outpouring of religious eloquence, which can most especially be seen in the
inspired writings of Ezekiel and Second Isaiah. There was a great longing
for the recovery of a Davidic kingdom. There was also a major shift from
land-owning and agrarian village life to urban professions such as trade and
banking. A substantial number of Jews chose to stay in Babylon after being
liberated, and many of them prospered there. From this point forward, there
would always be Jews in diaspora, or an "Israel abroad," which would live
spiritually on sacred memories, as well as dreams of restoration.

Cyrus' Liberation, Return of the Faithful Remnant (538–332 BCE)

Cyrus the Great of Persia, a Zoroastrian-inspired emperor, conquered Babylonia and made it a Persian province. Very soon after, he allowed Jewish exiles
to return to their homeland, Palestine. Why did he do this? At least part of
the answer may be that Cyrus perceived the God of the Jews to be the very
same Creator he recognized under the name of Ahura Mazda, the Wise Lord.
In addition to liberating the Jews, he committed himself and his successors to
helping them rebuild their Temple in Jerusalem. Zerubbabel led the returning "faithful remnant" in rebuilding the Temple, which was completed in 515
BCE. In the Second Temple, the invisible presence of God was no longer attached to a manmade object as it had been to the Ark of the Covenant. Ezra,
a priest who had been a scribe in the Persian government, and Nehemiah, a
former cupbearer for a Persian king, were both instrumental in reforming the
Jewish community and rebuilding Jerusalem as the capital city. For the next
few centuries, Jews survived as a tiny theocracy, attempting to live under the
precepts of the Torah, while giving allegiance to tolerant Persian rulers.

Hellenistic Domination (332–167 BCE)

Alexander of Macedonia subdued Palestine in 332 BCE as part of his massive
campaign to spread Greek culture throughout Europe, Egypt, and the near
East. By 301 BCE the Ptolemies controlled Egypt and Judea (old Judah),
while the Seleucids controlled Babylonia, Syria, and Asia Minor. The Ptolemies were relatively tolerant and allowed a Judean high priest to rule the
Jews in daily affairs by presiding over an advisory council of elders. In 198
BCE, the Seleucids gained control of Judea and were less tolerant of Jews,

trying to impose Greek culture and religion. In many cases, they lured Jews into more deeply Hellenistic practices, especially in Alexandria and Antioch. Diaspora Jews came to outnumber those in Judea, and the Bible transmitted to the later Christian church was the Greek version called the Septuagint.

Maccabean Revolt, Hasmonean Priest-Kings (167–63 BCE)

The Seleucid king, Antiochus Epiphanes, virtually transformed Jerusalem into a Greek city, killing many Judean protesters, banning the Torah and Sabbath observance, and rededicating the Temple to the Greek god Zeus. But Judas Maccabeas led a successful revolt that enabled Judeans to purify the Temple in 164 BCE. The Hasmonean dynasty then became the rulers of Judea. The Idumeans, who lived just south of Judea, were forcibly converted to Judaism. Pharisees rose to prominence during this period. They were strict adherents and teachers of the written and oral law attributed to Moses, and they became the center of opposition to the politically minded and culturally compromising Hasmonean rulers. Janneus, a tyrannical priest-king, ordered hundreds of executions of Pharisee leaders.

2 – Arising to Guide Humanity in the Worst of Times: Oppression under Rome and Herod (63 BCE–30 CE)

The Roman general Pompey seized Jerusalem in 63 BCE, and violated the inner sanctuary of the Temple. In 37 BCE Herod the Great was made king of the Jews by Roman decree, and he took Jerusalem by force from the last Hasmonean ruler. Most Jews felt oppressed both by their Roman overlords and by the assigned local ruler, Herod. Herod dealt harshly with his Jewish opponents, setting up a very controlling and efficient administration, employing Greek advisors and mercenary soldiers, and undertaking massive and expensive building campaigns. He hoped that erecting the greatest of all Temples on Mount Zion would consolidate his disputed kingship. He made many compromises with Rome to maintain his delicately balanced power over a Judea racked by sectarian tensions and messianic discontent.

Sectarian Tensions in Jesus' Day (7 BCE–30 CE)

A number of different sects developed within Judaism. The major sects that we know about are the Sadducees, the Pharisees, the Essenes, and the Zealots. The Sadducees were a priestly class and politically-minded aristocracy who officiated in the Temple. They also controlled the Sanhedrin, which functioned as a combination of supreme court and legislature, and was granted much freedom by Rome. They reduced religion to the written Mosaic law, and opposed the Pharisees' tendency to develop oral traditions. The Sadducees' concessions to the spirit of the times made them appear shallow to Pharisees. The Pharisees were the primary rivals of the Sadducees, deriving social standing from their detailed learning and devotion to both written and oral Torah, especially the Holiness Code. They taught in synagogues, often emphasizing the resurrection of the dead and messianic prophecies. The Pharisees advocated a separate Jewish nation, yet remained active in the debates of their day. The Essenes sought refuge in complete isolation from corrupt national life, maintaining a strict ethical and ascetic regimen in communal settings away from towns. The Dead Sea Scrolls offer an account of their practices and beliefs, including ritual bathing and emphasis on the end time or new spiritual advent. The Zealots advocated divinely-assisted armed revolt against their Roman oppressors and conceived of the Messiah in political-military terms. Their sporadic acts of resistance led to a major revolt that began in 66 CE and eventually resulted in the Roman destruction of the Second Temple and the fall of Jerusalem in 70 CE. Jesus' response to the conditions of His day was unlike any of the beliefs of these sects. His aim was to usher in a new divine kingdom—one that was open to all sects, classes, and nations.

3 – Advent Prophesied and Expected: John the Baptist Prepares the Way

The coming of Christ was heralded by John the Baptist, and John's coming was prophesied centuries ahead by Isaiah and Malachi, and months ahead by an angel. Isaiah said: *"A voice cries: 'In the wilderness prepare the way of the Lord, make straight in the desert a highway for our God."* [13] Malachi prophesied: *"Behold, I send my messenger to prepare the way before me."* [14] An angel spoke to the priest Zachariah about the coming of his son, John the Baptist. The angel said of Zachariah's son: *"he will be filled with the Holy Spirit, even from his mother's womb. . . . And he will go before him in the spirit of and power of Elijah . . . to make ready for the Lord a people prepared."* [15] Later, Zachariah would prophesy to his son: *"And you, child, will be called the prophet of the Most High; for you will go before the Lord to prepare his ways."* [16]

Some scholars suggest that John may have been an Essene, as the Essenes engaged in ritual bathing and were intensely focused on an "imminent end" and a "new beginning." However, John's message was not just to one sect, but to all who would hear; and he attracted many followers with his fiery preaching. What was John's message? He told the people, *"Repent, for the kingdom of heaven is at hand."* [17] He called Pharisees and Sadducees a "brood of vipers" and warned them: *"I baptize you with water for repentance, but he who is coming after me is mightier than I . . . he will baptize you with the Holy Spirit and with fire."* [18] Many were baptized in the Jordan River, confessing their sins. How did Jesus regard John the Baptist? He told the disciples, *"among those born of women there has arisen no one greater than John the Baptist. . . . He is Elijah who is to come."* [19] This is quite high spiritual praise. Yet all four gospels reported John's humility before Jesus, to the effect that he was unworthy to carry Jesus' sandals. John the Baptist said when speaking of Jesus, *"He must increase, but I must decrease."* [20]

4 – Auspicious Signs, Birth, and Intimations of Greatness: Virgin Mother, Davidic Lineage, Shepherds, Angels, Magi, and a Star

The gospels gave Jesus a lineage befitting a Messiah, linking Him to the royal House of David, as well as to the patriarch Abraham. They also refer back to Adam, connecting Jesus' bloodline to God. And John's gospel called Jesus the Word which was "in the beginning," and then *"became flesh and dwelt among us, full of grace and truth."* [21] The name Jesus was the Greek form of Joshua, which meant "God saves." Linked to this name throughout the New Testament is the title Christ, which means messiah, anointed one, or divinely appointed king. At the time of Jesus' birth, there was intense hope among many Jews that the Anointed One was about to come, and that he would be an ideal king standing alongside an ideal high priest, or perhaps embody both ideals.

The gospels agree on key features of Jesus' birth. Jesus' birth took place in Bethlehem, the city of David, and it occurred during the reign of Herod. The gospels also agree that Jesus was conceived through the Holy Spirit, and that He was destined to be the Savior of humanity. Matthew claimed that Jesus' birth fulfilled Isaiah's prophecy: *"Behold, a young woman shall conceive and bear a son, and his name shall be called Immanuel."* [22] In Luke, the angel Gabriel told Mary that her Son *"will be great, and will be called the Son of the Most High, and the Lord God will give to him the throne of his father David . . . and of his kingdom there will be no end."* [23] Later, Simeon, a devout man in Jerusalem, told Mary that Jesus would be *"a light for revelation to the Gentiles, and for glory to thy people Israel."*[24] Also in Luke, an angel said to some shepherds watching their flock at night, *"I bring you good news of a great joy which will come to all the people; for to you is born this day in the city of David a Savior, who is Christ the Lord."*[25] The note of universality is struck many times in Luke, where the appeal is to all people.

Matthew reported that *"wise men from the East came to Jerusalem, saying 'Where is he who has been born king of the Jews? For we have seen his star in the East, and have come to worship him.'"* They told Herod of the prophecy from Micah: *"O Bethlehem . . . from you shall come a ruler who will govern my people Israel."* The wise men followed the star, which *"came to rest over the place where the child was . . . and they fell down and worshipped him. Then, opening their treasures, they offered Him gifts, gold and frankincense and myrrh."*[26] Who were these wise men? Scholars now widely recognize them as magi—priest-astrologers and followers of Zoroaster. Zoroaster's teachings and vision of civilization were respected by Cyrus, who liberated the Jews from their Babylonian captivity in the sixth century BCE. The magi would have known Zoroastrian prophecies pointing to a new Savior at the time of Jesus. The episode of the magi preserves a major interreligious link—Jewish, Zoroastrian, and Christian scriptures converging on one world-changing event.

The gifts offered by the wise men were highly symbolic: gold was the sign of kingship, frankincense symbolized divinity, and myrrh indicated that one was destined for an early death. Isaiah had prophesied: *"A multitude of camels . . . shall bring gold and frankincense, and shall proclaim the praise of the Lord."*[27] A psalmist had exclaimed: *"may the kings of Sheba . . . bring gifts! May all kings fall down before him, all nations serve him!"*[28] Matthew preserved a very special story indeed, showing how the birth of Jesus could attract far-away dignitaries and experts in astrology and prophecy. Herod had asked the wise men to report to him about the exact location where the child could be worshipped, but the wise men were warned in a dream not to help Herod, and they never returned to him. Enraged by this development, Herod *"killed all the male children in Bethlehem and in all that region who were two years old or under. . . . Then was fulfilled what was spoken by the prophet Jeremiah: 'A Voice was heard in Ramah, wailing and loud lamentation, Rachel weeping for her children; because they were no more.'"*[29]

Another early sign of Jesus' spiritual station is described in Luke. Jesus and His parents attended a Passover celebration in Jerusalem when He was twelve years old. When His parents left Jerusalem, *"Jesus stayed behind. . . . After three days, they found him in the temple, sitting among the teachers, listening to them and asking them questions; and all who heard them were amazed at his understanding and his answers."* When Mary found Jesus, she was quite upset, but Jesus calmly replied: *"Did you not know that I must be in my Father's house? And they did not understand."* But upon returning to Nazareth, Jesus was *"obedient to them; and his mother kept all these things in her heart. And Jesus increased in wisdom and stature, and in favor with God and man."* [30]

5 – Divine Commission: Descent of a Dove and a Heavenly Voice

Just before the start of Jesus' ministry, a symbolic event is described in the Gospel of John. At a wedding celebration, Jesus turned water into wine. *"This, the first of His signs, Jesus did at Cana in Galilee, and manifested his glory."* [31] Though His mission had not formally been declared, the awareness was growing in His various social circles that He was not like other men. Jesus' divine calling was described in quite similar ways by Matthew, Mark, and Luke. John the Baptist, in the midst of his preaching and baptizing, and with great surprise, noticed Jesus, saying: *"I need to be baptized by you, and do you come to me?"* But Jesus humbly replied: *"it is fitting for us to fulfil all righteousness."* While being baptized by John, *"the heavens were opened and he saw the Spirit of God descending like a dove, and alighting on him; and lo, a voice from heaven, saying 'This is my beloved Son with whom I am well pleased.'"* [32] Now Jesus' providential and divinely guided mission began.

In a Qur'ánic version of this episode, God says to Jesus: *"Behold! I strengthened thee with the holy spirit, so that thou didst speak to the people in childhood and in maturity. Behold! I taught thee the Book and Wisdom, the Law and the Gospel."* [33] In the Bahá'í writings, Jesus is referred to as the *"essence"* of the Holy Spirit, Who *"was exalted above the imaginings of all that dwell on earth"* and Who brought a *"quickening power"* and a *"perfect example of love into the world."* [34]

6 – Struggling in Solitude:
Forty Days in the Wilderness, Satan's Offer

After receiving His divine call, Christ spent time in the desert and on a mountain—places that are associated with spiritual testing, purification, healing, and renewal. The basic belief behind this practice was that faith in God can be established by a serious test or trial. Three of the gospels described an event involving distinct demonic temptations. Matthew's account will suffice to show Christ's full understanding and command of the Mosaic revelation, as well as His spiritual readiness for a world transforming mission.

Christ was led *"by the Spirit into the wilderness to be tempted by the devil."* After fasting for *"forty days and forty nights,"* He was hungry, and the devil said: *"If you are the Son of God, command these stones to become loaves of bread."* He replied: *"Man shall not live by bread alone, but by every word that proceeds from the mouth of God."* This was victory over bodily needs. *"Then the devil took him to the holy city, and set him on the pinnacle of the temple, and said to him, 'If you are the Son of God, throw yourself down; for it is written, 'He will give his angels charge of you.'"* He replied: *"You shall not tempt the Lord your God."* This was victory over vanity and self-centeredness. *"Again, the devil took him to a very high mountain, and showed him all the kingdoms of the world and the glory of them; and he said to him, 'All these I will give you, if you will fall down and worship me.'"* He replied: *"Begone, Satan! for it is written, 'You shall worship the Lord your God and him only shall you serve.'"* This was victory over pride and ambition. *"Then the devil left him, and behold, angels came and ministered to him."* [35]

7 – Declaration and First Followers: Twelve Disciples Made Fishers of Men

Christ declared His mission and began recruiting followers in several places. *"Jesus began to preach, saying, 'Repent, for the kingdom of heaven is at hand.'"* To Peter and Andrew, who were casting a net into the Sea of Galilee, Jesus said, *"Follow me, and I will make you fishers of men."* [36] Two other nearby fishermen were recruited. There was initial activity in Nazareth, including to a fulfillment of Isaiah's prophecy. Jesus began preaching in the synagogues: *"The Spirit of the Lord is upon me, because he has anointed me to preach good news to the poor. He has sent me to proclaim release to the captives and recovering of sight to the blind, to see at liberty those who are oppressed, to proclaim the acceptable year of the Lord."* Everyone in the synagogue was rapt in attention. *"Today,"* He said, *"this scripture has been fulfilled in your hearing."* [37] All were impressed with these audacious words.

Luke described the process of spiritual deliberation used by Christ in selecting His disciples. He *"went out to the mountain to pray; and all night he continued in prayer to God. And when it was day, he called his leading disciples, and chose from them twelve, whom he named apostles.*"[38] Twelve seems to be a symbolic number, corresponding to the tribes of the earlier dispensation.

Mark offered other decisive moments of declaration. At Caesarea Philippi, Jesus asked the memorable question *"Who do men say that I am?"* Peter responded with a simple phrase, but one that captured centuries of spiritual yearning and expectation: *"You are the Christ."*[39] But then Jesus asked the disciples not to tell anyone about this yet, for the time of full disclosure was not yet at hand. Later, during His final week, *"the high priest asked him, 'Are you the Christ, the Son of the Blessed?' And Jesus said, 'I am; and you will see the Son of man seated at the right hand of Power, and coming with the clouds of heaven.'"*[40]

8 – Overcoming Powerful Opposition: Chief Priests, Elders, Scribes, Pharisees, and Romans

Instances of opposition and persecution abound in the gospels. The religious leaders and civil authorities of Christ's day opposed Him increasingly during His three-year ministry. Eventually, chief priests and elders conspired to kill Him and, with the assistance of local Roman authorities, had Him crucified. The persecution of the disciples and the early church are described in the Book of Acts in an historical mode, and in the Book of Revelation in an allegorical mode; but here we focus on the account in the gospels. Despite intense opposition, Christ's message and movement spread rapidly, and the new religious community took root across the lands surrounding the Mediterranean Sea. In less than four centuries, the Roman Empire had converted to the Christian Faith, which afterward spread to many other parts of the world.

The first signs of official opposition to Christ's ministry came when the Pharisees asked His disciples, *"'Why does your teacher eat with tax collectors and sinners?' But when he heard it, he said, 'Those who are well have no need of a physician, but those who are sick.'"*[41] After hearing Jesus say *"the Son of man is lord of the sabbath"* and *"it is lawful to do good on the sabbath"* then *"the Pharisees went out and took counsel against him, how to destroy him."*[42] When the people expressed amazement at His healing powers, the Pharisees said, *"It is only by . . . the prince of demons, that this man casts out demons."*[43] Jesus said to His opponents, *"I know that you are descendants of Abraham; yet you seek to kill me, because my word finds no place in you."*[44]

After Peter's confession of faith in Jesus as the Christ, *"Jesus began to show his disciples that he must go to Jerusalem and suffer many things from the elders and chief priests and scribes, and be killed, and on the third day be raised."*[45] At the beginning of His final week, *"Jesus entered the temple of God and drove out all who sold and bought in the temple, and he overturned tables of the money-changers. . . . He said to them, 'It is written, "My house shall be called a house of prayer"; but you make it a den of robbers.'"*[46] Then He taught and healed the people nearby.

The next day, the chief priests and elders challenged His authority to do these things. A high priest *"questioned Jesus about his disciples and his teaching. Jesus answered him, 'I have spoken openly to the world.' . . . Ask those who have heard me.' . . . One of the officers standing by struck Jesus with his hand, saying, 'Is that how you answer the high priest?' . . . Annas* [a leading elder] *then sent him bound to Caiaphas the high priest."*[47]

Before the last supper, *"the chief priests and the elders of the people gathered in the palace of the high priest, who was called Caiaphas, and took counsel together in order to arrest Jesus by stealth and kill him."*[48] John's gospel names the guilty and identifies their motivation. *"The Jews sought all the more to kill him, because he not only broke the sabbath, but also called God his own Father."*[49] In their deliberations they said: *"This man performs many signs. If we let him go on thus, every one will believe in him, and the Romans will come and destroy both our holy place and our nation."* Then the high priest said, *"it is expedient for you that one man should die for the people, and that the whole nation should not perish. . . . So from that day on they took counsel how to put him to death."*[50]

9 – Rejection by the People

Christ said the rejection He and His disciples would encounter had happened before in religious history, and would continue. *"Foxes have holes, and birds of the air have nests; but the Son of man has nowhere to lay his head."*[51] Village after village rejected Christ, despite being impressed with His teaching and charisma. When the Gadarenes saw Christ *"they begged him to leave their neighborhood."*[52] Some Jews said, *"He has a demon, and he is mad."*[53] So Christ prepared His disciples for rejection. *"And if any one will not receive you or listen to your words, shake off the dust from your feet as you leave that house or town. . . . Behold, I send you out as sheep in the midst of wolves. . . . Beware of men; for they will deliver you up to councils, and flog you in their synagogues, and you will be dragged before governors and kings for my sake. . . . You will be hated by all for my name's sake. But he who endures to the end will be saved."*[54]

But the message and ministry of Christ, despite banishment from town to town, took root in Palestine and moved both east and west. People said of Him: *"Behold, a glutton and a drunkard, a friend of tax collectors and sinners!"*[55] Even in His home town of Nazareth, Jesus was derided as merely *"the carpenter's son"* and despite being impressed with His wisdom, *"they took offense at him."* He replied: *"A prophet is not without honor except in his own country and in his own house."*[56] He reminded His disciples that history was repeating itself, that new words of God have always been rejected. *"Blessed are you when men revile you and persecute you and utter all kinds of evil against you falsely on my account. Rejoice and be glad, for your reward is great in heaven, for so men persecuted the prophets who were before you."*[57]

Luke refers to the pattern of persecution throughout history, striking a note of fate. He said that the Son of man *"must suffer many things and be rejected by this generation. As it was in the days of Noah, so will it be in the days of the Son of man."*[58] Christ warned His disciples: *"the hour is coming when whoever kills you will think he is offering service to God."*[59]

Not only did Christ encounter external opposition from religious leaders and the people, He also faced serious internal opposition from one of His disciples. Before the last supper, *"one of the twelve, who was called Judas Iscariot, went to the chief priests and said, 'What will you give me if I deliver him to you?' And they paid him thirty pieces of silver. And from that moment he sought an opportunity to betray him."*[60]

10 – Sacrificial Suffering

The theme of sacrifice—giving up things of worth for things of yet greater worth—gained momentum in the course of Jesus' ministry, and would reach a dramatic climax. Christ's sacrifice was announced early by John the Baptist: *"Behold, the Lamb of God, who takes away the sin of the world!"*[61] The purpose of Jesus' suffering would be to alleviate some of humanity's suffering by teaching humanity about the spiritual kingdom, by establishing a new covenant for believers in His mission, and by resurrecting His spirit in the disciples and the early church.

Jesus spoke often about the importance of sacrifice. Jesus taught that in order to follow Him, and to understand the teachings of God, people would need to sacrifice some part of their selves. *"If any man would come after me, let him deny himself and take up his cross and follow me. For whoever would save his life will lose it, and whoever loses his life for my sake will find it."*[62] Jesus explained that sacrifice was the greatest and noblest act that one could do for another: *"Greater love has no man than this, that a man lay down his life for his friends."*[63] Jesus also made reference to His future sacrifice on behalf of His followers, saying, *"I am the good shepherd. The good shepherd lays down his life for the sheep."*[64]

We do well to remember—each of us individually—that we are not morally above persecutors of the Saviors of humanity. Those who misunderstood and brought suffering to Christ and His disciples represent the corruptible side of human nature, our tendency to cling to the less perfect even after the more perfect has come. Caiaphas the high priest, for example, felt unable to relinquish his privileged position and his hardened views about the Messiah. Angry at Jesus' messianic claim, he said to the other chief priests: *"'You have now heard his blasphemy. What is your judgment?' They answered, 'He deserves death.' Then they spat in his face, and struck him."*[65] This reaction typifies humanity's tendency to persecute Founders, Whose suffering ultimately proves redemptive.

11 – Symbolic Language as a Test for Believers

Christ used many parables or comparisons as a way to challenge and elevate the understanding of His followers, as well as to weed out those with impure hearts and malevolent intentions. To His disciples Jesus said: *"To you it has been given to know the secrets of the kingdom of God; but for others they are in parables, so that seeing they may not see, and hearing they may not understand."*[66] Pharisees and Sadducees failed these tests, because their rigid interpretations of prophecies had been hardened into veils, preventing them from seeing new truths.

At one point in His ministry, Christ explained one of His parables, making each symbol crystal clear to the disciples. In the parable of the sower the seed is the Word of God; what is sown along the path is lost due to temptation; what is sown on the rock is lost due to lack of depth or faith; what falls among thorns is lost due to material attachments; but what is sown on good soil is held *"fast in an honest and good heart, and bring forth fruit with patience."*[67]

Paul summed up the challenge and tragedy of symbolic language very succinctly: *"the written code kills, but the Spirit gives life."*[68] Paul also spelled out the opportunity and danger in more detail.

Now we have received not with the spirit of the world, but the Spirit which is from God, that we might understand the gifts bestowed on us by God. And we impart this in words not taught by human wisdom but taught by the Spirit, interpreting spiritual truths to those who posses the Spirit.

The unspiritual man does not receive the gifts of the Spirit of God, for they are folly to him, and he is not able to understand them because they are spiritually discerned.[69]

Here Paul distinguished spiritual understanding from worldly wisdom, the former bringing light, but the latter bringing rigid doctrine and exclusive prejudice.

John's gospel included a profoundly mystical prayer of Christ, one that can be interpreted in exclusive or universal ways, depending on the degree of detachment brought to its contemplation. *"Father, the hour has come; glorify Thy Son that the Son may glorify Thee."* The prayer goes on to say, *"everything that thou hast given me is from thee."*[70] Was Jesus praying for Christians only? Or for people only of His own day? Or for all of humanity at all times? If God is one and loves all of humanity, this prayer must be viewed universally.

Over the centuries, some Christians have interpreted the symbols of their revelation rigidly and exclusively, thus preventing them from hearing later revelations—the Word of God as presented in the Islamic and the Bahá'í scriptures. This pattern of failing to penetrate the spiritual symbols of new revelation is not unique to any single faith tradition; rather, it has happened throughout world history. Among the most troublesome terms have been *resurrection, body of Christ, return of Christ,* and *Son of man coming on the clouds of heaven.* Interpretations of these key symbols have usually been literal, physical, and exclusive—thus separating Christians from later revelation. Those who awaited the literal return of Christ coming on clouds, in 1843 and 1844, were deeply disappointed. But figurative interpretations could link Christians to the broader providential patterns of world history.

Some of the most intense dispute and tragic distortion was generated in response to these verses: *"Immediately after the tribulations of those days the sun will be darkened, and the moon will not give its light, and the stars will fall from heaven, and the powers of the heavens will be shaken; then will appear the sign of the Son of man in heaven, and then all the tribes of the earth will mourn, and they will see the Son of man coming on the clouds of heaven with power and great glory."*[71] Taking this literally and awaiting such a cosmic catastrophe, followed by the historic Jesus descending from visible clouds to the tangible earth, led to deep and widespread spiritual anguish and disenchantment. But another interpretation could explain not only this passage, but countless similar ones in the world's scriptures that all point to the process by which the older dispensation comes to an end and a newer one begins.

What if the terms *sun, moon, stars, Son of man,* and *clouds* were to be interpreted more broadly, spiritually, and universally? Bahá'u'lláh taught that the terms *sun, moon,* and *stars* used in Biblical scriptures represent the worldly powers of their day and age—religious and civil leaders, priests, and kings—whose understanding became darkened due to their worldly attachments. These corrupt leaders inevitably "fell" because they became veiled from truth.

The term *Son of man* represents the new Divine Teacher Who, from nourishing clouds of heaven, brought a saving message. Christ's successors—Muḥammad and Bahá'u'lláh—like Christ Himself, inevitably produced tribulation and mourning at first, before a new religious civilization could be established. But the dying of the old order eventually brings the birth of the new order. Each new dispensation has inevitably brought progress, enriching "all the tribes of the earth" in a spiritual sense.

12 – Exemplary Women for All Ages: Mary the Nurturer, Mary Magdalene the Advocate

After learning of and fully embracing her divine purpose and mission, Mary, the future mother of Jesus, uttered these immortal and revelatory words called the Magnificat.

> *My soul magnifies the Lord, and my spirit rejoices in God my Savior, for he has regarded the low estate of his handmaiden. For behold, henceforth all generations will call me blessed; for he who is mighty has done great things for me, and holy is his name. And his mercy is on those who fear him from generation to generation. He has shown strength with his arm, he has scattered the proud in the imagination of their hearts, he has put down the mighty from their thrones, and exalted those of low degree; he has filled the hungry with good things, and the rich he has sent empty away. He has helped his servant Israel, in remembrance of his mercy, as he spoke to our fathers, to Abraham and to his posterity for ever.*[72]

Mother Mary became revered as the ultimate model of nurturance, purity, compassion, and patience. She became preeminent among saints. Her blessedness has been upheld outside the traditional boundaries of Christian Faith. She is mentioned with great reverence many times in the Qur'án. For example, one passage in the Qur'án says, *"Behold! The angels said: 'O Mary! God giveth thee glad tidings of a Word from Him: his name will be Christ Jesus, the son of Mary, held in honour in this world and the Hereafter and of (the company of) those nearest to God'"* She responded to the angel and said: *"'O my Lord! How shall I have a son when no man has touched me?' He said: 'Even so, God createth what He willeth'"*[73] The purity of Mary is also upheld in Bahá'í writings.

If Mother Mary was the exemplar of compassionate nurture, Mary Magdalene was the exemplar of communicative advocacy. Mary from Magdala was among several women who publicly supported Jesus and His disciples from early in their ministry through the time of the crucifixion, the resurrection, and the establishing of the early church. She had been healed by Jesus, and from that point forward was perhaps the most independent of those women following the teachings of Jesus. In John's gospel, she was the first to witness the resurrection, and she was asked by Christ to report it to the disciples. After He called her by name, she was able to distinguish Him from an angel. *"Jesus said to her 'Mary.' She turned and said to him in Hebrew, 'Rabboni!' (which means Teacher!) Jesus said to her, 'Do not hold me, for I have not yet ascended to the Father; but go to My brethren and say to them, I am ascending to my Father and your Father, to my God and your God.' Mary Magdalene went and said to the disciples, 'I have seen the Lord'; and she told them that he had said these things to her."*[74]

Mary Magdalene was called the "apostle of the apostles" by some early church theologians and historians. The longstanding traditional belief that she had been a prostitute was formally declared to be a mistake by the Roman Catholic Church in 1969. "Mary Magdalene is now recognized as a pioneering representative of women's ministry, for which there is much evidence in the New Testament, but which was rapidly suppressed by men in the Church until its spasmodic but accumulating recovery in the twentieth cent[ury]."[75]

13 – Dying and Ascending Victoriously: Crucifixion and Resurrection

Christ's death and ascension were more integral to His mission, message, and legacy than was the case for other Founders. A major portion of the gospel testimony is devoted to the elaborate story of His trial, crucifixion, and resurrection. We touch on the essentials of this story.

Trial and Crucifixion

Christ was identified and detained by Jewish authorities. *"Judas came, one of the twelve, and with him a great crowd with swords and clubs, from the chief priests and the elders of the people. Now the betrayer had given them a sign, saying, 'The one I shall kiss is the man; seize him.'"*[76] Then He was brought before the Roman governor Pilate. Chief priests and elders persuaded the people to ask for Barabbas to be spared, and for Jesus to be killed. In Mark's account, considerable guilt is imputed to the Romans as colluding with Jewish leaders in the execution. *"Pilate, wishing to satisfy the crowd . . . and having scourged Jesus . . . delivered him to be crucified."* Soon after this, the soldiers put a crown of thorns on His head, mocked and stripped Him, and *"led him out to crucify him."*[77]

In Matthew's account, Pilate seemed unwilling to crucify Christ. He asked the chief priests, *"'Then what shall I do with Jesus who is called Christ?" They all said, 'Let him be crucified.' And he* [Pilate] *said, 'Why, what evil has he done?' But they shouted all the more, 'Let him be crucified.'"* Seeing that the crowd had made its decision, Pilate *"washed his hands before the crowd, saying 'I am innocent of this man's blood; see to it yourselves."*[78] Then the soldiers of the governor stripped Him and mocked Him and then crucified Him. As they passed by Him they said, *"'If you are the Son of God, come down from the cross.' So also the chief priests, with the scribes and elders, mocked him, saying, 'He saved others; he cannot save himself. He is the King of Israel; let him come down now from the cross, and we will believe in him. He trusts in God; let God deliver him now, if he desires him, for he said, 'I am the Son of God.'"*[79]

Even after all of their taunts and mockery, Jesus was the essence of forgiveness. While dying on the cross, Christ said: *"Father, forgive them; for they know not what they do."* And later, right before he breathed His last breath, Jesus said, *"Father, into thy hands I commit my spirit!"*[80] At which point Christ's spirit ascended to the heavenly realm.

For Mother Mary, Mary Magdalene, the disciples, and the other grief-stricken followers gathered at Golgotha, the great promise of their Savior's life ended in seeming shame. No one fully grasped the significance of these events, though many present were aware that something momentous had happened when Christ yielded His spirit. *"The earth shook, and the rocks were split; the tombs also were opened, and many bodies of the saints who had fallen asleep were raised. . . . When the centurion and those who were with him, keeping watch over Jesus, saw the earthquake and what took place, they were filled with awe, and said, 'Truly this man was the Son of God!'"* [81]

The women helped with the wrapping of the body in linen and spices. His body was laid in the tomb, and the entrance was sealed with a large stone. The disciples were in despair, while Christ's opponents were satisfied that His dangerous movement was at last eliminated. It seemed that Christ's mission had ended in disgrace, with the hope for a new spiritual kingdom utterly shattered.

Ascension and Resurrection

None could have been prepared for the amazing and revelatory events that were to unfold over the next few days. The women who came to anoint Christ's body made the astonishing discovery that the tomb was empty. What could this mean? The women were told by angels, *"Why do you seek the living among the dead? Remember how he told you . . . that the Son of man must be delivered into the hand of sinful men, and be crucified, and on the third day rise.'"* [82] Post-resurrection appearances were soon to come. An angel told the women: *"You seek Jesus who was crucified. He is not here; for he has risen. . . . Tell his disciples that he has risen from the dead, and behold, he is going before you to Galilee; there you will see him."* [83]

Meanings and Mysteries of the Resurrection

Among the most influential stories about Christ inherited by humanity is that He conquered death, that His spirit transcended His bodily demise on the cross. Even His physical remains could not be held down by a large stone. The gospels report that shortly after the empty tomb was discovered, the risen Christ appeared to Mary Magdalene, to Peter, to two disciples walking to Emmaus, to His fearful disciples gathered in Jerusalem, to the doubting Thomas, to the fishermen in Galilee, and finally to Saul on the road to Damascus, the man later called Paul, the apostle to the Gentiles.

Christians also inherit the tradition that, though taken up to heaven, Christ left the promise that He would return. It seems unfortunate that rigidly literal interpretations of this story have prevented many from appreciating its profound spiritual significance, and its continuity with the legacies of other Founders and Saviors. It seems that another interpretation might be that the spirit of Christ's life and ministry had been resurrected and was present anew among the disciples and the early church. His qualities and powers returned, and invigorated them. It is also possible that after great Prophets and Saviors die, spiritual forces not fully explainable are released. Such spiritual forces would help account for how the Founders have been able to transform souls and societies, and generate new religious civilizations.

In the Qur'án, God said to Jesus: *"O Jesus! I will take thee and raise thee to Myself. . . . I will make those who follow thee superior to those who reject faith."* [84] The Qur'án also seems to say that Christ was not crucified, but this can be interpreted as meaning that though Jesus' body was crucified, His spirit or His spiritual station could not have been crucified, for it is eternal and divine.[85] In the Bahá'í writings, Christ's resurrection is interpreted spiritually. *"The Cause of Christ was like a lifeless body; and when after three days the disciples became assured and steadfast, and began to serve the Cause of Christ, and resolved to spread the divine teachings, putting His counsels into practice, and arising to serve Him, the Reality of Christ became resplendent and His bounty appeared. . . . In other words, the Cause of Christ was like a lifeless body until the life and the bounty of the Holy Spirit surrounded it."* [86] Though literal interpretations have often dominated theological thought regarding Christ's life and teaching, a spiritual interpretation should not be discounted. Religious scripture often contains many layers of meaning, and it often takes a sense of detachment from our preconceived ideas to understand the underlying spiritual meaning of the Founders' words and actions.

- 14 -
Christ: Teaching and Legacy

14 – Transformative Teaching and Healing: Words of Power, Good Deeds, and Miraculous Healing

Christ's transformative mission is said to have taken place in only three dramatic years, probably between the years 27–30 CE. This ministry included revolutionary teaching, healing work, and the ushering in of a spiritual kingdom. Peter once described Christ's mission in five simple words: *"he went about doing good."*[1] In several places, Jesus summarized His own mission briefly as well: *"the Son of man came to seek and to save the lost."*[2] Put in another way, He said, *"I did not come to judge the world but to save the world."*[3] Through powerful teaching and healing, Christ set out to lift the human race out of rigid, divisive legalism, out of violent oppressiveness, and up to new heights of spiritual awareness, compassion, and service.

We can divide the story of Jesus' life into three main periods: His early years, His ministry, and His final days. In the previous chapter we looked at His early years and final days. Here we explore His transformative ministry. There are a number of stories of Christ's ministry that are well-known and considered historically probable; but even if they are not strictly historical, their spiritual potency should not be denied. For example Jesus was said to have cleansed lepers, cured a paralytic and a deaf man, restored sight to the blind, and cast out demons. Beyond His miraculous ability to heal, Jesus also spent much of His time teaching. He is known for sharing the Word of God through parables, for preaching in synagogues, and for delivering the Sermon on the Mount.

This was a stunning record of "going about doing good," especially given the likelihood that other stories were omitted from gospel accounts. Jesus especially shared his spiritual teachings with His disciples, and they became trained as teachers and healers, and provided a powerful model of courage and steadfastness. Many of Christ's eyewitnesses concluded that a divine visitation had taken place. Some began to think of the "kingdom" in terms other than legal, political, or ritual-based interpretations that had previously been accepted as the only way to understand it. A new spiritual order was in the making. Christ's teaching set in motion a process at once transforming and disruptive, that spread to the Near East, as well as to Asia Minor, Greece, Rome, and later, many other countries across the globe.

15 – Delivering a Thematic and Complementary Message: Attaining the Kingdom of Heaven through Sacrificial Love

Christ's message to humanity, though placing more emphasis on inner transformation and less on ritual-legal guidance than Moses' message, was complementary to that of His predecessor. Jesus' central theme integrated teachings on love, salvation, and the kingdom of heaven. His concept of salvation applied both to the individual and to society, but it began with the individual and moved outward. The central theme of His teaching was that it was possible to attain the kingdom of heaven through sacrificial love, and He also enhanced the Mosaic focus on obedience to divine law. Christ offered a set of spiritual, social, and material guidelines with the power to generate a lofty religious civilization.

Sermon on the Mount

Scholars have surmised that Matthew collected summaries of many of Christ's sermons and placed most of them close together in his gospel. The set called the Sermon on the Mount offered the keynote for the kingdom Christ came to establish. The Beatitudes declared, in effect, that those who have been neglected—those who were referred to as the last or least—will be first and highest in the age to come. The wealthy and powerful were warned; the poor and downtrodden were lifted up. Since many were concerned about the relation between this new teaching and the Mosaic law, Christ put emphasis on fulfillment and completion, rather than replacement or abolishment. Inward qualities must now supplement outward observances and legal formalities. Prayer must now transcend empty phrases; it must align our will with God's, making earth *"as it is in heaven."*[4] Worldly treasures must be replaced with spiritual treasures of loving service and discerning justice.

Salvation and the Kingdom of Heaven

Many of Christ's most important teachings centered around "salvation" and the "kingdom of God," which are terms from the gospels of Mark and Luke, or the "kingdom of heaven," which is a term from the gospel of Matthew. The gospel of John used similar phrases, such as the "kingship not of this world" or the "glory of God." All these terms are ways of pointing to the process and attainment of ethical and spiritual fulfillment—a means and a goal primarily for the individual, but also for humanity as a whole. A special kind of love is required in this process, and there is no suggestion that it will be easy. Rather, it is a sacrifice. *"Whoever does not bear his own cross and come after me, cannot be my disciple. . . . Whoever of you does not renounce all that he has cannot be my disciple."*[5] Christ offered salvation, or the attainment of the kingdom of heaven, through sacrificial love. Humanity must become worthy of the great spiritual joy that accompanies the coming of the kingdom, and Jesus taught that this comes through repentance, steadfast faith, loving devotion, and service. This was a very different kind of kingdom than Jews were expecting, based on their memory of David's united kingdom, which was, in part, a political and military achievement.

Major questions arose about Jesus' kingdom in His own day, perplexities that have endured through the ages to our own day. What is the exact nature of the kingdom? What is required to attain it? To whom is it available? When and how will it come? This question was especially pressing, and Christ taught five different (or paradoxical) ideas about it: 1) it was always available—for children, or those who could adopt a child-like acceptance; 2) it was here and now, in Christ's presence—in the very midst of His followers; 3) it would come soon—when the new dispensation takes full effect; 4) it would come after death—as a heavenly reward after martyrdom; and 5) it would come at the end of the age—when *"the times of the Gentiles are fulfilled,"* accompanied by *"signs in sun and moon and stars."*[6] Most of Christ's references to the kingdom seem to relate to the present or to the immediate future, yet there is scriptural evidence for all of these interpretations. It seems best to view them all as carrying a kind of truth, while remembering that Jesus' teachings were intended to fulfill and complete the Mosaic law spiritually, rather than to entirely replace it.

Parables of the Kingdom

The method Christ used for conveying aspects of the kingdom was the parable—a comparison between a common image or incident of daily life and a lofty ethical and spiritual concept. Parables awakened the conscience and spirit, and inspired deeper commitment and faith. They were revelatory jolts, forcing listeners to examine life and ultimate reality in a new way. They pointed to the kingdom as the complete opposite of the world as ordinarily experienced. It was a realm of mind and spirit aligned with divine will and purpose.

How was the kingdom to be understood by ordinary people in everyday walks of life? What was it like? How did it feel? What changes would it bring about? In parables, Christ taught that it could be compared to rejoicing at a wedding, a seed sown and growing on good soil, harvesting at the end of the age, righteousness shining like the sun, treasure hidden in one's own field, a pearl of great price for which all else should be sold, neighborliness and mercy shown to an afflicted stranger, being invited to a great banquet, being once dead and now alive or being once lost and now found, a vineyard in which the owner gives some of the laborers more than promised, or bread from heaven giving life to this world. As we can see from these examples, Jesus used common images, such as agricultural practices or special events, to describe the heavenly realm and his new spiritual teachings to people in a way that could be easily understood.

Most of these metaphors for the kingdom of heaven in Christ's parables can be placed in three broad categories: 1) organic images of growth and renewal; 2) light images involving seeing, knowing, and discerning the hidden; and 3) love images of inclusion into the fold, or receiving sacrificial care.

Love and Sacrifice

Other summaries of Christ's essential message are given in passages of the gospels which do not employ parables. In one situation Jesus was asked which law was most important to follow, and Jesus replied in a very direct manner. A Pharisee asked Jesus, *"Teacher, which is the great commandment in the law?"* And Jesus replied: *"You shall love the Lord your God with all your heart, and with all your soul, and with all your mind. This is the great and first commandment. And a second is like it, You shall love your neighbor as yourself. On these two commandments depend all the law and the prophets."*[7] On this same theme,

Christ also taught: "*Love your enemies, do good to those who hate you, bless those who curse you, pray for those who abuse you. To him who strikes you on the cheek, offer the other also. . . . And as you wish that men would do to you, do so to them.*"[8] Jesus was clear—love was the most important law, and it needed to be shown not only to God but also to others.

16 – Renewing and Embodying Universal Virtues

Christ generated a dispensation that renewed and embodied universal virtues. Through a transformative ministry He reminded the world of abiding moral and spiritual verities, alluding to virtuous actions as good fruits and vice-based actions as bad fruits. He said, "*So, every sound tree bears good fruit, but the bad tree bears evil fruit. . . . Thus you will know them by their fruits.*"[9] Jesus here clarified that we are not "good" or "bad" based on words only, or on social or material status, but that our deeds and actions, our "fruits," are the true testament to the lives we live.

Spiritual Virtues in the Christian Revelation

Devotion-Faithfulness: "*Suffering produces endurance, and endurance produces character, and character produces hope, and hope does not disappoint us, because God's love has been poured into our hearts.*"[10]

Gratitude-Reverence: "*Rejoice always, pray constantly, give thanks in all circumstances.*"[11]

Self-discipline-Obedience: "*Blessed . . . are those who hear the word of God and keep it!*"[12]

Detachment-Patience: "*Do not be conformed to this world but be transformed by the renewal of your mind, that you may prove what is the will of God, what is good and acceptable and perfect.*"[13]

Wisdom-Discernment: "*The wisdom from above is first pure, then peaceable, gentle, open to reason, full of mercy and good fruits, without uncertainty or insincerity.*"[14]

Social Virtues in the Christian Revelation

Loving-kindness-Compassion: "*Love your enemies, do good to those who hate you, bless those who curse you, pray for those who abuse you.*"[15]

Service-Responsibility: "*Let each of you look not only to his own interests, but also to the interests of others.*"[16]

Respect-Tolerance: *"Put on then . . . compassion, kindness, lowliness, meekness, and patience, forbearing one another and, if one has a complaint against another, forgiving each other; as the Lord has forgiven you."*[17]
Justice-Righteousness: *"God shows no partiality, but in every nation any one who fears him and does what is right is acceptable to him."*[18]
Peace-Unity: *"Put your sword back into its place; for all who take the sword will perish by the sword."*[19]

Material Virtues in the Christian Revelation
Trustworthiness-Honesty: *"He who is faithful in a very little is faithful also in much; and he who is dishonest in a very little is dishonest also in much."*[20]
Moderation-Balance: *"Keep your life free from love of money, and be content with what you have."*[21]
Generosity-Hospitality: *"But if anyone has the world's goods and sees his brother in need, yet closes his heart against him, how does God's love abide in him?"*[22]
Creativity-Beauty: *"Having gifts that differ according to the grace given to us, let us use them."*[23]
Earthcare-Stewardship: *"Consider the lilies of the field, how they grow; they neither toil nor spin; yet I tell you, even Solomon in all his glory was not arrayed like one of these."*[24]

17 – Abrogating the Old and Establishing the New: Ritual and Legal Guidance
Christ ministered in a social context significantly different from that of Moses. Moses faced the challenge of teaching former slaves who were wandering in the wilderness of Sinai. Christ was teaching a people who had inherited nearly a millennium and a half of detailed religious legal traditions and ritual practices, and who were also embedded in a Roman civilization with another well-developed system of law firmly in place for over half a millennium. His context, then, or the society in which He lived, was overly legalistic, while Moses' context was not legally well-developed at all. Their tasks as Divine Educators differed. Christ abrogated many laws and rituals from the Mosaic dispensation because, over the course of many centuries, they had become dysfunctional.

For example, Sabbath laws were so restrictive that their original spiritual purpose was forgotten. In response to this Jesus reminded people that, *"The sabbath was made for man, not man for the sabbath."*[25] Christ made service

264

to others an acceptable form of devotion on the Sabbath, reminding people that the Sabbath was ultimately supposed to be spiritual in nature. Another example of the overly legalistic society that had developed could be seen in the marriage laws, which had become quite confusing, so Jesus abrogated them, returning to the original biblical teaching that *"the two shall become one flesh"* and added: *"What therefore God has joined together, let no man put asunder,"* allowing divorce only for reasons of adultery.[26] Whereas women had very restricted roles in Jewish tradition, Jesus treated them with great respect; and accordingly, women enjoyed important roles in the early church, including conducting worship.

Christ also abrogated many dietary laws, saying, *"for the sake of your tradition, you have made void the word of God."* He tried to change people's understanding of these laws, emphasizing their spiritual nature, when He explained, *"Not what goes into the mouth defiles a man, but what comes out of the mouth, this defiles a man."*[27] What people said and did to others, often in the name of these laws, was what was truly harmful. Jesus also lifted restrictive traditions about what classes of people one could properly join in "table fellowship" and other details of the purity code, thus widening the circles of socializing considerably. The practice of retaliatory justice was replaced by an ethic of forgiveness and love, and people were taught to *"love your enemies."*[28] Another law that was changed was the law of circumcision, which Paul relaxed, explaining that circumcision was actually a matter of the heart. It was taught that, *"He is a Jew who is one inwardly, and real circumcision is a matter of the heart, spiritual and not literal."*[29] These changes enabled Christianity to spread more rapidly.

Two rituals that Christ adapted to His cultural context in a spiritual way were baptism and communion. The degree to which these rituals were viewed literally or symbolically has been controversial in Christian history. For example, in terms of baptism, it is said that Jesus Himself did not physically baptize followers in the same way that John did. John the Baptist baptized believers by full immersion in water, and it is now believed that he may have been influenced by ancient Sabaean ritual bathing practices. John, recognizing Jesus' greater spiritual power in this regard said, *"I have baptized you with water; but he will baptize you with the Holy Spirit."*[30] However, in another passage Christ said, *"Unless one is born of water and the Spirit, he cannot enter the kingdom of God,"* which seems to emphasize the importance of being baptized by water.[31] And later, in Matthew's account of the post-resurrection "great commission," Jesus was reported as saying: *"Go therefore and make disciples of all nations, baptizing them in the name of the Father and of the Son and of the Holy Spirit."* [32] Perhaps because of these statements and John the Baptist's early actions, scholars believe that, "Baptism by full immersion was the rite of admission to the early Christian community."[33]

Christ's last supper as a modified Passover meal and as a basis for the ritual of communion seems more historically based. Bread and wine were made symbols of the sacrifice of His body and blood. Early Christian ritual meals were referred to as "the agape" or "love feast." Perhaps Paul's account has been the most influential: *"The Lord Jesus on the night when he was betrayed took bread, and when he had given thanks, he broke it, and said, 'This is my body which is for you. Do this in remembrance of me.' In the same way also the cup, after supper, saying, 'This cup is the new covenant in my blood. Do this, as often as you drink it, in remembrance of me.'"* [34] Communion as a symbol of thanksgiving for Christ's sacrifice, and baptism as a symbol of purification, have been powerfully inspirational rituals in Christian history.

18 – Human and Divine Qualities: Exemplifying a Dual Station

Scriptural evidence for the human and divine aspects of Christ can be found in the gospels. In fact, the relevant passages for both stations were usually placed close to one another, as if to clarify His potentially confusing dual station. Islamic and Bahá'í scriptures also confirm that Christ had a dual station. The Qur'án says, *"We gave Jesus . . . clear (Signs) and strengthened him with the holy spirit."* [35] A passage from the Bahá'í writings says, *"We testify that when He [Jesus] came into the world, He shed the splendor of His glory upon all created things."* [36] It is clear that Prophets Who came after Jesus did not discount Him, but instead recognized His spiritual nature, and the important role that He played.

Christ's Human Station

In many passages, Christ referred to His own frailties and subordination to God, Who He referred to as the Father. He said, *"I am gentle and lowly in heart"* [37] and later He also said, *"Why do you ask me about what is good? One there is who is good."* [38] It has been said that John's gospel, written later than the other gospels, reflects the theological understanding of the developing Christian community rather than the words and claims of the historical Jesus; and therefore John's estimation of Christ's station is much higher than in the other gospels. However, there is substantial evidence for Christ's human station in John. There are many passages where Jesus seems to refer to God as separate or distinct from Himself. Jesus said, *"I can do nothing on my own authority. . . . I seek not my own will but the will of him who sent me."* [39] He also said, *"My teaching is not mine, but his who sent me."* [40] Jesus explained that He came from God, *"I proceeded and came forth from God; I came not of my own accord, but he sent me,"* and that He does as God commands Him, *"I do as the Father has commanded me, so that the world may know that I love the Father."* [41]

The distance between Christ's two stations was especially wide when He faced His own death—alone with God in the Garden of Gethsemane, and when speaking to God while dying on the cross. Jesus, addressing God during his troubles, said, *"My Father, if it be possible, let this cup pass from me; nevertheless, not as I will, but as thou wilt.* [42] And in a very well-known passage describing the crucifixion, Jesus says, *"My God, my God, why hast Thou forsaken Me?* [43] Such testimonies, which show Jesus' physical pain and pleadings for divine assistance, suggest a human station.

Christ's Divine Station

We also find passages in the gospels suggesting that Christ's station was far above merely human, that He had divine authority and power over nature, a special intimacy with God the Father, and that in some respects He could be identified with God. When people encountered Jesus, they felt that there was something different about Him, saying, *"The men marveled, saying, 'What sort of man is this, that even winds and sea obey him?'"* [44] The gospels also say that Jesus was able to forgive the sins of others, *"The Son of man has authority on earth to forgive sins"* and that He had the ability to change the Sabbath laws, *"The Son of man is lord of the sabbath."* [45] It is also made clear that Jesus had a special relationship with God, *"No one knows the Son except the Father, and no one knows the Father except the Son."* [46] In these passages it is clear that Jesus had a power above other humans—He was able to perform miracles, had the ability to change God's laws, and had a unique and personal relationship with God.

Jesus' spiritual station can also been seen through what was described by Matthew, Mark, and Luke as His transfiguration. These three disciples witnessed Moses, Elijah, and Jesus talking with one another, all in radiant glory. When describing what they saw happen to Jesus, they said *"And he was transfigured before them, and his face shone like the sun, and his garments became white as light. And behold, there appeared to them Moses and Elijah, talking with him. . . . And a voice from the cloud said, 'This is My beloved Son, with whom I am well pleased; listen to him.'"*[47] Not only did His disciples witness Jesus having a special spiritual station, but at times Jesus described Himself in this way. In His final week, Christ told the chief priests and scribes that *"from now on the Son of man shall be seated at the right hand of the power of God."*[48] And to His disciples after the resurrection, He said *"All authority in heaven and earth has been given to me."*[49] These are among the clear scriptural affirmations of Christ's divine authority.

John's prologue also lifted up the divine status of Christ in language that impressed the Greek-speaking world. Christ was identified with the Logos or Word—the ordering power of all creation and the source of all revelation. The gospel of John starts out by saying, *"In the beginning was the Word, and the Word was with God, and the Word was God. . . . And the Word became flesh and dwelt among us, full of grace and truth; we beheld his glory, glory as of the only Son from the Father."*[50] Elsewhere in John's gospel were passages further clarifying the divinity of Christ. In various places Jesus refers to Himself as especially connected to God and the spiritual realm, at times even seeming to identify Himself as God. He said, *"You are from below, I am from above."*[51] He also linked Himself to previous dispensations, saying, *"Truly, truly, I say to you, before Abraham was, I am."*[52] And He explained that He and God were one, *"I and the Father are one. . . . The Father is in me and I am in the Father."*[53] And those who recognized Him recognized God, *"He who has seen me has seen the Father."*[54]

An especially controversial passage has been used frequently to espouse the exclusiveness and uniqueness of Christianity among all religions. This passage is interpreted to mean that salvation is only possible through Christ, and therefore, other religions have no spiritual power. Jesus said, *"I am the way, and the truth, and the life; no one comes to the Father, but by me."*[55] However, this can be interpreted as in continuity and harmony with claims of other Founders. It may mean that the most recent Mediator or Savior is the way, the truth, and the life; that humanity cannot receive divine grace except through the Mediator or Savior. It may also mean that the Messengers were one and united in that They shared the divine nature and could bring heavenly blessings to humanity. In this fought-over passage, Christ claimed that no one can receive divine blessings without One like Him—a Mediator, a Spiritual

Physician, a Divine Educator. By taking a more universal view, we can assume that this same statement could have been said by any of the Founders when they came to renew God's spiritual teachings to humanity. Since these Messengers are one and the same Spirit, this statement applies equally to all of Them.

19 – The Light and the Word

As with all major scriptural traditions, the Light and the Word are metaphors used frequently in the gospels. When describing Jesus' arrival in the world, the Gospel of John says, *"The true light that enlightens every man was coming into the world."* [56] Jesus referred to Himself as a light that will guide people out of darkness. *"I am the light of the world; he who follows me will not walk in darkness, but will have the light of life."* [57] Jesus, while talking to His companions, encouraged them to believe in and rely on the light of divine revelation. *"While you have the light, believe in the light, that you may become sons of light."* [58] And, of course, God Himself is described as the source of light. *"God is light and in him is no darkness at all."* [59] Light is a powerful metaphor that is used in all the major religious traditions to describe God, the Teacher, His revelation, or the station to which believers should strive to draw nearer.

20 – Affirming Four Realms: Divine, Revelatory, Human, Natural

New Testament writers assumed the same basic worldview as writers of ancient Israel's scriptures. We presented the Mosaic revelation as a four-level metaphysic. Christian revelation affirmed the same picture of the universe, adding details on certain aspects of the four realms.

The Natural Realm

Paul explained to Greco-Roman society that Christian teaching was not philosophically or scientifically backward, and that therefore, one need not be ashamed of the gospel. *"Ever since the creation of the world his invisible nature, namely, his eternal power and deity, has been clearly perceived in the things that have been made."* [60] This teaching suggested to the Western mind that the natural realm provides visible and tangible evidences of providential order—a view that encouraged empirical investigation for patterns and designs.

The Human Realm

New insights about the human spirit are provided in the Christian revelation. We are capable of reflecting heavenly virtues. *"The fruit of the Spirit is love, joy, peace, patience, kindness, goodness, faithfulness, gentleness, self-control."* [61] We have an inner nature or soul that is immortal, and can attend to invisible and higher realities. *"Though our outer nature is wasting away, our inner nature is being renewed every day. . . . We look not to the things that are seen but to the things that are unseen; for the things that are seen are transient, but the things that are unseen are eternal."* [62] Luke added, *"Do not rejoice in this, that the spirits are subject to you; but rejoice that your names are written in heaven."* [63] We are also creatures of choice and bodily limitation, capable of sin. *"I do not understand my own actions. For I do not do what I want, but I do the very thing I hate. . . . I see in my* [bodily] *members another law at war with the law of my mind and making me captive to the law of sin which dwells in my members."* [64] But the choice between higher and lower behavior is basically ours. *"For those who live according to the flesh set their minds on the things of the flesh, but those who live according to the Spirit set their minds on the things of the Spirit."* [65]

The Revelatory Realm

Christ's teaching on the revelatory realm does not seem significantly different from Moses'. Both were told what to say by God, suggesting that Their powers were at a lower level than God's, yet at a higher level than humanity as a whole. Humanity should live by revelatory guidance provided by Founders, that is, by *"every word that proceeds from the mouth of God."* [66] Jesus explained that His words did not come from Him alone, but from God. *"What I say, therefore, I say as the Father has bidden me."* [67] Christ also said, *"My kingship is not of this world"* [68] suggesting that the revelatory realm is higher than the kingdoms of the world. The author of Hebrews wrote that through the Son, God *"created the world. He reflects the glory of God and bears the very stamp of his nature, upholding the universe by his word of power."* [69] Such passages suggest that Christ's divine station includes His activity in shaping and sustaining the world. The terms *Spirit, Word,* and *Wisdom* in the Mosaic and Christian scriptures all point to the revelatory realm—an order of being higher than the highest stretches of human nature, but lower than and subordinate to God.

The Divine Realm

Some passages in Christian scriptures clearly suggest that God has aspects and powers that are even higher than the Son or the Word. All things, including the Revealers, proceed from the Ultimate Divine Mystery. For example, one passage states, *"There is . . . one God and Father of us all, who is above all and through all and in all."* [70] And in another similar passage it says, *"There is one God, the Father, from whom are all things and from whom we exist."* [71] There is also another passage where God is describing Himself as all-powerful. *"'I am the Alpha and the Omega,' says the Lord God, who is and who was and who is to come, the Almighty."* [72] God is clearly describing Himself as the Creator and Source of Revelation from which all else proceeds.

21 – Promising a Future Savior and a New Golden Age: Return of Christ, New Heaven and New Earth

There are many references in Christian scriptures to the "return" or "coming again" of the Son of man, as well as to "latter days" and a "new heaven and new earth." These passages are called succession prophecies and eschatological visions. They focus on the Future Savior and the fulfillment of divine promises in both the Jewish scriptures and the New Testament.

In the twenty-fourth chapter of Matthew, the disciples asked Christ very directly, *"What will be the sign of your coming and of the close of the age?"* And His answer was quite elaborate, and has been pondered, debated, and anticipated with varying degrees of intensity and longing over the last two millennia. The signs He mentioned explain that many will come in His name, but they will lead people astray; we will hear of wars and rumors of wars; nation will rise against nation; there will be famines and earthquakes; wickedness will be multiplied, and men's love will grow cold; the gospel will be preached throughout the whole world; and we will see the desolating sacrilege spoken of by Daniel when he said, *"upon the wing of abominations shall come one who makes desolate, until the decreed end is poured out on the desolator."* [73] Abominations might mean the intrusion of corrupt practices in both synagogues and churches; and we might recall that Luke wrote: *"Jerusalem will be trodden down by the Gentiles, until the times of the Gentiles are fulfilled."* [74]

Jesus mentioned other signs of His coming, describing a world where there will be great tribulation such as the world has never seen; immediately after the tribulation, the sun will be darkened, the moon will not give its light, the stars will fall from heaven, and the powers of the heavens will be shaken; the sign of the Son of man in heaven will appear; all the tribes of the earth will mourn; they will see the Son of man coming on clouds of heaven with power and great glory; but no one knows the day and hour, not even the Son of man, only the Father. Some millennial scholars concluded that these signs pointed to the year 1844, when Turkey allowed Jews to return to Jerusalem, and the "desolating sacrilege" of Jerusalem's being "trodden down" came to an end. By that time, also, Christian missionaries had reached all continents.

Signs like the darkening of the sun and moon, the falling of stars, and the powers of the heavens being shaken may be best interpreted as referring to the decline of religious guidance and authority. "Falling heavenly light" could be understood metaphorically, and could indicate the collapse of religious orthodoxies and establishments. "Clouds of heaven" may refer to new spiritual nourishment, or the "life-giving waters" of a new revelation.

The above references to the Son of man are perhaps best interpreted as pointing to the return of Christ's spiritual station rather than to His particular personhood. If the station of Christ, that is, His spiritual power and authority is the true reference, rather than the return of Jesus' historical body, then the figure of Bahá'u'lláh might be the fulfillment of Christ's prophecy.

There are also succession prophecies in John's gospel, where terms such as "Counselor" and "Spirit of Truth" were used, that may point to Muḥammad and Bahá'u'lláh, though Christians have interpreted these terms as referring either to the Holy Spirit working through the Church, or to a yet-to-appear literal return of Christ. Muslims and Bahá'ís have often interpreted these prophecies as referring to their communities of believers. For example, Jesus said, *"I have yet many things to say to you, but you cannot bear them now. When the Spirit of truth comes, he will guide you into all the truth; for he will not speak on his own authority."*[75] This passage, and others that refer to His return, seem to suggest that the spirit of Jesus was what would return rather than His physical body. In this way, it is possible to say that the spirit of Jesus returned in Muḥammad and Bahá'u'lláh.

Finally, there are prophecies depicting the end of the age, the new millennium, and the day of God. *"And in the last days it shall be, God declares, that I will pour out my Spirit upon all flesh. . . . And I will show wonders in the heaven above and signs on earth beneath. . . . And it shall be that whoever calls on the name of the Lord shall be saved."*[76] *"Then I saw a new heaven and a new earth. . . . And I saw the holy city, new Jerusalem, coming down out of heaven from God*

. . . . I heard a loud voice from the throne saying, 'Behold, the dwelling of God is with men. He will dwell with them, and they shall be his people, and God himself will be with them; he will wipe away every tear from their eyes, and death shall be no more, neither shall there be mourning nor crying nor pain any more, for the former things have passed away.[77] These passages point to a unified world, where spiritual maturity prevails and all nations enjoy justice and peace.

There has been some debate among Christians, Muslims, and Bahá'ís today as to whether these prophecies have been fulfilled already, and if not, how they will be fulfilled in the future. Some denominations of Christians believe that Christ would have returned in the middle of the nineteenth century, had the Christian world been morally and spiritually ready to receive Him. Muslims believe that Muḥammad fulfilled some of these prophecies, and that the Qá'im and Mahdi will fulfill them completely. Bahá'ís believe that Bahá'u'lláh has ushered in the era in which all of these prophecies will be fulfilled. We will revisit these challenging issues in later chapters.

22 – Essential Unity of the Revealers through the Ages

Each Faith can interpret its scriptures in an exclusive way, an approach to discerning God's will that separates them from the other Faiths in the world. Or they can interpret their scriptures in a way that links them to other scriptural traditions, as part of a more universal providential plan. In this study, we are taking the latter approach, which has the potential to bring interfaith understanding and cooperation, and to contribute to eventual world unity. In Luke's genealogy of Jesus, He is traced back through the scriptures of ancient Israel. Jesus was considered part of a lineage that included David, Abraham, Noah, and Adam, *"the son of God."*[78] This was a strong claim of essential unity among the Revealers down through the ages. The author of the Book of Hebrews put it this way: *"In many and various ways God spoke of old to our fathers by the prophets."*[79] When John's gospel declared that *"the Word became flesh and dwelt among us,"*[80] this might be interpreted as referring to more than one incarnation—perhaps the Word became flesh each time God sent a Revealer.

Christ taught that a prophet could return, not bodily, but in essential spiritual qualities. Jesus explained that John the Baptist was the return of the spirit of Elijah. *"I tell you that Elijah has already come, and they did not know him. . . . Then the disciples understood that He was speaking to them of John the Baptist."*[81] He also suggested that His own spiritual station has been available to humanity going back at least 2000 years before His day. Jesus said, *"Truly, truly, I say to you, before Abraham was, I am."* [82] Regarding His fulfillment of Jewish scripture, Christ asked His disciples: *"'Was it not necessary that the Christ should suffer these things and enter into his glory?' And beginning with Moses and all the prophets, he interpreted to them in all the scriptures the things concerning himself."* He said, *"Everything written about me in the law of Moses and the prophets and the psalms must be fulfilled."* [83] Thus, the unity of revelation is linked to fulfillment of prophecy.

Christ referred directly to His unity with Moses in these words: *"If you believed Moses, you would believe me, for he wrote of me."* [84] And He referred to His unity with future Revealers in these words: *"When the Counselor comes, whom I shall send to you from the Father, even the Spirit of truth, who proceeds from the Father, he will bear witness to me."* [85] This promise of Christ has been interpreted in Islamic and Bahá'í scriptures as referring to Muḥammad and to Bahá'u'lláh. Each scriptural tradition casts significant light on the others, and this is not surprising if we assume one God is the source of all revelation.

23 – Laying Enduring Foundations: Peter, Paul, Early Church, Constantine, Establishing Christian Society

What authoritative institutional arrangements did Christ make during His ministry? What were the major developments in the early Christian centuries? What led to the Christian Faith becoming the established religion of the Roman Empire? Here we summarize the early history of the Christian Faith, showing that Christ set in motion spiritual forces and provided enough institutional guidance to establish a new religious civilization—one which became strong enough, despite humble beginnings, to replace and supersede the power of Classical Antiquity.

Peter as the Rock

Christ tested His disciples on how they perceived his impact in Palestine, and how they personally perceived His station. Peter declared, *"You are the Christ, the Son of the living God."* And Jesus replied: *"Blessed are you , Simon Bar-Jona* [Peter]*! For flesh and blood has not revealed this to you, but my Father Who is in heaven. And I tell you, you are Peter, and on this rock I will build my church, and the powers of death shall not prevail against it. I will give you the keys of the kingdom of heaven, and whatever you bind on earth shall be bound in heaven, and whatever you loose on earth shall be loosed in heaven."* [86] This was quite a dramatic endowing of religious authority. But was the true foundation of the early church Peter as a person, or was it the qualities of faith and spirit that he manifested?

In John's account, Peter was assigned his enduring mission in very symbolic terms that suggested a sequence of institutional nurturance of the Faith. Jesus said to him, *"Feed my lambs. . . . Tend my sheep. . . . Feed my sheep."* [87] In Matthew, similar power to "bind and loose" was later bestowed on the disciples as a whole, along with the promise that if any two of them agree on an earthly request, it will be done for them in heaven by God. *"For where two or three are gathered in my name, there am I in the midst of them."* [88] These passages seem to be the primary basis on which churches were initiated.

Bestowing Spiritual Powers and the Great Commission

The disciples and the seventy elders were given the power to heal, and later they were also assured that, even without preparation, they would have *"wisdom, which none of your adversaries will be able to withstand or contradict."* [89] The final bestowal of authority described in the gospels is the Great Commission, in which Christ said to His disciples after the resurrection: *"All authority in heaven and on earth has been given to me. Go therefore and make disciples of all nations . . . teaching them to observe all that I have commanded you; and lo, I am with you always, to the close of the age."* [90]

The Growth of the Early Church

The Book of Acts describes the spread of the Christian Faith from Jerusalem, through Asia Minor and Greece, to Rome. Major turning-points included the Pentecost through which the curse of the Tower of Babel was temporarily lifted, and the Gospel message could be understood in the varied languages of the listeners; the martyrdom of Stephen; Peter's vision of a "great sheet from heaven" which revealed that *"What God has cleansed, you must not call common"* [91]; the Council in Jerusalem in about 50 CE when it was decided that circumcision was not a requirement for declaring oneself a Christian; and Peter's and Paul's heroic testimonies and ministries.

In Bahá'í writings, there is an intimate description of the spirit of consultation that helped empower the disciples before spreading out with their good news. 'Abdu'l-Bahá, the son of Bahá'u'lláh and leader of the Bahá'í Faith following His father's ascension, describes the meeting that took place among the disciples after Jesus had been crucified.

The most memorable instance of spiritual consultation was the meeting of the disciples of Jesus upon the mount after His ascension. They said, "Jesus Christ has been crucified, and we have no longer association and intercourse with Him in His physical body; therefore we must be loyal and faithful to Him, we must be grateful and appreciate Him, for He has raised us from the dead, He made us wise, He has given us eternal life. What shall we do to be faithful to Him?" And so they held council. One of them said, "We must detach ourselves from the chains and fetters of the world; otherwise, we cannot be faithful." The others replied, "That is so." Another said, "Either we must be married and faithful to our wives and children or serve our Lord free from these ties. We cannot be occupied with the care and provision for families and at the same time herald the Kingdom in the wilderness. Therefore let those who are unmarried remain so, and those who have married provide means of sustenance and comfort for their families and then go forth to spread the message of glad tidings." There were no dissenting voices; all agreed, saying, "That is right." A third disciple said, "To perform worthy deeds in the Kingdom we must be further self-sacrificing. From now on we should forego ease and bodily comfort, accept every difficulty, forget self and teach the Cause of God." This found acceptance and approval by all the others. Finally a fourth disciple said, 'There is still another aspect to our faith and unity. For Jesus' sake we shall be beaten, imprisoned and exiled. They may kill us. Let us receive this lesson now. Let us realize and resolve that though we are beaten, banished, cursed, spat upon and led forth to be killed, we shall accept all this joyfully, loving those who hate and wound us." All the disciples replied, 'Surely we will—it is agreed; this is right." Then they descended from the summit of the mountain, and each went forth in a different direction upon his divine mission.[92]

Following this meeting, the disciples all set about spreading the Word of Christ. Peter's work was centered in Jerusalem and directed mostly to Jews, as it was for James. Paul's work was directed more to the gentiles of the Roman Empire. By tradition, John and Matthew were credited for the later gospels which carried their names; Andrew preached in Scythia; Philip in various parts of Asia Minor; Bartholomew in Armenia; Thomas in India; and Judas the son of James in Persia. Christ's message took root less quickly among Jews who were trying to maintain their religious and cultural particularity, and more quickly among universalizing Jews who saw themselves as a "light to the nations." Gentile Christianity that grew in the early churches outside of Palestine soon dominated Jewish Christianity that was centered in synagogues in and around Palestine.

Paul as the Apostle to the Gentiles

Paul brought early Christians the belief that salvation came more from Christ's forgiveness, loving sacrifice, and the teachings of the heavenly kingdom than from the Mosaic law and the Holiness Code. Paul's letters to churches became an important addition to the New Testament, initiating the development of Christian doctrine. Paul also adapted the Christian message to Hellenistic minds, and his speech in Athens set the direction for the development of Christian theology. *"Men of Athens, I perceive that in every way you are very religious. . . . The God who made the world and everything in it, being Lord of heaven and earth, does not live in shrines made by man, nor is he served by human hands, as though he needed anything, since he himself gives to all men life and breath and everything. . . . Being then God's offspring, we ought not to think that the Deity is like gold, or silver, or stone, a representation by the art and imagination of man. The times of ignorance God overlooked, but now he commands all men everywhere to repent, because he has fixed a day on which he will judge the world in righteousness by a man whom he has appointed, and of this he has given assurance to all men by raising him from the dead."*[93] In this way, Paul was able to reach out to people of other cultural backgrounds and bring them Christian teachings.

Emperor Constantine and the Establishment of Christian Faith

How did Christian communities fare under the Roman Empire? The basic policy was that Christianity was illegal and punishable, but this policy was only intermittently enforced with varying degrees of severity. The worst persecutions for Christians were suffered under four emperors: Nero (54–68 CE), Domitian (81–96), Decius (249–51), and Diocletian (284–305). Constantine became emperor of the Western Empire in 306. In 313, he and the Eastern emperor Licinius proclaimed freedom for all religions. Constantine reunited the Roman Empire in 324 and ruled until 337. In 325, he convened the Council of Nicea, which established the Creed that became the core of later Christian doctrine.

It was reported that Constantine prayed before battle, and had a vision of a flaming cross with the inscription "By This Sign Conquer"; and also that Christ counseled him in a dream to place letter symbols of Christ on his soldiers' shields. Constantine won the battle and attributed victory to the Christian God. Moving his capital to Constantinople left the bishop of Rome as among the most powerful figures in Europe. In 381, the Edicts of Constantinople established Christianity as the state religion, prohibiting all pagan cults, ratifying the decisions of the Nicene Council, and adding the Holy Spirit to the Godhead.

What was Constantine's legacy? He helped transform the Church from a persecuted outcast sect into an institution of great power, wealth, and intellectual sophistication. Many beautiful churches and cathedrals were built, and monasteries and seminaries established. As the Church became stronger, so did its various helping agencies, such as schools, libraries, hospitals, orphanages, and shelters. Also under Constantine, state power was used to aid one side in theological debates, making heresy a punishable offense.

24 – Renewing Scriptural Guidance: The New Testament

Christian scripture is the entire New Testament: the four Gospels, the Acts of the Apostles, the nine Pauline Epistles, the twelve Pastoral Epistles, as well as the Book of Revelation. This amounts to twenty-seven books, which Christians publish together with the Hebrew scriptures, known as the Old Testament. Between the years 170 to 220 CE the four Gospels, Acts, and thirteen letters attributed to Paul became accepted as authentic and authoritative for Christians. There were questions about Hebrews, Revelation, and some of the smaller books; but by 382 CE a council in Rome listed the books now officially published as the New Testament.

25 – Generating Civilization Anew: Kingdom of Heaven on Earth

What sort of civilization did Christ envision? Matthew conveyed Christ's vision of a new spiritual civilization most especially in the Beatitudes and the Lord's Prayer. Christ de-emphasized ritual practices, sociopolitical institutions, and messianic liberation from oppressors. He emphasized the fashioning of a compassionate, spiritually-oriented dispensation, which would develop and cultivate inner qualities so as to transform society from the inside out. Christ said, *"Blessed are the poor in spirit, for theirs is the kingdom of heaven. Blessed are those who mourn, for they shall be comforted. Blessed are the meek, for they shall inherit the earth. Blessed are those who hunger and thirst for righteousness, for they shall be satisfied. Blessed are the merciful, for they shall*

278

obtain mercy. Blessed are the pure in heart for they shall see God. Blessed are the peacemakers, for they shall be called sons of God. Blessed are those who are persecuted for righteousness' sake, for theirs is the kingdom of heaven." [94] These blessings nurtured inner qualities that have born some of the best fruits of Christian civilization: compassion and caretaking, service to the poor and disadvantaged, purity and detachment from worldly power, humility before the majesty of God and the undeveloped capacities of the soul, an emphasis on peace, justice, and rewards of sacrificial devotion and love.

Two lines in the Lord's Prayer capture the essence of Christ's message and vision of civilization—humanity's collective task of making earth more heavenly. The prayer states, *"Thy kingdom come. Thy will be done, on earth as it is in heaven,"* [95] which emphasizes the need to build God's kingdom here on earth.

Luke conveyed some of Christ's vision of the new era through other voices, including Simeon's and Mary's. Both of these visions looked back in gratitude for saving acts for the people of Israel, as well as forward to a wider and more expansive era when the humble shall be exalted. Simeon shared this universal vision with Mary and Joseph, soon after Jesus was born: *"Mine eyes have seen thy salvation which thou hast prepared in the presence of all peoples, a light for revelation to the Gentiles, and for glory to thy people Israel. . . . Behold, this child is set for the fall and rising of many in Israel, and for a sign that is spoken against . . . that thoughts out of many hearts may be revealed."* [96] This last phrase, "that thoughts out of many hearts may be revealed," could refer to the many religious and cultural developments to unfold in the Christian dispensation under fresh divine guidance—the establishment of various institutions, schools, and libraries, the promotion of laws favoring the needy, the building of beautiful churches and cathedrals, and the spread of lofty ethical teachings.

We also get hints of Christ's vision of civilization in John, in passages referring to "bearing fruit," as well as a new kind of kingship that would differ from the Davidic vision by manifesting qualities of peacefulness and cooperation. *"By this my Father is glorified, that you bear much fruit, and so prove to be my disciples."* [97] He also said, *"My kingship is not of this world; if my kingship were of this world, my servants would fight, that I might not be handed over to the Jews."* [98]

Finally, we are given a glimpse of the "new heaven and new earth" in the closing book of the New Testament. The sea will disappear, as nations of the earth befriend one another, and all travel becomes free of fear. "All things will be made new" as all learning is shared and all obstacles to advancement are removed. The tears of social injustice and deprivation will be wiped away, as cooperation and compassion become the norms. Spiritual death will be no more when humanity reaches moral maturity and dwells with God. The glory of God will be the light by which the nations walk. And the nights of warfare and oppression will yield to the day of peace and righteousness.

15
Muḥammad: Background and Mission

More than a fifth of humanity reveres the Prophet Muḥammad. But for people in the West to appreciate the magnitude of His achievement—that a poor Arabian orphan rose in spiritual and political power and generated a new religious civilization within His lifetime—they need to become familiar with key features of His background and context. This requires a look at the history of the ancient Arabs, their connection to the religion of Abraham, the place of the Kaaba (the Meccan shrine of ancient Arabia), the imperial stand-off between Persia and Byzantium, and the rise of the Quraysh—the tribe from which Muḥammad emerged, and against which He struggled and eventually triumphed. Understanding and appreciating Muḥammad also requires that people in the West learn to reinterpret much of what the media presents of Islam. There are many layers of mutual prejudice separating peoples of the West and the Middle East, which has led to great misunderstanding about our respective religious and cultural backgrounds. It is hoped that this look into Muḥammad's life will help to break down some of these preconceptions.

1 – Continuity with Previous Dispensations: Abraham, the Hanifs, the Kaaba, and Imperial Influence

Muslims see themselves as completely continuous with previous dispensa-tions. God informed them: *"We sent thee inspiration, as We sent it to Noah and the Messengers after him."* [1] Muslims believe that Muḥammad comes from a long line of Messengers of God, dating back to the time of Noah. *"The same has He established for you as that which He enjoined on Noah—the which We have sent by inspiration to thee—and that which We enjoined on Abraham, Moses, and Jesus: namely, that ye should remain steadfast in Religion, and make no divisions therein."* [2] Such a message transformed the sense of history and destiny that the people of Arabia, to whom Muḥammad first taught His Faith, held. It made them see pre-Islamic Arabia as *Jahiliyyah*—the Age of

Ignorance—the time before God showed them the path to truth, the period before the year 610 CE when Muḥammad began to bring them the Word of God. Muslims describe their own pre-Islamic past as superstitious and prejudiced, crude and uncultivated, disorganized and violent, and morally corrupt and spiritually vacuous. But how did they actually live in the centuries and millennia before Muḥammad?

Ancient Arabia's Nomadic Tent-dwellers and Farmers

At one time the Arabs had been farmers in the more civilized lands of the Fertile Crescent. Some of them decided to brave the inhospitable steppes of the Arabian Peninsula. In summer they would graze their camels near tribally claimed water wells; in winter they wandered the steppes, which had enough vegetation to sustain them. The nomads and the farmers became interdependent—the nomads offered the farmers needed goods from their travels and raids, as well as protection through their warrior skills; while in return the farmers offered the nomads dates, wheat, and other staples.

Tribal solidarity was the only hope for survival under these conditions. An ethic of chivalry entailed protecting the weak, demonstrating courage in battle, and avenging the wrongs done to one's own tribe by other tribes. The threat of tribal revenge seemed the only means of providing a semblance of security, as the certainty of retaliation might make one hesitate to bring harm to another tribe. Most tribal chiefs were hereditary, but charisma and ability to protect influenced views of authority.

Only the strong could survive. Women were seen as property, and baby daughters were considered expendable, and they were sometimes killed without regret. An important aspect of the economy was the raid—a way of redistributing wealth that favored those tribes with the best warriors. Under these conditions, largesse or generosity was an important value, and was a way of demonstrating power and confidence. Such hospitality also served to deepen or extend tribal ties.

Tribal loyalty was a sacred value, and the poets, seers, and soothsayers had important roles in maintaining this standard. Through stories that praised heroic devotion, that interpreted events, and offered guidance and hope, they combined the functions of the arts and priesthood and united the tribe through these oral traditions. Seers sometimes claimed to be possessed by *jinn* (spirits that haunted the landscape), which gave them power to express and see important realities that others could not.

Some northern Arabs became Syrian Christians, but the Bedouin Arabs, or wandering tent-dwellers of Central Arabia, remained detached from and felt inferior to the "peoples of the Book"—Jews, Christians, and Zoroastrians who lived in the regions surrounding them.

Abraham's Temple and the Hanifs

Most ancient Arabs were polytheistic, believing in a remote high god, Allah, his daughters, and a few other deities, combined with a sense of fate. Even though they believed in various gods, they did not have a well-developed idea of an immortal soul or an afterlife. Yet in pre-Islamic Mecca, there were some who remained at least vaguely aware that they were descendents of Abraham, the Founder of a pure faith that believed in only one God. These somewhat halting believers in Abraham's God had enough of an identity to be given their own name, the *hanifs*. They had a weak but enduring understanding that one of Abraham's wives, Hagar, had given birth to a son Ishmael, a warrior-nomad who was their progenitor. They also believed that Abraham and Ishmael built the first temple of God, which became known as the Kaaba in Mecca.

However, the hanifs held only a marginal set of beliefs, and were unattached to any specific practices or teachings. They were the skeptics among the majority polytheists surrounding them, feeling that their idol-worshiping comrades had unfortunately forgotten the pure faith of belief in only one true God. A caravan merchant named Muḥammad also called Himself a hanif, that is, until His revelatory experience put His Abrahamic heritage in a vastly clearer and loftier perspective.

The Kaaba in Mecca

The ancient Arabs felt that certain places were holy, and these places became the sites of shrines. The most important of these shrines was the Kaaba, situated by the sacred spring of Zamzam in Mecca. The hanifs believed that Hagar was shown this spring by God as a merciful, saving act at the beginning of their racial and spiritual history. This was described in the Hebrew Bible in Genesis. *"The angel of God called to Hagar from heaven, and said to her, 'What troubles you, Hagar? Fear not; for God has heard the voice of the lad [Ishmael] where he is. Arise, lift up the lad, and hold him fast with your hand; for I will make him a great nation.' . . . And God was with the lad, and he grew up. . . . He lived in the wilderness of Paran [Arabia]; and his mother took a wife for him from the land of Egypt."*[3]

The Kaaba was a cube-shaped structure built around the Black Stone, probably a meteorite that once lit the sky as it fell, and may have been interpreted as a sign to the people who lived in the region that there was a link between heaven and earth. The Kaaba's square shape may have represented the four corners of the world. The Kaaba also had 360 symbols around it that may have come from the ancient Sumerian heritage, which had a year of 360 days and five extra holy days. It was an important religious gathering place for many tribes in Central Arabia over many centuries, and had been embellished with many inscriptions, artwork, symbols, and idols.

Pilgrims came to Mecca at certain months of their lunar year, at which time all violence was forbidden. Pilgrims came to perform certain ceremonies, including preparatory ritual cleansing, seven ritual circumambulations around the Kaaba following the direction of the sun, rushing to the valley of the thunder god, an all-night vigil on Mount Arafat, hurling pebbles at three sacred pillars, offering an animal sacrifice, and also visiting other shrines outside Mecca. All these activities were later interpreted by Muslims as related to the practices of Abraham.

Most pre-Islamic Arabs knew little about how these rituals had arisen or what they meant. But these rituals provided a regular means of spiritual reorientation, cleansing, connection to forebears, and enhanced tribal identity. Also, the relative freedom from attack in the area around the Kaaba enabled fair trading to take place, helping Mecca eventually become a commercial center conveniently located at the crossroads of busy trade routes.

Three nearby shrines were other sources of attraction to Mecca, which was described as a *"valley without cultivation"* in the Qur'án.[4] These shrines were dedicated to the daughters of Allah: al-Lat the Sovereign, al-Uzzah the Mighty, and Manat the Fateful. There was no well-developed mythology regarding these figures, and no personalized statues represented them, but instead large standing stones to which people would come to offer sacrifices and gifts. Though most believed that Allah created the heavens and the earth, this did not play a role in their devotions or worldview. Most knew that the Kaaba was dedicated to Allah, but it was His daughters that attracted attention.

Byzantine and Persian Influence

During the two centuries preceding the birth of Muḥammad, there were two superpowers—Persia and Byzantium—that dominated the region. Persia was a Zoroastrian empire centered in Babylon, and Byzantium was a

Christian empire centered in Constantinople. Though they were both people of the Book with scriptural guidance forming part of their backgrounds and beliefs, they were locked in a mutually debilitating struggle with each other for political and religious influence of the region.

In the early 500s CE, Byzantium encouraged the Abyssinian king to infiltrate South Arabia and thereby expand Christian influence. Abyssinia is now called Ethiopia, and was at that time a Christian culture. In 525 South Arabia became Abyssinian Christian. In 560 the governor of South Arabia built a magnificent Christian church to compete with Mecca, and because of his quest for power, began planning ways to destroy Mecca. Soon the Abyssinian army marched toward Mecca, and they used an elephant as part of their military strategy. Though prospects for Meccan survival seemed bleak, the Abyssinian army was stricken with a plague, the elephant refused to go forward, and a flock of birds dropped what has been referred to as "poisonous stones" on the Abyssinians. The Meccans felt they had been saved by Allah, and they referred to this time as the "Year of the Elephant." It was also the year that Muḥammad was born, 570 CE.

2 – Arising to Guide Humanity in the Worst of Times: The Quraysh and the Days of Ignorance

The leading tribe in Mecca in the Year of the Elephant was the Quraysh. Allah had saved them, and so it was believed He must have had a special purpose for them. They were also the most wealthy and powerful tribe in Central Arabia. How did they rise to their prestigious position? In the late 400s, the Quraysh settled in Mecca. Their ancestor, the Qusayy, had traveled in Syria and brought back with him the Nabatean god Hubal to take center stage at the Kaaba, along with the three daughters of Allah. The Quraysh expelled the previous guardian-tribe of Mecca, saying that they had failed in their sacred duties.

By Muḥammad's time, the Quraysh had developed into four sets of clans that were economically distinguishable. They added an increasingly vigorous trade to their traditional stock-breeding, built firm alliances with the Bedouins in the area, and were politically calculating enough to stay neutral in the tensions between Byzantium and Persia. By 600, the Quraysh were wealthier than they ever dreamed possible.

Along with this prosperity came some unanticipated social developments and serious challenges. The tribal ethic had been relatively egalitarian, but now a class structure began to develop. Whereas before orphans and widows had been taken care of, at this point there was a widening gap between rich and poor, significant problems related to the idea of social justice arose, and money had become a new form of salvation. Tribesmen in the roles of merchants, bankers, and financiers accumulated capital with a kind of religious zeal, and lost their sensitivity to the weaker members of various clans.

In response to the intensifying moral and spiritual tensions of the day, and in response to the new threats to the values of the old tribal ethic, the young and poor especially felt increasingly downtrodden and longed for a liberator. There were rumors of a new Prophet who might appear from among the Arabs. Could this Prophet elevate the lowly and unite the tribes on the basis of spiritual standards—that is, based on values higher than kinship, wealth, and power?

3 – Advent Prophesied and Expected: Former Prophets, Soothsayers, Holy Men, and Immediate Friends

Muḥammad's arrival had been prophesied by the Messengers Who came before Him. Moses had prophesied, envisioning the far distant future, that *"The Lord . . . shone from Mount Paran."*[5] Christ had referred four times to a figure He called the Counselor or Paraclete, which means illustrious, a term translated as Ahmad in Arabic, meaning praiseworthy, and a common title of Muḥammad was Ahmad, the Praiseworthy One. Muslims and Bahá'ís believe that these prophecies of Christ refer to Muḥammad and Bahá'u'lláh. The Bible contains a number of passages that seem to refer to the advent of Muḥammad. For example, the Gospel of John says, *"The Father . . . will give you another Counselor."*[6] The Gospel of John goes on to praise this future Counselor. It says, *"The Counselor, the Holy Spirit, whom the Father will send in my name, he will teach you all things,"* and *"When the Counselor comes, whom I shall send to you from the Father, even the Spirit of truth, who proceeds from the Father, he will bear witness to me."*[7] The Bible also explains that the Counselor would not come until some point in the future, *"If I do not go away, the Counselor will not come to you; but if I go, I will send him to you. And when he comes, he will convince the world concerning sin and righteousness and judgment."*[8]

In the days before Muḥammad's call and declaration, soothsayers in Mecca predicted the coming of a Prophet. They told their kinsmen repeatedly that the jinn (spirits) had brought them prophetic tidings, but most Meccans ignored these predictions. Around the same time a nearby tribe saw falling stars that startled them, for they believed such stars meant that Allah had a new purpose for them.

Jewish leaders in Mecca, Yathrib, and Khaybar told their pagan neighbors that the time of an Arabian Prophet had come, and that the Jews would conquer with this Prophet's aid. One Jewish leader pointed toward Mecca, saying the Prophet would come from that land. The most impressive Jewish prophecy at this time came from a holy man in Yathrib named Ibn al-Hayyaban, who proclaimed that he had left a land of bread and wine to come to this land of hardship and hunger for a special reason: the coming of the Prophet. Three Jewish youth who heard this prophecy became Muslims after Muḥammad's victory at the Battle of Badr.

In Mecca, Zayd ibn Amr, who was a hanif, a believer in Abraham's one God, and a skeptic regarding Arabian gods and goddesses and their associated practices, gave up idol worship in a dramatic fashion. He reproached the Quraysh for evil practices, especially for the killing of infant daughters, saying that the God of Abraham was the only proper object of worship. He expected a Prophet from the line of Ismail and Abdul Muttalib (Muḥammad's grandfather). Zayd ibn Amr described the Prophet so that others could recognize Him. The Prophet would be neither short nor tall, hair neither abundant nor sparse, and His name would be Ahmad. His birthplace would be Mecca, and this is where His mission would begin; but He would be driven out by the people, and forced to migrate to Yathrib, where He would eventually triumph.

Abu Bakr, Muḥammad's close friend (and Islam's first Caliph) heard news from Syria about the Prophet Ahmad who would arise in Central Arabia. Uthman, a young Meccan aristocrat (who later became Islam's third Caliph) heard a dream voice right before Muḥammad's call: *"Sleepers awake! for verily Ahmad has come forth in Mecca!"* [9]

4 – Auspicious Signs, Birth, and Intimations of Greatness: Qusayy's Lineage, a Voice and a Light, Virtuous Deeds

Five generations before Muḥammad, a man named Qusayy came, and he was known as the ancestor of the Quraysh tribe. Qusayy established two annual caravans: one north to Syria, and the other south to Yemen. Qusayy's son was Abd Manaf, whose son was Hashim, whose son was Abdul Muttalib—Muḥammad's charismatic and wealthy grandfather who rediscovered the sacred spring at Zamzam. Abdul Muttalib's youngest son was Abdullah, Muḥammad's father.

Abdullah married Amina, but died while Amina was still pregnant with Muḥammad. Amina said she heard a voice telling her she was carrying the Lord of the Arabs. She also saw a light issuing from her womb showing the castles of Syria (the direction in which Islam first grew). A Bedouin woman named Halima was called upon to nurse Muḥammad. Though hungry herself and having no milk, she said that milk began to flow from her breasts as soon as she held Muḥammad. A soothsayer also had a dream about Muḥammad in which a tree grew out of His back and reached the sky, stretching east and west and casting light upon Arabs and Persians.

Muḥammad's mother, Amina, died when He was six years old, and since His father had already passed away, this made Him an orphan at a very young age. Following the death of His mother, His grandfather, Abdul Muttalib, took care of Him until his death only two years later. So at age eight, Muḥammad came under the care of His uncle, Abu Talib, and remained under his uncle's care and protection until He married Khadija when he was twenty-five years old.

When Muḥammad was in His early youth, there was a meeting among some of the clans in response to local trading abuses. Those interested in justice and fair dealing were welcome to attend the meeting, which took place at the Kaaba. A pact was made called the League of the Virtuous, by which all participants swore to protect the wronged and oppressed. Muḥammad was present at this special meeting, and spoke favorably of this noble undertaking.

As a boy of twelve, Muḥammad was taken by His uncle Abu Talib on His first business trip to Syria. In Basra, a local Christian monk named Bahira saw a bright cloud over the caravan, suggesting to him that the Prophet was present. Bahira did not find signs of prophecy on anyone in the caravan, except when he turned to the young Muḥammad. Bahira questioned Muḥammad about His attitudes toward life's challenges, and was impressed with His responses. Bahira told Abu Talib to guard Muḥammad carefully against the Jews, who may do Him evil, though he predicted that Muḥammad would overcome all threats and have a great future.

In His youth, Muḥammad became a reliable and competent caravan merchant, as well as a skilled archer, swordsman, and wrestler. He became known as al-Amin, meaning the trustworthy, because His words and deeds corresponded perfectly. He looked directly at people with a bright expression when listening to them, acted decisively and fairly, and often gave to the poor and needy. He was described as shy and reserved, yet relaxed among His family and friends.

When Muḥammad was twenty-five, a wealthy and intelligent widow and merchant named Khadija, who was forty, offered Him a share of her profits if He would direct a caravan for her. Among the reports Khadija heard about Muḥammad's caravan was that a well-educated Christian claimed Muḥammad was the awaited Prophet. Khadija consulted her cousin, Waraqa, who had become a Christian well-versed in scriptural prophecies. Waraqa suggested to Khadija that Muḥammad must be the awaited Prophet. Khadija proposed marriage to Muḥammad and He eagerly accepted. Their marriage and family life were generally very happy, marred only by the early death of several sons, though such early deaths were quite common in the conditions of the day. One of their daughters, Fatima, would become very important in the history of Islam, and will be described later. It is said that Muḥammad enjoyed parenting, and was very affectionate with His children.

Not only was Muḥammad very caring toward His own family, but He often cared for others. A passage in the Qur'án beautifully summarized Muḥammad's upbringing, and describes how it influenced His actions later in life. *"Did He not find thee an orphan and give thee shelter (and care)? And He found thee wandering, and He gave Thee guidance. And He found Thee in need, and made Thee independent. Therefore, treat not the orphan with harshness, nor repulse the petitioner (unheard); But the bounty of thy Lord, rehearse and proclaim!"* [10] Because Muḥammad became an orphan when He was only a young child, He was deeply influenced by this experience and often reached out to help others. He recognized that His relatives had been there to take care of Him when He was in need, and as He grew older He did his best to help those He saw who were in need.

About five years before Muḥammad's divine call, the Quraysh decided to rebuild the Kaaba. A heated controversy arose over which clan should have the honor of placing the Black Stone in the center of the Kaaba. After much argument, they finally decided to accept the judgment of the next person to appear at the Kaaba. That person happened to be Muḥammad, the one worthy of praise, and they were pleased because they knew He would be fair. Muḥammad suggested that the Black Stone be placed on a cloak, and that representatives from each of the four clans hold a corner of the cloak and lift the Black Stone together back into its place. His decision was happily agreed to, and this story is pointed to as an early sign of his sense of fairness and justice.

There is another story, that of Salman the Persian, that is seen as an early sign of Who Muḥammad was to be come. Salman had been a Zoroastrian keeper of the sacred fire, but later became a Christian. A bishop told Salman that an Arabian Prophet would soon arise and migrate to a place where palm trees grew, perhaps to an oasis like Yathrib. Salman learned that the Prophet would not eat alms offerings. Years later, when Salman met Muḥammad, he offered Him food that Muḥammad immediately gave to others who needed it more than He did. When Salman told Muḥammad this story, He asked Salman to plant 300 trees in order to earn enough to buy his freedom from slavery, which he did with Muḥammad's help. All the planted trees lived, and Salman became a Muslim and advised Muḥammad at the Battle of the Trench. Bahá'í writings mention the story of Salman. A seer declared: *"Go to Ḥijáz for there the Daystar of Muḥammad will arise. Happy art thou, for thou shalt behold His face!"* [11]

5 – Divine Commission: Encounter with Gabriel on Mount Hira

By the time He was forty, Muḥammad was taking regular spiritual retreats on Mount Hira. This was a form of meditation, a way to take stock of His soul in solitude. It is said that He often pondered the deteriorating moral conditions in Mecca. His spiritual exercises involved prayer, fasting, and giving food to the poor from the limited provision He would bring with Him. Then one day while Muḥammad was meditating on Mount Hira an extraordinary event took place. It was the seventeenth night of Ramadan in the year 610 CE, when Muḥammad heard a Voice calling to Him. The Voice said to Him, *"O Muḥammad, thou art the apostle of God, and I am Gabriel!"* [12] Muḥammad fell to His knees trembling, wondering if He was possessed or going insane. Muḥammad saw the angel Gabriel on the horizon, and wherever He looked, there was Gabriel before Him—the embodiment of the Holy Spirit and the Word of God.

On this night, Gabriel also appeared to Muḥammad in His cave and said, *"Recite!"* Muḥammad, being illiterate, could only reply, *"I am not a reciter!"* The angel embraced Muḥammad in a powerful grip, pressing in upon Him to the limits of His capacity. Eventually, Muḥammad recited the earliest words of the Qur'án: *"Proclaim! (or Read!) in the name of thy Lord and Cherisher, Who created—created man, out of a (mere) clot of congealed blood: Proclaim! And thy Lord is Most Bountiful,—He Who taught (the use of) the Pen— taught man that which knew not."* *"We have indeed revealed this (Message) in the Night of Power: And what will explain to thee what the Night of Power is? The Night of Power is better than a thousand Months. Therein come down the angels and the Spirit by God's permission, on every errand: Peace! . . . This until the rise of Morn!"* [13]

6 – Struggling in Solitude: Doubts and Temptations

In great confusion and distress, Muḥammad hurried down the mountain to Khadija, and said, *"Cover me! cover me!"* [14] He felt scared and tried to explain what happened on Mount Hira. Khadija comforted Muḥammad and assured Him that God would never harm a man so trustworthy, kind, and noble. To reassure Him, she suggested they consult Waraqa, her Christian cousin who knew scriptures well, and could bring wider perspective to these events. Waraqa said, "There has come to him the greatest *namus* [Divine Law or Word of God] who came to Moses aforetime, and lo, he is the prophet of his people." [15]

After the first few revelations, Muḥammad experienced a period of divine silence that lasted a few years. Some Muslim writers called it a time of lonely, suicidal despair. Muḥammad began to wonder if He had been deluded. Maybe God found Him incompetent and had decided to abandon Him. It was a time of intense self-questioning and doubt. He spent more time alone, pondering the meaning of God's silence. But eventually, the revelations returned.

Once during the early opposition to His revelations, Muḥammad heard grievances from the Quraysh leaders, along with proposed means of reconciliation. They asked Muḥammad if He would cease His criticisms of their practices if He were offered money, if a physician were provided to help Him overcome His troubling jinn (or spirits), or if He could have a position of honor? Muḥammad stood firm against these temptations by revealing Surah 41, which declared: *"A Qur'án in Arabic, for people who understand;— giving Good News and Admonition. . . . It is revealed to me by inspiration, that your God is One God . . . and woe to those who join gods with God,—those who practice not regular Charity, and who even deny the Hereafter. For those who believe and work deeds of righteousness is a reward that will never fail."* [16] Muḥammad emphasized the principle of good works, and reiterated His teaching that there was only one God.

The Quraysh saw that Muḥammad's words could inspire as never before, and were told they should do nothing to hinder His reforming efforts. His message, they were warned, would set the tribes ablaze with moral passion, and then His victory and prosperity would be theirs as well. But the Quraysh concluded that all these were simply bewitching tales.

7 – Declaration and First Followers:
Family, Friends, Poor Meccans

Muḥammad's first followers included Khadija, His wife for nearly twenty-five years and His spiritual confidante; Ali, His cousin, future son-in-law, first Imam of the S̲h̲í'ah and fourth Caliph; Zayd, a freed slave and adopted son who remained in Muḥammad's household; Abu Bakr, a close friend and the first Caliph; Umar, a close friend, poet, and the second Caliph; Uthman, a rich aristocrat and the third Caliph; Abdullah ibn Masud, a friend and the first person to publicly recite the Qur'án; and Bilal, an Abyssinian slave who became the first muezzin or caller to prayer. In the first few years after the revelations began, there were about fifty Meccans who embraced Muḥammad's message. These were mostly family members and close friends, but they also included some of the poorer and weaker members of Meccan society.

8 – Overcoming Powerful Opposition: Meccan Merchants and
Chieftains, Medinan Hypocrites, Treacherous Jews

Given that Muḥammad was an orphan, illiterate, meek and shy in social settings, as well as marginal in social position and religious outlook, it appears miraculous that He could transform mutually hostile Arab tribes into a great spiritual nation in only twenty-two years. The forces arrayed against Him were utterly formidable, but the Word of God worked through Him to generate a lofty religious civilization. The Qur'án explains that Messengers of God have been and always will be rejected by those who hear Their message and see Their mission. God said to Muḥammad: *"Rejected were the Apostles before thee: with patience and constancy they bore their rejection and their wrongs, until Our aid did reach them."* [17]

Muḥammad faced three stages of opposition: early and intensifying opposition in Mecca, opposition in Medina from the Hypocrites and treacherous Jews, and opposition from the Quraysh armies and their affiliates in the holy war between 622 and 628. In Mecca, Muḥammad's messages were at first ignored, but when He conveyed God's view of the local goddesses as empty names and vain opinions, the Quraysh felt insulted and angry. They began persecuting the poorer Muslims and their slaves. Bilal, a black slave and follower of Muḥammad, had a heavy stone placed on his chest and was told to deny Muḥammad or die. But Bilal endured the pain patiently, saying only *"One, One!"* [18] testifying courageously to the unity of God. Abu Bakr then bought and freed Bilal, and so Bilal was then able to continue practicing his beliefs as a follower of Muḥammad.

The initial opposition in Mecca intensified steadily and sometimes dramatically. Some believers were beaten; others had their food withheld; many were mocked and insulted, including Muḥammad during His devotions at the Kaaba. Abu Talib, Muḥammad's uncle, was pressured to withdraw His protection of the Muslims so they would refrain from disparaging polytheism. But Abu Talib remained their protector, though he never became a Muslim himself. Then the Quraysh decided to sever all ties with Muḥammad's clan, the Hashim. This meant disallowing intermarriage, as well as a boycott on all buying and selling with the Hashim, causing great hardship for the Muslims. The physical and social abuses against Muḥammad and His followers continued to intensify. Thorns and garbage were thrown on the path of the Prophet, but His most anguishing affliction was their resistance to the truth about God and social justice.

In 619, both Khadija and Abu Talib died, leaving Muḥammad without His primary spiritual confidante and His elder tribal protector. This was a major turning point in Islamic history, for Muḥammad realized that the new Faith could not survive in Mecca. He tried to bring the message to the nearby town of Taif, but it was rejected there as well.

After the Quraysh heard that Muḥammad had made an alliance with the Yathribites, Abu Jahl, Muḥammad's archenemy, proposed that He be killed while sleeping. Abu Jahl's plan was that Muḥammad be killed by representatives of all the clans, so that retaliation would be impossible, given that the Hashim could not avenge all of the other clans collectively. But as we have seen elsewhere in Muḥammad's story, God had other plans. The new Faith would emigrate to Yathrib, which would be renamed Medina, City of the Prophet.

However, in Medina Muḥammad faced serious opposition as well, though it was a more subtle kind that required considerable political and military skill, as well as divine assistance, to overcome. Some Medinans, including their influential leader Ibn Ubayy, had declared allegiance to Muḥammad only as a matter of temporary convenience, and were therefore called Hypocrites because they did not truly believe in His teachings. Furthermore, the Hypocrites collaborated with disenchanted Jewish leaders in Medina, as well as with the Quraysh. This anti-Muslim collaboration and treachery amounted to an extremely formidable opposing force. It could not be tolerated if the new Faith were to survive.

In all these struggles, Muḥammad, through His unwavering faith in divine presence and justice, was able to transform a land and people with barbaric practices into a unified spiritual nation that would soon rule over an Islamic commonwealth stretching from the Atlantic to Pacific.

9 – Rejection by the People

Not only leaders and warriors opposed Muḥammad, but also ordinary people. He was mocked and heckled in public; garbage and dead animals were placed on His path and at doorways of the early Muslims; His poorest followers were beaten and food was withheld from them. When Khadija and Abu Talib died in 619, much of Muḥammad's spiritual and social support vanished with them, and there were escalating death threats against the Muslims. The Qur'án refers to the anti-Muslim Meccans as those who *"banish a party of you from their homes. . . . These are the people who buy the life of this world at the price of the Hereafter."* [19]

God described how this pattern of rejecting Messengers had happened before. *"Rejected were the Apostles before thee: with patience and constancy they bore their rejection and their wrongs, until Our aid did reach them."* [20] According to the Qur'án, the people will always reject a Messenger when He first begins to spread His message. They will not want to give up their old beliefs, and of the new beliefs they will say, *"'This is only a falsehood invented!' And the Unbelievers say of the Truth when it comes to them, 'This is nothing but evident magic!'"* [21] But the Hijrah, or emigration, to Medina would eventually lead to an increased number of receptive listeners who were willing to co-fashion a new Muslim society. Muḥammad's banishment would yield fruit for the new Islamic religious civilization, destined for greatness on the world stage.

10 – Sacrificial Suffering

In depths of despair, having lost Khadija and Abu Talib, and just before the Hijrah, Muḥammad turned to God for assistance. He saw no earthly way to bring divine guidance to leaders of Mecca or to a significant number of the people. Their hearts were not open to His teachings and their intentions against Him were malevolent. God saw that His Messenger contemplated a dramatic miracle to get their attention. God said the people must be made to hear, and assured Muḥammad that tribulation and adversity would be visited upon them, for the Divine Cause could not be thwarted indefinitely. *"We know indeed the grief which their words do cause thee. . . . If their spurning is hard on thy mind, yet if thou wert able to seek a tunnel in the ground or a ladder to the skies, and bring them a Sign, — (what good?) If it were God's Will, He could gather them together unto true guidance."*[22]

Muḥammad's suffering would prove to be sacrificial in that great bounties for humanity emerged from it. The success of the holy war against the Meccans, and their spiritual conversion in the next eight years may be seen as the fulfillment of God's assurance to Muḥammad in His hour of deepest despair.

11 – Symbolic Language as a Test for Believers

The symbolic material in the Qur'án, as in other scriptures, serves as a test to sort out those who receive its message with humility and understanding from those who receive it with arrogance and the desire to only follow their preconceived ideas of truth. The Qur'án explains that each revelation from God is for an appointed period of time, after which a new revelation will be offered by a new Messenger. The Qur'án also explains that only God can illumine the hidden meanings of scripture. Humanity's rigid and literalistic interpretations of symbolic material have served as a veil, preventing many from accepting later revelations. Because of rigid interpretation that developed over time, many Muslims have blocked themselves from appreciating the Messengers and the messages that came after the Qur'án.

Some of the terms posing obstacles to understanding in the Islamic dispensation, and that have been interpreted in very narrow, exclusive, and finalistic ways include: *seal of the prophets, the Book, the Mother of the Book, Islam, terms or periods of the Messengers, the Trumpet,* and *the Day of Resurrection.* Are these terms to be understood explicitly or implicitly, specifically or universally, categorically or analogically?

The Qur'án warns us that it contains both clear and difficult material, capable of providing illumination and judgment, as it sorts out receptive souls from contentious ones. *"We have propounded for men, in this Qur-an, every kind of Parable: but if thou bring to them any Sign, the Unbelievers are sure to say, 'Ye verily do nothing but talk vanities.' Thus does God seal up the hearts of those who do not understand."*[23] A passage in the Qur'án explains that there are different types of passages within it, and they need to be interpreted in different ways. *"He it is Who has sent down to thee the Book: in it are verses basic or fundamental (of established meaning); they are the foundation of the Book:*

others are allegorical. But those in whose hearts is perversity follow the part thereof that is allegorical, seeking discord . . . but no one knows its hidden meanings except God."[24] These passages warn that some will develop their own school of thought or ideological movement, leading many astray and proving divisive in the building of a divinely guided society.

Some passages in the Qur'án lend themselves to exclusive and dogmatic interpretations. *"Muhammad . . . is the Apostle of God, and the Seal of the Prophets."*[25] This has been widely interpreted by Muslims as meaning that God will send no more Messengers after Muḥammad, that He is the final one, and that revelation is therefore sealed. But the Qur'án distinguishes between a Prophet (*Rasul*), which means a Messenger, and a prophet (*nabi*), which means warners of the people. A Messenger, such as Jesus, reveals a new Book and generates a whole new religious dispensation. A prophet, such as John the Baptist, warns the people that times of divine judgment and opportunity are at hand. The Qur'án declares that Muḥammad is the seal of the *nabi*, or warners; it does not declare that He is the seal of the *Rasul*, or Messengers. Muḥammad served both as a warner and a Messenger.

There are other Qur'ánic texts used to claim that Islam is the final Word of God. *"If anyone desires a religion other than Islam (submission to God), never will it be accepted of him."*[26] The Qur'án also states, *"This day have I perfected your religion for you, completed My favour upon you, and have chosen for you Islam as your religion."*[27] These passages were interpreted as meaning no expression of faith other than the one generated by Muḥammad can have anything to do with the one and only God. However, *islam,* or a general belief in submission to God, is best interpreted as divine guidance offered throughout history by the same One God. Muḥammad's revelation is one of the expressions or dispensations of this islam. Another Qur'ánic passage seems to affirm this more universal view. *"The Religion before God is Islam (submission to His Will): nor did the People of the Book dissent therefrom except through envy of each other, after knowledge had come to them."*[28]

The Qur'án clarifies that God's messages come to humanity at intervals, and are sent to different locations. These messages are meant to endure for a certain period of time, after which they are replaced with a new message affirming the moral and spiritual basics of previous messages, but also providing distinctive and historically relevant changes. For example, the Qur'án says, *"For every Message is a limit of time,"*[29] implying that each revelation is only meant to last, or be followed, for a specific length of time. The Qur'án also says the arrival of another Messenger of God is inevitable. *"To every people is a term appointed: when their term is reached, not an hour can they cause delay."* [30] God reveals a particular set of teachings for different ages, and knowledge of all revelations lies with Him alone. *"For each period is a Book (revealed). God doth blot out or confirm what He pleaseth: with Him is the Mother of the Book."* [31] These passages suggest that divine guidance has been sent to all peoples, and that no single faith can claim to have the only and everlasting Word of God, for the Mother of the Book is God's alone, shared according to His providential plan.

The Day of Resurrection has also been an issue of controversy and contention. Is its reference earthly, heavenly, or a combination of both? Does it apply to individuals, collective bodies of people, or to humanity as a whole? And who or what is the Trumpet to be sounded beforehand? Are these specific or universal designations? To what degree are they meant to be historically interpreted, and to what degree spiritually interpreted? Do the Day and Trumpet refer to the end of time, the final judgment in the afterlife, the end of Muḥammad's dispensation, or to the coming of the Promised One of All Ages?

The mention of the Day and Trumpet in the Qur'án are probably symbols referring to several or all of these proposed meanings. *"The Trumpet shall be sounded, when behold! from the sepulchers (men) will rush forth to their Lord! . . . (A voice will say:) 'This is what (God) Most Gracious had promised. And true was the word of the apostles!'"* [32] Taken literally, this means that decomposed bodies will miraculously recompose, come alive, and step out of their graves. Figuratively and more probably it means the spiritually asleep will be quickened with a new divine message. *"And the Earth will shine with the glory of its Lord: the Record (of Deeds) will be placed (open); the prophets and the witnesses will be brought forward; and a just decision pronounced between them; and they will not be wronged (in the least)."* [33] This alludes to a time when the whole sweep of history will be evaluated in the light of progressive revelation—a time like ours.

12 – Exemplary Women:
Khadija the Nurturer, Aishah the Advocate

Khadija was the exemplary nurturing woman of the Islamic dispensation. As Muḥammad's first and only wife for their twenty-five years together, she was His greatest spiritual confidante, emotional supporter, and the first to accept His station and message. She comforted the Prophet greatly as He overcame the shock of His first revelations and dealt with the increasingly harsh reactions of the Meccan merchants and chieftains. Her wealth and social status also provided Muḥammad with recognition and respect, both before and after His divine commission in the year 610.

Four of their daughters survived into adulthood: Fatima, Ruqayya, Umm Khulthum, and Zaynab. Two of these daughters made very significant contributions to the early Muslim community. Fatima was the wife of Ali, the first Shī'ah Imam and the fourth Caliph; she was the mother of Hasan and Husayn, the second and third Shī'ah Imams; and she was also revered for her sublime character and spiritual radiance. Ruqayya and her husband Uthman, who became the third Caliph, were sent by Muḥammad to Abyssinia where they established a Muslim community, forming a constructive relationship with the Christian king.

Aishah was the exemplary assertive woman of the Islamic dispensation. She was the daughter of Abu Bakr, and the Prophet's second wife after the death of Khadija. She was very intelligent, well-educated, witty, and articulate. Aishah made many astute observations about Muḥammad and once described Him as "the walking Qur'án." "She did all that she could to preserve both the written Qur'an and the walking Qur'an, memorizing its verses and understanding them. . . . It was in large part due to her example that Hadith, or traditions or reports about the Prophet, became conjoined with the Qur'an."[34]

Two events in Aishah's life were extremely influential in the early development of Islam. Once she was on a mission with Muḥammad, and was left behind by mistake when the party moved on. Later, a young man found her alone and escorted her back to Medina. Gossip developed that she had behaved improperly with the young man. Among those who advocated returning her to her father's home was Ali. Muḥammad found this event upsetting and defended her reputation in public. Finally, some Qur'ánic verses came that clearly decreed her innocence. But Aishah's relationship with Ali was strained for several decades, leading to the second very influential event, the Battle of the Camel in 656.

Because of her excellent memory of Qur'ánic passages and sayings of the Prophet, Aishah became an extremely well-respected figure in the early Islamic community, and was called the Mother of the Believers. Her opinions were sought on all important matters. She opposed the rule of the third Caliph Uthman, but was also opposed to his assassination. She opposed the rule of Ali, the fourth Caliph and the first S̲h̲í'ah Imam. She helped lead a force of one thousand against Ali at the Battle of the Camel, which Ali won. Aishah, however, was treated with respect and honor. Eventually she and Ali became reconciled, but their earlier estrangement contributed to the S̲h̲í'ah / Sunni split that became formal at the Massacre of Karbala in 680, two years after Aishah's death. To this day, Aishah inspires Muslim women and elicits the respect of Muslim men.

13 – Dying and Ascending Victoriously: Achieving Arabian Peace and Unity, and Directing the Ummah Outward

Ummah means community, but due to Muḥammad's teaching this term came to have much greater visionary significance. Because God is one, all the communities, peoples, or religions that are truly under His guidance are united spiritually. This means that the truly faithful, those who accept God's continuing instruction and authority—despite any ethnic, cultural, linguistic, social, or geographic differences that abide among them—are ultimately one covenantal community. This trans-tribal vision of spiritual loyalty was unprecedented in Arabia and elsewhere in the world before Muḥammad started to receive His first revelations in 610.

In 632, shortly before He ascended, Muḥammad delivered a farewell address near Mount Arafat. He reminded Muslims of the basic themes of His message—that God sees all, expects social justice, and rewards each person fairly. Women, children, and the weak are to be treated kindly. Blood-feuds of the superstitious in the "days of ignorance" have been transcended by a new loyalty based on divine guidance, not on tribal bonds. The ummah's unity must reflect the divine unity, and all Muslims everywhere are brothers and sisters in God's family. Bridges of understanding and cooperation must be built with all people of good will. Muḥammad directed the ummah outward, far beyond the confines of Arabia. Later He said several times that Ali was to be His successor, though Sunni tradition has denied this.

After returning to Medina and falling ill, Muḥammad called His closest companions together and said, *"O people! Whoever hath me as his Lord verily hath this Alí as his Lord."*[35] Later, He called for the writing of a document so that *"you will never go astray after Me,"* but believing He was in great pain and delirious, they ignored this request. It was reported that He asked for Ali, but others said that Abu Bakr and Umar were sent to Him. These controversies are what eventually led to the Sunni / S͟hīʿah split.

The first to know that the Prophet would soon die, except for Muḥammad Himself, was Abu Bakr. Some of the others denied that the Prophet could ever die. Muḥammad's wives agreed to let Aishah care for Him in His weakest hours, because they knew that this was Muḥammad's wish. Soon after saying, *"Nay, the most Exalted Companion in paradise,"* [36] His spirit ascended from His body.

The news traveled quickly, and the Medinans gathered at the Mosque. Umar was passionately assuring everyone that Muḥammad's spirit would soon return to His body. But more serious attention was given to Abu Bakr, who reminded them that Muḥammad's teaching focused on the unity of God, the only true object of worship; and the Prophet warned them not to worship Him the way Christians worshiped Jesus. Abu Bakr clarified this teaching when He said, *"O men, if anyone worships Muḥammad, Muḥammad is dead. If anyone worships God, God is alive, immortal."* [37] Finally he quoted this verse from the Qurʾán, *"Muḥammad is no more than an Apostle: many were the Apostles that passed away before Him. If he died or were slain, will ye then turn back on your heels? . . . God (on the other hand) will swiftly reward those who (serve him) with gratitude."* [38]

Then the grieving community accepted the death of Muḥammad, the Prophet of God. Muḥammad's body was washed with His clothes on, as He rested on Ali's breast. He was buried the following day, exactly ten years after He had entered Medina. When He left Mecca for Medina, the fate of the new Faith seemed very uncertain, and Arabia was an unnoticed, disunited, and violent part of the world. When He departed this world, Arabia had become a spiritual nation, having attained a high degree of spiritual peace and political unity. Muslims were poised to become the center of world history for a time, and the builders of a great civilization.

- 16 -
Muḥammad: Teaching and Legacy

14 – Transformative Teaching and Healing:
Warning, Migration, War, Peace, Expansion, and Consolidation

Muḥammad's transformative ministry developed in four stages. The first stage included Muḥammad's Meccan years after His public declaration, a series of intensifying warnings to Meccans that God could see their actions and was displeased, negotiations with Yathribites, and the Hijrah, which involved breaking ties with the Quraysh and migrating to Yathrib. The second stage could be considered the true beginning of the Islamic era in Medina. This included the making of an Islamic Constitution in Medina and a holy war against Mecca, which involved key struggles at Badr, Uhud, and the Battle of the Trench. The third stage began with Muḥammad's peace initiative beginning at the sanctuary of Hudaybiyah, which, though broken by Meccans, led to the spiritual conquest of Mecca. And the fourth stage included Islam's early expansion, ending with the Prophet's farewell pilgrimage and addresses.

Warning the Meccans: 613–622

Muḥammad's early preaching clarified that there is only one God, the Creator of heaven and earth, Who will not tolerate the worship of false gods and goddesses. Muḥammad taught that God sees all things, and that nothing can be hidden from Him, including the greed and social injustices of wealthy Meccan merchants and chieftains. God judges each soul according to its deeds, both in this life and the next. God sees undistributed wealth as unfair. Instead, compassion should be shown to the poor, the widows, and the orphans. But a rigid kind of class system or social hierarchy had been established in Arabia, and Muḥammad taught that this was in complete violation of God's will. This corrupt system opposed the best aspect of old tribal ways, the mandate to care for members of one's own tribe.

Prior to Muḥammad's revelation, Arab paganism was failing both spiritually and socially. But it was to be replaced by a new revelation from God, one that was in continuity with earlier revelations from Abraham, Moses, and Jesus—a revelation now adapted to the highest aspirations, needs, and cultural patterns of Arabia. God's Messengers had been sent to many peoples, and Their messages were rejected by those holding the reins of authority. Now this same pattern was happening again in Mecca.

Muḥammad's message was rejected in ever more punitive ways by the Quraysh. However, some influential Yathribites became Muslims, and Muḥammad was willing to consult with these good neighbors to the north about the feasibility of migrating there. Yathrib, a city located to the north of Mecca, had grown weary of its own intertribal strife, and was now ready to receive the Prophet, Who could bring them a divinely guided system of justice. When the Muslim population of Yathrib had grown sufficiently large, and a significant number had pledged their willingness to defend Muḥammad with arms, He led a Muslim migration to Yathrib.

The Hijrah, the Constitution, and the Holy War: 622–628

This emigrating to Yathrib, known as the Hijrah, was not simply a relocation. It was unprecedented in Arabian culture. It was a permanent breaking of ties, an exodus to establish a society based on trans-tribal loyalty, a new concept of spiritual community (known as ummah), as well as a new religion of obedience to God and His Messenger. The Hijrah marked the start of the Islamic Era. By means of a document known as the Constitution of Medina, emigrants and helpers in Medina, as well as Jewish and Christian tribes living in an oasis formerly called Yathrib, now agreed to help and protect one another under Muḥammad's spiritual and political leadership. Medina means City of the Prophet, and the Hijrah marked the advent of Islamic society.

In 624, the first battle between Muslims and Mecccans took place southwest of Medina near the well of Badr. About 300 Muslims led by Muḥammad went to protect a caravan returning to Mecca and faced a Quraysh army 1000 strong. Though the Muslims were greatly outnumbered, they fought under unified command and with divine assistance, whereas the Quraysh used the old Arab style of fighting led by uncoordinated chiefs. This Muslim victory was understood not as some tribes defeating other tribes, but as the first sign of the Islamic conquest of

Arabia. It brought the hope that a new and more just social order might be established.

Abu Sufyan, one of the Meccan leaders at the Battle of Badr, vowed revenge on the Muslims. In 625, the Quraysh gathered a force of about 3000 near Mount Uhud. The Muslim army had about 1000 men. But the leader of the Hypocrites, a group that professed to be Muslims but proved faithless, and even treacherous when Muslims needed protection, withdrew 300 of his men upon seeing the force arrayed against them. In spite of this setback, the Muslims were winning during most of the fighting, but the archers, who were told not to abandon their positions, became greedy for booty. In the Battle of Uhud, seventy Muslims were killed, while only twenty-two Quraysh were killed. But the Quraysh did not follow up on their victory.

Questions arose about whether God was really on the side of the Muslims, but Muḥammad explained that disobedience caused their defeat. He ordered that two of the Jewish tribes, the Qaynuqah and the Nadir, be expelled from Medina because they had failed to fulfill their promises. The remaining Jewish tribe, the Qurayzah, formed a treacherous alliance with the Meccans. When Muḥammad heard of the growing preparations of the Quraysh, who had gathered a force of 10,000 for a march toward Medina, He took the advice of Salman the Persian and dug a trench around the southern side of Medina where it was most vulnerable. This novel strategy, combined with divine assistance—a storm blowing away the tents of the Quraysh, who had laid siege for two weeks—enabled the Muslims to emerge victorious at the Battle of the Trench in 627.

The Peace Initiative and the Spiritual Conquest of Mecca: 628–630

Despite all the hostilities, a daring peace initiative was undertaken by Muḥammad, which led to a positive perception of the Muslims, not only by the tribes surrounding Mecca and Medina, but also by the Quraysh. After the surprising success of the peace initiative, the number of Muslims doubled in only two years. In 628, Muḥammad invited His fellow Muslims to take a pilgrimage to the Kaaba in Mecca. A thousand of His followers agreed to join this risky venture. The Quraysh were suspicious of Muḥammad's motives, and sent troops to attack Him, even though, as pilgrims, the Muslims were virtually unarmed. But the Prophet evaded them and reached the sanctuary of Hudaybiyah, north of Mecca, where all violence was strictly forbidden.

The Quraysh felt pressured by the peace initiative to sign the Treaty of Hudaybiyah, whereby Muslims were forced to return home, but could have three days alone in Mecca the following year. The signing of this treaty led to a ten-year truce between Mecca, Medina, and all affiliated tribes. Muḥammad agreed to return any young Muslim who made the Hijrah without guardian consent. Muslims were shocked with the leniency of the Treaty, and some even considered rebellion; but faith in Muḥammad prevailed. In 630, Meccans violated the Treaty by failing to prevent one of their affiliated tribes from attacking one of the Muslims' affiliated tribes. Muḥammad gathered 10,000 Muslims for a march on Mecca. This mighty force was overwhelming to the Quraysh, and Mecca recognized its defeat and opened its doors to Muḥammad, Who entered the city without bloodshed. He then cleansed the Kaaba of idols. To the surprise of many Meccans and Muslims, He did not force conversions to Islam, but most Meccans declared their obedience to Muḥammad and to God. The spiritual conquest of Mecca was now complete; the spiritual conquest of Arabia was soon to come.

Expansion and Consolidation: 630–632

Three tribes had no intention of affiliating with the Muslims—the Hawazin, the Ahlaf, and the Banu Malik—and they feared domination by the Muslims. These tribes decided to attack the Muslims, and a collective force from these three tribes of about 4000 marched toward Mecca. In response to the impending attack, Muḥammad gathered an army of about 12,000. The battle at first went against the Muslims, partly because the newly converted Quraysh had doubts, and many of them fled. But Ali and others, with divine assistance, were able to overcome their enemies. Soon after this, delegations of the Hawazin and the Thaqif tribes accepted Islam.

Following this attack, it was rumored that the Byzantine emperor planned to conquer Mecca. Muḥammad gathered an army of about 30,000 and marched to present-day Jordan. Upon seeing such a vast army, the Byzantine emperor announced that he no longer had designs on Mecca. Islam continued to spread across the region, and in 631, what became known as the "year of delegations," many different tribes (including some Christian groups) sought to become Muslims, or to get help from the growing body of believers. By this time, nearly all of Arabia had embraced Islam, and most of those who had not were favorably impressed with this new Faith.

15 – Delivering a Thematic and Complementary Message: Submission to God and Building a Just and Spiritual Nation

The central theme of Muḥammad's message is that human beings should submit voluntarily to God. Such submission brings inner peace and enables people to establish a just social order, in which the gifts bestowed by God to humanity develop into a unified spiritual nation. Ten major themes are well-developed in the Qur'án. Usually several, and sometimes all these themes are woven together in any given surah, or chapter, of the Qur'án. The Qur'án contains 114 chapters, which are generally arranged by length, with longer ones in the beginning, with the exception of the short opening. The order of the Qur'án's content is neither historical nor thematic, and this often poses difficulties for Western readers, for whom the reading may feel like an oracular kaleidoscope of quickly-changing, confusing topics. But familiarity with major themes can help Westerners appreciate the profundity and scope of the Qur'án, and its harmony with other scriptures.

The Qur'án's Nature and Authority

The Qur'án describes itself as a revelation from God, a literary embodiment of archetypal truth, or the Mother of the Book. It provides guidance for humanity, and it confirms and illuminates previous scriptures. It seems that it is part of God's plan to test humanity in what He has given us, by forcing many of us to overcome prejudices before we can accept all the Messengers of God as equal and united. We need to ask ourselves: Can we learn from other scriptures and unite with all faithful communities? The Qur'án offers glad tidings to the righteous, but also warns the contentious. *"This is indeed a Qur-an most honourable . . . a Book well-guarded, which none shall touch but those who are clean: a Revelation from the Lord of the worlds."* [1] The Qur'án says we must be "clean" before we can read it, and this seems to be referring to a spiritual cleansing of sorts, similar to what was taught in previous revelations.

The Nature of God

The Qur'án teaches that there is only one God Who creates, sustains, and restores all beings in due proportion for just ends; Who is all-powerful, merciful, and just; Who is a majestic sovereign, and yet still personal in response to prayer. God's power is visible to a degree when we look at the vastness and beauty of creation, though we are limited in what we can see and understand.

There is continuity between levels of reality, with the various levels of the material and spiritual world interacting with one another, but everything ultimately depends on God. The Qur'án teaches that God is omniscient. He knows all our secrets and calls each soul to account, though He is forgiving of sins, and listens to the distressed and guides those who turn to Him. God loves those who choose to be kind and just, who make themselves pure, and who put their trust in Him. God has the ability to change evil into good, and has promised that one day He will gather all humankind together.

Messengers of God

Muḥammad taught that Messengers are sent to humanity by God in distinct stages, Each bringing more detailed revelations of spiritual reality and divine will, and fulfilling the promises of previous Messengers. Significant aspects of the missions and messages of Abraham, Moses, and Jesus are described in the Qur'án. Messengers have been sent to every people, and many more have come than are mentioned in the scriptures. They have been sent to centers of populations at distinct time periods, as the Qur'án says, *"for each period is a Book (revealed)."* [2] Scriptural dispensations have a preordained length. *"To every People is a term appointed: when their term is reached, not an hour can they cause delay."* [3] Messengers are endowed with special powers and explain divine mysteries that were previously beyond human understanding. A "band of witnesses," often a small group of devoted believers, is sent by God both before and after Them, to help spread the Word of God. Despite this, these great spiritual Teachers are inevitably rejected by the societies They visit. Yet due to divine assistance, They ultimately prevail and are able to sanctify Their peoples. Their coming is both a judgment and an opportunity, depending on whether Their message is rejected or embraced. Acceptance of the Messenger is understood as following the will of God, as the Qur'án says, *"He who obeys the Apostle, obeys God."* [4]

Faith and Devotional Practice

The Qur'án enjoins Muslims to *"believe in God and the Last Day, and the Angels, and the Book, and the Messengers; to spend of your substance, out of love for Him, for your kin, for orphans, for the needy . . . to be steadfast in prayer, and practice regular charity; to fulfill the contracts which ye have made; and to be firm and patient, in pain (or suffering) and adversity."* [5] The five pillars of faith, an important aspect of Islam, are viewed as necessary disciplines of submission that steadily align the believer's will with divine purpose. They are: 1) declaration of faith (*shahadah*), where a believer must affirm daily that he / she is a follower of Muḥammad by saying, "I declare there is no god but God, and Muḥammad is His Messenger"; 2) daily prayer (*salat*), where believers are to face Mecca five times daily in prayer; 3) charity (*zakat*), believers are encouraged in almsgiving to the poor and needy, and that charity should amount to 1/40 of one's surplus wealth after necessities; 4) fasting during Ramadan (*sawm*), which is when Muslims must refrain from food, drink, and sexual intercourse during daylight hours during the month of Muḥammad's initial revelation; and 5) pilgrimage to Mecca (*hajj*), which should be undertaken at least once in a lifetime for those who can afford the expense.

Human Capacities and Limitations

Muḥammad taught that human beings are the noblest creation of God, His vice-regents on earth, who are gifted with choice and reason and are meant to serve God through a covenantal relationship, and to develop a benevolent mastery over nature. Though we are all children of God, we have been created diverse in languages, colors, tribes, and nations, as a challenge to our growth and development. Though we can always learn more, we can never understand God comprehensively. Humanity tends to be ungrateful for our divine bounty, and forgets our servanthood to God through pride and sin. Threats to our survival and greed make us more disputatious and vulnerable to misconduct. Satan or evil is viewed as the force of temptation active in humanity, obscuring our understanding of divine will, strengthening our lower or animal nature, and leading us to choose a path of arrogance and injustice. Faith and devotional practice are needed to bring us back to our original moral and spiritual nature.

Women's Rights and Responsibilities

The Qur'án teaches that men and women were created of like nature, as mates and companions for one another as a divine favor, having mutual rights and responsibilities, and should live together on a basis of kindness and equity. Men are forbidden to inherit women against their will, must not treat them with harshness, must give them their dowers at least as prescribed, and allot to them all that they earn. In divorce, mutual agreements should be sought on an equitable basis, and women cannot be turned out of their houses. The spiritual equality of men and women is declared: *"For men and women who are patient and constant, for men and women who humble them-selves . . . for men and women who guard their chastity, and for men and women who engage in God's praise,—for them God has prepared forgiveness and a great reward."* [6] They must protect one another, and when they are both righteous, both enter Paradise.

Spiritual Laws

Among the most important spiritual laws in the Qur'án are those concerning the practice of remembering and submitting to the Will of God, remaining humble and truthful, seeking knowledge, and both fearing and loving God. The Qur'án says, *"Celebrate the praises of thy Lord again and again, and glorify Him in the evening and in the morning."* [7] Muḥammad also reminds us to be humble, *"Their hearts in all humility should engage in the remembrance of God and of the Truth."* [8] We are also taught to fear God, in order to better follow the teachings of God. *"Fear God, and (always) say a word directed to the Right: that He may make your conduct whole and sound."* [9] But ultimately we are told to follow God's teachings out of love, *"If ye do love God, follow me: God will love you and forgive you your sins."* [10]

Social and Economic Laws

The Qur'án supports and encourages family life, generosity, tolerance, equality, justice, consultative governance, and the defense of faith. We are called to alleviate suffering, help the afflicted, protect the weak, share wealth, extend kindness and charity, punish wrongdoing moderately, and to respect racial and cultural differences. Muḥammad taught that believers should refrain from spiritual conversion by force when He said, *"Let there be no compulsion in religion,"* [11] but at the same time, believers should bring society under divine law and build an ever-wider sense of religious community. Generosity is often mentioned in Muḥammad's teachings, and can be seen in this passage when He said, *"Give of the good things which ye have (honourably) earned, and of the fruits of the earth which We have produced for you."* [12] He also emphasized the importance of getting along with others, *"O Mankind! We created you from a single (pair) of a male and female, and made you into nations and tribes, that ye may know each other (not that ye may despise each other)."* [13] Kindness, charity, and justice are some of the central themes of Muḥammad's teachings.

Immortality of the Soul

The Qur'án teaches that upon death, our souls are judged and will endure. Human souls face the results of their intentions and actions. Each soul pays a price for what was misappropriated. *"Whether ye show what is in your minds or conceal it, God calleth you to account for it."* [14] Heaven and hell, or reward and punishment, are both physical and spiritual realities.

Day of Resurrection

A major theme in the Qur'án is the Day of Resurrection, or what is also called the Day of Judgment or Day of Renewal. These symbolic terms point to the end of the age. They suggest a time of turmoil and transition when profoundly important choices are made regarding a new revelation of God. Descriptions of this Day in the Qur'án share some elements of Christ's description of the Second Coming in the Gospel. The following passages show some of the depth and imagery of this Day, and the anguish and hope associated with it. They are best viewed in broad terms as pointing both to earthly and spiritual events, and as both within individuals and as encompassing all of humanity. When describing that Day, Muḥammad said, *"One Day everything that can be in commotion will be in violent commotion."* [15] Seemingly miraculous natural events are also used to describe that Day, *"When the sun (with its spacious light) is folded up; when the stars fall, losing their lustre; when the mountains vanish (like a mirage) . . . when the oceans boil over with a swell; when the souls are sorted out . . . when the Scrolls are laid open; when the World on High is unveiled... (then) shall each soul know what it has put forward."* [16] And it is described that on that Day, justice will reign: *"One day We shall call together all human beings with their (respective) Imams . . . and they will not be dealt with unjustly in the least."* [17]

16 – Renewing and Embodying Universal Virtues

Like Moses, Jesus, and all the other Founders, Muḥammad renewed and embodied universal virtues. Through teaching, care-giving, and fair administration, He reminded the world of abiding moral and spiritual verities, and established the basis of a lofty religious civilization. He said, *"Strive as in a race for all virtues."* [18] The collective body of virtues is often referred to as righteousness, and one of the most famous summaries is provided in this verse: *"It is righteousness . . . to spend of your substance, out of love for Him, for your kin, for orphans, for the needy, for the wayfarer, for those who ask, and for the ransom of slaves; to be steadfast in prayer, and practice regular charity; to fulfill the contracts which ye have made; and to be firm and patient, in pain (or suffering) and adversity."* [19]

Spiritual Virtues in the Islamic Revelation
Devotion-Faithfulness: *"Keep in remembrance the name of thy Lord, and devote thyself to Him whole-heartedly."* [20]
Gratitude-Reverence: *"It is He Who has spread out the earth for (His) creatures . . . then which of the favours of your Lord will ye deny?"* [21]
Self-discipline-Obedience: *"If any one obeyeth his own impulse to Good,—be sure that God is He Who recogniseth and knoweth."* [22]
Detachment-Patience: *"God is with those who patiently persevere."* [23]
Wisdom-Discernment: *"How many Signs in the heavens and the earth do they pass by? Yet they turn (their faces) away from them!"* [24]

Social Virtues in the Islamic Revelation
Loving-kindness-Compassion: *"What actions are most excellent? To gladden the heart of a human being, to feed the hungry, to help the afflicted, to lighten the sorrows of the sorrowful, and to remove the wrongs of the injured."* [25]
Service-Responsibility: *"Strive as in a race for all virtues."* [26]
Respect-Tolerance: *"Let there be no compulsion in religion."* [27]
Justice-Righteousness: *"Stand out firmly for justice, as witnesses to God, even as against yourselves, or your parents, or your kin, and whether it be (against) rich or poor."* [28]
Peace-Unity: *"The same religion has He established for you as that which He enjoined on Noah . . . Abraham, Moses and Jesus: namely, that ye should remain steadfast in Religion, and make no divisions therein."* [29]

Material Virtues in the Islamic Revelation
Trustworthiness-Honesty: *"This is a day on which the truthful will profit from their truth."* [30]
Moderation-Balance: *"God loveth not any arrogant boaster. And be moderate in thy pace, and lower thy voice."* [31]
Generosity-Hospitality: *"Give what is due to kindred, the needy, and the way-farer."* [32]
Creativity-Beauty: *"It is He Who hath made you (His) agents, inheritors of the*

earth: He hath raised you in ranks, some above the others: that He may try you in the gifts He hath given you."[33]
Earthcare-Stewardship: *"Thy Lord said to the angels: 'I will create a viceregent on earth.' . . . and He taught Adam the nature of all things."*[34]

17 – Abrogating the Old and Establishing the New: Ritual and Legal Guidance

As Jesus abrogated parts of Mosaic Law, spiritualized other parts, and redefined the kingdom, so did Muḥammad redefine the spiritual significance of the Kaaba in Mecca, while also generating a substantial body of new ritual and legal guidance. The necessity of change is mentioned in the Qur'án. *"None of Our revelations do We abrogate or cause to be forgotten, but We substitute something better or similar."*[35] How did Muḥammad revise the pilgrimage, transforming its framework from polytheistic to monotheistic, and from materialistic to spiritual purposes? In 624, He changed the direction (qiblah) of prayer from Jerusalem to Mecca. This was a significant change made under divine command, a declaration of independence from Jewish and Christian influence. It appealed to both Muslims and Arab pagans, redefining in one elegant gesture the spiritual meaning of the Kaaba's past and future.

In the Qur'án, the initially spiritual purposes of the Kaaba and the pilgrimage were declared. *"Behold! We gave the site, to Abraham, of the (Sacred) House, (saying): 'Associate not anything (in worship) with Me; and sanctify My House for those who compass it round, or stand up, or bow, or prostrate themselves (therein in prayer). And proclaim the Pilgrimage among men: they will come to thee on foot and (mounted).'"*[36] Muḥammad developed this ritual so as to integrate many different peoples and to level social classes, thereby treating kings and paupers as equals.

Pilgrimage takes place in the eleventh lunar month, and requires pilgrims to wear white plain cloth, to perform ritual cleansing, and to recite a special prayer. It calls for refraining from certain actions such as swearing, using perfume, and sexual intercourse. The pilgrimage includes regular prayers and prostrations, the circumambulation of the Sacred Mosque, the kissing of the Black Stone, and the commemoration of Hagar's desperate but divinely assisted search for a water spring. It involves casting stones at three pillars (symbolizing Abraham's rejection of temptations), as well as animal sacrifice. Custom also requires drinking from the well of Zamzam and visiting Medina's Mosque.

Islamic law takes new approaches and goes into more detail than previous dispensations regarding the following needs: giving to the poor, protecting the weak (including orphans, widows, and the sick), providing for education, fulfilling contracts, respecting women's rights, respecting racial equality, punishing wrongdoing appropriately, refraining from spiritual conversion by force, and refraining from initiating military violence. It also enjoins believers to refrain from alcohol, gambling, usury, prostitution, and eating pork. It requires defending the faith (by force if necessary), cleanliness, courtesy, and helping slaves to work their way to freedom.

18 – Human and Divine Qualities: Exemplifying a Dual Station

Partly in response to Christians who over-emphasized Christ's divine station, Muslims emphasized Muḥammad's human station at the expense of His divine station. It appears to Muslims and Jews that down through the centuries, Jesus was elevated by Christians, through doctrinal and theological development, to being considered identical with God. This is unacceptable to Muslims and Jews. In our view, all Founders were distinct and human in some respects, and united and divine in other respects.

Traditional sayings of Muḥammad referred to the dual station of all Messengers. *"Outwardly, we are the least of all, but inwardly we preceded everyone."*[37] In this teaching, Muḥammad was affirming the humility of all Prophets, as He describes Them as the "least of all." But He was also saying They shared a station where They came into being prior to humanity as a whole; They were manifestations of the divine Word and had transcendent powers. Attaining a balanced appraisal of Their dual station has proved to be very difficult, and has caused intense interreligious strife over many years. Another saying also points to the dual station of all Prophets. *"I am the closest of all people to Jesus, son of Mary, in this world and the Hereafter; for all prophets are brothers, with different mothers but one religion."*[38] The claim is that all Messengers are human by virtue of their birthplace and mothers, which can be termed the station of distinction; and They are divine by virtue of serving God's one religion together, for They all come from the station of unity.

Muḥammad's Human Station

Authentic traditions of Muḥammad depict a man of modesty and humility. He is said to have lived in a house made of clay, where He shared household duties with His wives, mended His clothes, cobbled His shoes, smiled and laughed often, and consulted others frequently about the best course of action. The Prophet said: *"Do not lavish praise on me as the Christians have lavished praise of the son of Mary; for I am only a slave. So call me God's slave and messenger."* And He went on to say, *"Do not consider me better than Moses, for all humankind will be struck unconscious on the Day of Resurrection, and I will be struck unconscious with them."* [39] The Qur'án specifies the Messengers' humanly distinct station. *"True, we are human like yourselves, but God doth grant His grace to such of His servants as He pleases. It is not for us to bring you an authority except as God permits."* [40] Muḥammad stated very clearly, *"I am but a man like yourselves."* [41] Muḥammad explained that His revelation came from God, and not from Himself, *"It is He Who has sent amongst the Unlettered an apostle from among themselves."* [42] Muḥammad emphasized His humanness, but clarified that His revelation came from God.

Muḥammad's Divine Station

Authentic traditions point directly to Muḥammad's divine station. Muḥammad said, *"Whoever sees me has seen God."* [43] Such sayings suggest that, for practical human purposes, Muḥammad's words and deeds may be viewed as divine. Muḥammad also said, *"He who obeys the Apostle, obeys God,"* [44] pointing to His unity with all Messengers. This parallels the Qur'ánic teaching that says, *"We make no distinction . . . between one and another of His apostles."* [45] Some Qur'ánic passages point to the exemplary nature of Muḥammad, serving as a model of the perfect man. *"Ye have indeed in the apostle of God a beautiful pattern (of conduct) for any one whose hope is in God and the Final Day."* [46] Muḥammad is described as possessing qualities beyond others, *"Thou (standest) on an exalted standard of character."* [47] Other passages point directly to Muḥammad's divine station. The Qur'án, when describing Muḥammad, states, *"Verily, those who plight their fealty to thee do no less than plight their fealty to God."* [49] Muḥammad is clearly described as holding a station that is beyond human.

Muḥammad's Night Journey

A dramatic portrayal of Muḥammad's divine station is the famous story of Muḥammad's "Night Journey" from Mecca to Jerusalem, from Jerusalem to Heaven, and back to Mecca. It was briefly referred to in the Qur'án, and then was further developed in Islamic traditions. Comparable to the transfiguration of Jesus in which He met with Moses and Elijah, the Night Journey is best viewed as a spiritual rather than a physical event. It is a symbolic story rather than a factual story. Its lessons are greater than mere history. The Qur'án says, *"Glory to (God) Who did take His Servant for a Journey by night from the Sacred Mosque to the Farthest Mosque, whose precincts We did bless,—in order that We might show him some of Our Signs."* [50]

The event inspiring this story (perhaps a dream) probably took place in the year 620. Muḥammad rose in the night and went to the Kaaba to pray. He decided to sleep there, but was later woken by the archangel Gabriel and lifted on a heavenly steed to Jerusalem. They alighted on the Temple Mount where a ladder appeared, enabling Muḥammad and Gabriel to climb the seven heavens and make the ascent to the throne of God. Adam presided over the first heaven. Jesus and John the Baptist were in the second heaven, Joseph in the third, Enoch in the fourth, Aaron in the fifth, Moses in the sixth, and Abraham in the seventh at the threshold of God's throne itself. The supreme vision was Paradise, underneath which a river flowed whiter than milk and sweeter than honey. Muḥammad reached a Lote-tree covered with jewels at the end of the garden, providing a limit beyond which even Messengers cannot pass.

The Night Journey played an important role in Islamic spirituality. Many mystics, theologians, philosophers, and poets pondered its meaning and significance. It depicts spiritual progress toward the heavenly abode. Authors, such as Dante, seem to have borrowed its general structure, and the Bahá'í writings include references to the Lote-tree beyond which there is no passing. Muḥammad's heavenly ascent and return serves as a kind of love poem linking humanity to God through the Prophets. It bridges dispensations and levels of reality. Sufis viewed Muḥammad as the perfect man, a glimpse of what we might become if our lower nature were perfectly managed and our spiritual qualities were completely developed.

19 – The Light and the Word

Christian tradition placed emphasis on the Revealer as the source of light, making Christ the focus of devotion, while Islamic tradition placed emphasis on the Revelation as the source of light, making the Qur'án the focus of guidance. This difference need not be seen as substantive, for it is a cultural matter, showing God's various means of educating people across the ages. The Qur'án says, *"We have made the (Qur-an) a Light, wherewith We guide such of Our servants as We will."* [51] God's light is described as mediated by the Messenger, offering guidance from a realm higher than human: *"A Book which we have revealed unto thee, in order that thou mightest lead mankind out of the depths of darkness into light."* [52] The Qur'án further describes this metaphor of God as the source of light. *"God is the Light of the heavens and the earth. The parable of His Light is as if there were a Niche and within it a Lamp: the Lamp enclosed in Glass: the glass as it were a brilliant star: lit from a blessed Tree, and Olive, neither of the East nor of the West, whose Oil is well-nigh luminous, though fire scarce touched it: Light upon Light!"* [53] The divine message is presented as the unlimited Word penetrating our ignorance, forgetfulness, and arrogance. *"Behold, this is the Word that distinguishes (Good from Evil)."* [54] God's revelation, the source of light, is described as endless, *"If the ocean were ink (wherewith to write out) the words of my Lord, sooner would the ocean be exhausted than would the words of my Lord."* [55] On that same note, the Qur'án also says, *"And if all the trees on earth were pens . . . yet would not the Words of God be exhausted."* [56]

20 – Affirming Four Realms: Divine, Revelatory, Human, Natural

The Qur'án presents the same basic metaphysical framework as the scriptures of ancient Israel and the New Testament. Human beings are given responsibility to cultivate the earth, and so are above it, while also being subject to many of its built-in limitations. Above us is the Word of God presented by Messengers. Above the Messengers is divine mystery.

The Natural Realm

Nature is designed in detail by God, using similar patterns at various levels, and building into everything evolutionary processes, which are discernible by conscientious investigators. Here we find considerable encouragement for the development of science. *"In the creation of the heavens and the earth . . . in the beasts of all kinds . . . are Signs for a people that are wise."* [57] However, even though we can study the world of nature, it is God Who is responsible for it. *"It is God Who causeth the seed-grain and the date-stone to split and sprout."* [58] Again, the Qur'án says, *"He created the sun, the moon, and the stars, (all) governed by laws under His Command."* [59] The Qur'án also describes the creation of humans, *"Man we did create from a quintessence (of clay); then We placed him as (a drop of) sperm in a place of rest, firmly fixed; then We made the sperm into a clot of congealed blood; then of that clot We made a (foetus) lump; then We made out of that lump bones and clothed the bones with flesh; then We developed out of it another creature.*" [60] The Qur'án explains that this entire creation follows God's Will, *"And among His signs is this, that heaven and the earth stand by His Command; then when He calls you, by a single call, ye (straightway) come forth."* [61]

The Human Realm

The Qur'án presents human nature as gifted with special divine favor, including abilities to name and understand various levels of reality, distinguish better from worse, make choices, and to continue growing after the body dies. The human tendency to forget our blessed endowment, and the accompanying need for tests, are also stressed. *"The (human) soul is certainly prone to evil, unless my Lord do bestow His Mercy."* [62] We are tested by both the good and the bad we experience in our lives, *"We test you by evil and by good by way of trial."* [63] God's gifts are continuously showered upon us, even though we do not always recognize it: *"Do ye not see that God has . . . made His bounties flow to you in exceeding Measure, (both) seen and unseen?"* [64]

The Revelatory Realm

Early Muslims understood the Qur'án to be God's direct speech to all who could hear, through Muḥammad, sometimes in response to issues arising between the faithful and their adversaries. But they also believed that much of the message had been delivered before to Abraham and other Prophets, to Jews and Christians before them, though it needed repeating because human beings easily forget and regress to old superstitions. *"It is He hath sent His Apostle with Guidance and the Religion of Truth, to proclaim it over all religion."* [65] The Qur'án was understood to be a miracle, because it was revealed through an "unlettered Prophet." Muslims believe that because Muḥammad was illiterate, that helped to assure the purity of the revelation, because one who could write might be easily tempted to tamper with the text. The Word of God was now considered unencumbered by merely human reception and transmission. Revelations came to Muḥammad in the midst of everyday activities, and spontaneous secretaries would often write them down on palm leaves, slates of stone, or skins of goats and sheep. The very sound of the Arabic Qur'án could have a healing and saving effect on its hearers. Reciting its lofty language became an oral art approaching the quality of the greatest music, bringing higher dimensions into human hearts, thereby lifting and transforming them.

316

The Divine Realm

God's ultimate nature is beyond human grasp, making Him an inexhaustible mystery. True glimpses of God depend on what Prophets convey to us. Muḥammad explained that we can never fully understand God, *"No vision can grasp Him, but His grasp is over all vision: He is above all comprehension, yet is acquainted with all things."* [66] God is considered to be all-knowing, *"He is the First and the Last, the Evident and the Immanent: and He has full knowledge of all things."* [67] The Qur'án also says that all of creation is designed to praise God, *"God is He, than Whom there is no other god;— the Sovereign, the Holy One, the Source of Peace. . . . Whatever is in the heavens and on earth doth declare His praises and Glory."* [68]

21 – Promising a Future Savior and a New Golden Age: The Return of Jesus, the Mahdi, the Qá'im, and the Day of Renewal

Muḥammad claimed to be foretold by Jesus, and Muḥammad in turn foretold Jesus' return at the Hour of Judgment. The following passage from the Qur'án related Jesus' promise that Ahmad would come, and Ahmad was another name for Muḥammad, as both names mean Praised One. *"Jesus, the son of Mary, said: 'O Children of Israel! I am the apostle of God (sent) to you, confirming the Law (which came) before me, and giving Glad Tidings of an Apostle to come after me, whose name shall be Ahmad.'"* [69]

In John's gospel, Jesus referred four times to the Counselor or Paraclete as His Successor. Muslims and Bahá'ís believe these are references to Muḥammad, and this seems reasonable in light of the Founders' capacity to prophesy, and in light of all the prophetic interconnections among the world's scriptures. The Promised Ones of Islam have been expected with varying degrees of intensity in Islamic history. They have been conceived of differently by Shí'ah and Sunni Muslims. Sunnis expect the Return of Jesus and the Mahdi or Guided One. This Figure will restore true religion, heralding the end of one age and the beginning of another. God will provide a Guide to bring humanity back to the straight way.

Shí'ah Muslims expect the Qá'im or "one who will arise from Muḥammad's family," who has also been called the Hidden Imam. The Twelver, or majority Shí'ahs, who affirm a sequence of twelve Imams, believe that the Twelfth Imam did not die, but has been waiting and guiding Muslims from a transcendent realm since the year 874 CE. The Qá'im or Hidden Imam has been expected to return to defeat the enemies of pure Islam, bringing justice and spiritual purification. Though the Hour cannot be known by mere human beings, "trumpet blasts" will awaken some who have been spiritually asleep. The Qur'án includes a number of references to these trumpet blasts that will be sounded on the Day of Judgment. The Qur'án says, *"And the Day that the Trumpet will be sounded . . . all shall come to His (Presence) as beings conscious of their lowliness."*[70] It also says, *"The Trumpet will (just) be sounded, when all that are in the heavens and on earth will swoon, except such as it will please God (to exempt). Then will a second one be sounded, when, behold, they will be standing and looking on! And the earth will shine with the glory of its Lord."*[71] The Qur'án also mentions the return of Jesus, saying, *"And (Jesus) shall be a Sign (for the coming of) the Hour (of Judgment): therefore have no doubt about the (Hour)."*[72]

These passages are interpreted by Muslims as pointing to the Promised Ones—Jesus, the Mahdi, and the Qá'im. The exact number and description of the Promised Ones have always been controversial. Bahá'ís interpret the two Trumpet sounds as referring to the declarations of the Báb in 1844 and Bahá'u'lláh in 1863. One of Muḥammad's traditional sayings described the returned Jesus as abrogating three sets of former laws—Jewish, Christian, and Islamic. *"The Hour will not be established until the son of Mary descends into your midst as a just arbitrator, whereupon he will break the cross, kill the swine, and set aside the special tax on non-Muslims citizens of Muslim lands."*[73]

Other traditional sayings describe the role of the Qá'im and the Mahdi, and the Mahdi is depicted as coming with a new cause, a new book, and a new law—just as Muḥammad came earlier, bringing a severe test to Arab leaders. *"He will fill the earth with equity and justice as it had been filled with oppression and tyranny. Those who dwell in heaven and those who dwell on earth will be pleased with him."*[74] Another tradition describes the beautiful future that awaits upon the Mahdi's arrival, *"The Imam who will create a world state . . . will bring succor to humanity. . . . He will revive the teachings of the Holy Qur'án. . . . He will protect and defend himself with resources of sciences and supreme knowledge. . . . He will establish an empire of God in this world."*[75]

The following hope-filled prophecies of the "new earth and new heaven" remind us of Christian prophecy in the book of Revelation, and may refer to a new dispensation embracing all peoples, global in scope and jurisdiction.

"One Day the Earth shall be changed to a different Earth, and so will be the Heavens, and (men) will be marshalled forth, before God."[76] God explains that this process of a new revelation coming will take place again, *"As We produced the first Creation, so shall We produce a new one: a promise We have undertaken: truly shall We fulfil it. Before this We wrote in the Psalms, after the Message (given to Moses): 'My servants, the righteous, shall inherit the earth.'"*[77] And it goes on to say: *"On that Day the Dominion will be that of God: He will judge between them: so those who believe and work righteous deeds will be in Gardens of Delight."*[78] That day will be a time when our actions will be judged by God, *"Our Lord will gather us together and will in the end decide the matter between us (and you) in truth and justice."*[79]

Bahá'ís believe these prophecies refer to today, when faith is being renewed, when a new divinely guided and global civilization is in the making, and the accomplishments of previous civilizations will be surpassed. *"Verily the Day of Sorting Out is a thing appointed, — The Day that the Trumpet shall be sounded, and ye shall come forth in crowds; And the heavens shall be opened as if there were doors, And the mountains shall vanish, as if they were a mirage."*[80]

22 – Essential Unity of the Revealers through the Ages

Islam can be interpreted universally and particularly. The universal reference is to the one and only religion of God—submission to the Divine Will in the past, present, and future. This universal religion of *islam* (obedience) has been conveyed to humanity through Messengers, beginning with Adam and continuing indefinitely. The more particular view of Islam limits it to the Qur'án, to the traditions of Muḥammad, to the official Shí'ah and Sunni interpretations, and to the historical experience of various Islamic communities since the Hijrah in 622. The universal view unites Islam with all authentic religion (dependence on God) in all eras. This study takes the universal view. But does the Qur'án support this broader perspective, that of the unity of Revealers through the ages? These passages point to a wider community of faith than Muslims. *"We believe in God and the revelation given to . . . (all) Prophets from Their Lord: we make no difference between one and another of them: and we bow to God (in Islam)."*[81] The Qur'án goes on to describe the oneness of all religions, *"The same religion has He established for you as that which He enjoined on . . . Abraham, Moses, and Jesus: namely, that ye should remain steadfast in Religion, and make no divisions therein."*[82]

23 – Laying Enduring Foundations: Succession Issues, Constitution, Imams, Caliphs, and Dynasties

Succession Controversy

As part of His farewell addresses at Ghadir Khumm, Muḥammad made comments that Shí'ah Muslims and Bahá'ís have interpreted as designating Ali as His successor. Muḥammad took the hands of Ali and raised them, saying: *"Whoever heartily receives me as his master, then to him 'Ali is the same. O Lord, befriend every friend of 'Ali, and be the enemy of all his enemies; help those that aid him, and abandon all that desert him."* Later, Muḥammad added: *"Next to me, 'Ali is your prince and leader, in following the commands of the Lord of the universe."* [83] Sunni Muslims, however, have denied this reporting of events, and have not recognized Ali's successorship.

The Constitution of Medina

In the pledges of Aqabah in 621 and 622, Medinans agreed to obey the Messenger, and to protect Him as they would their own families. Muḥammad asked them to choose nine from the tribe of Khazraj and three from the tribe of Aws, and asked these representatives to attend to their people's affairs. He compared them to Jesus' disciples. This prepared the way for other institutions to develop. The Constitution of Medina was the first formal attempt to establish a new ummah. It was an agreement among Muḥammad, Muslims, and those who cooperated with them. They were one community, or ummah, to the exclusion of all other affiliations. Originally this meant that all Muslims—those submissive and obedient to God—were brothers and sisters, one of another. No other social category could be more important. This covenantal relation had important implications for future relations between Muslims and other people of the Book. The Constitution regulated forays against God's enemies, established equity for all social groups in Medina, emphasized loyalty, condemned treachery, and referred all disputes and external affairs to Muḥammad. External affairs included the obligation to seek the widest possible peace. Jews and Christians had the same rights, but were expected to pay a tax for military protection. The Constitution was a model for shaping the ummah and guiding its growth.

Widening Affiliations

In 628, Muḥammad sent letters to neighboring kings, inviting them into the Faith to help administer divine justice. Among these kings were Heraclius of the Byzantine Empire, Khusrau II of the Persian Empire, the Negus of the Abyssinians, as well as rulers of Damascus, Alexandria, Bahrain, and Oman. The replies of Heraclius and the Negus were respectful and even affectionate, but their people were not prepared to follow a new religion. In 631, Muḥammad appointed Ali to proclaim the Declaration of Immunity (Surah 9), which defined future relations with pagan tribes, many of whom had broken pacts and could not be trusted. Muḥammad taught that all pacts mutually upheld must be fulfilled.

First Four Caliphs: The Rashidun

Muḥammad had led with divine assistance. His successors received less direct divine assistance, and their responsibilities were in some respects broader and more complex, because of the expanded territory and greater diversity of believers that had to be addressed. Abu Bakr was selected by the majority of the early Muslim community to serve as the first Caliph. He ruled for two years from 632 to 634, and faced the challenge of various tribes attempting to break away. He quelled these uprisings with wisdom and clemency, thus completing Arabian unification. Umar served as second Caliph from 634 to 644, leading a dramatic territorial expansion, including Iraq, Syria, Palestine, Egypt, and much of Persia. Jerusalem was brought under Muslim control in 638. There was a power vacuum in the region due to the exhaustion of the Byzantine and Persian empires. Muslims filled this vacuum with Islamic rule, and subject peoples usually welcomed their fair and responsible leadership. Umar established garrison towns for Muslim soldiers and officials in strategic locations in Iraq, Iran, and Egypt. In 644 Umar was murdered by a Persian prisoner of war. Uthman served as third Caliph from 644 to 656, continuing the expansion, reaching Azerbaijan, the eastern portion of the old Persian Empire, Cyprus, and part of North Africa. He alienated Muslims in Medina by offering positions to his own Umayyad clan, creating tensions that led to the first civil war. He was assassinated in a mutiny. Ali served as fourth Caliph from 656 to 661. Despite his high spiritual station, he was engaged in civil war during most of his rule. Aishah helped lead a rebellion against him, but when Ali overcame this resistance, he treated Aishah with respect and honor, and eventually they reconciled. Ali made Kufah in Iraq his new capital. Ali's rule was opposed by Mu'awiyah, the governor of Syria, who wanted Ali to punish Uthman's enemies more severely. Ali was assassinated by an extremist.

Diverging Shi'ah and Sunni Claims: Two Civil Wars

Ali was considered by Shí'ahs (partisans of Ali) to be the First Imam—the true spiritual successor of Muhammad. The first civil war was fought from 651 to 656, and brought defeat to the Shí'ahs, who have remained a minority in the Islamic world since then. Currently, Shí'ahs make up about 12% of the Muslim population. Sunnis, those who accepted the leadership of all Caliphs, have always been the majority. Twelve Shí'ah Imams served until 874, when the Twelfth Imam was said to enter occultation, a spiritual state from which the Hidden Imam guides the faithful until his return as the Qá'im (arising One) who will *"fill the earth with equity and justice."* [84] Mu'awiyah ruled from 661 to 680 as the first of the Umayyad Caliphs, and though he restored order, many Muslims in his day began to look back to the first four Caliphs as "rightly guided" (*rashidun*), faithful leaders who were unjustly opposed and brought low by those who strayed from true Islam.

In 680, Husayn, the son of Ali and the grandson of Muhammad, set out with a small group of followers including wives and children, toward Kufah, hoping to bring the ummah back to the guidance of Muhammad's family. On the plain of Karbala, Umayyad troops massacred Husayn and his entire party. This profound tragedy became a powerful symbol for Shí'ahs of the challenge and necessity of integrating spiritual guidance with political reality. Husayn's shrine in Karbala still evokes deep longing for Shí'ahs, longing for a new day of God. The second civil war stretched from 680 to 692. Ibn al-Zubayr rebelled against the Umayyads, and achieved widespread recognition as Caliph, but his forces were defeated and he was killed. The most positive achievement during these years was the Dome of the Rock in Jerusalem, completed in 692, the first major Islamic monument and a model for future architectural wonders. It marked the place of Abraham's near-sacrifice of His son, Solomon's Temple, and Muhammad's Night Journey.

Umayyads (661–750) and Abbasids (750–1258)

The Umayyads expanded the empire westward to the Pyrenees in Spain, and eastward to the Himalayas in India. The Abbasids, who replaced them in 750, traced their descent from the Prophet's uncle Abbas. They came into power on a wave of growing desire to place Muḥammad's family at the head of the Faith. The Abbasids ruled from 750 to 1258 from their beautiful capital in Baghdad. For half a millennium they offered the greatest cultural achievements of Islamic civilization, impressing the eyes of the world, and inspiring the European Renaissance. The magnificent cities of Baghdad, Damascus, Cairo, Cordoba, and Toledo generated great universities and became flowering centers of higher art and science where an array of topics were studied, including theology, ethics, jurisprudence, political theory, philosophy, mysticism, logic, algebra, chemistry, astronomy, medicine, architecture, poetry, history, geography, sociology, economics, horticulture, economics, and agronomy. This was what could be called "light upon light" shining for all of humanity.

24 – Renewing Scriptural Guidance: The Qur'án and the Hadith

Islamic scripture is the Qur'án. However, the collective body of hadith helped in interpreting the intent of the Prophet and in developing Islamic law and tradition. According to many Muslims, the Arabic Qur'án is the only authentic Islamic scripture. Many Muslims say the Qur'án cannot be adequately translated into any other language, but that interpretations are helpful in introducing it to non-Arabic-speakers. The hadith collected by Bukhari (d 870) and by Muslim (d 878) are considered authentic by most Muslims. Shí'ahs have their own collections of hadith. The two most accepted sources for the life of Muḥammad are the biographies of Ibn Ishaq (d 767) and Tabari (d 923).

Muslims claim the Qur'án is the final Word of God for humanity, and that there will not be any more divine revelations. How does the Qur'án itself explain its place in God's providential plan for humanity? *"None of Our revelations do We abrogate or cause to be forgotten, but We substitute something better or similar."* [85] This suggests that God can and will abrogate irrelevant aspects of the Qur'án, and replace them with "something better" in the future. *"When We substitute one revelation for another . . . the Holy Spirit has brought the revelation from thy Lord in Truth, in order to strengthen those who believe."* [86]

This suggests that God can and will substitute the Qur'ánic revelation for another, through the Holy Spirit, "in order to strengthen those who believe." The Qur'án itself seems to say that no revelation is meant to last forever, *"For every Message is a limit of time."* [87] This suggests that the Qur'án itself has a limit of time. The Qur'án also says, *"For each period is a Book (revealed)."* [88] This suggests that after the Islamic civilization, a new Book is to be revealed.

25 – Generating Civilization Anew: Ummah as Divinely Just Society

Muḥammad generated civilization anew, a beyond-human achievement that only Founders can accomplish. Royalty, statesmen, and thinkers—no matter how revered, wise, and competent—cannot generate civilization anew. Divine power and guidance is required. Muḥammad's vision was of the ummah, a divinely just society. This concept originally suggested an ever-expanding community of believers, with a sense of trans-tribal loyalty to a diverse social body, all sharing a vision of divine justice. This universal community abrogated old tribal bonds based on immediate kinship, and replaced them with a religious solidarity that had no theoretical limits. The ummah became a spiritual nation that, at its best, enjoyed peace, unity, and prosperity. This vision was reflected in the highest achievements of the Spanish Umayyads, the Abbasids, the Fatimids, the Ottomans, the Moghuls, and the Safavids.

We close with hopeful visions of the divinely just society described in the Qur'án and the hadith. *"The Believers are but a single Brotherhood: so make peace and reconciliation between your two (contending) brothers."* [89] Could the divisions referred to be separate world religions? Muḥammad also asked for forgiveness for others, and assistance in overcoming difficulties. *"Our Lord! Forgive us, and our brethren who came before us into the Faith, and leave not, in our hearts, rancour (or sense of injury) against those who have believed."* [90] *"And whenever people gather in one of the houses of God, read the book of God, and study it together, peace descends upon them, and mercy envelops them, and angels surround them, and God mentions them to those around."* [91]

- 17 -
Bahá'u'lláh: Background and Mission

The Bahá'í Faith is the newest world religion, and its Founder was Bahá'u'lláh. His name means the "glory of God," and His Faith emerged in Persia in the middle of the nineteenth century. His teachings emphasize world unity and the need to generate an ever-advancing global civilization. Because the Bahá'í Faith is the newest world religion, it is also the least known. But as the most recent in origin, it is also the best documented. Less than two centuries old, its founding events were more elaborately recorded than events surrounding Muḥammad, Christ, or any of the earlier Founders. The degree of historical truth in these records can also be more easily investigated since they happened so recently. Given that there is less familiarity with Bahá'u'lláh and the Bahá'í Faith, it is reasonable to ask if He has the same station as the other Founders. Is He significant enough in world history for a comparative study of this scope? Can it be shown that all the patterns we applied to the lives, missions, and messages of the other Founders apply to Bahá'u'lláh? Who is He?

1 – Continuity with Previous Dispensations:
Abraham's Family and the Blessing of All Nations
God promised Abraham: *"By you all the families of the earth shall bless themselves,"*[1] and these families include all the religions we are studying. The Bahá'í Faith emerged out of an Islamic background, just as Christianity emerged out of a Jewish background, and Buddhism emerged out of a Hindu background. Bahá'ís affirm the divine origins of all major religions and the authenticity of their revelations. All Founders are revered as agents of God's educational process. Christ and Muḥammad, for example, are seen as successive Manifestations of God and Their revelations are progressive. Bahá'u'lláh explains that these Messengers, or "Mirrors," will always come to reveal new

325

guidance to humanity. *"These Mirrors will everlastingly succeed each other, and will continue to reflect the light of the Ancient of Days."* [2]

As Christ was heralded by John the Baptist, Bahá'u'lláh was also heralded by a figure who warned people of His coming. The herald of Bahá'u'lláh was called the Báb—a title meaning "the Gate," and suggesting the "Gate of God." The Báb claimed to bring the culmination of Muḥammad's era, and the advent of the Promised Day for humanity. Bahá'ís regard the Báb as the Promised One of Islam—the Qá'im—the one who would arise from the family of Muḥammad to usher in an era of justice. Bahá'u'lláh is seen as the Promised One of All Ages—the Return of Christ, in a spiritual sense rather than physical—bringing a new dispensation that will establish world unity. Bahá'ís claim that a global civilization is now being ushered in by Bahá'u'lláh. All this will fulfill God's promise to Abraham 4000 years ago—the blessing of all nations as they learn to abide in peace.

2 – Arising to Guide Humanity in the Worst of Times: State and Religious Corruption in Persia

Islam began to change, or its teaching began to be distorted, as time passed from the days of Muḥammad. Persian clergy grew increasingly rigid and dominant after 1722, when Isfahan surrendered to attacking Afghan tribes. The Qajars seized control in 1794, and the clergy exercised oppressive powers unparalleled anywhere in the Muslim world. Persia was isolated culturally and technologically, and "the great majority of the population were poor peasant farmers, dominated both by the local urban elites and the nomadic and semi-nomadic tribal groups." [3] Western diplomats working with the government reported alarming degrees of corruption. Self-interest ruled the day, with trustworthiness and justice almost entirely absent. Both state and religious officials were defensive about any challenge, however reasonable, to their absolute power over the downtrodden masses. Given these conditions, intense messianic expectations emerged in Persia in the early decades of the nineteenth century.

3 – Advent Prophesied and Expected: The Promised One of Islam (the Báb), The Promised One of All Ages (Bahá'u'lláh)

Religious peoples from many traditions have longed for a World Redeemer. In the early nineteenth century, Christians and Muslims awaited the Return of Christ and the Promised One respectively. Historical events and scriptural prophecies indicated it was time for another Messenger to step onto the stage of history. More broadly, people in all times and places have been taught of a great day to come for humanity, an age when peace and prosperity will finally prevail. Jews await the Messiah or Lord of Hosts, Who will usher in the Divine Kingdom. Hindus await the return of Krishna, Who will usher in the Golden Age. Buddhists anticipate Maitreya or the Buddha of Universal Fellowship, Who will usher in the Pure Land. Zoroastrians await the Saoshyant or World Savior, Who will usher in the Final Restoration. There are also other spiritual traditions that contain prophecies about a future Promised One. The Chinese expect a Sage or True Man, Who will bring about the Grand Unity. Native Central Americans await the return of Quetzalcoatl, Who will fulfill the Rainbow Blessing. Native North Americans await a Holy Man sent by the Great Spirit, who will unite all the tribes on earth.

Christians led by messianic scholars who focused especially on certain prophetic biblical texts were expecting Christ to return in the years 1843 or 1844. The most expectant communities included Millerites and German Templars. Some of the scriptural titles for the Return of Christ included the King of Glory, the Glory of the Lord, the Prince of Peace, the Wonderful Counselor, the Spirit of Truth, and the Desire of All Nations. Preceding this New Day for humanity would be a period of darkness, suffering, and judgment.

Muslims expected the Mahdi—the Guide for the end of the age. *"He will fill the earth with equity and justice as it had been filled with oppression and tyranny."*[4] Another tradition gave some clues about who the Mahdi would be: *"The Mahdi will be of my family, of the descendents of Fáṭimah."*[5] Shí'ahs in particular expected the Qá'im, the One to arise from the Prophet's family, the Return of the Hidden Imam. And there were great expectations associated with the Qá'im, *"When the Qa'im arises, he will rule with justice and will remove injustice in his days. The roads will be safe and the earth will show forth bounties. Everything due will be returned to its rightful owner. And no people of religion will remain who do not show forth submission* (Islam) *and acknowledge belief* (Iman)."[6] The year 1260 of the Islamic lunar calendar, 1844 CE on the Western calendar, was a millennium after the Twelfth Imam disappeared, and for some, it was the expected hour of his return.

In the early nineteenth century, there were signs in the Muslim world that the expected Mahdi or Qá'im was imminent. "For centuries Muslims had been used to thinking of themselves as the most powerful advanced civilization in the world. Then, during this period, the Muslim world experienced a series of military defeats that made it clear that this was no longer the case: Napoleon's occupation of Egypt in 1798, Ottoman defeat at the hands of Russia in 1806, Iran's two disastrous wars against Russia, 1804–13 and 1826–8, the French occupation of Algiers in 1830 and the gradual British annexation of the Mughal Empire in India. In addition to military defeats there was the increasing evidence of the trading and manufacturing supremacy of the European states, forcing many merchants and craftsmen in the Middle East out of business. From the 1830s onwards cholera epidemics raged throughout the Muslim world. In all, many Muslims began to see in these events the signs of the Advent of the Mahdi. . . . It was in such circumstances that one of the prominent (religious leaders) of the period, Shaykh Aḥmad (d 1826) . . . began to preach a new doctrine that soon attracted a large number of followers. Among his doctrines was that the Traditions related to the coming of the Mahdi were to be understood as spiritual truths, not literal physical truths."[7]

Siyyid Kaẓim (d 1843) was Shaykh Aḥmad's successor, serving in the Shí'ah holy city of Karbala, Iraq. He taught the immediate advent of the Qá'im, and even refused to appoint a successor, telling his students to seek out the Promised One directly, for He had already appeared in the world.

The Forerunner of Bahá'u'lláh: The Báb

Though the Báb is the forerunner of the Bahá'í Faith, He is also viewed as a Manifestation of God. In this capacity He is called the Primal Point in humanity's spiritual evolution. We weave Him into our story of Bahá'u'lláh, using some of our standard patterns. Siyyid 'Alí-Muḥammad, known to history as the Báb, is the Founder of the Bábí Faith and the herald of Bahá'u'lláh. He was born in Shiraz, Persia in 1819, a direct descendant of Muḥammad.

Auspicious Signs in the Báb's Childhood

As with the other Founders, the Báb stood out from His peers, even from the very beginning of His life. "From His early childhood, the Báb was different from other children. He was always asking difficult questions and then giving the answers Himself in a way that astonished His elders. Often when other children were busy at play, He would be found wrapped in prayer under the shade of a tree or in some quiet spot."[8] Although from a merchant family, He became known for devoutness, wisdom, and nobility. At sixteen years of age, He began to work as a merchant, and quickly became known for His trustworthiness. Though His wisdom had not been learned from any teacher, He developed a "reputation as a holy ascetic, blessed with the grace of the Hidden Imam."[9]

The Báb's Declaration and First Followers

After Siyyid Kazim died, his followers spread out to find the Promised One. "A number of them under the leadership of a pious and learned young man, called Mullá Ḥusayn, spent 40 days in prayer and fasting, and then took the road to S͟híráz. . . . Near the gate of S͟híráz, Mullá Ḥusayn met a radiant young man who had come out to receive him. This young man was none other than the Báb. He invited Mullá Ḥusayn to His house, and there, on the 23rd of May, 1844, the Báb declared Himself the Promised One."[10] Mullá Ḥusayn recognized the Báb's words as revelation, and prostrated himself before the Báb as His first disciple. The Báb required seventeen others to recognize Him independently, and the first eighteen disciples were known as Letters of the Living. The Báb commissioned His disciples: *"Scatter throughout the length and breadth of this land, and, with steadfast feet and sanctified hearts, prepare the way for His coming."*[11] The Great Announcement was made of the Báb's immediate Successor, Who was referred to as "Him Whom God shall make manifest," which believers later understood to be an allusion to Bahá'u'lláh. The Báb's followers, called Bábís, saw the cycle of humanity's fulfillment as now initiated.

The Báb's Transformative Teaching: Independence from Islam

The Báb's purpose was to bring the corrupt and degraded condition of Islamic society to an end, and to prepare the way for Bahá'u'lláh to build a new world order. The Báb sent Mullá Ḥusayn with a letter to deliver to Bahá'u'lláh, Who immediately recognized the divine authority of the Báb and became His greatest supporter. In 1848, the Báb openly declared that Islamic law was now abrogated. In the summer of that year, Bahá'u'lláh organized a conference of eighty-one Bábís in Badasht in north-central Iran. Its purpose was to clarify the status of the Bábí cause. Was it a reform movement within Islam, or the beginning of a New Age for humanity? In a dramatic exercise planned by Bahá'u'lláh, Ṭáhirih—one of the attendees at the conference and the Báb's only female disciple—argued that a New Day for humanity was at hand. One day at the conference, Ṭáhirih appeared unveiled—an event unprecedented in the Islamic context. This event dramatized her claim that she was the Word that the Qá'im was to utter on the Day of Judgment. Her unveiling symbolized that the New Day of God had dawned and the break from Islam was complete. The occasion was marked by reciting a verse from the Qur'án: *"When the Event Inevitable cometh to pass . . . the earth shall be shaken to its depths, and the mountains shall be crumbled. . . . And those Foremost in Faith will be Foremost in the Hereafter."* [12]

The Báb's Theme: Breaking from the Cycle of Prophecy and Preparing for Bahá'u'lláh's Cycle of Fulfillment

Two major emphases of the Báb's teachings were the "prophetic cycle" and the "cycle of fulfillment." The idea of the prophetic cycle was that Messengers, or Prophets, had continuously come throughout history to teach humanity the Word of God. This process had guided humanity for six millennia, but the Báb taught that the prophetic cycle, and the competition that had existed among the different revelations, had now come to an end. In its place, the Báb explained that the cycle of fulfillment had begun, and would bring humanity into maturity. The Báb clarified that the "resurrection" of the previous Founder is the appearance of the present Founder—Christ is the resurrection of Moses; Muhammad is the resurrection of Christ; and the Báb is the resurrection of Muhammad. Henceforth, humanity will not need to establish new religions in the traditional sense, because we are now endowed with capacity to recognize progressive revelation. This is the advent of a qualitatively higher spiritual standard, accenting purity of heart. It is an advance in the spiritual evolution of humanity, and will truly be "a Day not followed by Night." Future declines will be far less degrading. Among the principles of the New Day are gender equality, elimination of poverty, transcending prejudices of all kinds, universal education, and the creative advance of sciences and arts. "Him Whom God shall make manifest" will usher in an ever-advancing global civilization, providing the means to discover and develop all that is needed for unending material and spiritual growth.

The Báb Overcomes Powerful Opposition: Dawn-Breakers

Forces opposing the Báb began to strengthen early in 1847 when the governor of Isfahan, the Báb's supporter, died. The rapid growth of the Báb's Cause angered religious and civil authorities, who saw Him as a dangerous heretic and a threat to their position. Bábís were brutally persecuted—20,000 of them sacrificed their lives. In 1848, the Báb was summoned to Tabriz for a trial, where He made this public declaration: *"I am, I am, I am the Promised One! I am the One whose name you have for a thousand years invoked, at whose mention you have risen, whose advent you have longed to witness, and the hour of whose Revelation you have prayed God to hasten. Verily I say, it is incumbent upon the peoples of both the East and the West to obey My word and to pledge allegiance to My person."* [13]

When commanded to recant, He refused, was beaten, and was then returned to prison. Three heroic battles in defense of the Báb's cause were fought in the last two years of His life. In Tabarsi, Nayriz, and Zanjan, the Bábís held out valiantly against vastly greater numbers. Even some of those who massacred them noticed a resemblance between their heroism and the heroism of Imam Ḥusayn and his fellow martyrs at Karbala in 680 CE. Tragically, a faith community that began with martyrdom over 1100 years earlier—Shí'ah Muslims—was now martyring others who spoke for the same God. The Bábís were the dawn-breakers of a New Day.

Exemplary Woman: Ṭáhirih Trumpets the Day of Gender Equality

Among the most remarkable women in religious history was the Báb's disciple, Ṭáhirih (1816–52), a title bestowed on her by the Báb meaning "the Pure." Her power was moral and spiritual, as well as intellectual and artistic. Ṭáhirih was renowned for her religious knowledge as well as her poetic talent, eloquence, courage, and beauty. Born into a prominent family of religious leaders, she engaged in higher Islamic studies, which was unusual for a woman in that time and place. Against family wishes she studied and embraced the teachings of Shaykh Aḥmad and Siyyid Káẓim, and agreed with their beliefs on the imminent coming of the Promised One.

In a dream, a young man appeared before Ṭáhirih with hands raised toward heaven, reciting wonderful verses in a beautiful voice. Upon waking, she wrote down one of these verses. Later, a friend gave her some of the writings of the Báb, and to her intense delight she saw the exact same words that she had written from her dream. She immediately wrote to the Báb, declaring her belief in Him as the Promised One foretold in the holy books. Ṭáhirih spread the Báb's message persuasively in Karbala, Baghdad, Tehran, and other cities. Early on she recognized the resistance that the Báb and His followers would face, and warned fellow Bábí leaders of coming sacrifices. She said, *"Let deeds, not words, be our adorning,"* [14] encouraging them to purify their lives and to teach the new Faith while there was still time.

Evidence of Ṭáhirih's high spiritual station is that she had foreknowledge of events to come and of revelations not yet revealed. She knew over a decade ahead of His revelation that Bahá'u'lláh would claim to be the One prophesied by the Báb, and also knew the significance of the ending of the prophetic cycle and the beginning the cycle of fulfillment before hearing these revelations. She also foresaw details of her own martyrdom.

Ṭáhirih's decision to remove her veil in Badasht was described as follows: "Suddenly the figure of Ṭáhirih, adorned and unveiled, appeared before the eyes of the assembled companions. . . . Her unruffled serenity sharply contrasted with the affrighted countenances of those who were gazing upon her face. . . . In language which bore a striking resemblance to that of the Qur'án, she delivered her appeal with matchless eloquence and profound fervour. . . . I am the Word which the Qá'im is to utter, the Word which shall put to flight the chiefs and nobles of the earth!'"[15]

In 1850, Ṭáhirih was arrested for her beliefs and was confined in Tehran, where she continued to teach the Báb's new Faith. A special government delegation questioned her during seven conferences. "When," she asked, "will you lift your eyes toward the Sun of Truth?" Shocked by her attitude and her refusal to recant her faith, they sentenced her to death. As the hour of her martyrdom approached, she declared boldly, "You can kill me as soon as you wish, but you cannot stop the emancipation of women!" Dressed in a gown of snow-white silk, she said "I am preparing to meet my Beloved . . . let no one disturb my devotions. I intend to fast . . . until I am brought face to face with my Beloved."[16] A silk handkerchief, as planned, was given to the executioner for her martyrdom. Strangled, her body was lowered into a well and covered with earth. She had sacrificed her life for the Báb's Cause, just as she had wished and foreseen.

The Báb Promises "He Whom God Shall Make Manifest"

Despite His lofty powers, the Báb made it clear that a greater Manifestation was very soon to come, the One Who had been referred to by the Báb as "Him Whom God shall make manifest." The Báb taught that this future Messenger's command would be equivalent to the command of God. "A thousand perusals of the Bayán [the Báb's primary scripture] were not equal to reading one of his verses. The Bayán was itself a gift to him, and revolved around his word."[17] The Báb's entire purpose and teachings revolved around the One Who would follow Him, and the Báb often praised this future Promised

One in His writings. The Báb prophesied: *"Know thou of a certainty that by Paradise is meant recognition of Him Whom God shall make manifest,"* and urged His followers to *"purge all thine acts and thy pursuits that thou mayest be nurtured in the paradise of pure love, and perchance mayest attain the presence of Him Whom God shall make manifest, adorned with a purity which He highly cherisheth, and be sanctified from whosoever hath turned away from Him and doth not support Him. Thus shalt thou manifest a purity that shall profit thee."* [18]

The Báb's Martyrdom: Proclaiming the New Age

The Báb, as was the case with other Messengers of God, was martyred for proclaiming a new revelation from God, and the dawn of a new age. The following is an account of His martyrdom.

After a brief six-year ministry, the Báb was executed under dramatic circumstances on July 9, 1850, in the city of Tabríz. On the day of execution, officers abruptly interrupted a conversation He was having with His secretary. He warned the officers that, until He had said all the things He wished to say, no "earthly power" could silence Him. The officers disregarded this warning and continued to carry out their duties. The Báb and a devoted young follower named Mírzá Muḥammad 'Alí were taken to the prison square. There they were suspended by ropes in front of a wall before some ten thousand onlookers. When the command for execution was given, a regiment of 750 soldiers opened fire. But when the smoke from the guns cleared, the Báb was not to be seen. The ropes that had held Him and His companion were completely severed, and Mírzá Muḥammad 'Alí stood alone and uninjured.

The Báb was discovered to be in His cell again, unhurt and unruffled, completing His interrupted conversation with His secretary. The colonel of the regiment ordered his soldiers to leave the scene and swore that he would never repeat what he had done. Another colonel volunteered for the duty, and a second regiment of soldiers was assembled.

When guards came to take the Báb away from His cell a second time, He told them He had finished His conversation. He said, *"Now you may proceed to fulfill your intention."* The Báb and Mírzá Muḥammad 'Alí were brought to the square again for execution in the same manner as before. *"O wayward generation!"* the Báb said in His last words to the thousands of onlookers,

Had you believed in Me every one of you would have followed the example of this youth, who stood in rank above most of you, and would have willingly sacrificed himself in My path. The day will come when you will have recognized Me; that day I shall have ceased to be with you.

The second regiment of soldiers formed a line and opened fire. This time the bodies of the Báb and Mírzá Muhammad 'Alí were riddled with bullets. But, surprisingly, their faces remained almost untouched.

Today a beautiful, majestic shrine stands over the Báb's resting place in Haifa, Israel. It is a special place of pilgrimage for Bahá'ís.[19]

4 – Auspicious Signs, Birth, and Intimations of Greatness: Bahá'u'lláh's Lineage, Prophetic Dreams, and Early Wisdom

Bahá'u'lláh was born in 1817 to a noble family in Tehran, the Persian capital. His given name was Mírzá Husayn 'Alí, and His father held a high-ranking position in the royal court. Bahá'u'lláh was also able to trace His lineage to some of the previous Founders of Faith. "He derived His descent, on one hand, from Abraham (the Father of the Faithful) through his wife Keturah, and on the other from Zoroaster, as well as from Yazdigird, the last king of the Sásáníyán dynasty. He was moreover a descendant of Jesse [David's father], and belonged, through His father, Mírzá 'Abbás, better known as Mírzá Buzurg—a nobleman closely associated with the ministerial circles of the Court of Fath-'Alí Sháh—to one of the most ancient and renowned families of Mázindarán."[20]

Accounts of Bahá'u'lláh's childhood describe His extraordinary knowledge, wisdom, kindness, generosity, eloquence, and magnetic personality. All who met Him were astonished and awe-stricken by His abilities, though He had no formal education. In His youth, He had a reputation for deep learning, and could discuss any subject and solve any problem presented to Him. His discussions entered into the domain of the theologian, but He never sounded presumptuous or arrogant, but rather always remained genial and modest.

Bahá'u'lláh grew up amidst riches and comfort, and *"the early part of His life was passed in the greatest happiness. His companions and associates were Persians of the highest rank, but not learned men."*[21] There were also great expectations for Bahá'u'lláh's future, as He was expected to follow in His father's footsteps and work in the court of the Sháh. But some were able to recognize that Bahá'u'lláh's future went far beyond serving the court. "The Grand Vizier . . . said that Mírzá Ḥusayn-'Alí was intended for a work of greater magnitude, and the arena of government was too small a field for His capacities."[22] Bahá'u'lláh's father had great love for his Son, and one night he had a special dream. He saw Bahá'u'lláh swimming in a vast ocean, with His long black hair floating in all directions. A multitude of fish gathered around Him, each holding on to one hair, yet not a single hair was detached, and Bahá'u'lláh moved freely, even above the waters, with all the fish following Him. His father asked a man renowned for his wisdom to explain this strange dream. The dream interpreter explained that the vast ocean in the dream was the larger world. Alone, Bahá'u'lláh would achieve sovereignty over it. The multitude of fish represented the turmoil He would arouse among the world's peoples. But with divine aid, He would prevail.

Some years later, an eminent jurist reported two dreams about Bahá'u'lláh. In one, the jurist made his way through a concourse of people to a house in which the promised Qá'im was engaged in a private conversation with none other than Bahá'u'lláh. In the other, he found himself in a library containing many books written by Bahá'u'lláh. Opening these books, he found that each letter and word was illumined with the most exquisite jewels.[23] Though these were only dreams, it was clear that early on some were able to perceive the high spiritual station that Bahá'u'lláh possessed.

Bahá'u'lláh's Young Adulthood: Serving the Báb's Cause
The royal family hoped Bahá'u'lláh would occupy a ministerial position, following in the footsteps of noble ancestors. When He showed no political inclinations they were surprised, but trusted His judgment, saying that He knew what He was doing and must have a loftier purpose. At age eighteen, He married Navváb, who shared His interest in tending to the poor and oppressed. When Bahá'u'lláh was twenty-two, His father passed away and the government asked Him to take His father's influential position. But Bahá'u'lláh chose to forego the life of luxury, and to instead dedicate Himself to serving the needy. He soon became known as Father of the Poor, and Navváb was called the Mother of Consolation. No deserving soul was refused their help and aid. Their three children were 'Abdu'l-Bahá (b 1844, the same night as the Báb's declaration), Bahíyyih Khánum (b 1846), and Mírzá Mihdí (b 1848).

Bahá'u'lláh took the Báb's Cause to His native province on the shore of the Caspian Sea, where He was able to challenge high-ranking clergy, persuade many of the truth of the Báb's Cause, and eventually aroused controversy because of these new teachings. Brilliant theological students sent to investigate Bahá'u'lláh were converted by Him, and such dramatic and unexpected conversions often helped to spread the new Faith. In 1848, Bahá'u'lláh organized the Conference of Badasht to help the scattered Bábí leaders clarify their central mission and their relation to Islam. Quddús, one of the Báb's Letters of the Living, favored a gradualist position, while Ṭáhirih propounded radical views. Although at first Bahá'u'lláh did not appear to have any official standing at the Conference, at the end, His was the decisive word: Ṭáhirih's "trumpet blast" must be understood as the will of the Báb. The time had come to close the prophetic cycle by breaking from Islam.

When Náṣiri'd-Dín Sháh came to the throne, he was far more ruthless toward the Bábís, and persecutions increased dramatically. Several hundred Bábís sought refuge in the Fort of Shaykh Ṭabarsí, and the clergy pressured the government to punish them harshly. Bahá'u'lláh was on His way to join the heroic Bábís at Ṭabarsí when He was stopped by government troops. The clergy preached death against the Bábís and stirred up mobs that thirsted for violent demonstrations against the Bábís. Bahá'u'lláh offered Himself instead of His friends, and He was physically abused by the angry crowd. After the Báb's martyrdom, Bahá'u'lláh rescued and concealed the remains of the Báb, which many years later would come to rest under a beautiful shrine on Mount Carmel in Haifa, Israel. And it was to Bahá'u'lláh that the Báb sent His seals, pen, rings, and vital papers—a symbolic transfer of great significance.

In 1852, three misguided Bábís sought to revenge the Báb's execution by killing Náṣiri'd-Dín Sháh. Though their poorly conceived attempt on the Sháh's life failed, it provided his government with an excuse to launch large-scale persecutions against the Bábís. When Bahá'u'lláh heard about the assassination attempt, He knew He would be sought by the government. While government officials were plotting His arrest, He came directly to them. The people of Tehran, who Bahá'u'lláh had served so graciously as Father of the Poor, now turned against Him as an angry mob. An old woman wanted to throw a stone at Bahá'u'lláh, and the guards had tried to quickly walk passed her, but Bahá'u'lláh said, *"Deny her not what she regards as a meritorious act in the sight of God."*[24]

A nation-wide massacre was conducted with unimaginable cruelty, beginning with the three youth who tried to kill the Sháh. One was cut into halves; the second had molten lead poured down his throat; and the flesh of the third was pierced, with lit candles placed in the holes. The suffering of thousands of Bábís was described in graphic detail by European officials who could hardly believe what they witnessed. Some Bábís suffered gouged-out eyes and amputated ears; others, crushed skulls; others still, skinned feet soaked in boiling oil. The fortunate victims were those merely used for target practice. Jeering crowds celebrated these unfathomable atrocities. Judgment Day had arrived, with the starkest evils brought into sharp contrast with a cause designed to save a depraved nation and elevate humanity to higher levels of spiritual maturity and material progress than ever before.

5 – Bahá'u'lláh's Divine Commission: Maid of Heaven in a Dungeon

Due partly to His family's noble reputation, and partly to Russian diplomatic pressure, but also to providence, Bahá'u'lláh was not executed. However, He was placed in such a dreadful prison, known as the Síyáh-Chál or Black Pit, that His survival was not expected. This was His punishment for His presumed role in the assassination attempt on the Sháh. The vermin-infested dungeon was, in Bahá'u'lláh's own words, *"foul beyond comparison."* The prison was *"wrapped in thick darkness,"* and filled with *"nearly a hundred and fifty souls: thieves, assassins and highwaymen."* [25] Around His neck they placed a very heavy chain, bending His whole frame. The Bábís were chained together in rows facing each other, and every night Bahá'u'lláh led them in chanting praises to God. They would sing, *"God is sufficient unto me. He, verily is the All-sufficing. In Him let the trusting trust."* [26] Day by day, an official would call out the names of those scheduled to be put to death, and every Bábí faced his fate with calm dignity, if not joy.

Bahá'u'lláh remained bound in the Black Pit for four months, but God made this darkness the setting for new light. While there, Bahá'u'lláh had a truly mystical experience. He described it in these words, *"One night, in a dream, these exalted words were heard on every side: 'Verily, We shall render Thee victorious by Thyself and by Thy Pen. Grieve Thou not for that which hath befallen Thee, neither be Thou afraid, for Thou art in safety. Erelong will God raise up the treasures of the earth—men who will aid Thee through Thyself and through Thy Name, wherewith God hath revived the hearts of such as have recognized Him.' . . . I felt as if something flowed from the crown of My head over My breast, even as a mighty torrent. . . . At such moments My tongue recited what no man could bear to hear."* [27] He went on to say, *"While engulfed in tribulations*

. . . I beheld a Maiden— the embodiment of the remembrance of the name of God—suspended in the air before Me. . . . Pointing with her finger to My head, she addressed all who are in heaven and all who are on earth, saying: 'This is the Best-Beloved of the worlds . . . the Beauty of God amongst you . . . the Cause of God and His glory.'" [28]

This was the divine commission of Bahá'u'lláh. Yet He was still a servant of the Báb's Cause and would not declare His own station and mission for another ten years. It soon became evident to His captors that Bahá'u'lláh was innocent of the assassination attempt. Unable to prove His guilt, they tried to poison His food, but upon tasting it, Bahá'u'lláh became quickly aware of their evil plan and avoided harm. Finally, they had no recourse other than to release Him, though He was never given His freedom again. Instead He and His family were exiled to Baghdad, in the hopes that this would help to extinguish the Cause of the Báb.

6 – Struggling in Solitude: Two Years in Sulaymaníyyih

Bahá'u'lláh emerged from the Black Pit ill and exhausted, with deep wounds on His neck from the heavy chain. His young son, 'Abdu'l-Bahá, was horrified to see his Father in this condition. After being given a short time to recover, He and His family embarked on a difficult three-month journey to Baghdad. While in prison, Bahá'u'lláh's property had been confiscated, and His family was forced to make the difficult trek with limited supplies. It was a bitterly cold winter, and they had to be content with little food and clothing, but after three months they arrived safely in Baghdad. It turned out that this exile was to be the first of many, as Bahá'u'lláh seemed to quickly win support wherever He went. His banishment from Iran was only the beginning of a series of exiles that endured for forty years, and were intended by His enemies to end the power and influence He had over people's hearts. Instead, the exiles served to spread His influence far and wide, fulfilling prophecies in Jewish, Christian, and Islamic scriptures. Before declaring His own station as the Promised One spoken of by the Báb, He led the scattered Bábí community for another ten years, completing the mission of the Báb.

At first opposition to the Bábí Faith had been external, but now began a long period when serious internal opposition was added to its challenges. Mírzá Yaḥyá, Bahá'u'lláh's jealous, ambitious, and cowardly half-brother, who believed himself the rightful leader of the Bábís, tried to cast doubt about Bahá'u'lláh's role and intention. So fierce was the conflict generated by Mírzá Yaḥyá that Bahá'u'lláh decided to retire from the scene. Without telling anyone, He left Baghdad for the mountain solitude of Kurdistan, near Sulaymáníyyih. This "withdrawal contemplated no return,"[29] for He wished not to contribute in any way to divisions in the cause. Bahá'u'lláh's self-imposed exile was a test. Was He the only Guide capable of showing the right path to the Bábís, the only One Who could restore to them their broken inner peace? If so, the passage of time and His absence would prove it conclusively.

Bahá'u'lláh stayed in a small cave and lived simply, praying and meditating most of the time. But gradually the people of Sulaymáníyyih and its theological school became aware of a Nameless One whose wisdom was rumored to be astonishing. Bahá'u'lláh's light could not keep from illuminating the people of Kurdistán. Eventually, word of the Sage reached the struggling Bábí community in Baghdad. 'Abdu'l-Bahá, who was destined to be the successor of Bahá'u'lláh and the Center of His Covenant, discerned that the Sage could be none other than His beloved Father. Emissaries were sent to implore Bahá'u'lláh to return. Providence had shown His indispensability.

7 – Declaration and First Followers: Garden of Riḍván

At the end of His time in Baghdad, Bahá'u'lláh moved to the Garden of Riḍván (Paradise), outside the city gates on the banks of the Tigris River. He knew His days in Baghdad were ending, the dispensation of the Báb nearing completion, and His second exile would soon begin. It was a time of great uncertainty for believers, as well as spectacular new achievements. The hour had arrived to declare Himself the Promised One of All Ages, He Whom God would make manifest, Christ Returned, the Lord of Hosts. Though we do not know the exact words spoken to those who first heard His declaration, Bahá'í writings provide their spiritual substance. *"The Revelation which, from time immemorial, hath been acclaimed as the Purpose and Promise of all the Prophets of God, and the most cherished Desire of His Messengers, hath now, by virtue of the pervasive Will of the Almighty and at His irresistible bidding, been revealed unto men."*[30] The announcement of Bahá'u'lláh's station was a joyous occasion. One description of the event says, "Heads were bent as the immensity of that Declaration touched the consciousness of men. Sadness had vanished; joy, celestial joy, prevailed."[31] During His stay in the Garden of Riḍván, multitudes of people of various backgrounds came to bid Him farewell, leaving flowers as tokens of their reverence. "So great would be the heap (of roses) that when His companions gathered to drink their morning tea in His presence, they would be unable to see each other across it."[32] When Bahá'u'lláh wrote of that time, He said, *"Rejoice with exceeding gladness, O people of Bahá, as ye call to remembrance the Day of supreme felicity."* [33]

8 – Overcoming Powerful Opposition: Persian and Turkish Leaders, and the Azalís

For almost half a century, Bahá'u'lláh faced varying degrees of persecution and constraint. Active opposition to Bahá'u'lláh lasted about thirty-three years, from the time He embraced the Báb's Cause in 1844, through His time in the Black Pit and His four subsequent banishments, until He was allowed to leave the prison-city walls of Akká in 1877. He taught very clearly the reasons for such opposition in religious history. A new revelation from God threatens both the religious and the political establishments, incites jealousy on the part of leaders, and generates disequilibrium for generations, if not centuries.

We touched on much of the opposition to Bahá'u'lláh when reviewing the Báb's mission, the persecution against Bábís coming after an attempt on the Sháh's life, Bahá'u'lláh's time in the Black Pit in Tehran, His exile to Baghdad, and the decision to withdraw to Kurdistan due to internal tensions within the struggling Faith. There would be further exiles by the Persian and Ottoman governments, who were manipulated by Muslim religious leaders. Here we focus on Mírzá Yaḥyá's internal opposition to Bahá'u'lláh, and how he colluded with government authorities to discredit Bahá'u'lláh.

Mírzá Yaḥyá (1832–1912), or Azal as he was known from some of his titles, was Bahá'u'lláh's younger half-brother, and was raised by Him after their father's death in 1839. The Báb appointed Mírzá Yaḥyá to preserve what was revealed in the Bayan, but from a Bahá'í perspective, this did not make Mírzá Yaḥyá the Báb's successor. Rather, it was an attempt to establish a temporary head for the Bábís, and to protect Bahá'u'lláh from receiving too much attention before His declaration in 1863. Mírzá Yaḥyá proved to be a very poor Bábí leader, due to his fearfulness in the face of threats, and an ever-deepening jealousy of Bahá'u'lláh's growing following. Mírzá Yaḥyá is viewed as the arch-breaker of the Bahá'í covenant, and is compared to Cain, Judas, and Abu-Jahl (Muḥammad's uncle).

In the early Baghdad years, a number of self-appointed "messiahs" brought great confusion to the Bábí community. Mírzá Yaḥyá was not only incompetent to deal with the challenge of leading the Bábís after the Báb's martyrdom, but also made things worse by allowing himself to be manipulated by other schemers against the new Faith. Especially in the later Baghdad years, Mírzá Yaḥyá made it easy for Iranian state and religious authorities to argue that Bahá'u'lláh should be exiled further away from the birthplace of their cause.

In Adrianople, Bahá'u'lláh openly proclaimed His station as "Him Whom God shall make manifest," the Promised One of All Ages. But when Mírzá Yaḥyá countered this proclamation, which caused great confusion among Bahá'ís, Bahá'u'lláh declared a Most Great Separation—a two-month period during which each believer needed to choose between following Bahá'u'lláh or Mírzá Yaḥyá. Almost all Bahá'ís chose to follow Bahá'u'lláh. About a year later, Mírzá Yaḥyá challenged Him to appear together at a mosque to await God's judgment on the true Founder of the new Faith. Bahá'u'lláh agreed, but Mírzá Yaḥyá failed to attend the meeting. Subsequently Mírzá Yaḥyá's followers, who became known as Azalís, tried to poison Bahá'u'lláh. They partially succeeded, for His hair turned white and He could no longer write without a shaking hand, but they were unable to end His life. Azalís also wrote anonymous letters to Constantinople, accusing Bahá'u'lláh of collusion with European powers in a plot to capture their capital. Ottoman rulers became fearful enough to condemn Bahá'u'lláh to perpetual banishment in Akká.

Bahá'u'lláh's sufferings at the hands of Azalís continued. Though He had enjoined forbearance regarding the few Azalís still in their midst, who had continued their treachery and the spreading of falsehoods, seven Bahá'ís reached their limit of tolerance and killed three Azalís. Bahá'u'lláh was appalled: *"My captivity cannot harm Me. That which can harm Me is the conduct of those who profess to love Me, who claim to be related to Me, and yet perpetrate what causeth My heart and My pen to groan. . . . That which can make Me ashamed is the conduct of such of My followers who profess to love Me, yet in fact follow the Evil One."*[34] Such events increased the hatred of the people around them, who Bahá'u'lláh called a "generation of vipers" and the "metropolis of the owl." However, over time 'Abdu'l-Bahá and Bahíyyih Khánum were able to gradually win respect and reverence from the people of Akká. 'Abdu'l-Bahá summarized Bahá'u'lláh's response to opposition: *"For fifty years Bahá'u'lláh faced His enemies like a mountain: all wished to annihilate Him and sought His destruction. A thousand times they planned to crucify and destroy Him, and during these fifty years He was in constant danger."* Throughout all these challenges, Bahá'u'lláh continued to share His message with the world, until *"His holy teachings penetrated all regions, and His Cause was established."* [35]

9 – Rejection by the People

In addition to Mírzá Yaḥyá, another Bábí, named Siyyid Muḥammad, colluded with the Azalís and helped to launch a campaign of lies against Bahá'u'lláh. Their motive was jealousy and the desire to eliminate the One Who won so much devotion and reverence, which, from their perspective, belonged to them. They spread rumors that Bahá'u'lláh had violated the instructions of the Báb and had plotted against the governors of Baghdad, Adrianople, and Akká. These "whisperings of Satan," as Siyyid Muḥammad's rumors became known, bore no resemblance to truth.

However, all these rumors and the confusion they created did have an effect. It was not only official religious and civil authorities who rejected Bahá'u'lláh. Many ordinary people assumed that anyone causing so much concern to leaders must be an evil-minded dissident and an enemy of religion. So Bahá'u'lláh was mocked and stoned by crowds along the paths of His ministry. Rejection by the people and by official leaders resulted in successive banishments that were intended to destroy His cause. The effects, however, assisted Bahá'u'lláh in pursuing His ultimate goal: to unify humanity.

10 – Sacrificial Suffering

There were thirty-three years of intense suffering—from 1844 to 1877—endured by Bahá'u'lláh and His closest family members and companions. When describing His suffering, Bahá'u'lláh said, *"I have, all the days of My life, been at the mercy of Mine enemies, and have suffered each day, in the path of the love of God, a fresh tribulation."* [36] He also mentioned how much sadness these troubles caused Him, *"My grief exceedeth all the woes to which Jacob gave vent, and all the afflictions of Job are but a part of My sorrows!"* [37] But all of this suffering proved redemptive. Not only did Bahá'u'lláh and his loved ones survive, but new revelatory teachings were spread that launched a new dispensation of ever wider unity and cooperation. Bahá'u'lláh stated, *"We have sustained the weight of all calamities to sanctify you from all earthly corruption."* [38]

11 – Symbolic Language as a Test for Believers

The pattern of scriptural language serving as a test and veil is a major theme of Bahá'u'lláh's Kitáb-i-Íqán, or "Book of Certitude." Throughout world history, religious leaders have become attached to and invested in certain distorted interpretations of scripture, veiling them from the deeper truths of their own scriptures, and blinding them to the new Revealer at the beginning of the new dispensation. Prophetic scriptural passages that are especially symbolic tend to be viewed in increasingly literal ways, which often leads to sectarian controversies and divisions.

But when this whole pattern is understood, each Founder can be seen as an integral part of progressive revelation. It then becomes possible for wider unity to be built, and the successive Messenger can be embraced as a renewer of one divine religion. Symbolic language would then be fully appreciated as providing improved access to higher, invisible realms. Today, the Bahá'í Faith is still in its early phase of growth, and it is difficult to see how this pattern will operate in the later part of this dispensation. Bahá'u'lláh taught that God always provides tests of the faithful, that the Bahá'í Faith itself will some day need to be renewed by another Manifestation of God, but the transition to the next dispensation will be less violent than in the past, because by then humanity will have fully entered its Age of Maturation and Fulfillment.

A few tentative points can be made about the testing and veiling process in the development of the Bahá'í Faith. Many Westerners, especially those with a more secular orientation, find the Bahá'í scriptures too flowery and poetic. The Bahá'í writings may strike them as archaic and unscientific, too elaborate and detailed, and some would add that these scriptures take prophecies too seriously for the modern mind. Such reactions might be viewed as ways of failing the test of a new revelation. God has the authority to speak as He chooses. We must learn to listen and elevate ourselves to a higher standard, even if it makes us uncomfortable at first.

It can be anticipated that some Bahá'ís, like believers in past dispensations, will become so attached to certain aspects of their faith—perhaps its Persian cultural origins, its institutions, or its shrines in the current Holy Land—that they will become blind to the next Manifestation, and will close themselves off from guidance needed for the next dispensation. But details of this process are of course invisible to mere mortals who ponder these possible developments centuries ahead of time.

12 – Exemplary Woman: Bahíyyih Khánum

The eldest daughter of Bahá'u'lláh and Navváb, and the sister of 'Abdu'l-Bahá, was Bahíyyih Khánum (1846–1932). She was given the title the "Greatest Holy Leaf," and was devoted to Bahá'u'lláh and her family. On several occasions she was entrusted as head of the Faith for a temporary period of time. From 1852 onward she shared the poverty, exiles, and sufferings of Bahá'u'lláh's family. She renounced marriage in order to completely dedicate herself to her Father's Cause. In Akká she managed most of the household affairs, cultivated positive relationships with wives of important officials, and helped to change initial hatred against the Bahá'ís into enduring respect and love.

After Bahá'u'lláh's ascension, Bahíyyih Khánum led the faithful family members who supported 'Abdu'l-Bahá, who Bahá'u'lláh had named as His successor in His Will and Testament, in His struggles with Muḥammad-'Alí, the arch-breaker of the Covenant. As the Faith continued to grow, her warm hospitality was enjoyed by an increasing number of pilgrims from East and West. She managed Bahá'í affairs in the Holy Land when 'Abdu'l-Bahá made His missionary journeys to Europe and North America (1911–13). She also oversaw extensive social service projects in Akká, and helped to prevent starvation in the community during difficult times, especially during World War I. After 'Abdu'l-Bahá's ascension in 1921, she supported and advised Shoghi Effendi during the early years of his Guardianship, and acted as head of the Faith during his absences from Haifa. The Guardian described her as a "pure angelic soul," attributing to her powers of intercession for all humanity. When she passed away, her funeral was massively attended by people of diverse backgrounds in the Holy Land.[39]

13 – Dying and Ascending Victoriously: Upon Completing Laws, Unifying Faith, and Clarifying Succession

At Bahjí, Bahá'u'lláh completed His book of laws intended to last until the next Messenger of God arrives, in no less than a thousand years, with further guidance for humanity. Now He was free to conclude His other important earthly tasks that would carry the Faith forward for a millennium. Though Bahá'u'lláh had visited Mount Carmel a few times before His final years, in 1891 He made an extended visit, and revealed the Tablet of Carmel—a dialogue between Bahá'u'lláh and the personified mountain, foretelling the establishment of the Bahá'í World Center and the Universal House of Justice (God's Ark) there. In the Tablet, Bahá'u'lláh states, *"Call out to Zion, O Carmel, and announce the joyful tidings: He that was hidden from mortal eyes is come! His all-conquering sovereignty is manifest; His all-encompassing splendour is revealed. Beware lest thou hesitate or halt. Hasten forth and circumambulate the City of God that hath descended from heaven, the celestial Kaaba round which have circled in adoration the favoured of God, the pure in heart, and the company of the most exalted angels. . . . Ere long will God sail His Ark upon thee, and will manifest the people of Bahá who have been mentioned in the Book of Names."* [40]

Bahá'u'lláh's words on Mount Carmel point to the fulfillment of Isaiah's age-old prophecy, calling all nations and religions to the "mountain of the house of the Lord," where they may learn divine ways and dwell in peace. The Bible prophesied the importance of Mount Carmel. *"It shall come to pass in the latter days that the mountain of the house of the Lord shall be established . . . and all nations shall flow to it, and many peoples shall come."* [41]

Bahá'u'lláh showed 'Abdu'l-Bahá the exact spot on Mount Carmel where the Shrine of the Báb was to be built. "Today, on the very spot indicated by Bahá'u'lláh, stands a mausoleum of glorious beauty, surmounted by a golden dome reflecting many hues of the sea and sky, and surrounded by gardens that ravish the eyes and enchant the soul."[42] It was also in 1891 that Bahá'u'lláh wrote His last major work, Epistle to the Son of the Wolf, which was addressed to a prominent Iranian clergyman who had persecuted Bahá'ís, calling upon him to repent and ask for God's forgiveness. This important book also summarizes many of Bahá'u'lláh's teachings, citing passages from His own earlier revelations. It points to the transforming power of His teachings, which inspired militant Bábís to turn away from sedition toward good deeds. It also details biblical prophecies that have been fulfilled by Bahá'u'lláh's earthly mission in the Holy Land.

Among the many guests who met Bahá'u'lláh at the mansion of Bahjí was the distinguished Cambridge scholar, Edward Granville Browne. He created a pen-portrait of Bahá'u'lláh, and it is the only one of its kind. Browne, when describing Bahá'u'lláh said, "The face of him on whom I gazed I can never forget, though I cannot describe it. Those piercing eyes seemed to read one's very soul; power and authority sat on that ample brow. . . . No need to ask in whose presence I stood, as I bowed myself before one who is the object of a devotion and love which kings might envy." Browne continued by describing his visit, "A mild dignified voice bade me be seated, and then continued: *'Praise be to God that thou hast attained! . . . Thou hast come to see a prisoner and an exile. . . . We desire but the good of the world and happiness of the nations; yet they deem us a stirrer up of strife and sedition worthy of bondage and banishment. . . . That all nations should become one in faith and all men as brothers; that the bonds of affection and unity between the sons of men should be strengthened; that diversity of religion should cease, and differences of race be annulled—what harm is there in this? . . . Yet so it shall be; these fruitless strifes, these ruinous wars shall pass away, and the "Most Great Peace" shall come. . . . These strifes and this bloodshed and discord must cease, and all men be as one kindred and one family. . . . Let not a man glory in this, that he loves his country; let him rather glory in this, that he loves his kind.'"* [43]

Bahá'u'lláh's last testament, what is known as The Book of the Covenant, was written during His final illness in 1892. It explicitly appoints 'Abdu'l-Bahá as His successor. All Bahá'ís should turn to 'Abdu'l-Bahá as the Greatest Branch, the Center of the Covenant. It also exhorts Bahá'ís to fear God and perform praiseworthy deeds. God's religion should never be made the cause of enmity and conflict is forbidden. While God's domain is the hearts of men, worldly governance is entrusted to kings. Bahá'u'lláh clarified that Bahá'ís should be led by "rulers," who would be elected decision-makers, and by the "learned," who would be appointed teachers within the Faith. [44]

Nine months before His ascension, Bahá'u'lláh, expressed His desire to part from this world, and thereafter made it increasingly clear that His time in this earthly realm was drawing to a close. Six days before He passed away, He gathered together His family and closest friends for their last meeting with Him in the Mansion of Bahjí. *"I am well pleased with you all,"* He said. *"Ye have rendered many services, and been very assiduous in your labours. Ye have come here every morning and every evening. May God assist you to remain united. May He aid you to exalt the Cause of the Lord of being."* [45] Everyone who had gathered around him was deeply moved by His words, and tears streamed from their eyes.

"Bahá'u'lláh left His human temple on the 29th of May, 1892. A telegram bore the news to the Sultan of Turkey: 'The Sun of Bahá has set.' Yet It shines dazzlingly in the full meridian." For Bahá'ís, Bahá'u'lláh's shrine at Bahjí is the point of adoration and direction for prayer, and is considered the holiest place on earth. After Bahá'u'lláh had passed away, many came to pay their respects. "For a full week a vast number of mourners, rich and poor alike, tarried to grieve with the bereaved family. . . . Notables, among whom were numbered Shí'ahs, Sunnis, Christians, Jews and Druzes, as well poets, ulamas and government officials, all joined in lamenting the loss, and in magnifying the virtues and greatness of Bahá'u'lláh. . . . These glowing testimonials were, without exception, submitted to 'Abdu'l-Bahá, Who now represented the Cause of the departed Leader, and Whose praises were often mingled in these eulogies with the homage paid to His Father."[46]

- 18 -
Bahá'u'lláh: Teaching and Legacy

14 – Transformative Teaching and Healing

Though Bahá'u'lláh's exiles took Him ever further from His homeland, and though these exiles were designed by His enemies to eliminate His influence and destroy His cause, they served to expand and strengthen it. As was the case with the other Founders, human opposition was made to serve a divine purpose. During the first exile in Baghdad (1853–63), Bahá'u'lláh revived the ailing Bábí Faith, making it more vigorous than ever before, without formally declaring His station until the eve of departure to Constantinople in 1863. During His five years in Turkey (1863–68), Bahá'u'lláh gave initial shape to the distinctive Bahá'í Faith, now an independent Faith that developed after the Bábí Faith, and was able to address the larger world. In His final exile to 'Akká in the Holy Land (1868–92), new laws were revealed for a new world order, sites were established for a new world center of the Faith, and succession was clarified and bound by a new covenant aimed at world unity.

First Exile: Baghdad (1853–63)

While Bahá'u'lláh withdrew to Sulaymáníyyih, the Bábí cause sunk lower. But upon His return to Baghdad in 1856, He revived spirits and reminded believers of their mission—to prepare the world for Him Whom God shall make manifest. A sign of the Faith's renewal was a gathering of the most distinguished clergy in Baghdad—Muslim ulama, Jewish rabbis, and Christian monks—called to expose Bahá'u'lláh as a fraud and thereby justify destroying the Bábí Cause. But to every question posed to Him by the leaders of these faiths, Bahá'u'lláh gave a convincing reply, forcing them to admit He was without peer in all fields of learning. The clergy asked for a miracle on Bahá'u'lláh's part to show the divine power of His cause. He replied that, although they had no right to ask this, *"for God should test His creatures, and they*

349

should not test God," He would allow it under certain conditions. Bahá'u'lláh said they must all agree on one miracle to be performed, and write that after its performance, their doubts must cease and they will declare loyalty to His cause; but if the miracle is not performed, Bahá'u'lláh will be convicted as an impostor. *"They consulted together and said, 'This man is an enchanter; perhaps he will perform an enchantment, and then we shall have nothing more to say.' Acting on this belief, they did not dare to push the matter further."*[1] This story spread far and wide, giving the Bábí Faith new adherents.

In the Seven Valleys, Bahá'u'lláh's greatest mystical work, He uses a framework similar to the Persian writer, Aṭṭár (d 1229). One's spiritual search is described as a journey moving through seven valleys. The first stage of the spiritual journey is the Valley of Search, requiring seekers to "ride the steed of patience" in quest of the Beloved. The second is the Valley of Love, a passionate quest bringing sacrificial pain and glory to the wayfarer. The third is the Valley of Knowledge, which brings certitude and understanding on the interrelatedness of all creation. The fourth is the Valley of Unity, which transcends worldly distinctions, and passage through it allows people to gaze "upon all things with the eyes of oneness." The fifth is the Valley of Contentment where God transforms our sorrow into joy, our grief into happiness. The sixth is the Valley of Wonderment, where transience and complexity throw us into a state of bewilderment. Finally, the Valley of True Poverty and Nothingness is a state of "dying from self and living in God." Bahá'u'lláh concludes: *"These journeys have no visible ending in the world of time, but the severed wayfarer—if invisible confirmation descend upon him and the Guardian of the Cause assist him—may cross these seven stages in seven steps, nay rather in seven breaths, nay rather in a single breath, if God will and desire it."*[2]

The Hidden Words, which was revealed in 1857–58, is Bahá'u'lláh's preeminent ethical work, inviting sincere seekers into a divinely guided moral transformation. It is "written in a lucid and captivating prose, presenting those eternal verities at the core of every revealed religion."[3] Bahá'u'lláh said when describing it, *"This is that which hath descended from the realm of glory, uttered by the tongue of power and might, and revealed unto the Prophets of old. We have taken the inner essence thereof and clothed it in the garment of brevity."*[4] It assures readers that God loves humanity and has made our hearts His home, our spirits the place of His revelation. We are invited to detach ourselves from *"that which perisheth"* and commune with God, freeing ourselves from the *"prison of self."* We are enjoined to follow divine law and accept trials for God's sake. We should neither fear abasement nor rejoice in prosperity. We should see the poor as God's trust, and when able, bestow God's wealth upon them. We should avoid covetousness, envy, and malice, planting only "the rose of love" in the garden of the heart. We may behold the "new garden," learn its mysteries and wisdom, seizing our chance before the "fleeting moment" of life ends.[5]

The Book of Certitude, which was revealed in 1862, is Bahá'u'lláh's outstanding doctrinal work. It is a logical essay on the theological interpretation of past and present scriptures. It explains why the same pattern of rejection occurred and recurred with all Founders. Religious leaders had limited understanding of Their teachings, and felt threatened by the spiritual authority that the Founders possessed. The veil of literalism has been a major obstacle to unity and understanding, but spiritual interpretation, as given in later revelations, illumines earlier ones. God tests humanity repeatedly regarding our tradition-bound outlook. If we can approach scripture with a pure heart, cleansed from worldly standards, understanding becomes possible. Proofs of a Founder's authenticity are His verses, His steadfastness despite persecution, His ability to inspire steadfastness in His followers, and His ability to prophesy future developments.[6]

Bahá'u'lláh's ten years in Baghdad were very productive, as followers absorbed and acted on His teachings, and great opposition was overcome. However, clouds of uncertainty and new trials loomed ahead. He described a dream in which He saw *"the Prophets and the Messengers gather and seat themselves around Me, moaning, weeping and loudly lamenting . . . Thereupon the Concourse on high addressed Me saying: '. . . Erelong shalt Thou behold with Thine own eyes what no Prophet hath beheld. . . . Be patient, be patient.'"*[7] Enemies conspired to exile Bahá'u'lláh yet further from the Faith's birthplace. Fear seized the Bábís as word got out of Bahá'u'lláh's imminent departure. But joy replaced dread when they heard of His declaration that He was the One foretold by the Báb. They believed the world's long ages of waiting had ended, and the Day of Days had arrived. Humanity's maturing and unifying process began, despite whatever trials may ensue.

Second and Third Exiles: Constantinople and Adrianople (1863–68)
Constantinople was the capital of the Ottoman Empire, and Bahá'u'lláh called it the "throne of tyranny"[8] in which the foolish ruled the wise. He prophesied that its outward splendor would soon perish, and that its heedless

people would lament what their hands had wrought. "With the arrival of Bahá'u'lláh in Constantinople . . . the grimmest and most calamitous and yet the most glorious chapter in the history of the first Bahá'í century may be said to have opened."[9] Though it was customary for distinguished visitors to ask to meet the Sultan, often to seek favors from government officials, Bahá'u'lláh had no favor to solicit, and only came at the command of the government. They could seek Him if they had anything to convey. This upset the members of court because Bahá'u'lláh was brining attention to the corruption He saw engulfing the current government practices. He saw the court as surrounded by intriguers, and refused all association with their designs.[10]

In Constantinople as in Baghdad, Bahá'u'lláh's wisdom and charisma attracted multitudes. Again the clergy felt threatened and advocated another exile. When Sultan 'Abdu'l-Aziz issued an exile order, Bahá'u'lláh replied: *"Hearken, O King, to the speech of Him that speaketh the truth. . . . Lay not aside the fear of God, and be thou of them that act uprightly. . . . Overstep not the bounds of moderation, and deal justly with them that serve thee."* [11] He prophesied that conditions would "wax grievous" for the Sultan, and what they boasted of would perish. He knew the coming exiles would bring His cause much suffering. *"They expelled Us . . . with an abasement with which no abasement on earth can compare . . . The eyes of the enemies wept over us."* But He comforted followers, saying, *"whatever may befall us, great shall be our gain."* [12]

After a few months in Constantinople, Bahá'u'lláh and His family were exiled to Adrianople, a remote part of the Ottoman Empire near the edge of Europe, where they spent five years experiencing both great suffering and achievement. Bahá'u'lláh openly proclaimed Himself Revealer of a new message from God that would transform the world, but not without great social and political turmoil. He declared a worldwide mission through a series of letters to individual kings and rulers, and to all of them collectively, calling them to embrace the new Faith, reminding them that the poor were their trust, for whom they would answer to God. Kings must dedicate themselves to the welfare of their people, and to world peace. Bahá'u'lláh said, *"Be reconciled amongst yourselves, that ye may need no more armaments save in a measure to safeguard your territories and dominions. . . . Be united, O kings of the earth, for thereby will the tempest of discord be stilled amongst you . . . . Should any one among you take up arms against another, rise ye all against him, for this is naught but manifest justice."* [13] He warned that if they did not heed His counsel, divine chastisement would follow. Christian monarchs were called to be faithful to Jesus' call to follow the promised Spirit of Truth (Bahá'u'lláh).

He wrote the lengthiest individual letter to the S͟háh of Iran, the tyrant who launched a violent attack against Bábís, and exiled Bahá'u'lláh to Baghdad. Bahá'u'lláh mentioned His unfair suffering, and asked the S͟háh to tolerate Bahá'ís in Iran, for they were obedient subjects. He insisted that militant Bábís abandon any seditious plans. If the S͟háh wished, He would return to Iran, consult with the clergy to establish the truth. If the S͟háh responded positively, he would attain a great spiritual station. In order to remember the importance of humility before God, the S͟háh was reminded that the skeletal remains of kings and paupers are the same. Many wished the honor of delivering this letter to the S͟háh, and the chosen bearer was a youth named Badí', who faced his martyrdom with fortitude. The S͟háh tried to commission the clergy to meet His religious challenge, but was disgusted with their evasion as they warned that Bahá'u'lláh was a political threat.

There were many struggles between Bahá'u'lláh and Mírzá Yaḥyá, and between Bahá'ís and Azalís. These developments alerted Ottoman authorities to religious and social unrest, prompting them to condemn both Bahá'í and Azalí leaders to perpetual banishment and imprisonment. Bahá'u'lláh, His family, and a few Azalís were exiled to the prison-city of Akká, Palestine, while Mírzá Yaḥyá and other Azalí leaders were exiled to the island of Cyprus. After the first leg of their journey to Akká, Bahá'u'lláh foresaw grievous trials ahead, and gave His companions the opportunity to depart and be sheltered from tests, because thereafter they would be unable to leave. All ignored this warning, and went forward together to the Most Great Prison.

Fourth Exile: 'Akká and the Holy Land (1868–77)

'Akká is a city over 3000 years old, having had many times of high and low fortune. By the time of Bahá'u'lláh's arrival, "Akka was a penal colony to which murderers, highway robbers, and political agitators were sent from all over the Turkish Empire. It had no source of fresh water within its gates and was notorious for being flea-infested, damp, and filthy. It had a reputation for being more desolate, unsightly, and detestable than any other city. According to popular lore, 'Akká's air was so putrid that a bird flying over it would drop dead."[14]

However, the arrival of Bahá'u'lláh in the Holy Land fulfilled ancient prophecies. David referred to 'Akká as the "strong city," and in Psalm 24

353

wrote, *"Lift up your heads, O ye gates . . . and the King of glory shall come in. Who is this King of glory? The Lord of Hosts, He is the King of glory."* [15] Hosea called 'Akká a *"door of hope."* [16] Micah prophesied, *"In that day they will come to you, from Assyria . . . from sea to sea and from mountain to mountain. But the earth will be desolate."* [17] Ezekiel prophesied, *"the glory of the God of Israel came from the east."* [18] Isaiah prophesied, *"Carmel . . . shall see the glory of the Lord."* [19] Muḥammad declared: *"Blessed the man that hath visited 'Akká, and blessed he that hath visited the visitor of 'Akká."* [20] All these prophecies seem to be references to Bahá'u'lláh and His banishment to 'Akká.

Bahá'u'lláh foretold victory: *"Upon Our arrival We were welcomed with banners of light, whereupon the Voice of the Spirit cried out saying: 'Soon will all that dwell on earth be enlisted under these banners.'"* [21] Yet the first two years in 'Akká were a time of severe suffering for Bahá'u'lláh, His family, and their companions. The most tragic event was the sudden death of His son, Mírzá Mihdí, who, while absorbed in prayer on the roof, fell through a skylight onto a wooden crate, piercing his ribs. Before his passing, Bahá'u'lláh asked him his wish. He replied, "I wish the people of Bahá to be able to attain Your presence." *"And so it shall be"* pronounced Bahá'u'lláh; *"God will grant your wish."* [22] Although restrictions against the Bahá'ís were extremely severe at first, these were gradually relaxed so that visitors were able to come to see Bahá'u'lláh. Mírzá Mihdí's wish had been fulfilled.

Letters written to individual kings that Bahá'u'lláh had begun in Adrianople were resumed in 'Akká. He wrote twice to Napoleon III, the most politically powerful figure in the world at the time. In the first letter, He asked him to inquire into the justice of His imprisonment, but Napoleon's reaction was disdainful and arrogant. Hearing no reply, Bahá'u'lláh wrote again saying *"thy kingdom shall be thrown into confusion, and thine empire shall pass from thine hands. . . . Hath thy pomp made thee proud? By My life! It shall not endure; nay it shall soon pass away, unless thou holdest fast by this firm Cord."* [23] This letter was sent in 1869 and a year later Napoleon met his defeat. Bahá'u'lláh's prophecy about Napoleon became widely known and was a factor in the growth of the Faith.

To Queen Victoria, Bahá'u'lláh wrote: *"We have been informed that thou hast forbidden the trading in slaves, both men and women. This, verily, is what God hath enjoined in this wondrous Revelation. God hath, truly, destined a reward for thee, because of this. . . . We have also heard that thou hast entrusted the reins of counsel into the hands of the representatives of the people. Thou, indeed, hast done well, for thereby the foundations of the edifice of thine affairs will be strengthened, and the hearts of all that are beneath thy shadow, whether high or low, will be tranquillized."* [24] The Queen's was the only reasonably positive reply. She said, "If this is of God, it will endure; if not, it can do no harm." [25]

To Pope Pius IX, Bahá'u'lláh wrote: *"Rend the veils asunder. He Who is the Lord of Lords is come overshadowed with clouds. . . . Dwellest thou in palaces whilst He Who is the King of Revelation liveth in the most desolate of abodes? . . . Call thou to remembrance Him Who was the Spirit (Jesus), Who, when He came, the most learned of His age pronounced judgment against Him in His own country, whilst he who was only a fisherman believed in Him. . . . Consider those who opposed the Son (Jesus), when He came unto them with sovereignty and power. . . . The Word which the Son concealed is made manifest. It hath been sent down in the form of the human temple in this day. . . . The Father is come, and that which ye were promised in the Kingdom is fulfilled!"* [26]

Bahá'u'lláh wrote to Czar Alexander II of Russia, to Emperor Francis Joseph of Austria, and to William I, the German Emperor, mentioning to the latter: *"O banks of the Rhine! We have seen you covered with gore, inasmuch as the swords of retribution were drawn against you; and you shall have another turn. And we hear the lamentations of Berlin, though she be today in conspicuous glory."* This seemed to prophesy two World Wars, over four decades ahead of the first War. To the Americas, Bahá'u'lláh wrote: *"Hearken ye, O Rulers of America and the Presidents of the Republics therein. . . . Adorn ye the temple of dominion with the ornament of justice and of the fear of God. . . . Bind ye the broken with the hands of justice, and crush the oppressor who flourisheth with the rod of the commandments of your Lord."* [27]

Bahá'u'lláh called upon world leaders to inaugurate the Most Great Peace by uniting under His banner. This opportunity was refused, so He challenged them and their posterity to establish the Lesser Peace, which He described as a humanly wrought system of collective security that would assure a measure of peace and justice. Bahá'u'lláh also appended a copy of His Chapter of the Temple to His letters to the Pope, Napoleon III, the Czar, the Queen, and the Sháh. In this passage, the voice of God addresses Bahá'u'lláh as the promised biblical Temple of God.

Bahá'u'lláh's nine years within the walls of Akká also yielded the Kitáb-i-Aqdas, or the Most Holy Book, which was revealed in 1873. It is known as His Book of Law, and is also referred to as the Charter of His New World Order and envisioned as "a new heaven and a new earth." [28] He described this book as the "unerring Balance" testing the peoples of the world, and providing the "mightiest stronghold for the protection of the world." It is "not a mere code of laws," but rather the "choice Wine," containing laws that are the "breath of life" and should be followed out of love for Bahá'u'lláh.[29]

Bahá'u'lláh teaches that true liberty can be won through obedience to these laws. Specific laws may be categorized as: 1) personal obligations toward God, 2) regulation of personal status and contracts, 3) community life, 4) prohibitions, 5) exhortations, and 6) punishments for crime. Islamic rulings on ritual impurity and music are abrogated, and leaders are warned not to prevent people from recognizing Bahá'u'lláh.

Freedom to Build the Cause of God: Mazra'ih and Bahjí (1877–92)

It became ever clearer to 'Akká's leaders that their "Chief Prisoner was not an ordinary man, that they had in their custody a Personage of vastly superior gifts and powers. They became enamored of His majestic bearing, of His amazing knowledge of human affairs, of His disarming charity and forbearing nature. Their prisoner He was, but a time came when it was almost impossible to realize the fact, or to enforce the harsh and drastic injunctions of the government in Constantinople."[30] As Bahá'u'lláh's dying son hoped, Bahá'ís came from afar and were able to see Him. The mufti of 'Akká, experts on law within Sunní Islam, were converted from hatred to allegiance. The governor offered to help Bahá'u'lláh personally, but was asked to repair the aqueduct instead, leading to fresh water and better air in the city. A later governor told Him that He was free now to live in the countryside.

In the first two years in 'Akká, Bahá'u'lláh had declared, *"Fear not. These doors shall be opened. My tent shall be pitched on Mount Carmel, and the utmost joy shall be realized."* Then one day Bahá'u'lláh, a lover of nature, told His son 'Abdu'l-Bahá, *"I have not gazed on verdure for nine years. The country is the world of the soul, the city is the world of bodies."*[31] Accordingly, 'Abdu'l-Bahá rented a house in Mazra'ih, and also a garden on an island in a nearby river, a garden called Riḍván to evoke the memory of His declaration.

After two years at Mazra'ih, Bahá'u'lláh moved to a mansion in Bahjí, where He spent His remaining thirteen years on earth, except for a few visits to Mount Carmel. 'Abdu'l-Bahá took on more managerial and diplomatic roles, and acquired the Bahjí mansion for His beloved Father. The view from Bahá'u'lláh's window included the pure blue of the Mediterranean, minarets of the prison-city, and the gentle slope of Mount Carmel. From 1852 to 1877, Bahá'u'lláh showed the glory of God in a state of hardship and persecution. Now He would show the glory of God in a state of honor and prosperity. Officially He was still a prisoner, though in reality He was more revered than a king.

Protected and relieved by the superb administration of 'Abdu'l-Bahá, Bahá'u'lláh devoted these peaceful years to extensive writing, and also received many guests. In the Lawh-i-Aqdas, or Most Holy Tablet, Bahá'u'lláh addressed all Christians, declaring that He was the Return of Christ, the Spirit of Truth who had come to lead them to all truth. He asked them to avoid the mistake of the Pharisees, the most learned in their day, who could not recognize Christ, yet a humble fisherman did. He summoned priests to leave their churches and proclaim His cause, and invited monks to abandon their cloisters and work to benefit the souls of all as *"heirs of My Kingdom."* He prophesied the fall of bishops by divine justice, but said they could become *"stars of the heaven of My knowledge"* if they recognized Him.[32]

15 – Delivering a Thematic and Complementary Message: World Unity and an Ever-Advancing Global Civilization

The central theme of Bahá'u'lláh's revelation is to generate world unity and an ever-advancing global civilization. As with all revelatory systems, there are several major themes in the Bahá'í Faith, but unity is the theme that integrates all of Bahá'u'lláh's teachings. Humanity's primary responsibility in this Day is to create a sense of unity—a coming together spiritually, socially, and materially of all peoples—and to establish a new world order based on divine guidance. This process will generate a diverse, but unified and ever-advancing civilization. Implied in this concept of world unity is the unity of God, the unity of religion, and the unity of humanity. These three kinds of unity are supported by many complementary principles, including progressive revelation, the independent investigation of truth, the harmony of science and religion, overcoming prejudice, racial and gender equality, support for family life, equality, universal education, consultative problem-solving, a universal auxiliary language, collective security, world government, the elimination of extremes of wealth and poverty, the search for spiritual solutions to economic problems, and care for the earth.

16 – Renewing and Embodying Universal Virtues

The Bahá'í writings clarify that virtues originate in divinely-generated religion, rather than in human rationality or social institutions. Virtues are embedded in scripture, and are the basis of the civilization-building process. *"It is religion . . . which produces all human virtues, and it is these virtues which are the bright candles of civilization."*[33]

Spiritual Virtues in the Bahá'í Revelation

Devotion-Faithfulness: *"Create in me a pure heart, O my God, and renew a tranquil conscience within me."*[34]

Gratitude-Reverence: *"Praised be Thou, O Lord my God! Every time I attempt to make mention of Thee I am hindered by the sublimity of Thy station and the overpowering greatness of Thy might."*[35]

Self-discipline-Obedience: *"Man should know his own self and recognize that which leadeth unto loftiness or lowliness, glory or abasement, wealth or poverty."*[36]

Detachment-Patience: *"Disencumber yourselves of all attachment to this world and the vanities thereof."*[37]

Wisdom-Discernment: *"Knowledge is one of the wondrous gifts of God. It is incumbent upon everyone to acquire it."*[38]

Social Virtues in the Bahá'í Revelation

Loving-kindness-Compassion: *"Ye are the fruits of one tree, and the leaves of one branch. Deal ye one with another with the utmost love and harmony, with friendliness and fellowship."*[39]

Service-Responsibility: *"Man's merit lieth in service and virtue and not in the pageantry of wealth and riches."*[40]

Respect-Tolerance: *"Consort with the followers of all religions in a spirit of friendliness and fellowship"*[41]

Justice-Righteousness: *"If thine eyes be turned towards justice, choose thou for thy neighbour that which thou choosest for thyself."*[42]

Peace-Unity: *"It is incumbent upon all peoples of the world to reconcile their differences, and, with perfect unity and peace, abide beneath the shadow of the Tree of His care and loving-kindness."*[43]

Material Virtues in the Bahá'í Revelation

Trustworthiness-Honesty: *"Truthfulness is the foundation of all human virtues."*[44]

Moderation-Balance: *"Whatsoever passeth beyond the limits of moderation will cease to exert a beneficial influence."*[45]

Generosity-Hospitality: *"Be generous in prosperity . . . a treasure to the poor, an admonisher to the rich, an answerer to the cry of the needy"*[46]

Creativity-Beauty: *"Arts, crafts and sciences uplift the world of being, and are conducive to its exaltation."* [47]

Earthcare-Stewardship: *"Every part of the universe is connected with every other part by ties that are very powerful and admit of no imbalance, nor any slackening whatever."* [48]

17 – Abrogating the Old and Establishing the New: Laws for a New World Order

Like Christ, Muḥammad, and other Manifestations of God, Bahá'u'lláh abrogated rituals and socioeconomic guidelines from the previous dispensation. Islamic laws, except where specifically reiterated, were abrogated and replaced with the laws revealed by Bahá'u'lláh in the Kitáb-i-Aqdas. Part of the reason for such abrogation is that many rituals have been initiated by priests, and deviate markedly from original divine teachings. The main reason for new rituals and laws is that historical conditions change, and humanity's capacities develop.

Bahá'u'lláh provided many guidelines leading to a new world order. Some areas of guidance include prayer, marriage, teaching the faith, devotions, consultation, work and professions, education, institutional gatherings, administrative institutions, funding religion, pilgrimage, rights and responsibilities, economics, social service, equity and justice, scholarship, secular law, security, peacemaking, and global governance.

Bahá'í law teaches gradualism, diversity, individual conscience, and the importance of maintaining principles above details. One study of the Bahá'í Faith says, "Bahá'u'lláh himself stated that observance of his law should be subject to 'tact and wisdom' so as not to cause 'disturbance and dissension.' Humankind should be guided to 'the ocean of true understanding' in a 'spirit of love and tolerance.'" Some laws have been applied "extemely gradually in those countries in which they go against established social patterns. . . . It is attraction to Bahá'u'lláh, combined with the fear of God, that is intended to be the primary motivation for obedience. With the exception of behavior that is criminal or liable to bring the Bahá'í community into disrepute, compliance is a matter of individual conscience. . . . Bahá'í law is often presented in the form of general principles which each individual must apply as they best see fit in their own lives."[49] It is understood that although Bahá'í laws are extremely important, it may take some time before we learn how to completely apply them to our lives, so the goal is always to learn, grow, and strive to do one's best.

18 – Human and Divine Qualities: Exemplifying a Dual Station

Bahá'u'lláh's Human Station

Bahá'u'lláh claimed to be living a human life while acting as a divine agent. *"I was but a man like others, asleep upon My couch, when lo, the breezes of the All-Glorious were wafted over Me, and taught Me the knowledge of all that hath been. This thing is not from Me, but from One Who is Almighty and All-Knowing. And He bade Me lift up My voice between earth and heaven."* [50] Bahá'u'lláh was called to be a Revealer by God, and spoke to humanity not of His own accord. He spoke of His divine / human roles or dual station in this passage: *"When I contemplate, O my God, the relationship that bindeth me to Thee, I am moved to proclaim to all created things 'verily I am God!'; and when I consider my own self, lo, I find it courser than clay!"* [51] Evidence of Bahá'u'lláh's human station can be found in His many years of suffering. He emerged from the dungeon in Tehran walking with great difficulty, with a very bruised and swollen neck, His back bent from the weight of the chain. When describing His life, Bahá'u'lláh explained that although He had been raised with great privileges, He was also made to endure great suffering for God. *"The throat Thou didst accustom to the touch of silk Thou hast, in the end, clasped with strong chains, and the body Thou didst ease with brocades and velvets Thou hast at last subjected to the abasement of a dungeon."* [52]

Bahá'u'lláh's Divine Station

Bahá'ís regard Bahá'u'lláh as the Manifestation of God for our present age. His divine station is intrinsic to the claim that He is the fulfillment of the prophetic Promise of All Ages, the bearer of God's Greatest Name, the Glory of God, the Everlasting Father, Lord of Hosts, Spirit of Truth, and Desire of the world. "Whilst Bahá'u'lláh had spoken with the voice of God, this was not to be misconceived or misinterpreted: he was a great Being, and incarnated the names and attributes of God to an extraordinary degree, but His 'human temple' remained 'entirely distinguished' from that 'eternal Essence of Essences' that was God."[53] The Bahá'í writings are clear that Bahá'u'lláh, along with the other Messengers of God, occupied a unique position in that He was human, but was also a perfect reflection of God's attributes.

19 – The Light and the Word

In the Bahá'í writings, God is identified as a heavenly light from which all forms, bounties, and splendors radiate. *"Within every atom are enshrined the signs that bear eloquent testimony to the revelation of that Most Great Light."* [54] Founders are compared to the various dawning-points of the sun. They are one in Their capacity to convey divine light, but They also vary in Their times and places of rising. In different historical and cultural settings, They have been the light of the world in that They brought teachings that illumined higher realms, uplifted our spirits, and inspired the loftiest achievements of civilization. Their teachings are also the Word of God, guiding us to break free of ignorance and attain ever higher and deeper wisdom.

20 – Affirming Four Realms: Divine, Revelatory, Human, Natural

The metaphysics taught in the Bahá'í revelation can be interpreted as four-leveled. God is the highest level, and the Messengers or Manifestations of God occupy the second level. Humanity is below but has access to the revelatory level, yet is above the physical creation by virtue of spiritual, rational, and creative powers. As human beings, we are at the lower level of the spiritual realm, being souls able to aspire upward to higher levels of reality, or to sink downward to more material levels. 'Abdu'l-Bahá refers to a three-leveled metaphysic very succinctly in this passage: *"Know that the conditions of existence are limited to the conditions of servitude, of prophethood, and of Deity."* [55] Servitude includes the natural creation and humanity. Prophethood refers to the revelatory realm, which involves many sub-levels. Deity points to the unknowable Source of all realms.

The Natural Realm

The physical universe is divinely created, with traces of its Creator discernible throughout. It consists of the mineral realm, with a special power of attraction; the plant realm, with a special power of augmentation or growth; and the animal realm, with a special power of sensation. Human bodies are part of the physical universe. All parts of the physical universe are interdependent and evolutionary. Capacities are built-in by the Creator, but unfold gradually as conditions become conducive. The Bahá'í writings explain that everything in this world points to God. *"Know thou that every created thing is a sign of the revelation of God."* [56] We are all part of God's design: *"All beings, whether large* or small, were created perfect and complete from the first, but their perfections appear in them by degrees. The organization of God is one; the evolution of existence is one; the divine system is one." [57] The Bahá'í writing also explain that there might be life in other parts of the universe: "*Know thou that every fixed star hath its own planets, and every planet its own creatures, whose number no man can compute.*" [58] In the 1990s astronomers discovered that stars other than our own sun have planetary systems. Whether there is life on other planets, by a wider conception of life, remains an open question. Bahá'í teachings are compatible with science. "*Religion and science are the two wings upon which man's intelligence can soar into the heights, with which the human soul can progress. . . . Should a man try to fly with the wing of religion alone he would quickly fall into the quagmire of superstition, whilst on the other hand, with the wing of science alone he would also make no progress, but fall into the despairing slough of materialism.*" [59] The Bahá'í writings emphasize the harmony of science and religion, and explain that if the two are at odds with each other, it is because of human misunderstanding and superstition.

The Human Realm

Humans share some qualities in common with the natural realm and with the spiritual realm. The spiritual realm includes the lower angelic order, souls progressing beyond bodily life, and the realm in which divine commands are carried out. With rational and imaginative faculties we can discern new and higher truths, and can fashion new techniques and artistic forms. The terms human reality and soul are used interchangeably in the Bahá'í writings. But the writings explain that our true self is our soul. "*Man—the true man—is soul, not body.*" [60] We are natural and spiritual creatures, with capacities to choose and reflect unlimited spiritual qualities. "*Upon the reality of man . . . He* [God] *hath focused the radiance of all of His names and attributes, and made it a mirror of His own Self. Alone of all created things, man has been singled out for so great a favor, so enduring a bounty.*" [61] The main purpose of individual human existence is to know and to love God. Our collective purpose is to co-fashion an ever-advancing civilization, using the guidance of the most recent Founder. Human life on earth is seen as a stage of our eternal journey in the worlds of God. The Bahá'í writings explain, "The progress of the soul does not come to an end with death. It rather starts along a new line. Bahá'u'lláh teaches that great far-reaching possibilities await the soul in the other world. Spiritual progress in that realm is infinite, and no man, while on this earth, can visualize its full power and extent."[62]

The Revelatory Realm

In the Bahá'í writings the revelatory or spiritual realm is described as having three sub-levels: 1) *malakut*—the lower angelic order or the Concourse on High; 2) *jabarut*—the higher angelic order or the All-Highest Paradise, in which the revealed God acts within creation and makes commands; and 3) *lahut*—the names and attributes of Divine Consciousness, the Tongue of Grandeur, also called the Word, Logos, Holy Spirit, or Primal Will. The Manifestations traverse the human realm and the revelatory realm. This range of capacities is far beyond our comprehension. Higher still, something separates lahut (the Word) from hahut (the Divine Mystery). This boundary is the Lote Tree beyond which there is no passing, even for Manifestations. The Word of God originates in the revelatory realm, and comes to humanity at intervals of about 1000 years. It is the primary proof of the Manifestations' status, enabling Them to unseal obscure scriptural passages. Revelation has come to us in this Day with greater abundance than ever before, due to our expanded capacity. The actual process by which Bahá'u'lláh and His son 'Abdu'l-Bahá revealed verses is described in various ways. There were unpredictable visions, but guidance often came in response to questions and events. It brought an aura of vibrancy and power, and was sometimes chanted as a kind of heavenly language. Tablets sometimes appeared in Their mind's eye, showing Them what was revealed in past holy books. Bahá'í revelation has also been called a Spirit breathing new life into every frame, and an ocean of light illuminating not only what it reflects directly, but also many previously hidden mysteries.

The Divine Realm

Bahá'í writings call God the Unknowable Essence, the Hidden Treasure, the central Orb of the universe, and many other titles. But God as *hahut* cannot be known in any way, even by the Manifestations of God. *"The way is barred and to seek it is impiety."*[63] The Divine Reality might be thought of as the Source of all sources, but nothing substantive can be affirmed of this Ultimate Realm. To fully recognize our complete inability to reach this absolute height is considered a very lofty spiritual attainment. *"Far be it from*

His glory that human tongue should adequately recount His praise, or that human heart comprehend His fathomless mystery. He is, and hath ever been, veiled in the ancient eternity of His Essence, and will remain in His Reality everlastingly hidden from the sight of men."[64] Although the Manifestations of God come to explain guidance and teachings from God, it is beyond humanity's capacity to truly understand who or what God is. Instead, we are able to look to these Founders as examples and guides for our own lives.

21 – Promising a Future Savior and the Renewal of Civilization

Bahá'u'lláh taught that the Manifestations of God, Who are a reflection of God's beauty, *"will continue to the 'End that knoweth no end.'"*[65] And also, *"Once in about a thousand years shall this City* [the Word of God] *be renewed and readorned."*[66] There will always be a new set of divine teachings to guide humanity, and the next Manifestation will appear no sooner than 1000 years from 1852, when Bahá'u'lláh received His divine commission. Bahá'u'lláh explained that before then, we should not believe anyone who claims to be a Messenger from God. *"Whoso layeth claim to a Revelation direct from God, ere the expiration of a full thousand years, such a man is assuredly a lying impostor."*[67] This point is further explained, "The intimation of His [God's] Revelation to Bahá'u'lláh in the Síyáh-Chál [Black Pit] of Ṭihrán, in October 1852, marks the birth of His Prophetic Mission and hence the commencement of the one thousand years or more that must elapse before the appearance of the next Manifestation of God."[68]

22 – Essential Unity of the Revealers through the Ages

The essential unity of the Revealers is strongly emphasized in the Bahá'í writings, giving it a crucial voice in interfaith understanding and cooperation. One God has sent all the Founders, so all authentic religions are one. Bahá'u'lláh explains, *"This is the changeless Faith of God, eternal in the past, eternal in the future."*[69] God is now calling upon all people to recognize all His Manifestations. *"Know assuredly that the essence of all the Prophets of God is one and the same. Their unity is absolute. God, the Creator, saith: 'There is no distinction whatsoever among the Bearers of My Message. They all have but one purpose; their secret is the same secret. To prefer one in honor to another, to exalt certain ones above the rest, is in no wise to be permitted.'"* Although outwardly They may appear distinct, inwardly the essence of Their spirit is one and the same: *"All the Prophets are Temples of the Cause of God, Who have appeared clothed in divers attire . . . all abiding in the same tabernacle, soaring in the same heaven, seated upon the same throne, uttering the same speech, and proclaiming the same Faith."*[70] Wide recognition of these truths would eliminate the religious basis of conflict, and be a major step in uniting the world and establishing peace.[71]

23 – Laying Enduring Foundations: Greater and Lesser Covenants

Generally, covenants are agreements whereby God bestows bounties on humanity in the form of Prophets guiding our moral and spiritual well-being, in return for our recognition of Them and obedience to Their guidance. The Bahá'í writings refer to two covenants—the Greater and Lesser Covenants. The Greater Covenant is the agreement between a Manifestation and His followers regarding the promise of the next Manifestation. This assures humanity that it will always be sent new guidance, but requires our promise to live accordingly. The Lesser Covenant is a more specific agreement regarding the Manifestations' immediate successor, requiring followers to accept the authority of these successors, so as to maintain unity and integrity of the faith community. Historically, the challenge of sustaining loyalty to authorized successors has vexed humanity. Divisions darkened the history of all religions before Bahá'u'lláh. Bahá'ís believe that as part of humanity's maturation, current guidance avoids divisions and creates global unity. The coming peace was prophesied as the Day that would not be followed by night.

'Abdu'l-Bahá: Center of the Covenant (1892–1921)

Bahá'u'lláh designated 'Abdu'l-Bahá (1844–1921) as His immediate successor, making him a divinely-inspired interpreter of Bahá'í teachings. At a very young age, 'Abdu'l-Bahá, which is a title meaning the "servant of Bahá," recognized his father's station, devoted himself to serving the Cause despite great hardship, and from his early twenties onward became Bahá'u'lláh's closest companion and protector, carrying out important work on his father's behalf. Bahá'u'lláh called 'Abdu'l-Bahá the Master, the Center of the Covenant, as well as the Mystery of God—titles suggesting the ability to blend human and divine qualities. Bahá'ís regard 'Abdu'l-Bahá as the perfect exemplar of every Bahá'í ideal.

In the early part of His ministry (1892–1908) 'Abdu'l-Bahá's authority was rejected by his half-brother, Muḥammad-'Alí, which lead to recurrent problems with Turkish authorities, including the reimposition of confinement in 'Akká. Muḥammad-'Alí and his associates were denounced as covenant-breakers and were excommunicated from the Faith. During this period, 'Abdu'l-Bahá wrote his Will and Testament, in which he designated his eldest grandson, Shoghi Effendi, as the Guardian of the Faith after his passing. Throughout his life, 'Abdu'l-Bahá facilitated the formation of locally elected assemblies, as well as some national bodies. He also encouraged educational, medical, and economic development among Eastern Bahá'ís, and began the construction of the Shrine of the Báb on Mount Carmel.

In the middle part of His ministry (1908–14) 'Abdu'l-Bahá was freed from imprisonment in the Young Turk Revolution, and then moved to Haifa where he was able to complete the initial Shrine of the Báb. Then from 1910 to 1913 he went on successful missionary journeys to Egypt, Europe, and the United States and Canada. Fledgling Western Bahá'í communities were greatly strengthened, positive publicity was generated, and the body of Bahá'í scripture was expanded. Through some 27,000 letters written during his lifetime, he guided and expanded the Faith.

In His final years (1914–21) he overcame threats from the Turkish army chief, provided famine relief in the Holy Land during World War I, was awarded a knighthood for his social services, and became recognized as the head of an international religious movement. Among His most influential writings are *The Secret of Divine Civilization, Some Answered Questions, Paris Talks, The Promulgation of Universal Peace, Tablets of the Divine Plan* (which inspired many Bahá'ís to leave their home and native land, and spread the Faith throughout the world), and his Will and Testament. This final work extended Bahá'u'lláh's Covenant by giving further explanation of the "twin successors" that would be established following the passing of 'Abdu'l-Bahá. The twin successors who were to lead the Faith after 'Abdu'l-Bahá were the Guardian and the Universal House of Justice. 'Abdu'l-Bahá put great emphasis on the importance of the Covenant, calling it the *"sure handle"* that we should cling to.[72]

Shoghi Effendi: The Guardian (1921–57)
'Abdu'l-Bahá chose his eldest grandson, Shoghi Effendi (1897–1957), as his successor when Shoghi was a child, and he attended closely to the child's preparation for his future role as the Guardian. Shoghi Effendi was educated at the American University in Beirut and Oxford University in England, where he was able to master the English language. Whereas Bahá'u'lláh's and

'Abdu'l-Bahá's writings are considered scripture, Shoghi Effendi's are viewed as authoritative and binding, but not scriptural. 'Abdu'l-Bahá called him the *"priceless pearl"* and the *"sacred bough that branched from the Twin Holy Trees,"* because in him, the families of the Báb and Bahá'u'lláh were joined together.[73] He was the *"sign of God," "under the care and protection of the Abhá Beauty* [Bahá'u'lláh]."[74]

At the age of twenty-four, Shoghi Effendi became head of the Bahá'í Faith in 1921 when 'Abdu'l-Bahá passed away. Though initially shocked and overwhelmed with his responsibility, he recovered with Bahíyyih Khánum's support, and very soon developed a clear vision of the future progress of the Faith. The Guardian's productive thirty-six-year ministry ensued. His first major focus was systematizing and expanding the Bahá'í administrative order, with its two branches: the "rulers" (elected decision-makers) and the "learned" (appointed teachers and counselors). Then he developed a scripturally grounded vision of the coming World Order, translating a number of Bahá'u'lláh's and 'Abdu'l-Bahá's writings. From the late 1930s onward, the Guardian developed systematic plans by which the Faith expanded and consolidated throughout the world. These plans proved very effective. When 'Abdu'l-Bahá's ministry ended, there were Bahá'ís in thirty-five countries; and when the Guardian's ministry ended, the Faith had spread to 251 countries and territories, including all those proposed by 'Abdu'l-Bahá.

In the 1940s a serious conflict developed between the Guardian and several members of his extended family, due to their deepening contacts with Covenant-breakers, and they were eventually excommunicated. Despite some of these personal setbacks, Shoghi Effendi was able to dedicate himself to the expansion of the Faith, as well as the construction of Bahá'í sites in the Holy Land. "In the late 1940s and 1950s he began a series of major developments at the Bahá'í World Center (construction of the superstructure of the Shrine of the Báb and the International Archives building, extension and beautification of the gardens at Bahjí). During the 1950s he again turned to matters of administration: establishing the International Bahá'í Council (1950) as a precursor of the Universal House of Justice, and Auxiliary Boards (1954); and appointing Hands of the Cause (1951–57)."[75]

The Guardian's most ambitious plan was the Ten Year Spiritual Crusade. It began in 1953 and aimed to settle Bahá'ís in every nation and significant territory throughout the world, to increase markedly the number of local and national assemblies, and the number of Bahá'í centers and languages with

Bahá'í literature. The results of this endeavor surpassed expectations. Shoghi Effendi also spent a lot of time writing—he translated works of Bahá'u'lláh and 'Abdu'l-Bahá, and he also wrote many letters to Bahá'ís around the world, answering their questions and encouraging them in their service to the Bahá'í Faith. Beside his translations of scripture, the Guardian's most important writings were monograph letters, which have been published under the titles *The World Order of Bahá'u'lláh*, *The Advent of Divine Justice*, and *The Promised Day is Come*. 17,500 letters are credited to him. He also wrote a history of the first century of the Bahá'í Faith in a book titled *God Passes By*, and translated an early history of the Bábí Faith called *The Dawn-Breakers*.

'Abdu'l-Bahá established the Guardianship as hereditary, but because Shoghi Effendi had no children, no successor could be named. When he unexpectedly passed away in 1957, the Hands of the Cause, who made up the institution of the "learned" and were designated as the Bahá'í world's "chief stewards," guided and protected the Faith until the Universal House of Justice was elected in 1963.

Formation and Guidance of the Universal House of Justice (1957 =>)
Bahá'u'lláh ordained the Universal House of Justice in His writings, promising that God would inspire its members. 'Abdu'l-Bahá and the Guardian considered establishing it during their ministries, but discerned that national assemblies were not yet strong enough. Bahá'u'lláh and 'Abdu'l-Bahá had both appointed Hands of the Cause during their lives, and the Guardian continued to expand this institution by appointing twenty-seven Hands of the Cause during his life, and designating them as chief stewards of the Faith. When Shoghi Effendi passed away, the Hands of the Cause elected a temporary nine-member body called the "custodians" to head the Faith, focusing on the extensive preparations needed to elect the Universal House of Justice. Other Hands of the Cause scattered throughout the world to help complete the Ten Year Spiritual Crusade. To celebrate the completion of the Crusade, the election of the first Universal House of Justice successfully took place. The same year the worldwide Bahá'í community also celebrated that centennial of Bahá'u'lláh's declaration with a great festival and a Bahá'í world congress, held in London in 1963, with over 6200 people from all over the world in attendance.

The other main purpose of the Bahá'í world congress was the establishment of the Universal House of Justice. The electors of the Universal House of Justice were the members of the fifty-six National Assemblies in existence in 1963. Since that election, the Universal House of Justice has acted as the supreme Bahá'í administrative body. In the absence of a living Guardian, which would have been its "twin institution," the Universal House of Justice is the permanent head of the Bahá'í Faith.

Among the purposes of the Universal House of Justice are to ensure the continuity of divine guidance, to safeguard unity of the Faith, and to maintain the integrity and flexibility of its teachings. The duties and powers of the Universal House of Justice all have a textual basis in the writings as interpreted by the Guardian. These duties include promoting progress of the Faith, preserving Bahá'í writings and safeguarding their inviolability, enacting laws and ordinances not expressly recorded in the writings, and promulgating and applying laws and principles of the Faith. Its nine members are elected every five years by members of the National Spiritual Assemblies around the world at an international convention.

After the election of the Universal House of Justice, it was decided that they had not been entrusted with the capacity to elect new Hands of the Cause of God. In response to this, the Universal House of Justice created new institutions known as the Continental Boards of Counselors and the International Teaching Center. One description of the Bahá'í administrative order states, "The seat of the Universal House of Justice is located at the Bahá'í World Center on Mount Carmel in Haifa, Israel. . . . In 1964 the Universal House of Justice determined that it could not legislate to make it possible to appoint more Hands of the Cause of God. To extend the work of the Hands into the future after the Guardian's passing, the Universal House of Justice created the institutions of the Continental Boards of Counselors in 1968 and the International Teaching Center in 1973. The International Teaching Center coordinates and directs the work of the Continental Boards of Counselors. The Counselors' work is to stimulate, counsel and assist National Spiritual Assemblies and to keep the Hands of the Cause and the Universal House of Justice informed about the condition of the Faith around the world."[76]

The Guardian made a plan to construct five buildings in a harmonious architectural style, arranged as an Arc centering on the resting-places of the Holy Family on Mount Carmel, where Navváb, Bahíyyih Khánum, and Mírzá Mihdí are buried. These buildings include the Seat of the Universal House of Justice, the International Teaching Center, the International Bahá'í Archives, the Center for the Study of the Texts, and the International Bahá'í

Library. "The building projects on Mount Carmel are far more than a construction project meant to handle the growing physical needs of the Bahá'í World Center. They have deep spiritual significance." The Universal House of Justice describes the buildings on the Arc on Mount Carmel as "the visible seat of mighty institutions whose purpose is no other than the spiritualization of humanity and the preservation of justice and unity throughout the world." The importance of the construction of these buildings on Mount Carmel goes far beyond outward appearances. "The beauty and splendor of the terraces and gardens on Mount Carmel symbolize the nature of the transformation that will occur both in the hearts of the world's peoples and in the physical environment of our planet."[77]

24 – Renewing Scriptural Guidance: Book of Law, Book of Certitude, Hidden Words, Letters to Kings

All the writings of Bahá'u'lláh and the Báb are regarded as divine revelation by Bahá'ís. The writings of 'Abdu'l-Bahá are also regarded as scripture. Some of Bahá'u'lláh's most important works include the Kitáb-i-Aqdas (The Most Holy Book), the Kitáb-i-Íqán (The Book of Certitude), and the Hidden Words. Also among the most important writings are the letters to kings, which are included in a volume entitled *The Summons of the Lord of Hosts*, as well as *Gleanings from the Writings of Bahá'u'lláh*, Epistle to the Son of the Wolf, and a tablet titled Kitáb-i-'Ahd (Book of the Covenant).

25 – Generating Civilization Anew: An Ever-advancing Process

In a talk given in North America, 'Abdu'l-Bahá provided a glimpse of the coming global civilization. *"From the standpoints of both material and spiritual civilization, extraordinary progress and development will be witnessed. In this present cycle there will be an evolution in civilization unparalleled in the history of the world. The world of humanity has, heretofore, been in the stage of infancy; now it is approaching maturity. Just as the individual human organism, having attained the period of maturity, reaches its fullest degree of physical strength and ripened intellectual faculties so that in one year of this ripened period there is witnessed an unprecedented measure of development, likewise the world of humanity in this cycle of its completeness and consummation will realize an immeasurable upward progress."*[78]

What are some of the most important aspects of civilization, as understood in Bahá'í teachings? "A true and 'ever-advancing' civilization is based on the development of virtues which enhance human dignity. 'Abdu'l-Bahá emphasized that human success and prosperity depend on the combination of material progress (including wise laws; just government; the promotion of the arts and sciences; discovery; the expansion of trade; the development of industry; and the beautification of the country) with spiritual and moral guidance."[79]

Shoghi Effendi identified key structural elements of the coming global civilization, and explained that the future world commonwealth must consist of a world legislature, a world executive, a world tribunal, a mechanism of world intercommunication, a world metropolis, a world language, a world script, a world literature, and a uniform and universal system of currency, of weights and measures. "In such a world society," he states, "science and religion, the two most potent forces in human life, will be reconciled, will cooperate, and will harmoniously develop. . . . A world federal system, ruling the whole earth and exercising unchallengeable authority over its unimaginably vast resources, blending and embodying the ideals of both East and West, liberated from the curse of war. . . . A system in which Force is made the servant of Justice, whose life is sustained by its universal recognition of one God and by its allegiance to one common Revelation—such is the goal towards which humanity, impelled by the unifying forces of life, is moving."[80] There may soon arise a commonly accepted interpretation of the place of the Bahá'í Faith in the last two centuries of world history. It would need to demonstrate the impact of a new divine religion, and identify key developments in the emergence of global civilization. We live in a time of unprecedented opportunity to nurture the family of humanity. We can co-fashion an earth that reflects ever more beautifully the glory of heaven.

—

Appendix:

Patterns in the Backgrounds, Missions, Teachings, and Legacies of the Founders of Faith

Background: Heritage and Context

1 - Continuity with Previous Dispensations

Moses: claimed to fulfill the promises of Abraham, Isaac, Jacob, and Joseph

Zoroaster: claimed to fulfill the promises of ancient Persian prophets including Yima, Spitama, and Manuschir

Krishna: claimed to be in line of the ancient Indian Avatars, and to be the return of Rama

Buddha: claimed to be in line of ancient the Indian Buddhas, and to be the return of Kassapa

Christ: claimed to fulfill the promises of Moses, David, and Isaiah

Muḥammad: claimed to fulfill the promises of Jesus regarding a Counselor to come

Bahá'u'lláh: claimed to fulfill promises of Abraham, Moses, David, Zoroaster, Isaiah, Jesus, and Muḥammad

2 - Arising to Guide Humanity in the Worst of Times

Moses: arose under Egyptian Pharaoh's oppression

Zoroaster: arose during violent nomadic raids and priestly corruption in eastern Persia

Krishna: arose under the tyrant King Kamsa who oppressed and terrorized northern India

Buddha: arose during intense restlessness, economic exploitation, and
inter-tribal violence in northeast India

Christ: arose under Roman oppression and Herod's oppression

Muḥammad: arose under the Quraysh tribe's oppression, exploitation,
and spiritual abuse

Bahá'u'lláh: arose under Iranian oppression, official corruption, and
degradation

3 - *Advent Prophesied and Expected*

Moses: the Egyptian court's soothsayers prophesied that a Hebrew king
would arise

Zoroaster: the soul of creation (the voice of the earth) called out for a
righteous Savior

Krishna: a heavenly voice prophesied that King Kamsa would be killed
and righteousness would be restored

Buddha: the seer Asita prophesied that Gautama would be a world ruler
or a world redeemer

Christ: wise men from the east (Zoroastrian magi) and John the Baptist
anticipated a Savior

Muḥammad: Bahira the Christian and Salman the Persian foresaw the
coming of an Arabian Prophet

Bahá'u'lláh: Shaykhi visionaries and the Báb prophesied the coming of
the Promised One of All Ages

4 - *Auspicious Signs, Birth, and Intimations of Greatness*

Moses: set afloat on the Nile as an infant, rescued by Pharaoh's daughter, and showed early sense of righteousness

Zoroaster: virgin birth, received divine protection from evil forces, and
went through a vision quest

Krishna: born in dungeon, received divine assistance, miraculously escaped, slew demons, and bested the gods

Buddha: his mother dreamed that a white elephant entered womb, and
he made early meditative discoveries

Christ: born of a virgin, there was a star over Bethlehem, came from
Davidic heritage, at age twelve found conversing in Temple

Muḥammad: mother heard great voice and saw bright light, and at age twelve he joined the League of the Virtuous

Bahá'u'lláh: descent from David and Zoroaster, dreams of sovereignty, showed early brilliance

Mission: Purpose and Story

5 - Divine Commission

Moses: a burning bush appeared and a divine voice spoke

Zoroaster: led by an archangel to the Wise Lord's heavenly court, where He was shown visions and commissioned to teach

Krishna: called to leave childhood home, to kill King Kamsa, and to restore righteousness

Buddha: called to leave the pleasure palace, sought answers in the forest, and became enlightened under the Bodhi Tree

Christ: saw the descent of a dove during baptism by John, and a divine voice spoke

Muḥammad: had an encounter with the archangel Gabriel on Mount Hira

Bahá'u'lláh: saw a vision and heard the voice of the maid of heaven while in a dungeon

6 - Struggling in Solitude

Moses: had doubts about abilities, said He was not eloquent, went on a solitary journey back to Egypt

Zoroaster: lived in a cave, was tempted by the Evil Spirit, and feared spiritual failure

Krishna: tempted to return to childhood home due to the power of His love for family and friends

Buddha: doubts haunted His six-year spiritual search, and was tempted by the Evil One under the Bodhi Tree

Christ: experienced temptations by the devil in the wilderness

Muḥammad: had concerns about possession by spirits, and suffered a few years of divine silence

Bahá'u'lláh: withdrew to the mountains of Kurdistan, and contemplated no return

7 - Declaration and First Followers

Moses: brother Aaron and the Elders of Israel in Egypt

Zoroaster: King Vishtaspa, Queen Hutaosa, and their royal court

Krishna: the Pandava brothers and their shared wife Draupadi

Buddha: the five monks of the early forest search, and later Sariputta and Mogallana

Christ: twelve disciples who are made "fishers of men"

Muḥammad: family and close friends in Mecca

Bahá'u'lláh: small group of followers in the Garden of Riḍvan in Baghdad

8 - Overcoming Powerful Opposition: Religious and Civil Leaders

Moses: Pharoah, royal priests, and Egyptian soldiers

Zoroaster: corrupt wizards, magi, and oppressive Turanians

Krishna: Vedic priests, and oppressive kings, including Kamsa, Jara-sandha, and Duryodhana

Buddha: an evil follower, and evil princes, including Devadatta and Ajatasattu

Christ: Scribes, Pharisees, the Elders of Israel, and Roman officials

Muḥammad: Quraysh chieftains and Meccan merchants

Bahá'u'lláh: Iranian and Turkish leaders

9 - Rejection by the People

Moses: Hebrew murmurers and regression to idolatry through the golden calf incident, but their wandering through the desert brought moral training

Zoroaster: forced out by villagers, but His wandering brought spiritual strength and revelations

Krishna: many clans and kingdoms rejected Him, but war against oppressive leadership yielded cleansing and righteousness

Buddha: abused and mocked by villagers, but His teachings on the new Dharma spread

Christ: mocked and taunted by townspeople and crowds in Jerusalem, and betrayal of Judas, but the Gospel spread

Muḥammad: betrayal by hypocrites, treacherous Jews, and faithless followers, but Islam expanded

Bahá'u'lláh: angry onlookers, Mírzá Yaḥyá and his followers, but the Faith spread

10 - Sacrificial Suffering

Moses: forty years of wandering in the wilderness with "stiff-necked" people

Zoroaster: twelve years of rejected teaching and two holy wars brought despair

Krishna: sons' failure to recognize Him, and failed inter-clan diplomacy brought despair

Buddha: terrifying experiences in forest and hurtful words brought suffering

Christ: three years of abuse by Jewish and Roman authorities, then crucified

Muḥammad: social exclusion, death threats, and aggressive military opposition

Bahá'u'lláh: forty-nine years of persecution, exile, imprisonment, internal opposition

11 - Symbolic Language as a Test for Believers

Moses: followers misinterpreted the terms *sovereign, throne,* and *Messiah*

Zoroaster: followers misinterpreted the terms *fire, pollution,* and *Son of Zoroaster*

Krishna: followers misinterpreted the terms *rebirth, caste,* and *Return of Krishna*

Buddha: followers misinterpreted the terms *relics, Buddhas,* and *Maitreya Buddha*

Christ: followers misinterpreted the terms *Counselor, Spirit of Truth, Son coming in clouds*

Muḥammad: followers misinterpreted the terms *Seal of Prophets* and *Day of Resurrection*

Bahá'u'lláh: warned and taught that there would be tests and veils of symbolic language

12 - Exemplary Women for All Ages: The Nurturer and the Advocate

Moses: Miriam, His sister and a poetess, and Deborah, a judge and prophetess

Zoroaster: Dughdao, His saintly mother, and Poruchista, His fearless missionary daughter

Krishna: Rukmini, His sacrificial wife, and Draupadi, a courageous peacemaker disciple

Buddha: Mahamaya His saintly mother, and Mahaprajapati, who established an order of nuns

Christ: Mother Mary, a preeminent saint, and Mary Magdalene, who
was referred to as the apostle to apostles

Muḥammad: Khadijah, His wife and encourager, and Fatima, His
daughter and a teacher and leader

Bahá'u'lláh: Bahíyyih, His daughter and exemplar, and Ṭáhirih, a
prophetess and heroine

13 - Dying and Ascending Victoriously

Moses: upon delivering divine law, renewing Covenant, and reaching
Promised Land

Zoroaster: martyrdom at fire temple, having purified devotion and established righteous rule

Krishna: arrow in Achilles heel, having purified devotion and established righteous rule

Buddha: upon spreading the sangha and Dharma, and offering farewell lessons

Christ: upon training and empowering disciples, establishing the
church, and being crucified and resurrected

Muḥammad: upon achieving transtribal spiritual unity, and consolidating and expanding the ummah (spiritual community)

Bahá'u'lláh: upon unifying the Faith, renewing the Covenant and divine law, and appointing a successor

Teaching: Message and Guidance

14 - Transformative Teaching and Healing

Moses: delivered Hebrews from bondage, gave divine law, and reached
the Promised Land

Zoroaster: established royal patronage, abolished corruption, shared
new divine wisdom, and trained magi

Krishna: inspired devotion, trained Pandavas, won holy war, and established righteous rule

Buddha: taught new Dharma (path), healed suffering, and established
the sangha

Christ: preached the "Good News," and healed and empowered marginal groups

Muḥammad: warned Meccans, revealed the Qur'án, and established trans-tribal ties

Bahá'u'lláh: synthesized and harmonized divine guidance, wrote letters to kings, and revealed new divine laws

15 - Delivering a Thematic and Complementary Message

Moses: obeying the Covenant and divine law

Zoroaster: good thoughts, good words, and good deeds

Krishna: devotion to the Avatar and selfless action

Buddha: awakening in compassion for suffering and the attainment of nirvana

Christ: sacrificial love is a means to attain the kingdom of heaven

Muḥammad: submission to God and building a trans-tribal spiritual nation

Bahá'u'lláh: unity of Faith and humanity while building a global civilization

16 - Renewing and Embodying Universal Virtues

a) Spiritual Virtues: 1) Devotion-Faithfulness, 2) Gratitude-Reverence, 3) Self-Discipline-Obedience, 4) Detachment-Patience, 5) Wisdom-Discernment

b) Social Virtues: 1) Loving-kindness-Compassion, 2) Service-Responsibility, 3) Respect-Tolerance, 4) Justice-Righteousness, 5) Peace-Unity

c) Material Virtues: 1) Trustworthiness-Honesty, 2) Moderation-Balance, 3) Generosity-Hospitality, 4) Creativity-Beauty, 5) Earthcare-Stewardship

17 – Abrogating the Old and Establishing the New: Ritual and Legal Guidance

Moses: modified and reinterpreted cultic practices and legal precedents

Zoroaster: abolished polytheistic form of worship and established ethical monotheism

Krishna: simplified Vedic ritual, law, and caste practices; purified yoga and devotion

Buddha: eliminated castes and Brahmanism and established ethical and spiritual practices

Christ: abrogated the Mosaic holiness and purity code and emphasized inner purity

Muḥammad: abrogated and reinterpreted pagan and Judeo-Christian
practices
Bahá'u'lláh: abrogated and universalized Islamic ritual and legal precedents

18 - Human and Divine Qualities: Claiming and Exemplifying a Dual Station
Moses: meek and humble, but was also "entrusted with God's house"
Zoroaster: despaired of failure to teach many people, but also revealed
and manifested divine power
Krishna: bound by love and karma, but was also a World Teacher
Buddha: demonstrated ordinary fears, temptations, and pains, but was
also one with Dharma
Christ: did as the Father commanded, but also claimed "I and the Father are one"
Muḥammad: claimed to be "only a mortal the like of you," but also said
"whoever sees me has seen God"
Bahá'u'lláh: said He was "but a servant of God," but also represented
the "Glory of God"

19 - The Light and the Word
Moses: revealed "the Lord is my light" and "Thy Word is my lamp"
Zoroaster: described light and growth as good and darkness and decay
as bad
Krishna: revealed "Light of all lights shines beyond darkness" and that
holy names sanctify the speaker and hearer
Buddha: described light as a path and darkness as confusion and material attachment
Christ: revealed "I am the light of the world" and "In the beginning was
the Word"
Muḥammad: revealed "God is the light of heavens and earth" and "His
words are inexhaustible"
Bahá'u'lláh: revealed "He is a light not followed by darkness" and "the
Word of God endureth forever"

20 - Affirming Four Levels of Reality:
1) Divine, 2) Revelatory, 3) Human, 4) Natural
Moses: 1) The Most High, 2) Law Giver, 3) heart / mind / soul, 4) earth /
life / firmament

Zoroaster: 1) Ahura Mazda, 2) Prophets, 3) conscience, 4) world of light / dark

Krishna: 1) Brahman-Atman, 2) Avatars, 3) soul, 4) illusory material realm

Buddha: 1) Unborn, Unconditioned Realm, 2) Buddhas, 3) inner observer, 4) transient things

Christ: 1) Father / Creator, 2) Son / Word, 3) spirit / flesh, 4) earth / principalities / world

Muḥammad: 1) Eternal / Absolute, 2) Messenger / Truth, 3) heart / soul, 4) earth / creation

Bahá'u'lláh: 1) Unknowable Essence, 2) Divine Manifestations, 3) human realm, 4) nature

Legacy: Influence & Impact

21 - Promising a Future Savior and the Age of Spiritual Maturation

Moses: the Messiah will bring about the Divine Kingdom

Zoroaster: the Saoshyant will bring about the Final Triumph and Restoration

Krishna: the Kalki Avatar will bring about the New Golden Age

Buddha: the Maitreya Buddha will bring about the Pure Land of the Western Paradise

Christ: the Returned Christ will bring about the New Millennium

Muḥammad: the Promised Ones will bring about the Day of Renewal and Resurrection

Bahá'u'lláh: claimed that "the Promised Day has come," and that in the future the Most Great Peace will come, and that another Manifestation of God will appear in "not less than one thousand years"

22 - Essential Unity of the Revealers through the Ages

Moses: said "The Most High fixed the bounds of the people according to number of sons of God"

Zoroaster: said that a line of Prophets leads to the Final Triumph and Restoration

Krishna: said "I am born in every age"

Buddha: said there was "no distinction between any of the Buddhas"

Christ: said "If you believed Moses, you would believe Me" and "Before Abraham was, I am"

Muḥammad: said "Abraham, Moses, Jesus . . . no difference do We make between them"

Bahá'u'lláh: said "All the Prophets are the Temples of the Cause of God . . . seated on same throne"

23 - Laying Enduring Foundations

Moses: established Torah Laws, a Covenant, the Elders, the Judges, the Tabernacle, and the Ark of the Covenant

Zoroaster: established new laws for the Persian Empire, reformed the magi, built fire temples, and made prophecies about the Sons of Zoroaster

Krishna: renewed Eternal Law, purified devotion and yogas, and established guruship and kingship

Buddha: developed sangha discipline, moral precepts, spiritual practices, and compassionate service

Christ: established church and eucharist (communion) through Peter and Paul, and created service agencies

Muḥammad: left Qur'ánic laws, the Constitution of Medina, Hadiths, the five pillars of Islam, and Imams

Bahá'u'lláh: established a book of laws, the Center of Covenant, the Guardian, and the Universal House of Justice

24 - Renewing Scriptural Guidance

Moses: the Torah, the Prophets, and the Writings

Zoroaster: the Gathas (Divine Songs) and the Avesta (Divine Injunction)

Krishna: wrote the Bhagavad Gita (Celestial Song) and the Uddhava Gita (Farewell Address)

Buddha: the Tripitaka (Three Baskets), especially the Dhammapada (Path of Truth)

Christ: the Gospel (Good News) and the Epistles

Muḥammad: the Qur'án (Recitation) and the Hadiths (Sayings)

Bahá'u'lláh: the Kitáb-i-Aqdas (Most Holy Book), the Kitáb-i-Íqán (the Book of Certitude), the Hidden Words, and the Summons of the Lord of Hosts

25 - Generating Civilization Anew

Moses: from the "tabernacle of God" to a "holy nation," the "righteous city" of David's kingdom

Zoroaster: from small kingdom to the Persian Empire of Cyrus and Darius

Krishna: from exiled disciples to Yudishthira's righteous empire

Buddha: from a few monks to Asoka's compassionate realm based on Dharma, which eventually spread the Dharma across Asia

Christ: from small loving communities to Constantine's and Justinian's empires, which led to the eventual spread of the Gospel to most of the world

Muḥammad: from Medina, Mecca, and Arabia to ummah, a universal community of faith

Baháʾuʾlláh: from exile to a new world order, a world commonwealth, and an ever-advancing global civilization

Notes

Chapter 1

1. Written on behalf of the Universal House of Justice, *Century of Light*, p. 137.
2. Wilson, ed., *World Scripture*, p. 773.
3. The Báb, quoted in Nábil-i-A'zam, *The Dawn-Breakers*, p. 94.
4. Black Elk, *Black Elk Speaks*, p. 43.
5. Daniel 7:27.
6. Bundahishn, cited in Zaehner, ed. *Concise Encyclopedia of Living Faiths*, pp. 148–50.
7. Vishnu Purana 4.24:25–9, quoted in Momen, *The Phenomenon of Religion*, p. 252.
8. Digha Nikaya 3:76, quoted in Wilson, ed., *World Scripture*, p. 786.
9. Classic of Rites 7.1.2, quoted in Chew, *The Chinese Religion and the Bahá'í Faith*, p. 75.
10. Revelation 21:1–2, 23.
11. Qur'án 21:104.
12. 'Abdul-Bahá, *Selections from the Writings of 'Abdul-Bahá*, no. 65.2.

Chapter 2

1. Bahá'u'lláh, *Gleanings*, no. 19.1.
2. Taherzadeh, *The Revelation of Bahá'u'lláh*, Vol 1, pp. 1, 3.
3. Balyuzi, *Bahá'u'lláh*, p. 9.
4. Toynbee, *A Study of History*, pp. 319, 334, 350.
5. See Toynbee, *Christianity among the Religions of the World*, p. 104.
6. Toynbee, *A Study of History*, p. 350.

Chapter 3

1. See Kuhn, *The Structure of Scientific Revolutions*.
2. See Eck, *Encountering God: A Spiritual Journey from Bozeman to Banaras*.
3. Fenton, "Religious Founders," *The Perennial Dictionary of World Religions*, p. 262.

Chapter 4

1. Wilson, ed., *World Scripture: A Comparative Anthology of Sacred Texts*, p. 473.
2. Fenton, "Religious Founders," *The Perennial Dictionary of World Religions*, p. 263.

3. Bahá'u'lláh, The Kitáb-i-Íqán, ¶162.
4. Genesis 12:3.
5. Genesis 50:24.
6. Momen, *The Phenomenon of Religion*, p. 243.
7. Ma'ṣúmián, *Divine Educators*, p. 1.
8. Momen, *The Phenomenon of Religion*, pp. 304–305.
9. Matthew 3:11.
10. Bahá'u'lláh, The Kitáb-i-Íqán, ¶66.
11. Momen, *The Phenomenon of Religion*, p. 304.
12. Conze, *Buddhist Scriptures*, p. 36.
13. Luke 1:38.
14. Luke 2:13.
15. Fenton, "Religious Founders," *The Perennial Dictionary of World Religions*, p. 263.
16. Luke 3:22.
17. Qur'án 96:1.
18. Bahá'u'lláh, Epistle to the Son of the Wolf, p. 21
19. Momen, *The Phenomenon of Religion*, p. 305.
20. Ma'ṣúmián, *Divine Educators*, p. 8.
21. Exodus 4:10.
22. Vanamali, *The Play of God: Visions of the Life of Krishna*, p. 228.
23. Matthew 4:1–8.
24. Bahá'u'lláh, The Kitáb-i-Íqán, ¶278.
25. Momen, *The Phenomenon of Religion*, p. 305.
26. Exodus 5:1.
27. Matthew 4:19.
28. Bahá'u'lláh, The Kitáb-i-Íqán, ¶15.
29. Momen, *The Phenomenon of Religion*, p. 312.
30. Ma'ṣúmián, *Divine Educators*, p. 64.
31. Ibid., p. 84.
32. Bahá'u'lláh, *Gleanings from the Writings of Bahá'u'lláh*, no. 141.2.
33. Wilson, ed., *World Scripture*, p. 574.
34. Bahá'u'lláh, The Kitáb-i-Íqán, ¶75.
35. Momen, *The Phenomenon of Religion*, p. 442.
36. Qur'án 54:55.
37. Fenton, "Religious Founders," *The Perennial Dictionary of World Religions*, pp. 261–64.
38. Schaefer, *Beyond the Clash of Religions: The Emergence of a New Paradigm*, p. 56.
39. 'Abdu'l-Bahá, *The Secret of Divine Civilization*, p. 98.
40. Deuteronomy 6:4–5.
41. Psalm 133:1.
42. Leviticus 19:11.
43. Yasna 28.10, quoted in Wilson, ed., *World Scripture*, p. 595.
44. Yasna 60.5 quoted in Ibid., p. 198.

45. Ibid.

46. Bhagavad Gita 6.35.

47. Ibid., 9.29.

48. Ibid., 16.1.

49. Dhammapada 145.

50. Dhammapada 199.

51. Dhammapada 52.

52. Matthew 6:10.

53. Mathew 5:9.

54. Acts 24:16.

55. Hadith, quoted in Wilson, ed., *World Scripture*, p. 523.

56. Qur'án 3:103.

57. Qur'án 16:91.

58. Bahá'u'lláh, Hidden Words, Arabic, no. 1.

59. Bahá'u'lláh, *Gleanings from the Writings of Bahá'u'lláh*, no. 117.1.

60. Bahá'u'lláh, quoted in *Compilation of Compilations, vol. II*, no. 2046.

61. Momen, *The Phenomenon of Religion*, pp. 309, 311.

62. Wilson, ed., *World Scripture*, p. 465.

63. Fenton, "Religious Founders," *The Perennial Dictionary of World Religions*, p. 263.

64. Numbers 11:14, 12:3, 12:8.

65. Vanamali, *The Play of God*, p. 374.

66. See Anguttara Nikaya 4.36; Vinaya Maharagga 1.6; Majjhima Nikaya 92.17; Digha Nikaya 13.38.

67. Matthew 26:39; John 8:12; John 10:30.

68. Qur'án 41:6; 17:85; Hadith of Bukhari and Muslim, quoted in Wilson, ed., *World Scripture*, p. 465.

69. Ma'súmián, *Divine Educators*, p. 54.

70. Wilson, ed., *World Scripture*, p. 596.

71. Psalms 27:1; 119:105.

72. Bhagavad Gita 13:17.

73. Samyutta Nikaya 442, quoted in Ma'súmián, *Divine Educators*, p. 56.

74. John 1:5, 9; 9:5.

75. Qur'án 24:35; 59:23–24.

76. Bahá'u'lláh, *Tablets of Bahá'u'lláh*, p. 108; Hidden Words, Arabic, no. 12.

77. Momen, *The Phenomenon of Religion*, p. 199.

78. Wilson, ed., *World Scripture*, p. 574.

79. Exodus 4:12.

80. 'Abdu'l-Bahá, *Some Answered Questions*, p. 230.

81. Wilson, ed., *World Scripture*, p. 783.

82. Momen, *The Phenomenon of Religion*, p. 251.

83. Deuteronomy 18:18; 1 Samuel 10:1.

84. Bhagavad Gita 4:7–8, quoted in Wilson, ed., *World Scripture*, p. 474.

85. John 14:28.

86. Qur'án 43.61; Mishkat al-Masabih 3:1114, quoted in Momen, *The Phenomenon of World Religion*, p. 253.

87. Bahá'u'lláh, *Gleanings from the Writings of Bahá'u'lláh*, no. 125.10.
88. Bahá'u'lláh, The Kitáb-i-Íqán, ¶162.
89. Ma'súmián, *Divine Educators*, p. 35.
90. Exodus 3.15; Deuteronomy 18.15.
91. Bhagavad Gita 4.8.
92. Milandapaṅha, quoted in Ma'-súmián, *Divine Educators*, p. 36
93. John 5:46; Revelation 21:6.
94. Qur'án 2:136.
95. Bahá'u'lláh, *Gleanings from the Writings of Bahá'u'lláh*, no. 34.3.
96. Fenton, "Religious Founders," *The Perennial Dictionary of World Religions*, pp. 263–64.
97. Ibid., p. 262.
98. Deuteronomy 17:15.
99. Wilson, ed., *World Scripture*, p. xiii.
100. Ibid., p. 789.
101. Exodus 19:6; Isaiah 1:26.
102. Bahman Yast 3:39, quoted in Momen, *The Phenomenon of Religion*, p. 252.
103. Vishnu Purana 4:24, quoted in Ibid.
104. Matthew 6:10.
105. Bahá'u'lláh, *Gleanings from the Writings of Bahá'u'lláh*, no. 109.2.

Chapter 5

1. Genesis 3:17.
2. Genesis 4:26.
3. Bowker, ed., *The Oxford Dictionary of World Religions*, p. 16.
4. Romans 7:13–15.
5. Qur'án 2:30.
6. Qur'án 2:36.
7. Newby, *A Concise Encyclopedia of Islam*, p. 18.
8. 'Abdul-Bahá, *Some Answered Questions*, pp. 122–26.
9. *The New Oxford Annotated Bible (RSV)*, pp. 9–10, fn 7:18–20.
10. Genesis 6:9.
11. Genesis 9:20.
12. Acts 15:15–17.
13. Acts 21:15–26.
14. Qur'án 11:26.
15. Vendidad 2:22-41.
16. Bhagavad Purana 8:24.
17. Qur'án 7, 11, 26; Bahá'u'lláh, The Kitáb-i-Íqán, ¶5, 9.
18. Qur'án 7, 17, 26.
19. Qur'án 34:15, 17.
20. 1 Kings 10:9.
21. Isaiah 45:14.
22. *The Oxford Dictionary of World Religions*, p. 611.
23. Genesis 11:31.
24. Genesis 15:18; 12:3.
25. Exodus 6:3.
26. Genesis 15:5.
27. Hebrews 11:10.
28. Genesis 32:28.

29. Genesis 41:38-40.
30. Genesis 50:24.
31. Daiches, *Moses: The Man and His Vision*, p. 19.
32. Exodus 3:15.
33. See Jack, *The Date of the Exodus in the Light of External Evidence.*
34. Exodus 2:23–24.
35. Genesis 50:24.
36. Bahá'u'lláh, The Kitáb-i-Íqán, ¶68.
37. See Jack, *The Date of the Exodus in the Light of External Evidence.*
38. Exodus 2:13–14.
39. Exodus 2:19.
40. Exodus 3:5.
41. Exodus 3:8.
42. Exodus 3:11-12.
43. Exodus 3:14.
44. Exodus 3:18.
45. Bahá'u'lláh, The Kitáb-i-Íqán, ¶57.
46. Exodus 4:28.
47. Exodus 4:31.
48. Bahá'u'lláh, The Kitáb-i-Íqán, ¶57.
49. Exodus 5:22–23.
50. Exodus 7:16.
51. Qur'án 40:28.
52. Bahá'u'lláh, The Kitáb-i-Íqán, ¶12.
53. 'Abdu'l-Bahá, *Some Answered Questions*, p. 50.
54. Exodus 14:11–13.
55. Exodus 15:24–25.
56. Exodus 16:3-4.
57. Numbers 14:2–3,
58. Numbers 14:19–20.
59. Exodus 32:4.
60. Exodus 32:9.
61. Exodus 32:12–14.
62. Exodus 32:19–20.
63. Exodus 32:25–33.
64. Exodus 17:3, 6.
65. Numbers 11:1–2.
66. Numbers 11:4–5, 11, 16–18, 31.
67. Deuteronomy 9:16–18, 26.
68. Isaiah 6:9.
69. Isaiah 6:10.
70. Jeremiah 1:10.
71. Jeremiah 1:13–14.
72. Judges 5:3,9.
73. Deuteronomy 34.4–6.

Chapter 6

1. Exodus 12:35–36.
2. Exodus 14:9, 13, 16.
3. Exodus 14:21–31.
4. Exodus 12:11–14.
5. Exodus 12:11.
6. Deuteronomy 5:12.
7. Daiches, *Moses*, p. 104.
8. Ibid., p. 78.
9. Exodus 6:6–7.
10. Exodus 19:16–18.
11. Exodus 24:12.
12. Exodus 20:1–17.
13. Exodus 24:7–8.
14. Leviticus 24:22.
15. Deuteronomy 1:17.
16. Exodus 24:7.
17. Exodus 29:7.

18. Exodus 25:22.
19. Exodus 29:44–45.
20. Exodus 40:35–38.
21. Deuteronomy 1.10–11.
22. Daiches, *Moses*, p. 131.
23. Leviticus 26:9–17.
24. Numbers 6:24–26.
25. Numbers 14:10–12.
26. Numbers 14:20–24.
27. Numbers 23:21, 24:17.
28. Deuteronomy 5:33.
29. Deuteronomy 5:24–26.
30. Deuteronomy 6:4–7.
31. Deuteronomy 10:12–13.
32. Deuteronomy 12:8–12.
33. Deuteronomy 28:1–2.
34. Deuteronomy 28:15.
35. Deuteronomy 28:47–48.
36. Deuteronomy 30:19–20.
37. Psalms 139:23–24.
38. Psalms 104:24.
39. Proverbs 16:32.
40. Psalms 23:1.
41. Psalms 111:10.
42. Leviticus 19:18.
43. Micah 6:8.
44. Malachi 2:10.
45. Deuteronomy 1:17.
46. Isaiah 2:4.
47. Exodus 20:16.
48. Proverbs 22:16.
49. Proverbs 3:27.
50. Psalms 66:1.
51. Genesis 1.28.
52. Exodus 4:10.
53. Numbers 11:14.
54. Numbers 12:3.
55. Exodus 4:15.
56. Exodus 20:19.
57. Exodus 33:11; Deuteronomy 34:10.
58. Exodus 24:2.
59. Exodus 34:29–30.
60. Isaiah 42:6–7.
61. Isaiah 60:1, 3.
62. Isaiah 60:19.
63. Genesis 1:3, 6, 9.
64. Psalm 19:1.
65. Genesis 1:12
66. Genesis 2:9.
67. Genesis 1:20, 24.
68. Genesis 1:26.
69. Psalm 8:5–6.
70. Isaiah 1:18.
71. Genesis 3:7.
72. Genesis 3:17–19.
73. Isaiah 64:8.
74. Job 5:6–7.
75. Psalms 49:15, 23:6.
76. Deuteronomy 18:18.
77. Job 28:12–13, 23–24.
78. Deuteronomy 32:10–11.
79. Psalm 146:8, 145:9.
80. Psalms 33:11.
81. Exodus 33:20.
82. Psalms 145:3.
83. Isaiah 44:6.
84. Isaiah 55:8–9.
85. Job 11:7–9.
86. Deuteronomy 18:15.
87. Psalms 24:9–10.
88. Cohn-Sherbok, *A Concise Encyclopedia of Judaism*, p. 130.
89. Isaiah 9:6–7.

90. Isaiah 11:1–2.
91. Isaiah 66:18.
92. Isaiah 65:17.
93. Isaiah 2:4.
94. Daniel 7:13–14.
95. Deuteronomy 33:2.
96. Deuteronomy 33:26–27.
97. Exodus 18:21–23.
98. Numbers 11:16–17.
99. Genesis 15:18.
100. Numbers 27:18–20.
101. Deuteronomy 31:23.
102. 'Abdu'l-Bahá, *The Secret of Divine Civilization*, p. 76.
103. Deuteronomy 17:15–20.
104. 1 Samuel 16:12–13.
105. Qur'án 38:20.
106. Exodus 19:6.
107. Amos 5:24.
108. Isaiah 1:26.
109. Isaiah 40:4–5.

Chapter 7

1. See Eliade, *Encyclopedia of Religion*; Bowker, *The Oxford Dictionary of World Religions*.
2. Greenlees, *The Gospel of Zarathushtra*, p. xlvi.
3. Mehr, *The Zoroastrian Tradition: An Introduction to the Ancient Wisdom of Zarathustra*, pp. 49, 55.
4. Greenlees, *The Gospel of Zarathushtra*, pp. l–li.
5. Ibid, p. liii.
6. Ballou, *The Portable World Bible*, p. 166.

7. Greenlees, *The Gospel of Zarathushtra*, p. lv.
8. Ibid, p. lvi.
9. Ibid. p. lvii.
10. Ibid.
11. Noss, *Man's Religions*, p. 347.
12. Greenlees, *The Gospel of Zarathushtra*, p. lix–lx.
13. Ibid, p. lxx.
14. Yasna 46.1, quoted in Wilson, ed., *World Scripture*, p. 432.
15. Yasna 48.10.
16. Yasna 43.11, quoted in Ma'ṣúmián, *Divine Educators*, p. 85.
17. Yasna 34.4, quoted in Wilson, ed., *World Scripture*, p. 609.
18. Yasna 30.2, 46.10, and 53.5–9.
19. Greenlees, *The Gospel of Zarathushtra*, p. lxxiii.

Chapter 8

1. Greenlees, *The Gospel of Zarathushtra*, p. lxvi.
2. Ibid., p. lxvii.
3. Ibid., p. lxxi.
4. Shoghi Effendi, *God Passes By*, p. 183.
5. Yasna 45.2.
6. Mehr, *The Zoroastrian Tradition: An Introduction to the Ancient Wisdom of Zarathustra*, p. 29.
7. Ibid., p. 27.
8. Ibid., p. 23.
9. Yasna 34.3, quoted in Wilson, ed., *World Scripture*, p. 366.
10. Yasna 45.5, quoted in Ibid., p. 105.

11. Yasna 33.1, quoted in Ibid., p. 243.
12. Yasna 34.6, quoted in Jacques Duchesne-Guillemin, *The Hymns of Zarathustra*, p. 43.
13. Yasna 53.3, quoted in Ibid., p. 153.
14. Yasna 60.5, quoted in Wilson, ed., *World Scripture*, p. 198.
15. Sad-Dar 8.10.
16. The Counsels of Adhurbadh, Son of Mahraspand 12, 16, quoted in Zaehner, ed., *Concise Encyclopedia of Living Faiths*, p. 102.
17. The Counsels of Adhurbadh, Son of Mahraspand 5, quoted in Ibid.
18. Yasna 60.5, quoted in Wilson, ed., *World Scripture*, p. 198.
19. Mihir Yasht 10.2, quoted in Ibid., p. 41.
20. Shikand Gumani Vazar 1.11–14, quoted in Zaehner, ed., *Concise Encyclopedia of Living Faiths*, p. 86.
21. Yasna 51.21, quoted in Wilson, ed., *World Scripture*, p. 545.
22. Some Sayings of Adhurbadh, Son of Mahraspand 66, quoted in Zaehner, ed., *Concise Encyclopedia of Living Faiths*, p. 115.
23. Ibid., no. 63.
24. Yasna 29.7, quoted in Wilson, ed., *World Scripture*, p. 223.
25. Yasna 50.1, quoted in Duchesne-Guillemin, *The Hymns of Zarathustra*, p. 29.
26. Yasna 46.1, quoted in Ma'ṣúmián, *Divine Educators*, p. 65.
27. Yasna 50.6–7, quoted in Duchesne-Guillemin, *The Hymns of Zarathustra*, p. 31.
28. Yasna 34.1, quoted in Ibid., p. 41.
29. Yasna 46.3, quoted in Wilson, ed., *World Scripture*, p. 432.
30. Bowker, ed., *The Oxford Dictionary of World Religions*, p. 1070.
31. See Yasna 44.5, 19.3–4, 31.7, 1.16, 30.1, and 46.1.
32. Yasna 44.3, quoted in Wilson, ed., *World Scripture*, p. 80.
33. Yasna 50.10.
34. Yasna 30.2.
35. Yasna 48.4.
36. Yasna 46.10-11.
37. Yasna 29.8.
38. Yasna 28.5.
39. Mehr, *The Zoroastrian Tradition*, p. 43.
40. Yasna 31.3.
41. Yasna 31.8.
42. Yasna 43.5.
43. Yasna 46.9.
44. Mehr, *The Zoroastrian Tradition*, pp. 25–26.
45. Ibid., p. 38.
46. Bahman Yast 2.37.
47. Dinkard 7.8.2–10.

48. Yasna 45.11.
49. Yasna 46.3, quoted in Wilson, ed., *World Scripture*, p. 432.
50. Yasna 48.12, quoted in ibid., p. 741.
51. Yasna 51.9, quoted in Mehr, *The Zoroastrian Tradition*, p. 120.
52. Dinkard 7.
53. Bahman Yast 3.39–40.
54. Dinkard 9 and Bundahishn 34.
55. Bidez and Cumont, *Les Mages Hellenises: Zoroastre Ostanes et Hystaspe, Tome II*. Translation available online.
56. Dinkard, quoted in Ferraby, *All Things Made New*, p. 171.
57. Noss, *Man's Religions*, p. 352.
58. Bowker, ed., *The Oxford Dictionary of World Religions*, pp. 647–48.
59. Ibid., p. 1071.
60. Bahman Yast 3.39.
61. Yasna 51.1–8.
62. Yasna 51.16, 19–20.
63. Dinkard, quoted in Zaehner, ed., *Concise Encyclopedia of Living Faiths*, p. 96.
64. Mehr, *The Zoroastrian Tradition*, pp. 113–14.

Chapter 9

1. Wilson, ed., *World Scripture*, p. 10.
2. Laws of Manu 1.85, quoted in Wilson, ed., *World Scripture*, p. 307.
3. Rig Veda 1.164.46, quoted in Wilson, ed., *World Scripture*, p. 35.
4. Bhagavad Gita 4.1 (Eknath Easwaran translation).
5. Fozdar, *The God of Buddha*, p. 16.
6. Srimad Bhagavatam 10.5, quoted in Wilson, ed., *World Scripture*, p. 546.
7. Vanamali, *The Play of God*, p. 98.
8. Ibid., p. 103.
9. Ibid., p. 106.
10. Ibid., p. 164.
11. Ibid., p. 175.
12. Bhagavad Gita 7.3.
13. Rig Veda 1.164.45, quoted in Wilson, ed., *World Scripture*, p. 576.
14. Bhagavad Gita 2.42–43.
15. Bhagavad Gita 3.38.
16. Kena Upanishad 2.3, quoted in Wilson, ed., *World Scripture*, p. 56.
17. Mundaka Upanishad 1.1.6, quoted in Ibid.
18. Srimad Bhagavatam 11.3, quoted in Ibid., p. 40.
19. Vanamali, *The Play of God*, p. 334.
20. Ibid., pp. 334–35.
21. Uddhava Gita 1.1, 21–22, 26.
22. Uddhava Gita 1.29–30.
23. Vanamali, *The Play of God*, p. 361.
24. Ibid., p. 364.

Chapter 10

1. Vanamali, *The Play of God*, p. 175.
2. Ibid., pp. 186–87.
3. Ibid., pp. 203–204.
4. Ibid., p. 222.
5. Ibid., p. 223.
6. Ibid., pp. 256–58.
7. Ibid., pp. 303–304.
8. Ibid., pp. 337–38.
9. Ibid., p. 311.
10. Ibid., p. 296.
11. Ibid., p. 230.
12. Ibid., p. 307.
13. Bhagavad Gita 3.3, 6.25, 10.10.
14. Vanamali, *The Play of God*, p. 60.
15. Ibid., p. 75.
16. Ibid., p. 174.
17. Bhagavad Gita 16.5.
18. Bhagavad Gita 9.34.
19. Bhagavad Gita 18.57.
20. Bhagavad Gita 5.23.
21. Bhagavad Gita 2.48.
22. Bhagavad Gita 2.55.
23. Bhagavad Gita 12.13.
24. Bhagavad Gita 3.19–20.
25. Bhagavad Gita 9.32.
26. Mahabharata, Anussana Parva 113.8, quoted in Wilson, ed., *World Scripture*, p. 114.
27. Bhagavad Gita 15.15.
28. Bhagavad Gita 16.1.
29. Bhagavad Gita 6.16–17.
30. Bhagavad Gita 17.20.
31. Bhagavad Gita 3.10.
32. Bhagavad Gita 9.10.
33. Bhagavad Gita 17.11.
34. Bhagavad Gita 12.12.
35. Bhagavad Gita 9.26–28.
36. Bhagavad Gita 9.16.
37. Bhagavad Gita 9.32.
38. Vanamali, *The Play of God*, p. 228.
39. Ibid., p. 374.
40. Bhagavata Purana 1.3.27, quoted in Bowker, ed., *The Oxford Dictionary of World Religions*, p. 559.
41. Bhagavad Gita 5.16.
42. Bhagavad Gita 10.11, 10.38.
43. Bhagavad Gita 13.33, 8.13.
44. Uddhava Gita 20.24–25.
45. Bhagavad Gita 13.20–21.
46. Uddhava Gita 19.18.
47. Bhagavad Gita 14.11–13.
48. Bhagavad Gita 18.65.
49. Bhagavata Purana 1.3.27, quoted in Bowker, ed., *The Oxford Dictionary of World Religions*, p. 559.
50. Vanamali, *The Play of God*, pp. xv–xvi.
51. Ibid, p. 230.
52. Bhagavad Gita 8.18.
53. Bhagavad Gita, 10.33–41.
54. Bhagavad Gita 4.7–8.
55. Srimad Bhagavatam 1.1, quoted in Wilson, ed., *World Scripture*, p. 467.
56. Vishnu Purana 4.24, quoted in Momen, *The Phenomenon of Religion*, p. 252.
57. Mahabharata, quoted in Narasimhan, *The Mahabharata: An English Version Based on Selected Verses*, p. 195.

58. Mahabharata 12.56.44–45, quoted in Zimmer, *Philosophies of India*, p. 127, fn 43.
59. Vanamali, *The Play of God*, p. 327.
60. Bhagavad Gita 10.41.
61. Uddhava Gita 20.2, 5.

Chapter 11

1. Samyutta Nikaya 2.106, quoted in Wilson, ed., *World Scripture*, p. 473.
2. Conze, *Buddhist Scriptures*, p. 19.
3. Ibid., p. 24.
4. Anagatavamsa, quoted in Wilson, ed., *World Scripture*, p. 786.
5. Digha Nikaya 3.76, quoted in Ibid., p. 786.
6. Armstrong, *Buddha*, p. 20.
7. Strong, *The Buddha: A Short Biography*, p. 35.
8. Conze, *Buddhist Scriptures*, pp. 36–37.
9. Ibid., p. 36.
10. Smith, *The World's Religions*, pp. 82–83.
11. Strong, *The Buddha: A Short Biography*, p. 45.
12. Conze, *Buddhist Scriptures*, pp. 41–43.
13. Strong, *The Buddha: A Short Biography*, p. 52.
14. Ibid., pp. 52–53.
15. Smith, *The World's Religions*, p. 84.
16. Fozdar, *The God of Buddha*, pp. 2–4.
17. Conze, *Buddhist Scriptures*, p. 46.
18. Ibid., pp. 47–48.
19. Mahavagga, quoted in Momen, *The Phenomenon of Religion*, p. 306.
20. Smith, *The World's Religions*, pp. 86–87.
21. Strong, *The Buddha: A Short Biography*, p. 76.
22. Dhammapada 154.
23. Majjhima Nikaya 5.26, quoted in Fozdar, *The God of Buddha*, p. 11.
24. Mahavagga 1.6, quoted in Ibid., p. 12.
25. Anguttara Nikaya 2.193, quoted in Wilson, ed., *World Scripture*, p. 431.
26. Armstrong, *Buddha*, pp. 164–72.
27. Mahavagga 1.43, quoted in Wilson, ed., *World Scripture*, p. 431.
28. Dhammapada Commentary, quoted in Wilson, ed., *World Scripture*, pp. 431–32.
29. Smith, *The World's Religions*, p. 85.
30. Dhammapada 320.
31. Dhammapada 11–12.
32. Majjhima Nikaya 63, quoted in Coward, *Scripture in the World Religions: A Short Introduction*, p. 153.
33. Crim, ed., *Perennial Dictionary of World Religions*, p. 808.
34. Smith, *The World's Religions*, p. 99.

Chapter 12

1. Strong, *The Buddha: A Short Biography*, p. 88.
2. Ibid.
3. Ibid, p. 90.
4. Samyutta Nikaya 35.28, quoted in Wilson, ed., *World Scripture*, p. 271.
5. Smith, *The World's Religions*, p. 91.
6. Strong, *The Buddha: A Short Biography*, pp. 90–91.
7. Fozdar, *The God of Buddha*, p. 15.
8. Strong, *The Buddha: A Short Biography*, p. 99.
9. Ibid, pp. 96–97.
10. Ibid., pp. 101–107.
11. Smith, *The World's Religions*, pp. 99–112.
12. Dhammapada 326.
13. Dhammapada 327.
14. Mahavagga 1.1, quoted in Armstrong, *Buddha*, p. 107.
15. Armstrong, *Buddha*, pp. 107–108.
16. Udana 80 quoted in Wilson, ed., *World Scripture*, p. 48.
17. Majjhima Nikaya 26, 36, 85, 100.
18. Sutta Nipata 118, quoted in Wilson, ed., *World Scripture*, p. 160.
19. Dhammapada 168.
20. Paramita: The Ten Perfections, quoted in Powers, *A Concise Encyclopedia of Buddhism*, p. 161
21. Dhammapada 24.
22. Anguttara Nikaya 1.61, quoted in Wilson, ed., *World Scripture*, p. 556.
23. Dhammapada 14.
24. Dhammapada 83.
25. Dhammapada 59.
26. Khuddaka Patha, Metta Sutta, quoted in Wilson, ed., *World Scripture*, p. 685.
27. Itivuttaka 65, quoted in Wilson, ed., *World Scripture*, p. 698.
28. Dhammapada 50.
29. Dhammapada 132.
30. Dhammapada 100.
31. Dhammapada 257.
32. Dhammapada 8.
33. Dhammapada 177.
34. Sutta Nipata 261, quoted in Wilson, ed., *World Scripture*, p. 564.
35. Dhammapada 49.
36. Wilson, ed., *World Scripture*, p. 191, fn Dhammapada 393, 396.
37. Dhammapada 396.
38. Anguttara Nikaya 4.44–45, quoted in Wilson, ed., *World Scripture*, p. 617.
39. Sutta Nipata 249, quoted in Ibid., p. 614.
40. Udana 6, Ibid.
41. See Bowker, ed., *The Oxford Dictionary of World Religions*; Crim, ed., *The Perennial Dictionary of World Religions*.

42. Buddhacarita 28.69, quoted in Wilson, ed., *World Scripture*, p. 609.
43. Strong, *The Buddha: A Short Biography*, pp. 5–6.
44. Anguttara Nikaya 2.69–70.
45. Digha Nikaya 3.61, quoted in Wilson, ed., *World Scripture*, p. 751.
46. See Carus, comp., *The Gospel of Buddha*, ¶5, 6, 12.
47. Dhammapada 271–72.
48. Majjhima Nikaya 92.17, 19, quoted in Borg, ed., *Jesus and Buddha: The Parallel Sayings*, p. 211.
49. Digha Nikaya 3.84, quoted in Fozdar, *The God of Buddha*, p. 16.
50. Samyutta Nikaya 3.120, quoted in Wilson, ed., *World Scripture*, p. 465.
51. Vajracchedika 176, 11a, quoted in Fozdar, *The God of Buddha*, p. 20.
52. Udana 73, quoted in Wilson, ed., *World Scripture*, p. 454.
53. Digha Nikaya 14.1.17, quoted in Borg, *Jesus and Buddha*, p. 195.
54. See Eliade, ed., *Encyclopedia of Religion*; Powers, ed., *A Concise Encyclopedia of Buddhism*.
55. Sutta Nipata 654, quoted in Wilson, ed., *World Scripture*, p. 102.
56. Dhammapada 160–61.
57. Dhammapada 166.
58. Samyutta Nikaya 3.120, quoted in Wilson, ed., *World Scripture*, p. 465.
59. Digha Nikaya 3.135, quoted in Fozdar, *The God of Buddha*, p. 26.
60. Digha Nikaya 1.46, quoted in Fozdar, *The God of Buddha*, p. 23.
61. Lankavatara Sutra 61, quoted in Wilson, ed., *World Scripture*, p. 102.
62. Lion's Roar of Queen Srimala 5, quoted in Wilson, ed., *World Scripture*, p. 466.
63. Digha Nikaya 3.76, quoted in Wilson, ed., *World Scripture*, p. 786.
64. Conze, *Buddhist Scriptures*, p. 237.
65. Conze, *Buddhist Scriptures*, pp. 238–42.
66. Milandapanha, quoted in de Bary, *The Buddhist Tradition in India, China and Japan*, pp. 31–32.
67. Sukhavativyuha, in Conze, *Buddhist Scriptures*, pp. 232–36.
68. Fozdar, *The God of Buddha*, p. 14.
69. Milandapanha, p. 285, quoted in Ibid., p. 14.
70. Samyutta Nikaya 2.106, quoted in Wilson, ed., *World Scripture*, p. 389.

71. Armstrong, *Buddha*, pp. 157–58, a translation of Dhammapada 183–85.
72. Bowker, ed., *The Oxford Dictionary of World Religions*, pp. 100, 304.
73. Strong, *The Buddha: A Short Biography*, pp. 117–20, 8–10.
74. Momen, *The Phenomenon of Religion*, p. 10.
75. Maitreya-vyakarana, quoted in Momen, *The Phenomenon of Religion*, p. 252.
76. Digha Nikaya 3.59–62, quoted in Wilson, ed., *World Scripture*, p. 200.
77. Anguttara Nikaya 2.75, quoted in Ibid., p. 757.
78. Golden Light Sutra 12, quoted in Ibid., p. 750.

Chapter 13

1. John 5:45–46.
2. Matthew 5:17.
3. Hebrews 1:1–2.
4. Isaiah 22:17–18.
5. Isaiah 7:13–14
6. Isaiah 9:6–7.
7. Jeremiah 13:20.
8. Jeremiah 31:31.
9. Ezekiel 12:13
10. Ezekiel 12:15.
11. Ezekiel 37:26.
12. Daniel 7:13–14.
13. Isaiah 40:3.
14. Malachi 3:1.
15. Luke 1:15–17.
16. Luke 1:76.
17. Matthew 3:1.
18. Matthew 3:11.
19. Matthew 11:11, 14.
20. John 3:30.
21. John 1:14.
22. Isaiah 7:14.
23. Luke 1.32–33.
24. Luke 2:32.
25. Luke 2:10–11.
26. Matthew 2:1–11.
27. Isaiah 60:6.
28. Psalms 72:10–11.
29. Matthew 2:16–18.
30. Luke 2:41–52.
31. John 2:11.
32. Matthew 3.14-17
33. Qur'an 5:110.
34. Smith, *A Concise Encyclopedia of the Bahá'í Faith*, p. 214.
35. Matthew 4:1–11.
36. Matthew 4:17–19.
37. Luke 4:18–21.
38. Luke 6:12–14.
39. Mark 8:29.
40. Mark 14:61–62.
41. Matthew 9:11–12.
42. Matthew 12:8–14.
43. Matthew 12:24.
44. John 8:37.
45. Matthew 16:21.
46. Matthew 21:12–13.
47. John 18:19–23.
48. Matthew 26:3-4.
49. John 5:18.

50. John 11:47–53.
51. Matthew 8:20.
52. Matthew 8:34.
53. John 10:20.
54. Matthew 10:16–22.
55. Matthew 11:19.
56. Matthew 13:54–57.
57. Matthew 5:11–12.
58. Luke 17:25-26.
59. John 16:2.
60. Matthew 26:14–16.
61. John 1:29.
62. Matthew 16:24–25.
63. John 15:13.
64. John 10:11.
65. Matthew 26:65–67.
66. Luke 8:10.
67. Luke 8.15.
68. 2 Corinthians 3:6.
69. 1 Corinthians 2:12–14.
70. John 17:1, 7.
71. Matthew 24:29–30.
72. Luke 1:46–55.
73. Qur'án 3:45, 47.
74. John 20:16–18.
75. Bowker, ed., *The Oxford Dictionary of World Religions*, p. 625.
76. Matthew 26:47–48.
77. Mark 15:15, 20.
78. Matthew 27:20–24
79. Matthew 27:39–43.
80. Luke 23:34, 44-46.
81. Matthew 27:51–54.
82. Luke 24:5–8.
83. Matthew 28:5–7.

84. Qur'án 3:55.
85. Qur'án 4:157.
86. 'Abdu'l-Bahá, *Some Answered Questions*, p. 104.

Chapter 14

1. Acts 10:38.
2. Luke 19:10.
3. John 12:47.
4. Matthew 6:10.
5. Luke 14:27, 33.
6. Luke 21:24–25.
7. Matthew 22:36–40.
8. Luke 6:27–31.
9. Matthew 7:17, 20.
10. Romans 5:3–4.
11. I Thessalonians 5:16–18.
12. Luke 11:28.
13. Romans 12:2.
14. James 3:17.
15. Luke 6:27–28.
16. Philippians 2:4.
17. Colossians 3:12–13.
18. Acts 10:34.
19. Matthew 26:52.
20. Luke 16.10.
21. Hebrews 13:5.
22. 1 John 3:17.
23. Romans 12:6.
24. Matthew 6:28–29.
25. Mark 2:27.
26. Matthew 19:5–6.
27. Matthew 15:6, 11.
28. Matthew 5:44.
29. Romans 2:29.
30. Mark 1:8.

31. John 3:5.
32. Matthew 28.19.
33. Parrinder, *A Concise Encyclopedia of Christianity*, p. 34.
34. 1 Corinthians 11:23–25.
35. Qur'án 2.87.
36. Baháu'lláh, *Gleanings*, no. 36.2.
37. Matthew 11:29.
38. Matthew 19:17.
39. John 5:30.
40. John 7:16.
41. John 8:42; 14:31.
42. Matthew 26:39.
43. Matthew 27:46.
44. Matthew 8:27.
45. Matthew 9:6; 12:8.
46. Matthew 11:27.
47. Matthew 17:2–5.
48. Luke 22:68.
49. Matthew 28:18.
50. John 1:1, 14.
51. John 8:23.
52. John 8:58.
53. John 10:30, 38.
54. John 14:9.
55. John 14:6.
56. John 1.9.
57. John 8:12.
58. John 12:36.
59. 1 John 1:5.
60. Romans 1:20.
61. Galatians 5:22–23.
62. 2 Corinthians 4:16–18.
63. Luke 10:20.
64. Romans 7:15, 23.
65. Romans 8:5.
66. Matthew 4:4.
67. John 12:50.
68. John 18:36.
69. Hebrews 1:3.
70. Ephesians 4:6.
71. 1 Corinthians 8:6.
72. Revelation 1:8.
73. Daniel 9:27.
74. Luke 21:24.
75. John 16.12–13.
76. Acts 2:17–21.
77. Revelation 21:1–4.
78. Luke 3:38.
79. Hebrews 1:1.
80. John 1:14.
81. Matthew 17:12–13.
82. John 8:58.
83. Luke 24:26–27, 44.
84. John 5:46.
85. John 15:26–27.
86. Matthew 16:15–19.
87. John 21:15–17.
88. Matthew 18:20.
89. Luke 21:15.
90. Matthew 28:18–20.
91. Acts 10:15
92. 'Abdu'l-Bahá, *Promulgation of Universal Peace*, pp. 100–101.
93. Acts 17.22–31.
94. Matthew 5:3–10.
95. Matthew 6:10.
96. Luke 2:30–35.
97. John 15:8.
98. John 18:36.

Chapter 15

1. Qur'án 4:163.
2. Qur'án 42:13.

3. Genesis 21:17–21.
4. Qur'án 14:37.
5. Deuteronomy 33:2.
6. John 14:16.
7. John 14:26, 15:26.
8. John 16:7–8.
9. Hadith, quoted in Armstrong, *Muhammad: A Biography of the Prophet*, p. 103.
10. Qur'án 93:6–11.
11. Bahá'u'lláh, The Kitáb-i-Íqán, ¶71.
12. Hadith, quoted in Armstrong, *Muhammad: A Biography of the Prophet*, p. 83.
13. Qur'án 96:1–5, 97:1–5.
14. Hadith, quoted in Armstrong, *Muhammad: A Biography of the Prophet*, p. 84.
15. Ibid., p. 85.
16. Qur'án 41:3–8.
17. Qur'án 6:34.
18. Monajem, *Stories of the Life of Muhammad*, p. 42.
19. Qur'án 2:85–86.
20. Qur'án 6:34.
21. Qur'án 34.43.
22. Qur'án 6.33–35.
23. Qur'án 30:58–59.
24. Qur'án 3:7.
25. Qur'án 33:40.
26. Qur'án 3:85.
27. Qur'án 5:3.
28. Qur'án 3:19.
29. Qur'án 6:67.
30. Qur'án 7:34.
31. Qur'án 13:38–39.
32. Qur'án 36:51–52.
33. Qur'án 39:69.
34. Lawrence, *The Qur'an: A Biography*, p. 53.
34. Hadith, quoted in Monajem, *Stories of the Life of Muhammad*, p. 213.
36. Ibn Ishaq, quoted in Armstrong, *Muhammad: A Biography of the Prophet*, p. 256.
37. Ibn Ishaq, Sirat Rasul Allah, no. 1012, quoted in Ibid., p. 257.
38. Qur'án 3:144.

Chapter 16

1. Qur'án 56:77–80.
2. Qur'án 13:38.
3. Qur'án 7:34.
4. Qur'án 4:80.
5. Qur'án 2:177.
6. Qur'án 33:35.
7. Qur'án 3:41.
8. Qur'án 57:16.
9. Qur'án 33:70–71.
10. Qur'án 3:31.
11. Qur'án 2:256.
12. Qur'án 2:267.
13. Qur'án 49:13.
14. Qur'án 2:284.
15. Qur'án 79:6.
16. Qur'án 81:1–14.
17. Qur'án 17:71.
18. Qur'án 5:48.
19. Qur'án 2:177.
20. Qur'án 73:8.
21. Qur'án 55:10–13.

22. Qur'án 2:158.
23. Qur'án 2:153.
24. Qur'án 12:105.
25. Hadith of Bukhari and Muslim, quoted in Novak, ed., *The World's Wisdom: Sacred Texts of the World's Religions*, p. 315.
26. Qur'án 5:48.
27. Qur'án 2:256.
28. Qur'án 4:135.
29. Qur'án 42:13.
30. Qur'án 5:119.
31. Qur'án 31:18–19.
32. Qur'án 30:38.
33. Qur'án 6:165.
34. Qur'án 2:30–31.
35. Qur'án 2:106.
36. Qur'án 22:26–27.
37. Hadith of Bukhari, quoted in Wilson, ed., *World Scripture*, p. 466.
38. Hadith of Bukhari and Muslim, quoted in Cleary, *The Wisdom of the Prophet*, p. 24.
39. Ibid., pp. 19, 24.
40. Qur'án 14:11.
41. Qur'án 18:110.
42. Qur'án 62:2.
43. Hadith of Bukhari and Muslim, quoted in Wilson, ed., *World Scripture*, p. 465.
44. Qur'án 4:80.
45. Qur'án 2:285.
46. Qur'án 33:21.
47. Qur'án 68:4.
49. Qur'án 48:10.

50. Qur'án 17:1.
51. Qur'án 42:52.
52. Qur'án 14:1.
53. Qur'án 24:35.
54. Qur'án 86:13.
55. Qur'án 18:109.
56. Qur'án 31:27.
57. Qur'án 2:164.
58. Qur'án 6:95.
59. Qur'án 7:54.
60. Qur'án 23:12–14.
61. Qur'án 30.25.
62. Qur'án 12:53.
63. Qur'án 21:35.
64. Qur'án 31:20.
65. Qur'án 9:33.
66. Qur'án 6:103.
67. Qur'án 57:3.
68. Qur'án 59:23–24.
69. Qur'án 61:6.
70. Qur'án 27.87.
71. Qur'án 39:68–69.
72. Qur'án 43:61.
73. Hadith, quoted in Cleary, *The Wisdom of the Prophet*, p. 29.
74. Mishkat al-Masabih 3:1141, quoted in Momen, *The Phenomenon of Religion*, p. 253.
75. Nahjul Balagha Sermon 141 and 187, quoted in Wilson, ed., *World Scripture*, p. 785.
76. Qur'án 14:48.
77. Qur'án 21:104–105.
78. Qur'án 22:56.
79. Qur'án 34:26.
80. Qur'án 78:17-20.

81. Qur'án 2:136.
82. Qur'án 42:13.
83. Hadith (Shí'ah Collection), quoted in Nasr, *Muhammad: Man of God,* pp. 64, 67.
84. Mishkat al-Masabih 3:1141, quoted in Momen, *The Phenomenon of Religion,* p. 253.
85. Qur'án 2:106.
86. Qur'án 16:101–102.
87. Qur'án 6:67.
88. Qur'án 13:38.
89. Qur'án 49:10.
90. Qur'án 59:10.
91. Hadith of Bukhari and Muslim, quoted in Cleary, *The Wisdom of the Prophet,* p. 118.

Chapter 17
1. Genesis 12:3.
2. Bahá'u'lláh, *Gleanings from the Writings of Bahá'u'lláh,* no. 30.1
3. Smith, *A Concise Encyclopedia of the Bahá'í Faith,* p. 204.
4. Mishkat al-Masabih 3.1141 quoted in Momen, *The Phenomenon of Religion,* p. 253.
5. Abú Dáwud, Sunan, Kitab al-Mahdi, Vol 2, p. 422, quoted in Momen, *Islam and the Bahá'í Faith,* p. 120.
6. Kitab al-Irshad, quoted in Momen, *The Phenomenon of Religion,* p. 253.
7. Momen, *Islam and the Bahá'í Faith,* pp. 187, 189.

8. Fathea'zam, *The New Garden,* p. 27.
9. Smith, *A Concise Encyclopedia of the Bahá'í Faith,* p. 56.
10. Fathea'zam, *The New Garden,* pp. 27–28.
11. The Báb, quoted in Nabil-i-A'zam, *The Dawn-Breakers,* p. 94.
12. Qur'án 56:1, 4–5, 10.
13. The Báb, quoted in Nabíl-i-A'zam, *The Dawn-Breakers,* pp. 315–16.
14. Ṭáhirih, quoted in Ibid., p. 286.
15. Ibid., pp. 294–95.
16. Ṭáhirih, quoted in Sears, *Release the Sun,* pp. 115–20.
17. Smith, *A Concise Encyclopedia of the Bahá'í Faith,* p. 180.
18. Balyuzi, *Bahá'u'lláh,* p 27; The Báb, *Selections from the Writings of the Báb,* nos. 3:8:1, 3:27:1.
19. Prepared by the National Spiritual Assembly of the United States, *So Great an Honor: Becoming a Bahá'í,* pp. 12–13.
20. Shoghi Effendi, *God Passes By,* p. 94.
21. 'Abdu'l-Bahá, *Some Answered Questions,* p. 27.
22. Balyuzi, *Bahá'u'lláh,* p. 10.
23. Townshend, *The Promise of All Ages,* p. 106.
24. Bahá'u'lláh, quoted in Nabíl-i-A'zam, *The Dawn-Breakers,* p. 608.

25. Bahá'u'lláh, Epistle to the Son of the Wolf, pp. 20–21.
26. Balyuzi, *Bahá'u'lláh*, p. 17.
27. Bahá'u'lláh, Epistle to the Son of the Wolf, pp. 21–22.
28. Bahá'u'lláh, quoted in Shoghi Effendi, *God Passes By*, pp. 101–2.
29. Balyuzi, *Bahá'u'lláh*, p. 21.
30. Bahá'u'lláh, *Gleanings from the Writings of Bahá'u'lláh*, no. 3.1.
31. Balyuzi, *Bahá'u'lláh*, p. 35.
32. Shoghi Effendi, *God Passes By*, p. 153.
33. Bahá'u'lláh, *Gleanings from the Writings of Bahá'u'lláh*, no. 14.18.
34. Bahá'u'lláh, quoted in Shoghi Effendi, *God Passes By*, p. 190.
35. 'Abdu'l-Bahá, *Some Answered Questions*, pp. 35, 31.
36. Bahá'u'lláh, *Gleanings from the Writings of Bahá'u'lláh* no. 100.6.
37. Bahá'u'lláh, Epistle to the Son of the Wolf, p. 77.
38. Bahá'u'lláh, *Gleanings from the Writings of Bahá'u'lláh*, no. 141.2.
39. See Smith, *A Concise Encyclopedia of the Bahá'í Faith*, pp. 86–87.
40. Bahá'u'lláh, *Tablets of Bahá'u'lláh*, pp. 4–5.
41. Isaiah 2:2–3.
42. Balyuzi, *Bahá'u'lláh*, p. 65.
43. Bahá'u'lláh, in *Compilation of Compilations*, vol. II, no. 1578.
44. Smith, *A Concise Encyclopedia of the Baha'i Faith*, pp. 114–15.
45. Bahá'u'lláh, quoted in Shoghi Effendi, *God Passes By*, p. 222.
46. Shoghi Effendi, *God Passes By*, pp. 222–23.

Chapter 18
1. 'Abdu'l-Bahá, *Some Answered Questions*, p. 30.
2. Bahá'u'lláh, The Seven Valleys, p. 65.
3. Balyuzi, *Bahá'u'lláh*, p. 26;
4. Bahá'u'lláh, The Hidden Words, p. 3.
5. Smith, *A Concise Encyclopedia of the Bahá'í Faith*, p. 181.
6. Hatcher, *The Ocean of His Words*, pp. 247–52.
7. Bahá'u'lláh, quoted in Shoghi Effendi, *God Passes By*, p 147.
8. Bahá'u'lláh, The Kitáb-i-Aqdas, ¶89.
9. Shoghi Effendi, *God Passes By*, p. 157;
10. Balyuzi, *Bahá'u'lláh*, p. 36.
11. Bahá'u'lláh, *Summons of the Lord of Hosts*, no. 5.58–59.
12. Bahá'u'lláh, quoted in Shoghi Effendi, *God Passes By*, p. 161.
13. Bahá'u'lláh, *Summons of the Lord of Hosts*, no. 1.180–82.

14. Prepared by the National Spiritual Assembly of the United States, *So Great an Honor: Becoming a Bahá'í,* pp. 17–18.
15. Psalms 24:9–10.
16. Hosea 2:15.
17. Micah 7:12–13.
18. Ezekiel 43:1.
19. Isaiah 35:2
20. Bahá'u'lláh, Epistle to the Son of the Wolf, p. 179
21. Bahá'u'lláh, quoted in Shoghi Effendi, *God Passes By,* p. 184.
22. Balyuzi, *Bahá'u'lláh,* pp. 311, 313.
23. Bahá'u'lláh, *Summons of the Lord of Hosts,* no. 1.138.
24. Bahá'u'lláh, *Summons of the Lord of Hosts,* no. 1.172–73;
25. Balyuzi, *Bahá'u'lláh,* p. 51.
26. Bahá'u'lláh, *Summons of the Lord of Hosts,* nos. 1.102–3, 1.106, 1.113.
27. Bahá'u'lláh, The Kitáb-i-Aqdas, ¶90, 88.
28. Revelation 21:1
29. Smith, *A Concise Encyclopedia of the Bahá'í Faith,* pp. 43–44.
30. Balyuzi, *Bahá'u'lláh,* p. 58.
31. Esslemont, *Bahá'u'lláh and the New Era,* p. 41.
32. Bahá'u'lláh, *Tablets of Bahá'u'lláh,* p. 14
33. 'Abdu'l-Bahá, *The Secret of Divine Civilization,* p 98.
34. Bahá'u'lláh, *Prayers and Meditations,* p. 248.
35. Bahá'u'lláh, in *Bahá'í Prayers,* p.140.
36. Bahá'u'lláh, *Tablets of Bahá'u'lláh,* p. 35.
37. Bahá'u'lláh, *Gleanings from the Writings of Bahá'u'lláh,* no. 128.3.
38. Bahá'u'lláh, *Tablets of Bahá'u'lláh,* p. 39.
39. Bahá'u'lláh, *Gleanings from the Writings of Bahá'u'lláh,* no. 132.3.
40. Bahá'u'lláh, *Tablets of Bahá'u'lláh,* p. 138.
41. Ibid., p. 22.
42. Ibid., p. 64.
43. Bahá'u'lláh, *Gleanings from the Writings of Bahá'u'lláh,* no. 4.1.
44. Bahá'u'lláh, quoted in Shoghi Effendi, *Advent of Divine Justice,* p. 26.
45. Bahá'u'lláh, *Tablets of Bahá'u'lláh,* p. 169.
46. Bahá'u'lláh, *Gleanings from the Writings of Bahá'u'lláh,* no. 130.1.
47. Bahá'u'lláh, Epistle to the Son of the Wolf, p. 26.
48. 'Abdu'l-Bahá, *Selections from the Writings of 'Abdu'l-Bahá,* no. 137.2.
49. Smith, *A Concise Encyclopedia of the Bahá'í Faith,* p. 224.
50. Bahá'u'lláh, Epistle to the Son of the Wolf, p. 11.
51. Bahá'u'lláh, Kitáb-i-Aqdas, Notes, no. 160.

52. Bahá'u'lláh, quoted in Shoghi Effendi, *God Passes By*, p. 109.

53. Smith, *A Concise Encyclopedia of the Bahá'í Faith*, p. 79.

54. Bahá'u'lláh, *Gleanings from the Writings of Bahá'u'lláh*, no. 90.1.

55. 'Abdu'l-Bahá, *Some Answered Questions*, p. 230.

56. Bahá'u'lláh, *Gleanings from the Writings of Bahá'u'lláh*, no. 93.1.

57. 'Abdu'l-Bahá, *Some Answered Questions*, p. 198.

58. Bahá'u'lláh, *Gleanings from the Writings of Bahá'u'lláh*, no. 82.11.

59. 'Abdu'l-Bahá, *Paris Talks*, no. 44.14.

60. 'Abdu'l-Bahá, *Paris Talks*, no. 28.6.

61. Bahá'u'lláh, *Gleanings from the Writings of Bahá'u'lláh*, no. 27.2.

62. Written on behalf of Shoghi Effendi, *Lights of Guidance*, no. 683.

63. Bahá'u'lláh, The Seven Valleys, p. 37;

64. Bahá'u'lláh, *Gleanings from the Writings of Bahá'u'lláh*, no. 19.1.

65. Bahá'u'lláh, The Kitáb-i-Íqán, ¶178.

66. Bahá'u'lláh, *Gleanings from the Writings of Bahá'u'lláh*, nos. 125.10.

67. Ibid., no. 166.1.

68. Bahá'u'lláh, The Kitáb-i-Aqdas, Notes, no. 62.

69. Bahá'u'lláh, *Tablets of Bahá'u'lláh*, p. 196.

70. Bahá'u'lláh, *Gleanings from the Writings of Bahá'u'lláh*, nos. 34.3, 22.3.

71. See Isaiah 60:11; Revelation 21:22–25.

72. 'Abdul-Bahá, *Selections from the Writings of 'Abdu'l-Bahá*, no. 177.3.

73. 'Abdu'l-Bahá, Will and Testament, p. 3.

74. Ibid., p. 11.

75. Smith, *A Concise Encyclopedia of the Bahá'í Faith*, p. 316.

76. Prepared by the National Spiritual Assembly of the United States, *So Great an Honor*, pp. 25–26.

77. Ibid., p. 31.

78. 'Abdu'l-Bahá, *Promulgation of Universal Peace*, p. 52.

79. Smith, *A Concise Encyclopedia of the Bahá'í Faith*, p. 106.

80. Shoghi Effendi, *The World Order of Bahá'u'lláh*, pp. 203–4.

Bibliography

World Religions: General Sources

Armstrong, Karen. *A History of God: The 4000-Year Quest of Judaism, Christianity and Islam.* New York: Ballantine Books, 1993.

_____. *The Battle for God: A History of Fundamentalism.* New York: Ballantine Books, 2000.

_____. *The Great Transformation: The Beginnings of Our Religious Traditions.* Toronto: Alfred A Knopf, 2006.

Beversluis, Joel, ed. *Sourcebook of the World's Religions: An Interfaith Guide to Religion and Spirituality.* Novato, CA: New World Library, 2000.

Bowker, John, ed. *The Oxford Dictionary of World Religions.* New York: Oxford University Press, 1997.

Braybrooke, Marcus. *Pilgrimage of Hope: 100 Years of Global Interfaith Dialogue.* New York: Crossroads, 1992.

_____. *Faith and Interfaith in a Global Age.* Grand Rapids, MI: CoNexus Press, 1998.

Campbell, Joseph. *The Masks of God: Occidental Mythology.* New York: Penguin Compass, 1991.

_____. *The Masks of God: Oriental Mythology.* New York: Penguin Compass, 1991.

_____. *The Hero with a Thousand Faces.* New York: Princeton University Press, Bollingen Series, 1973.

Coward, Harold. *Scripture in the World's Religions.* Oxford: Oneworld Publications, 2000.

_____. Pluralism in the World's Religions. Oxford: Oneworld Publications, 2000.

Crim, Keith, ed. *The Perennial Dictionary of the World's Religions.* San Francisco: HarperSanFrancisco, 1981.

Eck, Diana C. *Encountering God: A Spiritual Journey from Bozeman to Banaras.* Boston: Beacon Press, 1993.

Eliade, Mircea, ed. *Encyclopedia of Religion.* 1st ed. New York: Macmillan, 1987.

_____. *Essential Sacred Writings from Around the World.* San Francisco: HarperSanFrancisco, 1977.

Ferguson, John. *War and Peace in the World's Religions.* New York: Oxford University Press, 1977.

Gier, Nicholas F. *The Virtue of Nonviolence: From Gautama to Gandhi.* Albany, NY: State University of New York, 2004.

Hick, John. *God and the Universe of Faiths.* Oxford: Oneworld Publications, 1993.

Kung, Hans. *Global Responsibility: In Search of a New World Ethic.* New York: The Continuum Publishing Company, 1993.

Ma'ṣúmián, Farnaz and Bijan. *Divine Educators.* Oxford: George Ronald, 2005.

Merton, Thomas. *Thoughts on the East.* New York: New Directions Bibelot, 1995.

Mische, Patricia and Melissa Merkling, eds. *Toward a Global Civilization: The Contribution of Religions.* New York: Peter Lang Publishing, Inc., 2001.

Momen, Moojan. *The Phenomenon of Religion: A Thematic Approach.* Oxford: Oneworld, 1999.

Nhat Hanh, Thich. *Living Buddha, Living Christ.* New York: Riverhead Books, 1995.

Noss, John B. *Man's Religions.* 4th ed. New York: The Macmillan Company, 1971.

Novak, Philip, ed. *The World's Wisdom: Sacred Texts of the World's Religions.* San Francisco: HarperSanFrancisco, 1994.

Popov, Dan. *Divine Virtues and Spiritual Qualities: A Compilation from the Sacred Texts.* Salt Spring Island, BC, Canada: Wellspring International Educational Foundation, 1995.

Popov, Linda Kavelin. *The Virtues Project Educator's Guide: Simple Ways to Create a Culture of Character.* Austin, TX: Pro-Ed, Inc., 2000.

_____. *Sacred Moments: Daily Meditations on the Virtues.* Fountain Hills, AZ: Virtues Communications, Inc, 1996.

Rohani, M.K. *Accents of God: Selections from the World's Sacred Scriptures.* Oxford: Oneworld Publications. 1993.

Rosen, Harold. *Universal Questions: Exploring the Mysteries of Existence.* North Vancouver, BC, Canada: Running Water Productions, 1997.

_____. *Rainbowmaking: Intercultural and Interfaith Outreach for Canadian Unitarians and Universalists.* Toronto: Canadian Unitarian Council, 1994.

Runzo, Joseph. *Global Philosophy of Religion: A Short Introduction.* Oxford: Oneworld Publications, 2001.

Runzo, Joseph and Nancy M. Martin, eds. *The Meaning of Life in the World's Religions.* Oxford: Oneworld Publications, 2000.

Savi, Julio. *For the Sake of One God: Notes on Philosophy of Religion.* New Delhi: Royal Falcon Books, Bahá'í Publishing Trust, 2005.

Schaefer, Udo. *Beyond the Clash of Religions: The Emergence of a New Paradigm.* Prague: Zero Palm Press, 1995.

Seager, Richard Hughes, ed. *The Dawn of Religious Pluralism: Voices from the World's Parliament of Religions,* 1893. LaSalle, IL: Open Court Publishing Company, 1994.

Smart, Ninian. *The World's Religions.* Cambridge: Cambridge University Press, 1993.

Smith, Huston. *The World's Religions.* San Francisco: HarperSanFrancisco, 1991.

_____. *Beyond the Post-Modern Mind.* Wheaton, IL: The Theosophical Publishing House, 1992.

Smith, Wilfred Cantwell. *Towards a World Theology: Faith and the Comparative History of Religion.* Philadelphia: Westminster Press, 1981.

Traer, Robert. *Faith in Human Rights: Support in Religious Traditions for a Global Struggle.* Washington, DC: Georgetown University Press, 1991.

_____. *Quest for Truth: Critical Reflections on Interfaith Cooperation.* Aurora, Colorado:
The Davies Group, Publishers, 1999.

Wilson, Andrew, ed. *World Scripture: A Comparative Anthology of Sacred Texts.* New York: Paragon House, 1995.

Zaehner, Robert C., ed. *Concise Encyclopedia of Living Faiths.* 3rd ed. London: Hutchinson, 1977.

World History: General Sources

Alexander, Fran, ed. *Oxford Encyclopedia of World History*. New York: Oxford University Press, 1998.

Brown, D.M., ed. *Lost Civilizations* (21 volumes). Richmond, VA: Time-Life Books Series, 1995.

Duiker, William and Spielvogel, Jackson. *World History, Volume 1: To 1800*. Belmont, CA: Wadsworth/Thomson Learning, 2000.

Hocking, William Ernest. *The Coming World Civilization*. New York: Harper & Brothers Publishing, 1956.

Huntington, Samuel, *The Clash of Civilizations and the Remaking of World Order*. New York: Touchstone, 1996.

Roberts, J.M. *A Short History of the World*. New York: Oxford University Press, 1997.

Sorokin, Pitirim A. *The Crisis of Our Age*. Oxford: Oneworld Publications, 1992.

Stearns, Peter, ed. *The Encyclopedia of World History*. New York: Houghton Mifflin Company, 2001.

Teeple, John B. *Timelines of World History*. New York: DK Publishing, 2002.

Toynbee, Arnold and Jane Caplan. *An Historian's Approach to Religion*. New York: Oxford University Press, 1979.

_____. *A Study of History: 1ˢᵗ Abridged 1-Volume Edition*. Oxford: Oxford University Press, 1972.

_____. *Change and Habit: The Challenge of Our Time*. Oxford: Oneworld Publications, 1992.

_____. *Christianity Among the Religions of the World*. New York: Charles Scribner's Sons, 1957.

Wright, Ronald. *A Short History of Progress*. Scarborough, Ontario: CBC Massey Lectures, HarperCollins Canada Ltd., 2004.

Religious Sources

JEWISH FAITH

Cohn-Sherbok, Dan. *A Concise Encyclopedia of Judaism*. Oxford: Oneworld Publications, 1998.

Daiches, David. *Moses: The Man & His Vision*. New York: Praeger Publishers, 1975.

Feiler, Bruce. *Abraham: A Journey to the Heart of Three Faiths.* New York: HarperCollins, 2004.

Jack, James W. *The Date of the Exodus in the Light of External Evidence.* Edinburgh: T & T Clark, 1925.

Kung, Hans and Kasper, Walter, editors. *Christians and Jews.* New York: Seabury Press, 1974.

May, Herbert G. and Bruce M. Metzger, eds. *The New Oxford Annotated Bible (Revised Standard Version).* New York: Oxford University Press, 1977.

Roth, Cecil, ed. *Encyclopedia Judaica.* Jerusalem: Keter Publishing House, 1972.

Steinsaltz, Adin. *The Essential Talmud.* Translated by Chaya Galai. London: Weidenfeld and Nicolson, 1976.

ZOROASTRIAN FAITH

Ballou, Robert O. *The Portable World Bible.* New York: Penguin Books, 1984.

Boyce, Mary. *Zoroastrians: Their Religious Beliefs and Practices.* London: Routledge & Kegan Paul, 1984.

Duchesne-Guillemin, Jacques. *The Hymns of Zarathustra.* Translated by M. Henning. London: Butler & Tanner, 1952.

Greenlees, Duncan. *The Gospel of Zarathushtra.* Adyar, India: The Theosophical Publishing House, 1951.

Mehr, Farhang. *The Zoroastrian Tradition: An Introduction to the Ancient Wisdom of Zarathustra.* Rockport, MA: Element Inc, 1991.

Taraporewala, Irach J.S. *The Divine Songs of Zarathushtra.* Bombay: Hukhta Foundation, 1993.

Zaehner, Robert C. *The Dawn and Twilight of Zoroastrianism.* New York: G.P Putnam's Sons, 1961.

_____. *The Teachings of the Magi: A Compendium of Zoroastrian Beliefs.* New York: Oxford University Press, 1972.

HINDU FAITH

Klostermaier, Klaus. *A Concise Encyclopedia of Hinduism.* Oxford: Oneworld Publications, 1998.

Krishna. *The Bhagavad Gita.* Translated by Eknath Easwaran. New York: Vintage Spiritual Classics, Random House, 2000.

_____. *The Uddhava Gita*. Translated by Ambikananda Saraswati. Berkeley, CA: Seastone, 2002.

Manchester, Frederich and Prabhavananda. *The Upanishads: Breath of the Eternal*. New York: Penguin Books, 1975.

McGreal, Ian P., ed. *Great Thinkers of the Eastern World*. New York: HarpcrCollins, 1995.

Momen, Moojan. *Hinduism and the Bahá'í Faith*. Oxford: George Ronald, 1990.

Narasimhan, Chakrvarthi V. *The Mahabharata: An English Version Based on Selected Verses*. New York: Columbia University Press, 1998.

Radhakrishnan, Sarvepalli and Charles A. Moore. *A Sourcebook in Indian Philosophy*. Princeton, NJ: Princeton University Press, 1973.

Vanamali. *The Play of God: Visions of the Life of Krishna*. San Diego, CA: Blue Dove Press, 1998.

BUDDHIST FAITH

Armstrong, Karen. *Buddha*. New York: Penguin Putnam, 2001.

Borg, Marcus and Kornfield, Jack. *Jesus and Buddha: The Parallel Sayings*. Berkeley, CA: Seastone, 1999.

Buddha. *The Dhammapada: The Path of Perfection*. Translated by Juan Mascaro. New York: Penguin Books, 1973.

Burtt, E. A. *The Teachings of the Compassionate Buddha*. New York: Penguin Putnam, 1982.

Carus, Paul, comp. *The Gospel of Buddha*. Chicago and London: The Open Court Publishing Company, 1915.

Chew, Phyllis Ghim Lian. *The Chinese Religion and the Bahá'í Faith*. Oxford: George Ronald, 1993.

Conze, Edward. *Buddhist Scriptures*. New York: Penguin Putnam, 1959.

De Bary, Theodore William. *The Buddhist Tradition in India, China and Japan*. New York: Random House, 1969.

Fozdar, Jamshed K. *Buddha-Maitrya-Amitabha Has Appeared*. New Delhi: Bahá'í Publishing Trust, 1976.

_____. *The God of Buddha*. New York: Asia Publishing House, 1973.

Momen, Moojan. *Buddhism and the Bahá'í Faith*. Oxford: George Ronald, 1995.

Powers, John. *A Concise Encyclopedia of Buddhism*. Oxford: Oneworld Publications, 2000.

Strong, John S. *The Buddha: A Short Biography*. Oxford: Oneworld Publications, 2002.

Bibliography

CHRISTIAN FAITH

Borg, Marcus J. and Jack Kornfield. *Jesus and Buddha: The Parallel Sayings.* Berkeley, CA: Seastone, 1999.

Borg, Marcus J. and N.T. Wright. *The Meaning of Jesus: Two Visions.* San Francisco: HarperSanFrancisco, 1999.

Borg, Marcus J. *Meeting Jesus Again for the First Time.* San Francisco: HarperSanFrancisco, 1995.

Bromiley, Geoffrey, ed. *The International Standard Bible Encyclopedia.* Grand Rapids, Michigan: Eerdmans Publishing Company, 1979.

Douglas-Klotz, Neil. *Prayers of the Cosmos: Meditations on the Aramaic Words of Jesus.* San Francisco: HarperSanFrancisco, 1990.

Gardner, Joseph L, ed. *The Story of Jesus.* New York: The Reader's Digest Association, Inc., 1993.

Green, Joey. *Jesus and Muhammad: The Parallel Sayings.* Berkeley, CA: Seastone, 2003.

May, Herbert G. and Bruce M. Metzger, eds. *The New Oxford Annotated Bible (Revised Standard Version).* Oxford University Press, New York, 1977.

Neil, William. *One Volume Bible Commentary.* Toronto: Hodder and Stoughton, 1973.

Parrinder, Geoffrey. *A Concise Encyclopedia of Christianity.* Oxford: Oneworld Publications, 1998.

Tillich, Paul. *Christianity and the Encounter of the World Religions.* New York: Columbia University Press, 1963.

Townshend, George. *Christ and Bahá'u'lláh.* Oxford: George Ronald, 1990.

ISLAMIC FAITH

Armstrong, Karen. *Islam: A Short History.* Toronto: Random House, Inc., 2000.

_____. *Muhammad: A Biography of the Prophet.* San Francisco: HarperSanFrancisco, 1992.

Balyuzi, Hasan. *Muhammad and the Course of Islam.* Oxford: George Ronald, 1976.

Cobb, Stanwood. *Islamic Contributions to Civilization.* Washington, DC: Avalon Press, 1963.

Esack, Farid. *The Qur'án: A Short Introduction.* Oxford: Oneworld Publications, 2002.

Forward, Martin. *Muhammad: A Short Biography.* Oxford: Oneworld Publications, 1997.

Glasse, Cyril. *The Concise Encyclopedia of Islam.* San Francisco: Harper Books, 1991.

Green, Joey. *Jesus and Muhammad: The Parallel Sayings.* Berkeley, CA: Seastone, 2003.

Lawrence, Bruce. *The Qur'án: A Biography.* Vancouver: Douglas & McIntyre, Inc., 2006.

Lewis, Bernard. *The Middle East: 2000 Years of History from the Rise of Christianity to the Present Day.* London: Phoenix Press, 1995.

Momen, Moojan. *Islam and the Bahá'í Faith.* Oxford: George Ronald, 2000.

Monajem, Jamshid. *Stories of Muhammad: A Selection.* New Delhi: Bahá'í Publishing Trust, 1999.

Muhammad. *The Holy Qur'án.* Translated by Abdullah Yusuf Ali. Elmhurst, New York: Tahrike Tarsile Qur'án, Inc., 2002.

_____. Translated by Muhammad Pickthall. Beltsville, Maryland: Amana Publications, 1996.

_____. Translated by Arthur Arberry. Oxford: Oxford University Press, 1998.

_____. Translated by Thomas Cleary. Edison, NJ: Castle Books, 1998.

Nasr, Seyyed Hossein. *Muhammad: Man of God.* Chicago: Kazi Publications, Inc., 1995.

Newby, Gordon D. *A Concise Encyclopedia of Islam.* Oxford: Oneworld Publications, 2002.

Schimmel, Annemarie. *Islam: An Introduction.* Albany, NY: State University of New York Press, 1992.

Watt, William Montgomery. *A Short History of Islam.* Oxford: Oneworld Publications, 1996.

Bahá'í Faith

Works of Bahá'u'lláh

Epistle to the Son of the Wolf. Translated by Shoghi Effendi. 1st pocket-size ed. Wilmette, IL: Bahá'í Publishing Trust, 1988.

Gleanings from the Writings of Baha'u'llah. Translated by Shoghi Effendi. New ed. Wilmette, IL: Bahá'í Publishing, 2005.

The Hidden Words. Translated by Shoghi Effendi. Wilmette, IL: Bahá'í Publishing, 2002.

Kitáb-i-Aqdas: The Most Holy Book. Wilmette, IL: Bahá'í Publishing Trust, 1993.

Kitáb-i-Íqán: The Book of Certitude. Translated by Shoghi Effendi. Wilmette, IL: Bahá'í Publishing, 2003.

The Seven Valleys and the Four Valleys. Wilmette, IL: Bahá'í Publishing Trust, 1991.

The Summons of the Lord of Hosts: Tablets of Baha'u'llah. Wilmette, IL: Bahá'í Publishing, 2006.

Tablets of Bahá'u'lláh revealed after the Kitáb-i-Aqdas. Compiled by the Research Department of the Universal House of Justice. Translated by Habib Taherzadeh et al. Wilmette, IL: Bahá'í Publishing Trust, 1988.

Works of 'Abdu'l-Bahá

Paris Talks: Addresses Given by 'Abdu'l-Bahá in Paris in 1911. Wilmette, IL: Bahá'í Publishing, 2006.

The Promulgation of Universal Peace: Talks Delivered by 'Abdu'l-Bahá during His Visit to the United States and Canada in 1912. Compiled by Howard MacNutt. Wilmette, IL: Bahá'í Publishing Trust, 2007.

The Secret of Divine Civilization. 1st pocket-size ed. Translated by Marzieh Gail and Ali-Kuli Khan. Wilmette, IL: Bahá'í Publishing, 2007.

Selections from the Writings of 'Abdu'l-Bahá. Compiled by the Research Department of the Universal House of Justice. Translated by a Committee at the Bahá'í World Center and by Marzieh Gail. 1st pocket-sized ed. Wilmette, IL: Bahá'í Publishing, 2010.

Some Answered Questions. Compiled and translated by Laura Clifford Barney. Wilmette, IL: Bahá'í Publishing Trust, 2004.

Works of Shoghi Effendi

The Advent of Divine Justice. New ed. Wilmete, IL: Bahá'í Publishing Trust, 2006.

God Passes By. Rev. ed. Wilmette, IL: Bahá'í Publishing Trust, 1974.

The Promised Day is Come. 1st pocket-sized ed. Wilmette, IL: Bahá'í Publishing Trust, 1996.

The World Order of Bahá'u'lláh: Selected Letters. New ed. Wilmette, IL: Bahá'í Publishing Trust, 1991.

Bibliography

Works of the Universal House of Justice
Century of Light. Thornhill, Ontario: National Spiritual Assembly of the Bahá'ís of Canada, 2001.
One Common Faith. Thornhill, Ontario: Bahá'í Canada Publications, 2005.

Compilations from the Bahá'í Writings
Bahá'í Prayers: A Selection of Prayers Revealed by Bahá'u'lláh, the Báb, and 'Abdu'l-Bahá. Wilmette, IL: Bahá'í Publishing Trust, 2002.

Other Bahá'í Works
Balyuzi, Hasan. *Bahá'u'lláh.* New Delhi: Mirat Publications, 1998.

Brown, Keven, ed. *Evolution and Bahá'í Belief: 'Abdu'l-Bahá's Response to Nineteenth Century Darwinism.* Los Angeles: Kalimat Press, 2001.

Cederquist, Druzelle. *The Story of Bahá'u'lláh: Promised One of All Ages.* Wilmette, IL: Bahá'í Publishing, 2005.

Dunbar, Hooper C. *A Companion to the Study of the Kitáb-i-Íqán.* Oxford: George Ronald, 1998.

Fathea'zam, Hushmand. *The New Garden.* New Delhi: Karan Press, 1999.

Fazel, Seena and John Danesh, eds. *Reason and Revelation: New Directions in Bahá'í Thought.* Los Angeles: Kalimat Press, 2002.

Ferraby, John. *All Things Made New: A Comprehensive Outline of the Bahá'í Faith.* London: Bahá'í Publishing Trust, 1975.

Hatcher, John and Hemmat, Amrollah. *The Poetry of Táhirih.* Oxford: George Ronald, 2002.

Hatcher, John. *The Ocean of His Words: A Reader's Guide to the Art of Bahá'u'lláh.* Wilmette, IL: Bahá'í Publishing Trust, 1997.

Hatcher, William and Douglas Martin. *The Bahá'í Faith: The Emerging Global Religion.* Wilmette, IL: Bahá'í Publishing, 2002.

Hershel, Ron. *Evolution of Human Spirituality.* Unpublished manuscript.

Hornby, Helen Bassett, compiler. *Lights of Guidance: A Bahá'í Reference File.* New Delhi: Bahá'í Publishing Trust, 1994.

Ma'súmián, Farnaz and Bijan. *Divine Educators.* Oxford: George Ronald, 2005.

McLean, Jack A. *Dimensions in Spirituality: Reflections on the Meaning of Spiritual Life and Transformation in Light of the Bahá'í Faith.* Oxford: George Ronald. 1994.

_____. "Prolegomena to a Bahá'í Theology". The Journal of Bahá'í Studies. (Volume 5, Number 1.) Toronto. March-June, 1992.

_____, ed. *Revisioning the Sacred: New Perspectives on a Baha'i Theology.* Los Angeles: Kalimat Press, 1997.

Momen, Moojan, ed. *The Bahá'í Faith and the World's Religions.* Oxford: George Ronald, 2003.

____. *Scripture and Revelation.* Oxford: George Ronald, 1997.

Monjazeb, Shahrokh. *Bahá'u'lláh: A Brief Survey of His Life and His Works.* Ottawa: Furutan Academy Publications, 2007.

Nábil-i-A'zam. *The Dawn-Breakers: Nabil's Narrative of the Early Days of the Baha'i Revelation.* Translated and edited by Shoghi Effendi. Wilmete: IL: Baha'i Publishing Trust, 1932.

Saeidi, Nader. *Logos and Civilization: Spirit, History, and Order in the Writings of Bahá'u'lláh.* Bethesda, MD: University Press of Maryland, 2000.

_____. *Gate of the Heart: Understanding the Writings of the Báb.* Waterloo, Ontario: Wilfrid Laurier University Press, 2008.

Sears, William. *Thief in the Night: The Case of the Missing Millennium.* Oxford: George Ronald, 1997.

_____. *Release the Sun.* New ed. Wilmette, IL: Bahá'í Publishing, 2003.

_____. *The Prisoner and the Kings.* Wilmette, IL: Bahá'í Publishing, 2007.

_____. *The Wine of Astonishment.* Oxford: George Ronald, 2008.

Smith, Peter. *A Concise Encyclopedia of the Bahá'í Faith.* Oxford: Oneworld Publications, 2000.

Sours, Michael. *Without Sound or Syllable: The World's Sacred Scriptures in the Bahá'í Faith.* Los Angeles: Kalimat Press, 2000.

Taherzadeh, Adib. *The Revelation of Bahá'u'lláh* (4 Volumes). Oxford: George Ronald, 1977–87.

Townshend, George. *The Promise of All Ages.* Oxford: George Ronald, 1972.

OTHER FAITHS

Bopp, Judie and Michael, Lee Brown, and Phil Lane. *The Sacred Tree: Reflections on Native American Spirituality* (Fourth Edition). Twin Lakes, WI: Lotus Press, 2004.

Hoople, E.H, R.F. Piper, and W.P. Tolley. *Preface to Philosophy: Book of Readings.* New York: The Macmillan Company, 1947.

Hubbard, Barbara Marx. *Conscious Evolution: Awakening the Power of Our Social Potential.* Novato, CA: New World Library, 1998.

Bibliography

Kuhn, Thomas S. *The Structure of Scientific Revolutions.* (Third Edition.) Chicago: University of Chicago Press, 1996.

Neihardt, John G. *Black Elk Speaks.* Lincoln, Nebraska: University of Nebraska Press, 1979.

Willoya, William and Visno Brown. *Warriors of the Rainbow: Strange and Prophetic Dreams of the Indian Peoples.* Happy Camp, CA: Naturegraph Publishers, Inc, 1962.

Wright, John W. *The New York Times Guide to Essential Knowledge.* New York: The New York Times, 2004.

PUBLISHING

Bahá'í Publishing and the Bahá'í Faith

Bahá'í Publishing produces books based on the teachings of the Bahá'í Faith. Founded over 160 years ago, the Bahá'í Faith has spread to some 235 nations and territories and is now accepted by more than five million people. The word "Bahá'í" means "follower of Bahá'u'lláh." Bahá'u'lláh, the founder of the Bahá'í Faith, asserted that He is the Messenger of God for all of humanity in this day. The cornerstone of His teachings is the establishment of the spiritual unity of humankind, which will be achieved by personal transformation and the application of clearly identified spiritual principles. Bahá'ís also believe that there is but one religion and that all the Messengers of God—among them Abraham, Zoroaster, Moses, Krishna, Buddha, Jesus, and Muḥammad—have progressively revealed its nature. Together, the world's great religions are expressions of a single, unfolding divine plan. Human beings, not God's Messengers, are the source of religious divisions, prejudices, and hatreds.

The Bahá'í Faith is not a sect or denomination of another religion, nor is it a cult or a social movement. Rather, it is a globally recognized independent world religion founded on new books of scripture revealed by Bahá'u'lláh.

Bahá'í Publishing is an imprint of the National Spiritual Assembly of the Bahá'ís of the United States.

For more information about the Bahá'í Faith,
or to contact Bahá'ís near you,
visit http://www.bahai.us/
or call
1-800-22-unite

Other Books Available from Bahá'í Publishing

AMERICA'S SACRED CALLING
BUILDING A NEW SPIRITUAL REALITY
John Fitzgerald Medina
$14.00 U.S. / $16.00 CAN
Trade Paper
ISBN 978-1-931847-79-7

A call to action for America to embrace a new society that honors the spiritual reality of the human soul.

America's Sacred Calling describes a blueprint for creating a new society that uplifts and honors the spiritual reality of the human soul while fostering the conditions for humankind to transcend the existential fears, anxieties, and petty concerns of this temporal physical world. Author John Medina examines the Western-dominated worldview that pervades so much of the modern world as we know it, and perceives a rampant materialism that is detrimental to the psychological and spiritual development of humankind. At the same time, Medina explores the writings of the Bahá'í Faith and uncovers prophecies that foreshadow a glorious destiny for the United States and its peoples. Focusing on the activities of the American Bahá'í community and the mission given to its members, Medina finds a great source of hope for the future—a future in which the American nation "will lead all nations spiritually" and play a key role in the unification of the entire planet.

FOUNTAIN OF WISDOM

A Collection of the Writings from Bahá'u'lláh

Bahá'u'lláh

$14.00 U.S. / $16.00 CAN

Trade Paper

ISBN 978-1-931847-80-3

A timeless collection of writings penned by the Prophet-Founder of the Bahá'í Faith with a universal message that all humanity is one race, destined to live in peace and harmony.

Fountain of Wisdom is a collection of the writings of Bahá'u'lláh, the Prophet-Founder of the Bahá'í Faith, in which He explains some of the "precepts and principles that lie at the very core of His Faith." Revealed during the final years of His ministry, the sixteen tablets contained in this volume cover a wide range of topics and place emphasis on principles such as the oneness and wholeness of the human race, collective security, justice, trustworthiness, and moderation in all things.

PROMISES FULFILLED

CHRISTIANITY, ISLAM, AND THE BAHÁ'Í FAITH

Nabil I. Hanna

$16.00 U.S. / $18.00 CAN

Trade Paper

978-1-931847-77-3

An examination of the promises made in both the Bible and the Qur'án concerning the coming of the Promised One.

Promises Fulfilled examines the promises made in both the Bible and the Qur'án concerning the coming of the Promised One, and sheds light on the principal objections that prevent Christians and Muslims from accepting the Bahá'í Faith. The book also discusses some of the verses in the Bible and Qur'án that are the cause of tension between Christians and Muslims. Such verses may appear to differ on the topics of Christ's crucifixion, His ascension, and the meaning of Sonship. As Promises Fulfilled demonstrates, however, no contradiction exists between the sacred texts. In addition, this book introduces explanations from the Bahá'í writings that can bridge misunderstandings that have arisen between Muslims and Christians, and demonstrates the shared values between the two religions. Some of the topics covered include the Word of God, the Day of Resurrection and Judgment, salvation, the meaning of life and death, miracles, parables, and the meaning of the phrase "the seal of the Prophets."

SPIRIT OF FAITH
THE ONENESS OF GOD
Bahá'í Publishing
$12.00 U.S. / $14.00 CAN
Hardcover
ISBN 978-1-931847-76-6

The new Spirit of Faith *series presents a selection of uplifting prayers and writings that focus on the oneness and unity of God for spiritual seekers of all faiths.*

Spirit of Faith: The Oneness of God is a compilation of writings and prayers that offers hope for a better future—one filled with unity, understanding, and acceptance between all peoples and religions of the world. This collection of sacred scripture demonstrates that we are all part of a single, unfolding, divine creation. The *Spirit of Faith* series will explore important spiritual topics—such as the unity of humanity, the eternal covenant of God, the promise of world peace, and much more—by taking an in-depth look at how the writings of the Bahá'í Faiths view these issues. The series is designed to encourage readers of all faiths to think about spiritual issues, and to take time to pray and meditate on these important spiritual topics.

To view our complete catalog,
Please visit http://books.bahai.us

FOUNDERS
OF FAITH